I0210909

Georg Hermann
A Writer's Life

LEGENDA

LEGENDA is the Modern Humanities Research Association's book imprint for new research in the Humanities. Founded in 1995 by Malcolm Bowie and others within the University of Oxford, Legenda has always been a collaborative publishing enterprise, directly governed by scholars. The Modern Humanities Research Association (MHRA) joined this collaboration in 1998, became half-owner in 2004, in partnership with Maney Publishing and then Routledge, and has since 2016 been sole owner. Titles range from medieval texts to contemporary cinema and form a widely comparative view of the modern humanities, including works on Arabic, Catalan, English, French, German, Greek, Italian, Portuguese, Russian, Spanish, and Yiddish literature. Editorial boards and committees of more than 60 leading academic specialists work in collaboration with bodies such as the Society for French Studies, the British Comparative Literature Association and the Association of Hispanists of Great Britain & Ireland.

The MHRA encourages and promotes advanced study and research in the field of the modern humanities, especially modern European languages and literature, including English, and also cinema. It aims to break down the barriers between scholars working in different disciplines and to maintain the unity of humanistic scholarship. The Association fulfils this purpose through the publication of journals, bibliographies, monographs, critical editions, and the MHRA Style Guide, and by making grants in support of research. Membership is open to all who work in the Humanities, whether independent or in a University post, and the participation of younger colleagues entering the field is especially welcomed.

ALSO PUBLISHED BY THE ASSOCIATION

Critical Texts
Tudor and Stuart Translations • *New Translations* • *European Translations*
MHRA Library of Medieval Welsh Literature

MHRA Bibliographies
Publications of the Modern Humanities Research Association

The Annual Bibliography of English Language & Literature
Austrian Studies
Modern Language Review
Portuguese Studies
The Slavonic and East European Review
Working Papers in the Humanities
The Yearbook of English Studies

www.mhra.org.uk
www.legendabooks.com

GERMANIC LITERATURES

Editorial Committee
Chair: Professor Ritchie Robertson (University of Oxford)
Dr Barbara Burns (Glasgow University)
Professor Jane Fenoulhet (University College London)
Professor Anne Fuchs (University College Dublin)
Dr Jakob Stougaard-Nielsen (University College London)
Professor Annette Volfing (University of Oxford)
Professor Susanne Kord (University College London)
Professor John Zilcosky (University of Toronto)

Germanic Literatures includes monographs and essay collections on literature originally written not only in German, but also in Dutch and the Scandinavian languages. Within the German-speaking area, it seeks also to publish studies of other national literatures such as those of Austria and Switzerland. The chronological scope of the series extends from the early Middle Ages down to the present day.

Managing Editor
Dr Graham Nelson, 41 Wellington Square, Oxford OX1 2JF, UK
www.legendabooks.com

Georg Hermann's Bookplate

Georg Hermann

A Writer's Life

❖

John Craig-Sharples

l

LEGENDA
Germanic Literatures 19
Modern Humanities Research Association
2019

Published by Legenda
an imprint of the Modern Humanities Research Association
Salisbury House, Station Road, Cambridge CB1 2LA

ISBN 978-1-78188-855-1 (HB)
ISBN 978-1-78188-856-8 (PB)

First published 2019
Paperback edition with minor corrections 2021

All rights reserved. No part of this publication may be reproduced or disseminated or transmitted in any form or by any means, electronic, mechanical, photocopying, recording or otherwise, or stored in any retrieval system, or otherwise used in any manner whatsoever without written permission of the copyright owner, except in accordance with the provisions of the Copyright, Designs and Patents Act 1988, or under the terms of a licence permitting restricted copying issued in the UK by the Copyright Licensing Agency Ltd, Saffron House, 6–10 Kirby Street, London EC1N 8TS, England, or in the USA by the Copyright Clearance Center, 222 Rosewood Drive, Danvers MA 01923. Application for the written permission of the copyright owner to reproduce any part of this publication must be made by email to legenda@mhra.org.uk.

Disclaimer: Statements of fact and opinion contained in this book are those of the author and not of the editors or the Modern Humanities Research Association. The publisher makes no representation, express or implied, in respect of the accuracy of the material in this book and cannot accept any legal responsibility or liability for any errors or omissions that may be made.

Trademark notice: Product or corporate names may be trademarks or registered trademarks, and are used only for identification and explanation without intent to infringe.

© Modern Humanities Research Association 2019

Copy-Editor: Dr Birgit Mikus

CONTENTS

❖

Litera scripta manet

ACKNOWLEDGEMENTS

❖

Discovering more about the life of my great-grandfather, Georg Hermann, has been a deeply rewarding experience. A number of people have helped me along the way by reading earlier drafts and their comments and suggestions proved invaluable. In particular, I would like to thank Ritchie Robertson, Godela Weiss-Sussex, Birgit Mikus and Graham Nelson. I am also grateful for the help I have received from Lisette Buchholz, Cilli Kasper-Holtkotte, Evelyn Weissberg, Hermann Ebling, Stephan Kraft, Michael Simonson of the Leo Baeck Institute, Jelle Tromp of the National Library of the Netherlands, Emma Quinlan of the Nuffield College Library, Oxford, and Simone Langer. My uncle, George Rothschild and cousin, Eilam Ben-Dror, along with my brother Tony and sister Jeanette, have also helped and encouraged me.

Despite having her own book to complete, Laureen Nussbaum showed great kindness in reading an early draft of my manuscript in its entirety and providing me with detailed comments. Exchanging emails with Laureen as I worked on the text proved a real pleasure. Her encouragement has meant a great deal to me and I would like to express my special gratitude to Laureen.

My grandmother often spoke about her father and her former life in Neckargemünd. We joked that we knew more about her childhood than our own but I realize now that the stories she told kept the past alive for us. I hope that this book will help my children, Gemma, Ben, Jake and Hannah, to understand more about their talented great-great grandfather and why our shared past is something that we should all hold on to.

Finally I should like to thank my wife, Fiona, for her patience and support during the long period that I have been working on this biography.

J. C-S., London, April 2019

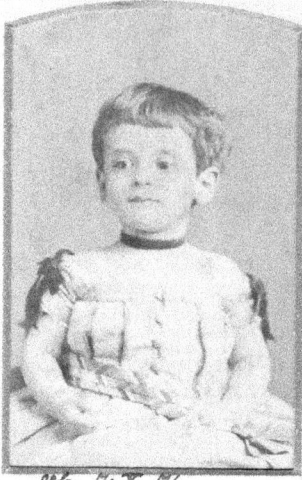

geb. 7. 8. 91
Georg Borchardt

Georg Borchardt

Martha Borchardt geb. Heynemann
Frau von Georg B.

Unter den Linden 134

geb. 19 October 1875 Berlin
gest. 26 März 1955 in Purley Engl.

Olga Borchardt
geb. 1901 gest. 1901

The Borchardt Family Album

PREFACE

❖

One afternoon during the long dry summer of 1976, I remember my grandmother showing me the old family photograph album. Enormous and with a shiny white cover, it seemed to me to be, like her, extremely aged. As Eva turned the pages and reminisced about the people in the photographs, I felt it unlikely that there could be any connection between them and me. The serious looking men, with thick beards and the women in their crinolines belonged to another world, one where everybody and everything had been black and white. And their names — all these Heinrichs and Siegfrieds, Lottes and Claras — how could there be any link between their lives and mine, a schoolboy growing up in Maidstone, Kent, removed by time and place?

I have the album now in my hands. It has shrunk in the meantime and, strangely, also turned from white to brown. The thick pages are trimmed with red and golden-edged. The worn leather cover is embossed with an ornate pattern, like a carving in wood, a tapestry of acorns and leaves which frames a classical figure on the front. There was once a metal clasp to keep the thick cardboard pages closed, but it is long broken.

More than forty years have passed since that summer's day but the same faces still stare out of the album's pages, the secrets of their lives still largely concealed within it. There is nobody left alive now who knew Anna Lademann, who looks out from the third page of the album; Anna who was Hermann and Berta Borchardt's housekeeper for many years in Berlin, before the crash. And the pages where the photographs have been taken out from the elaborate frames into which they were once slotted — pictures of Onkel Ludwig as a boy that Eva sent to his wife Mimi after his sudden death in Paris and which today are in Cairo, in the Swiss Institute for Egyptian Architectural and Archaeological Research.

I know now that the album which as a boy I assumed was my grandmother's actually belonged to her father, Georg. He penned some of the inky German hieroglyphics underneath the photos which Eva later annotated and the album is full of pictures of his family and friends. In fact there are no pictures of Eva; it belongs to a time before she was born. There are just two photographs of Georg, whose album this must have been. In the first he is a little boy, maybe three or so years old, with dark ribbons on his shoulders. Underneath the picture, Eva has written 'geb. 7. X. 71, Georg Borchardt'. In the opposite corner there is a photograph of a smartly dressed Georg when he was in his late twenties perhaps (there is no date). He already looks a little portly in his suit and tie. His dark hair has only just started to recede and he sports a bushy moustache. On the same page there are two other

The Borchardt Family Album

photographs. 'Martha Borchardt geb. Heynemann, Frau von Georg B.' Eva has written below a picture of her mother as a young woman. It is a studio picture, the address of the photographer is still visible (Unter den Linden 194). 'geb. 19 October 1875 Berlin; gest. 26 März 1955 in Purley, Engl.' In the fourth corner of the page there is a picture of a pretty baby girl, Ilse Borchardt, sitting in a plush looking chair. Underneath her sister's name, Eva has written 'geb. 1901; gest. 1901.'

Georg's album, once Eva's, never my mother's but now mine, is a family treasure, deeply private and personal as any collection of family photographs. But it is more than that. To explore the lives of the people captured in its pages is also to discover the times in which they lived. In the introduction to his short history of the twentieth century, Eric Hobsbawm writes that, for historians of his generation, 'public events are part of the texture of our lives. Public events are what formed our lives, private and public.'[1] For Hobsbawm, with his schoolboy memories of walking home one winter's afternoon and seeing the headline that Hitler had become Chancellor of Germany, the past, he writes, is part of his permanent present. 'Der Augenblick ist Ewigkeit.' [The moment is eternity].[2]

Even for those of us born after 1945, there persists a very real sense that the past is part of our permanent present, too. Discovering more about my great-grandfather, Georg Hermann, a writer who was acutely sensitive to the interplay between the old and the new, and whose life was shaped no less by public events than private, is to better understand the world in which we live now. Hermann's world, along with that of the others whose pictures are contained in the album, may be lost to us but it should not be forgotten. Just as he once hoped in the preface to his most famous novel, *Jettchen Gebert*, to spare his grandparents' generation the injustice of sinking into nothingness, the injustice that, 'a mere fifty or sixty years after our life in this doubtful place, when we have withdrawn from life's scene, not a living soul should breathe our story, not a wind of heaven whisper it'[3], so I hope to recapture something of Hermann's life and times. To seek, in Tennyson's phrase, to 'beat the twilight into flakes of fire'.[4]

Notes to the Preface

1. Eric Hobsbawm, *Age of Extremes* (London: Abacus, 1994), p. 4. Hobsbawm was born in 1917.
2. Johann Wolfgang von Goethe, *Selected Poems* (Evanston, IL: Northwestern University Press, 1998), pp. 150–51.
3. Georg Hermann, *Hetty Geybert*, trans. by Anna Barwell (London: George Allen & Unwin, 1924), pp. 9–10.
4. Alfred Tennyson, 'Tithonus', in *Tennyson Poems*, selected by Peter Washington (New York, NY: Knopf, 2004), pp. 91–93.

Georg Hermann Family Tree

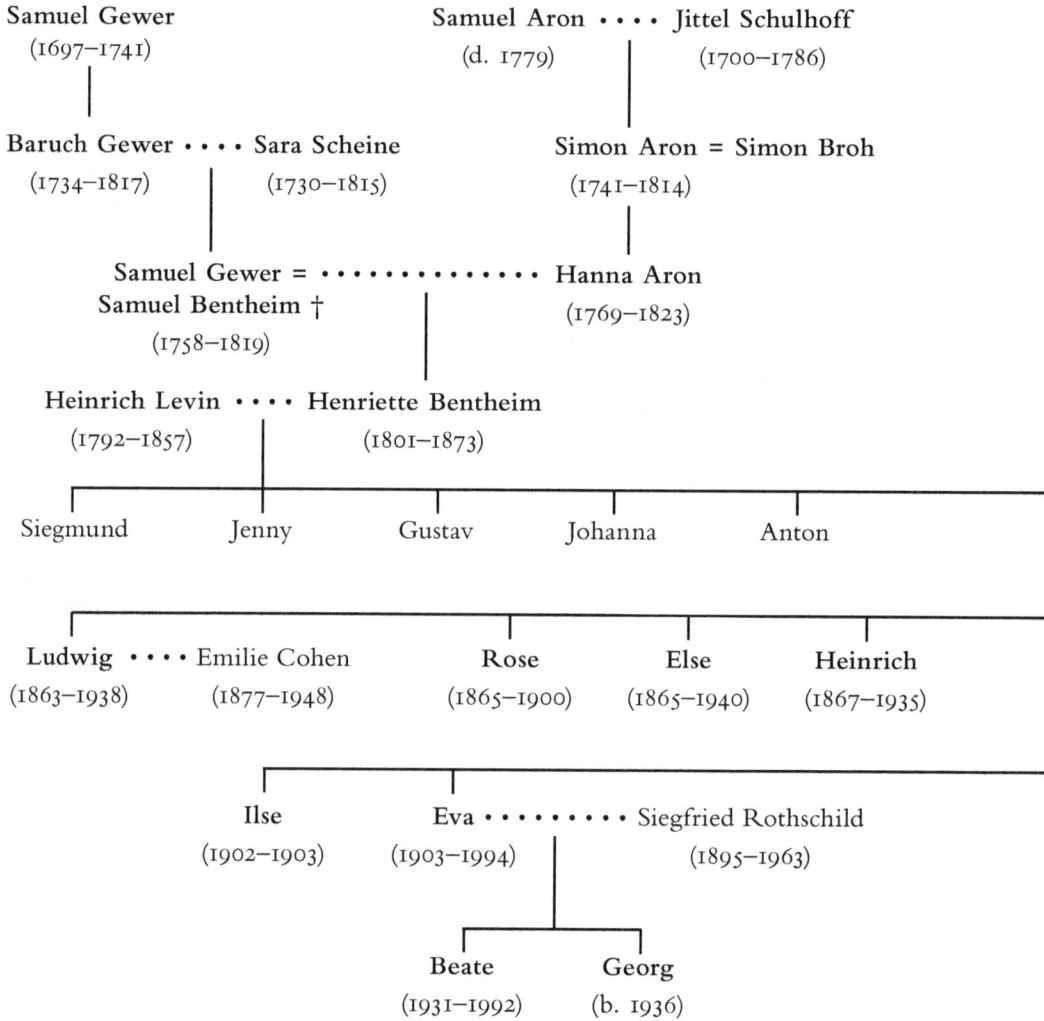

Samuel Gewer
(1697–1741)

Samuel Aron ···· Jittel Schulhoff
(d. 1779)   (1700–1786)

Baruch Gewer ···· Sara Scheine
(1734–1817)   (1730–1815)

Simon Aron = Simon Broh
(1741–1814)

Samuel Gewer = ·············· Hanna Aron
Samuel Bentheim †   (1769–1823)
(1758–1819)

Heinrich Levin ···· Henriette Bentheim
(1792–1857)   (1801–1873)

Siegmund   Jenny   Gustav   Johanna   Anton

Ludwig ···· Emilie Cohen   Rose   Else   Heinrich
(1863–1938)   (1877–1948)   (1865–1900)   (1865–1940)   (1867–1935)

Ilse   Eva ········· Siegfried Rothschild
(1902–1903)   (1903–1994)   (1895–1963)

Beate   Georg
(1931–1992)   (b. 1936)

† Samuel changed his surname from Gewer to Bentheim in 1812 when his daughter, Henriette was 11 years old.

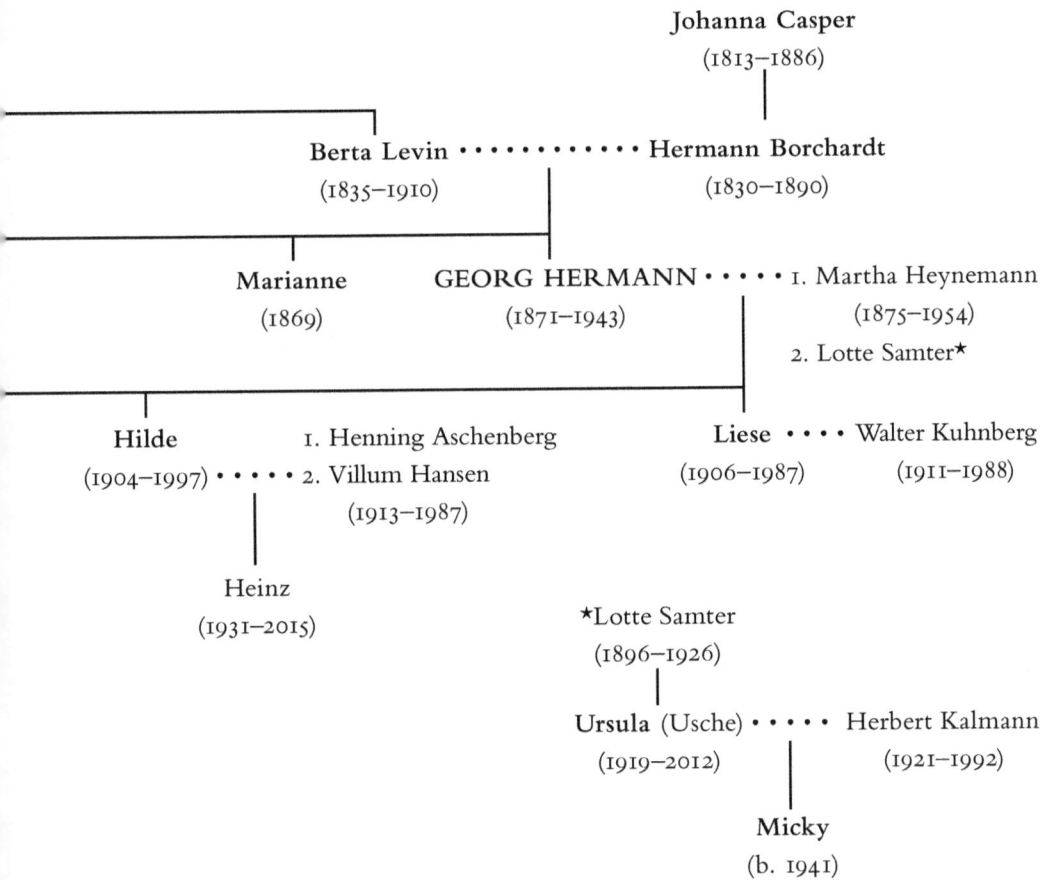

Johanna Casper
(1813–1886)

Berta Levin • • • • • • • • • • • Hermann Borchardt
(1835–1910)   (1830–1890)

Marianne   GEORG HERMANN • • • • • 1. Martha Heynemann
(1869)   (1871–1943)   (1875–1954)
                                                   2. Lotte Samter★

Hilde   1. Henning Aschenberg   Liese • • • • Walter Kuhnberg
(1904–1997) • • • • • 2. Villum Hansen   (1906–1987)   (1911–1988)
                      (1913–1987)

Heinz
(1931–2015)

★Lotte Samter
(1896–1926)

Ursula (Usche) • • • • • Herbert Kalmann
(1919–2012)   (1921–1992)

Micky
(b. 1941)

PART I

❖

1871–1933

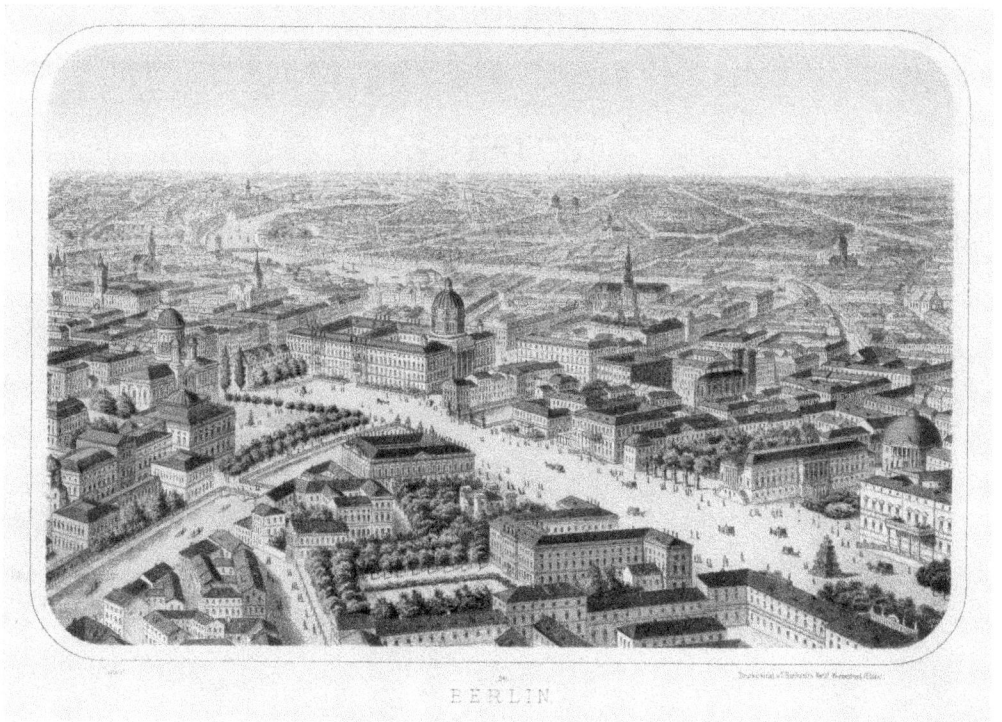

FIG. 1.1. Berlin, *c.* 1870.

CHAPTER 1

❖

An Impecunious
Childhood

In 1870 the famous historian Heinrich Graetz felt able to finish the eleventh and final volume of his history of the Jewish people on an upbeat note. He wrote in the preface that he was concluding

> with the joyous feeling that in the civilized world the Jewish tribe had found, at last, not only justice and liberty but also a certain recognition. Now at long last it had unlimited freedom to develop its talents, not as an act of mercy but as a right acquired through thousandfold sufferings.[1]

In January 1871, the unification of Germany under the Prussian King, now rebranded as Emperor Wilhelm I, was proclaimed in Versailles and soon afterwards the new Reichstag abolished all restrictions on civil and political rights based upon religious differences.

It was on 7 October that auspicious year that my great-grandfather Georg Hermann was born, a third son to Hermann and Berta Borchardt. He was Berta's sixth child in eight years. Georg joined his two brothers, the eight-year-old Ludwig and four-year-old Heinrich and his twin sisters, Else and Rose, who were six, in the family's home in Heilige-Geist-Straße in Berlin-Mitte.[2] A third daughter, Marianne, born two years previously had died when only a few days old.

At the time of Georg's birth, his mother's family had already been living in Berlin for about 150 years. They were representative of that thirty per cent of urban German Jews who had absorbed secular culture the fastest and often achieved the most financial and social success. My grandmother, Eva, always maintained that her father's family, prior to settling in Berlin, had originated from Spain and that they were among the 200,000 Sephardic Jews expelled in 1492. Georg Hermann's biographer, Cornelis Geraard van Liere, believed that the family had come to Germany from Austria but Eva disputed this and in the margin of her copy of his book she has written that they came from the Netherlands.[3]

Subsequent research, most notably by the genealogist Paul J. Jacobi, indicates that she was probably right about this.[4] Following the expulsion from Spain, a number of Jews made their way to the relative tolerance of the Netherlands. The family's earliest known ancestors are two brothers, Daniel and Moses I, who lived in the old Friesland market town of Jever in the seventeenth century. Daniel's son, Jacob, was born in 1706 in Jever but we know that he left and came to Berlin in 1723. Moses I's son, Samuel, was born nine years before Jacob, also in Jever and made the same journey to Berlin, arriving in 1720. At the time, Jews were not permitted to take surnames and generally called themselves by their place of origin. Samuel was known as 'Samuel von Gewer' or 'Samuel Gewer', for short.

Before 1669 Jews had been banned from settling in Berlin and indeed from anywhere in the adjacent region. But after the Austrian Emperor Leopold I expelled all of the Jews from Vienna and Lower Austria in that year, Friedrich I of Prussia had accepted fifty of the richest Viennese Jews. To become one of Friedrich's *Schutzjuden*, each had to pay him 2000 thaler, agree to set up certain businesses and not to establish a synagogue.[5] They were required by law to be recognisable from a distance. It was not until 1710 that Friedrich Wilhelm I agreed to abolish the Jews' mandatory yellow patch in return for a payment of 8000 thaler each. Five years later, just before Samuel Gewer came to live in Berlin, the Prussian King sold his Jews the right to build a synagogue, with the proviso that it should be inconspicuous.

Samuel, like his cousin, Jacob, and as later would Moses Mendelssohn, entered Berlin via the Rosenthal Gate which was reserved for Jews and cattle. There was no right of entry and the cousins must have had some connection with one of the resident Jewish families which enabled them to enter and then remain. In their original charter, privileged Jews had been able to bring with them their household personnel and a number of teachers, rabbis and other dependents. In this way the community had grown since 1669 but in 1737 the king, alarmed at the increase, decreed that only 120 of the richest and best Jewish families could remain in Berlin. Both Samuel and Jacob were among those who stayed.

Van Liere includes a portrait of one 'Rabbi Schemuel' in his biography, which he maintains is Samuel Gewer, this early ancestor of Georg Hermann. Eva has written 'Nicht in unserer Familie!' [not in our family!] under his picture. My grandmother, a profoundly secular woman of science, had no space for this rabbi in the family tree. Jacobi doubts that Samuel actually was a rabbi. Rather, the records suggest he was a pawnbroker who was active in the church hierarchy and reached the position of Gabbai Tzedakah, a lay synagogue official with responsibility for the collection and disbursement of alms.[6] Samuel married twice; first to a widow from Brandenburg, five years after he settled in Berlin and then, after her death, again in 1737. But the marriage was short-lived. He died in 1741 at the age of forty-six.

Amongst the children from Samuel's first marriage were two sons, Moses (1726–1798) and Baruch (1734–1817), both of whom were born and lived in Berlin. In 1756 Baruch married Sara Scheine (*c.* 1730–1815) who came from the prestigious Viennese Reiss-Öttingen family. On their marriage certificate Baruch describes himself as a *Publique-Bedienter*. At the time, Jews were classified into six groups. At the top were the *General-Priviligierter* who were the wealthiest financiers and near to citizenship. Then came *Ordentlicher Schutzjude* (merchants); *Ausserordentlicher-Schutzjude* (e.g. physicians); *Publique-Bedienter* such as Baruch (public servants dependent on employment like rabbis); *Tolerierter* (tolerated younger offspring not married); and finally *Bedienter* (servants). The records indicate that Baruch was a *Krankenwärter* (an orderly in a Jewish hospital) before becoming a successful businessman.[7]

FIG. 1.2. Samuel Gewer.

In 1790, Baruch and Sara's son, Samuel (1758–1819) married Hanna Aron (1769–1823), the daughter of Simon Aron (1741–1814) who was also known as Simon Broh.[8] Van Liere describes Simon Broh as the son of Samuel Gewer but this is incorrect, as Eva indicated in her copy of his book. Simon's parents were actually Jitel (née Schulhoff) and Samuel Aron who ran a boutique selling old clothes from the family's home in Rätzengasse. The records also show that in 1774 Simon Broh lost his status as a *Schutzjude* and for a long period of time was threatened with expulsion from the country.[9] The reason for this is not clear but Simon appears to have been somebody who lived life to the full. According to family legend, he had thirty-six children, although a long lost family tree apparently only showed twenty-four. In an essay about his parents, Georg Hermann recalls his mother Berta telling her cousin, '... wir hier alle von Simon Broh abstammen, der um siebzehnhundert fünfzig in der Kleinen Hamburger Straße wohnte und mit alten Kleidern handelte.' [... we are all descended from Simon Broh who lived at 1750 Kleinen Hamburger Straße and traded in old clothes].[10]

Hermann's awareness of his family's long association with Berlin, was due in part to Berta's habit of sharing stories that had been passed down through the generations. It is from one of these tales which Hermann related many years later as 'Die Reise nach Massow' [The Journey to Massow] that we learn a little more about Simon Broh, Hermann's great-great-grandfather.[11] In addition to trading in old clothes and second-hand uniforms, without taking undue care about how he acquired them,

FIG. 1.3. Simon Broh.

the other business streams Simon Broh exploited elude our knowledge, Hermann writes, but it is a fact that he was a wealthy man. One of Simon's favourite sayings was, 'Von jedem Essen hab' ich dreimal Vergnügen: Ich werde essen, ich esse, und ich habe gegessen.' [From every meal I have thrice pleasure: I will eat, I eat and I ate].[12] He married several times. The wife who endured him for the longest period was apparently never without her knitting bag and needles:

> Sie knippelte und knüpfte den ganzen lieben langen Tag. Und wenn man sie fragte, für wen sie die *Strümpfe* da stricke, dann sagte sie: "Für Jakob". Und wenn man dann meinte, daß die Strümpfe für Jakob doch viel zu groß seien, dann antwortete sie friedfertig: "Nu, dann kriegt se eben Louis oder Nathan" und knippelte weiter.

> [She knitted the whole day long. And should you ask for whom she was knitting those stockings, she'd say: "for Jakob." And if you said, "but those stockings are much too big for Jakob!" then she'd reply peaceably, "Nu — then they'll be for Louis or Nathan" and carried on knitting.][13]

According to Hermann, Samuel Bentheim (who changed his surname from Gewer in 1812) was an accomplished silversmith and jeweller.[14] His portrait, which is still in the family's possession, shows Samuel elegantly attired in a blue jacket and wrinkled jabot. His face is clean-shaven and his features are smart and sharp. In 'Die Reise' Hermann retells a story from 1814 when Samuel, on horseback, rode to the Brandenburg Gate at the head of the city's merchants, who were also on their

FIG. 1.4. Samuel Bentheim.

horses, as part of a ceremony to mark the triumphant return of Friedrich Wilhelm III and his entourage, following the Allied troops' occupation of Paris. But the affair did not go off well, for when the military band started playing, the merchants' horses were startled and reared up. More confident with their ledgers than they were certain in the saddle, the merchants struggled to control their horses and came forward at high speed from the left and the right in a disgracefully disorderly fashion:

> Der Urgroßvater aber, der mit Pferden gut umzugehen wußte [...] stellte sich in den Steigbügeln auf, wandte sich halb um und brüllte über den Pariser Platz ein Kommando, das wohl niemals bisher und auch nie später auf einem preußischen Kasernenhof erklungen war, nämlich: "Ganze Eskadron Schande!" Das heißt, er rief gar nicht "Schande!" sondern er rief "Charpes!" was dasselbe besagen will und in seinen Urtiefen von dem Gros der Kaufmannschaft weit besser verstanden wurde als das langweilige hochdeutsche Wort "Schande".

> [My great-grandfather who knew well how to deal with horses [...] stood in his stirrups, half-turned and shouted out over Pariser Platz a command which had never been heard before and has never been heard since on a Prussian parade-ground. "Whole squadron, Schande!" [Disgrace!] Except that he cried not "Schande!" but "Kharpe!" which in the depth of their hearts the merchants understood much better than the dull High German word, "Schande".][15]

Samuel Bentheim may have been more sophisticated than Simon Broh but he only managed to father ten children:

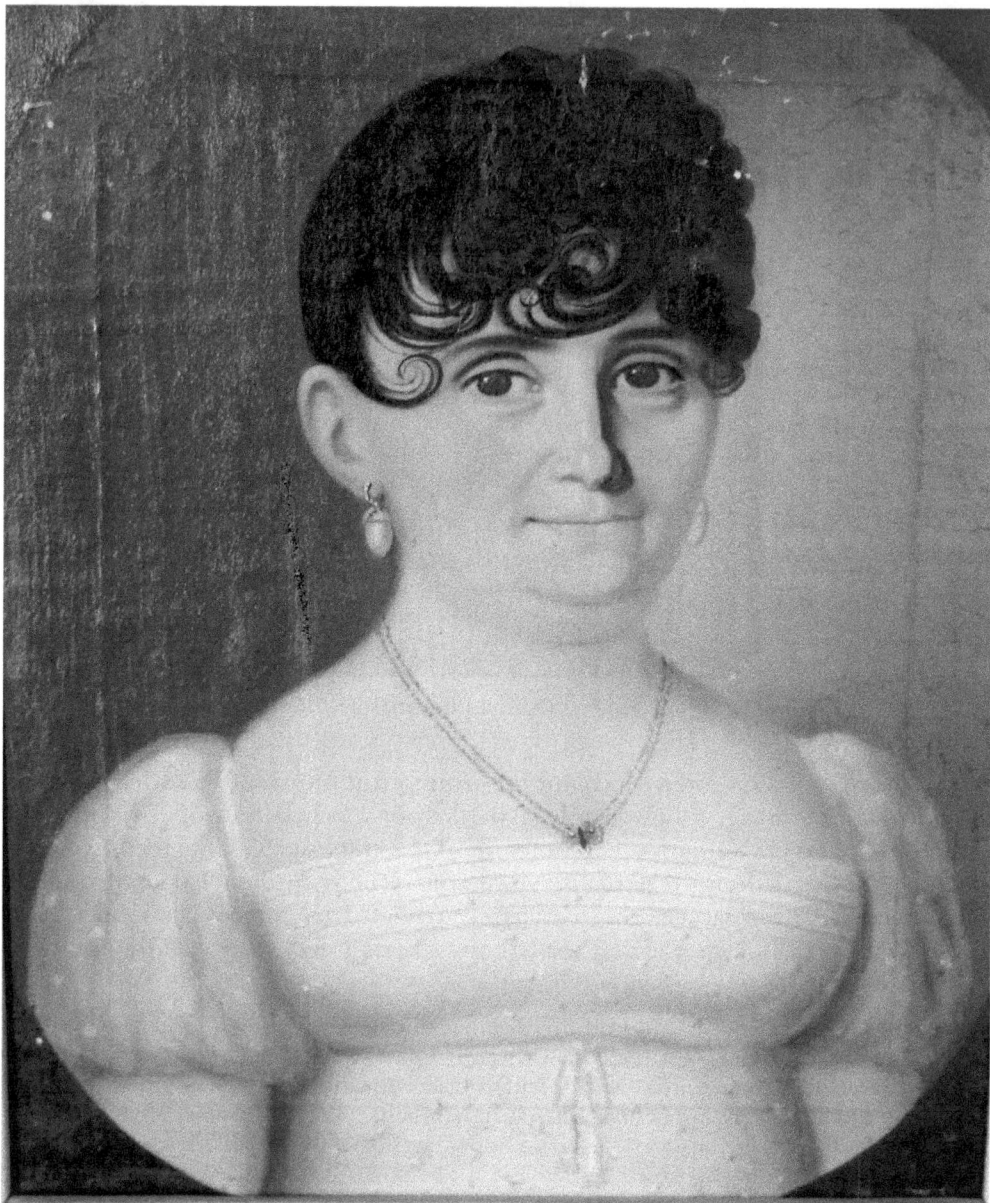

FIG. 1.5. Hanna Bentheim.

Hanne, Rike, Mine, Fieke, Jette waren die Mädchen — und Jason, Eduard, Ferdinand, Salomon und ... also das ist ja gleich. Genug, wenn er wirklich noch zwei, drei lumpige Kinder gehabt hätte, er hätte doch nur als trauriger Stümper gegenüber seinem Herrn Schwiegervater bestehen können.

[Hanne, Rike, Mine, Fieke, Jette, they were the girls and Jason, Eduard, Ferdinand, Salomon and ... so, that's more or less the same. In any case even if he'd had two or three more measly children, he would still have been a sad bungler, compared with his father-in-law.][16]

Hanna, Samuel's wife, was a tough woman. In her picture she has sharp thin lips which apparently narrowed when her maid failed to dress her beautiful hair to her satisfaction. Their youngest daughter, Jette, married Heinrich Levin, a Berlin silk draper who came from Massow in Pomerania.[17] Hermann writes that Heinrich left home at the age of twelve and lived in Hamburg and Leipzig before settling in Berlin. According to Hermann, by the time of the marriage, Heinrich was already in his thirties and Jette was just sixteen. But when Hanna was asked by an acquaintance how she could marry the child so early, she said, 'Ich finde das gerade spät genug.' [I think it is just late enough!].[18]

Heinrich had established a successful business in Berlin making shawls, scarves and jackets which he exported to South America. In 'Die Reise' we are told that he was a short fat man with a little beard who exuded a trustworthy air. He had a fantastic imagination and would make up wonderful stories to tell his children. Storytelling seems to have been something that ran in the family through the generations.

Heinrich and Jette had six children spread over sixteen years. Three (Siegmund, Jenny and Gustav) were born in quick succession in the early years of the marriage but then there was a long gap before the three younger children (Johanna, Anton

FIG. 1.6. Heinrich Levin.
FIG. 1.7. Henriette (Jette) Levin.

and Berta) were born. Had Simon Broh still been alive, Hermann writes, he would surely have cursed Heinrich for only fathering a paltry six children, spread out over so many years.

The memorable journey to Massow which Hermann recounts in 'Die Reise' took place towards the end of the 1820s, in the interval between the birth of the first three children and their siblings' arrival. Heinrich had decided that he must show his wife Massow and besides, he himself wanted to see his childhood home again. She would find Massow to be quite an important town of a very modern character, he told Jette. They would be able to admire the giant ancient tower where he used to go. His mother would prepare food for them — all of his old favourites — one could not taste anything so wonderful even in the finest restaurants in London and Paris.

In preparation for the trip the family are kitted out in the most elegant and fashionable clothes. Jette and Jenny wear white cashmere dresses with pink and blue designs, wide collars and big puffy sleeves, decorated with red and green satin ribbons. They even wear some of the best scarves from the family business. Jette thinks that all this finery is unnecessary but Heinrich insists, she should think of Massow, she would find it a thoroughly modern town. In Massow you could not appear other than at your absolute best.

And so on a beautiful May morning they set off in a big landau from Spandauer Straße. The whole neighbourhood is watching them leave, as if seeing a bride departing for her wedding. The children immediately begin to squabble about who is going to sit by the window while Heinrich tells the family of the wonders that await them in Massow and how happy he feels to be seeing his old parents again. Gustav, the youngest child, is already proving a pest and Jette complains that half an hour, let alone a whole day, in his company is enough to bring on her biliary colic.

Hermann describes their long journey via the port at Stettin and Heinrich's persistent belief on the second day of the trip that they must soon arrive. They ride on and on through fields and barren heath. Each time Heinrich asks the coachman how much further it is to Massow, 'Only a little way now', comes the reply. Eventually Heinrich starts to recognize where he is and sure enough they come upon the ancient tower. But it is situated by some non-descript lakes and is so small a tower that it is hardly worthy of the name. 'Gott, hat sich das hier verändert!' sagte der Großvater. 'Früher jedenfalls sah es ganz anders hier aus.' [God, the changes here!' exclaimed Grandfather. 'It used to look very different.'].[19]

At last they reach the small town. The sun has not yet set and the people in Massow are very surprised to see a landau come rattling through the streets. In front of the house sit Heinrich's parents, and some of his brothers and sisters:

> Und wie die Mutter ihren Sohn erkannte, der da als leibhaftiger Herr mit Kind und Kegel in einem richtigen Landauer angefahren kam, da lief sie sofort hinein und holte einen Stuhl heraus und trug ihn an den Wagen. Denn sie hatte noch niemals in ihrem Leben einen Wagen gesehen, der einen Tritt und eine Kutschtür zum Aufmachen hatte. Alle Wagen in Massow waren so, daß man nur hinein- und herauskletterte.
>
> Großvater winkte ab, wurde rot und sah mit einem sehr ängstlichen Blick

zu seiner großstädtischen Frau herüber. Ach Gott, kam ihm das alles klein und eng und kümmerlich vor. Aber das Essen — auf das freute er sich; das war doch etwas! Wie seine Mutter kochte, das konnte seine Frau nicht.

Und richtig — da kam auch gleich seine Lieblingsspeise auf den Tisch. Großvater nahm eine Riesenportion und steckte einen tüchtigen Happen von der pommerschen Grütze in den Mund, während die Kinder, die das nicht kannten, protestierten: sie wollten etwas anderes haben; und Großmutter sich bezwang und ein Löffelchen davon an die Lippen führte.

Aber seltsam . . . auch Großvater bekam den Bissen nicht herunter. Und, mit Verlaub zu sagen, er spuckte ihn ganz verstohlen wieder auf den Teller und sagte: 'Höre mal, Mutterchen, das hast du doch früher ganz anders gekocht?'

Aber die alte Frau versicherte mit Tränen, daß sie es früher ganz genauso gekocht hätte.

[And as grandfather's mother realized who it was that was approaching, she and the others brought out a chair and carried it to the carriage — for she had never seen in her life a carriage door which could open. All of the carriages in Massow were such that you had to scramble in and out of them.

Grandfather shook his head, blushed and looked anxiously at his big-city wife. Ach! This home, it was all so small and cramped and miserable. Still, the food — that he could look forward to, that would be something. His wife could not cook like his mother.

And yes, there on the table was all of his favourite food laid out. Grandfather took a huge portion of Pomeranian jelly and put a hearty bite of it into his mouth while the children who had never tasted the jelly before protested that they wanted something else, and grandmother forced herself to take a spoonful to her lips.

But strange... grandfather couldn't swallow his mouthful and had to stealthily spit it back out onto his plate. He said, 'Listen, little mother, you used to cook very differently.'

The old woman, with tears in her eyes, assured him that her cooking had not changed.][20]

What has changed, of course, is Heinrich, after so many years of living away from his family home. A few days later, he tells his wife that although he personally feels incredibly well in Massow he recognizes that she, being a native Berliner, is more accustomed to the conditions of the big city. And so the visit is curtailed and they return to Spandauer Straße, sooner than anyone had expected, with much less fanfare than had attended their departure. When pressed about the journey by friends, we are told that Heinrich summed it up in the admirable phrase, 'Gott soll hüten vor kleinen Städten!' [God should beware of small towns!][21]

In contrast to his mother's family, Georg Hermann knew almost nothing about the family of his father Hermann Borchardt. In a letter written to his daughter, Hilde in April 1939, Hermann explains '... die Borchardt Legende ist dunkel und verliert sich schnell nach rückwärts. Und der Name gibt keinerlei Garantie für wirkliche Verwandtschaft.' [... the Borchardt legend is obscure and soon lost when you trace it back. The name doesn't guarantee any real relationship].[22] Hermann Borchardt, who was born in 1830, was illegitimate and the identity of his father is unknown. In the letter Georg speculates that, based on research done by his brother

FIG. 1.8. Hermann Borchardt.

Ludwig and Eva, he may have been a Spanish soldier in Napoleon's army who had been involved in the 1812 Russian campaign and had remained in Germany after it. This, he writes, would explain his and his siblings pronounced Spanish features.[23]

> Vater ist 1830 geboren. Jedenfalls ist er [...] von irgendeinem Manne (Onkel?) namens "Borchardt" adoptiert worden und nannte sich dann nach ihm. [...] Seine Mutter heiratete dann [...] einen Herrn Kohn in Schwerin an der Warthe, von dem sie zahlreiche Kinder hatte...

> [Father was born in 1830. In any case, he was adopted [...] by some man (uncle?) named "Borchardt" and took the man's name. [...] His mother then married [...] a Mr. Kohn in Schwerin an der Warthe, by whom she had several children ...][24]

Hermann Borchardt's half-siblings all lived in Berlin and there are photographs of them and their children in the family album.

More detail about Hermann Borchardt's adoption only came to light in 2014 when the Borchardt genealogist, François Cellier discovered that, although

Hermann's mother, Johanna Casper (1813–1886), grew up in Schwerin, Hermann's adoptive father came from Jastrow, a town further to the east.[25] Using old Berlin address books, Cellier uncovered that Johanna's sister Mathilda was married to one Max Borchardt and that it was they who adopted Hermann. This Uncle Max died in the cholera epidemic of 1847 and that same year, Mathilda died after giving birth to their fourth child. A younger brother of Max adopted his four small children but did not take Hermann Borchardt, who by this time was seventeen. Instead he went to live with his mother, her husband (Hirsch Seckelsohn) and his half-siblings.

Max Borchardt and his brothers had established the first company in Berlin which used machines to produce men's shirts. Two of his sons, Salomon and Max Junior further modernized the company and were able to produce shirts more cheaply than many of their competitors, becoming quite wealthy in the process. Hermann Borchardt also went into the clothing business, setting up his own company selling crinolines in 1865 but he was not able to match the success of his cousins.

Hermann Borchardt and Berta Levin had married two years earlier. We know from Georg Hermann's essay 'Meine Eltern' [My Parents] that Berta came with a large dowry and possibly some of this was used to establish the crinoline business.[26] Her father, Heinrich Levin, was according to Hermann of 'unerschütterlicher Wohlhabenheit' [unshakable wealth][27] and Berta's brothers were also extremely rich and died millionaires. She had enjoyed a pampered affluent youth — breakfast, for instance, would be served on a silver tray by one of the family's numerous servants — but was also very well educated. Berta spoke English, French and Italian, and Hermann describes her as the family's 'lebendes Lexikon' [living encyclopedia].[28] She was, he writes, an observant woman who grasped the deeper subtleties of life. Her conversation was always enriching and she enjoyed regaling family and friends with stories of her earlier life and experiences. Apparently, she had an idiosyncratic way of talking and would pepper her speech with original images and similes.

Eva was only seven years old when Berta died but she had strong memories of her and always compared Berta favourably with her other grandmother, Elise Heynemann. Where Berta was short and roundish, Elise was tall and thin. Berta was the more jovial figure. Eva recollected that she saw everything in positive terms, whereas Elise, although twenty-two years younger, was a pessimist.[29] There was a sweet tenderness about Berta, which according to Hermann, she never lost despite the hardships she endured when the comforable affluence she had known all her life was shattered by the collapse of her husband's business in 1876. The collapse was a cataclysmic event in the family's life and had an impact, not only on Hermann's childhood but his whole world view.

In 'Also — ein Jubiläum' [So — An Anniversary], an evocative essay about his early childhood, Georg Hermann remembers when, as a boy of five, he went to the Spandauer Straße synagogue.[30] The family was living at the time in Blumeshof in Tiergarten. Georg's kindergarten was at the corner of Karlsbader Privat Straße. His world, he writes, was bound by the grassy banks of the Landwehr Canal and the elm-lined towpath leading to Potsdam Bridge. The outer limit was the green wall of the zoo where Bendlerstraße ended.[31] Hermann recalls playing in a nearby

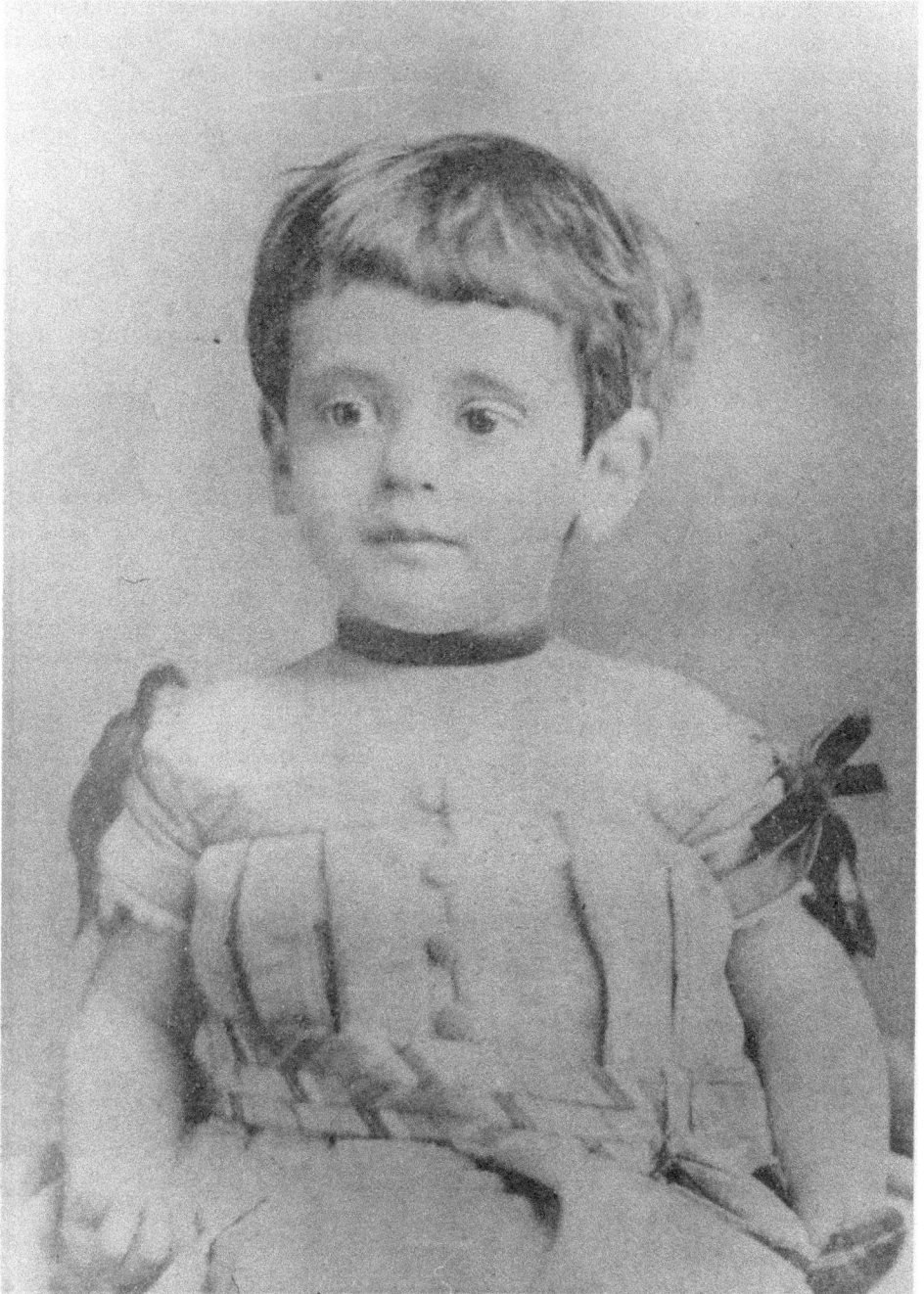

FIG. 1.9. Georg Hermann

garden which extended almost as far as Hildebrandstraße. He would climb the sturdy lilac bushes in the garden and, making a seat from a convenient fork in the branches, lodge the tips of his feet against the garden's iron railings. From this comfortable perch, he would survey the long sunny street which stretched out far into the distance.

There were walnut trees in the garden and Hermann recalls that if one was lucky and came early, before the path had been swept, you could find the nuts which had fallen during the night. There was also *Mehläpfelchen* [dogwood] with its small red-cheeked fruits that taste sweet and sour at the same time and which, Hermann recalls, seemed as desirable to him in those days as the apples of the Hesperides. Horse chestnut trees, too. Hermann remembers his childhood delight at the exquisite beauty of the conkers when they had just broken out of their cases, shiny, smooth and brown, veined and banded with lighter tones; cool and wonderful to the touch.[32]

Having described a little of this childhood world, Hermann focuses on the particular day in question. That it was special he knew not only because there was more food on the evening dinner table than the family would normally eat at lunchtime but also because he was wearing his gold-buttoned sailor suit and an especially beautiful blue and white cravat. There was even talk of an autumn coat, a real coat, fit for a gentleman, which he would be wearing for the first time, that night. Hermann continues,

> Und als wir nun bei Tisch saßen, alle miteinander, und das waren mit dem Fräulein Seifert acht, da sagte mein Vater zu mir, das heißt, er sagte es zu den anderen, verkündete es ihnen, ohne mich dabei auch nur anzusehen oder zu beachten, als unabweisbaren Beschluß: "Also der Junge kommt auch mit in die Schule" (schon ein peinlicher Begriff), "das erste Mal, und wir bleiben die ganze Nacht da bis morgen abend um diese Zeit, und er muß auch *mitfasten*."

> [As we sat down to table (we made eight with the young Fräulein Seifert), my father said to me, that is, he announced it to the others, as if he had reached an incontrovertible decision and did not even look in my direction, "So, my little boy, for the first time you will be coming with me to the synagogue (already an embarrassing word), we must stay there all night until this time tomorrow and you must take part in the fast."][33]

His two older brothers, Ludwig and Heinrich, chime in to say that they too had fasted. His mother tries to comfort Georg by saying it won't be as bad as all that and Fräulein Seifert pronounces 'Ja, ja, bei uns war das nie anders' [yes, yes, with us it was no different].[34] But this does not seem credible to Georg, because Fräulein Seifert wears an ivory brooch in the shape of a cross. Then his father is speaking again and saying that children have starved to death as a result of having to go the whole long night and the following day without eating anything. This is the point at which Georg realizes how desperate his situation is and asks for some more veal and potatoes. His mother protests that he shouldn't be eating so much in the evening, especially not so much meat. But Georg's father says he is quite right to eat while he can. Then, all at once, it is time to get ready to leave:

Ich aber warf einen schmerzlichen Blick auf sie zurück. Hier war noch alles die Hülle und Fülle. Brötchen, Knüppel, Semmel, Salzkuchen, silberne Obstschalen voll Birnen, Pflaumen und Weinbeeren, Kalbskeule und Kompott und Gurkensalat. Und ich würde heut nacht verhungern. Elend zugrunde gehen. Eingesperrt sein. Morgen früh, wenn es zu spät wäre, würde sich meine ganze Familie über meine armselige, langsam erkaltende Leiche werfen und weinen. Und das wäre ihre gerechte Strafe für die Grausamkeit ihrer harten Herzen, mich dem Hungertod auszusetzen.

[I took a painful lingering look back at the table. There everything was in abundance. Rolls, sticks, bread, *salzkuchen*,[35] silver fruit bowls full of pears, plums, and grapes, leg of veal and stewed fruit and cucumber salad. And yet I was to starve, to perish miserably and be imprisoned. Tomorrow morning, when it was too late, my family would see my poor, cold lifeless corpse and weep. And that would be just punishment for the cruelty of their hard hearts in exposing me to starvation.][36]

But when there are five children it takes a bit of time to leave the house. For instance, there are caps to be found and 'do you think you can go out with such hands? You look like you've been shovelling coal!' So there is more delay and washing of hands while Georg stands in his new coat, smart and clean as Adonis. Amid the commotion, he takes the opportunity to go back into the dining room to get some emergency rations — putting two bread rolls and a *salzkuchen* in one of the pockets of his coat and three handfuls of plums in the other.

Wenn sie meinten, daß ich so leicht und kampflos mein Leben hergäbe, irrten sie sich. Und ehe noch die Schottenmütze meiner Schwester Rose gefunden war (im Schirmständer), da war ich längst wieder zurück.

[If they thought that I was going to give up my life so easily without a fight, they were wrong. And before my sister's missing tam-o'-shanter had been found (in the umbrella stand), I was already back.][37]

Along the way to the synagogue in Spandauer Straße, Georg collects some acorns because he knows from fairy tales that *in extremis* you can survive on them. He remembers the synagogue as being strangely magical and exciting. Men stood in their overcoats, swaying rhythmically in prayer and further back, dim, behind wooden lattices, were the blurred faces of women. The half-chanting, half-speaking of the men made a muffled but beautiful and melodious sound (although, Hermann writes, surely no one understood the words). For a while, it all seemed quite pleasant but,

... es würde die ganze Nacht so weitergehen. Und man würde dabei langsam, aber schrecklich verhungern müssen. Und es schien gar keine Möglichkeit, hierbei zu den Knüppeln, dem Schusterjungen, den Pflaumen und den Eicheln zu gelangen. Die Eicheln würde ich zuletzt essen, nur in höchster Not.

[... it was to last all night. And one was to starve slowly and terribly. And there seemed to be no way to get at the bread rolls, the plums and the acorns. The acorns I would only eat as a last resort.][38]

Suddenly the chanting surges to an angry murmur and the congregation throws itself down between the benches on the ground. As Hermann does likewise he manages to extricate some plums from his coat pocket. Unfortunately at the same time as he is stuffing the plums into his mouth, a few acorns tumble out and roll across the dark trampled floor. Still, he feels, at least for the next half hour he is saved from starvation. But then everyone is back up again and soon the men are restless and noisily closing their books, turning to each other and starting to chat, shaking hands and getting slowly out of their seats. Georg's father says,

> "Na, komm nach Hause, mein Söhnchen ... es ist aus", sagte mein Vater. "Was hast du denn, du bist doch so rot?" "Ich bin müde", schluckte ich. [...] Draußen blinzelten in einer tiefblauen feuchten Nacht die Laternen, und ich streute im Gehen so langsam eine Pflaume nach der anderen, eine Eichel nach der anderen fort. Die Knüppelchen bröselte ich auf und warf die Krümchen ganz heimlich hinter mich, spielte, mich nachziehen lassend, müde und schlaftrunken einen Fuß vor den anderen setzend, Hänsel und Gretel im wilden Wald.

> ["So, my son, it is over, we can go home now. But what did you do, why are you so red?" "I'm tired," I gulped. [...] And blinking at the lights of the lanterns as we stepped outside into the damp blue of the wet night, I steadily ate my way through one plum after another. I crumbled up the bread rolls throwing the crumbs secretly behind me, and drowsily put one foot in front of the other, like Hansel and Gretel stepping into the wild forest.][39]

The comfortable family life Hermann depicts in 'Also — ein Jubiläum' was to be shattered only a few months afterwards by the collapse of his father's business. By the 1870s Hermann Borchardt was making his living as a broker but he was to lose almost all the family's money in the speculative boom of the Gründerzeit. In the heady economic climate of the time, as Germany experienced a great economic upswing, it had been possible for entrepreneurs like Borchardt to become rich overnight, but in May 1873 came a stock market crash. The German economy had become over-heated, mainly as a result of the billions pouring into it in French war reparation payments. The crash, which provoked a wave of anti-Semitic agitation, ushered in Germany's longest recession of the nineteenth century and tens of thousands of middle-class and aristocratic families lost everything.[40] Whether or not Hermann Borchardt's financial demise had its roots in the crash is not altogether clear but we do know that within a couple of years, the family had to move first to Bendlerstraße and then to Bülowstraße. In the years thereafter they moved home repeatedly (perhaps in an attempt to steer clear of creditors), as they slid inexorably down the social pecking order.

The family's financial ruin had a nightmarish impact on the young Hermann. In an autobiographical essay 'Im Spiegel' [In the Mirror] first published in *Das literarische Echo* in 1914, Hermann reflects that as a consequence, he quickly learned some hard lessons about the nature of life.[41] Describing his father's bankruptcy, Hermann writes that he was very conscious as a child of the change in the family's situation and that the experience has stayed with him. Where previously life had been secure, now everything was hanging in the air, all that remained was the outer façade of bourgeois respectability with nothing substantive to underpin it.

As 'Im Spiegel' shows, financial ruin was not just about sudden impoverishment.

Fig. 1.10. Berta Borchardt.

For the Borchardts there was also the social stigma to be endured. Something of what this would have meant is captured in Thomas Mann's *Buddenbrooks* (1901). When Tony is told that her entrepreneur husband Grünlich is bankrupt, she sinks back into her seat:

> In that minute all that was involved in the word "bankrupt" rose clearly before her: all the vague and fearful hints which she had heard as a child. "Bankrupt" — that was more dreadful than death, that was catastrophe, ruin, shame, disgrace, misery, despair. "He is bankrupt," she repeated.[42]

Given Berta's affluent upbringing and the comfortable bourgeois world in which she had always lived, the disgrace of bankruptcy and its associated miseries must have been severe. She found herself now, at the age of forty-one and with five small children, having to cope with the family's suddenly straitened circumstances. Georg Hermann writes of his vivid memories of bailiffs coming to the family home and taking away all of the furniture (including the piano) and of officers searching for his father who periodically was taken away and imprisoned for debt.[43] What brought his father to bankruptcy, Hermann never fully understood. It seems that he was simply not a very good businessman and failed to maintain adequate savings. It may have been the consequence of a failed speculation. As Uncle Eli points out in *Jettchen Gebert*, 'a merchant [...] can throw away all his property and his wife's as well in two speculations.'[44] What is clear is that Hermann Borchardt never recovered. His own children likened him to the ever-hopeful but debt-laden Micawber in *David Copperfield*. In 1884 Borchardt suffered a stroke which left him very ill and prematurely aged. At fifty-four he was a broken man, both mentally and physically.

The years after the financial collapse of Hermann Borchardt's business were very difficult for the family. According to Hermann, it was Berta's strength of character which kept the family afloat. 'Wenn wir trotzdem nicht verproletarisierten, sondern immer noch wenigstens am äußeren Rand der Gesellschaft uns bewegten, so war es wohl der Geist der Mutter, der uns davor behütete.' [That we were not wholly impoverished and managed to remain on the outer fringes of society was due to the spirit of my mother, who sheltered us from a great deal].[45]

His father's bankruptcy and its impact on the family are major themes in Hermann's first semi-autobiographic novel, *Spielkinder*. He came to believe that his whole outlook on life had been shaped by these formative experiences. It gave him a profound empathy for the vulnerable, a natural sympathy with the weak and unsuccessful. Later in life, Hermann was to express his infinite gratitude to his father for the financial hardship he inflicted on the family because otherwise he might have become a safe and conventional citizen, materialistic and shallow.[46]

Georg Hermann's career at school was not marked by success. He went first to the Askanisches Gymnasium in Hallesche Straße and then to the Friedrichswerdersche Gymnasium in Dorotheenstraße. From Hermann's own account, this change of schools was not a straight-forward transition but because he was asked to leave.[47] Despite his struggles at school, there was no money to give the young Hermann any additional support, as might have been the case in a wealthier family with

FIG. 1.11. Curt Gitschmann, *Georg Hermann* (1891).

fewer children. He was thirteen when his father suffered the stroke which left him permanently incapacitated, and with this further deterioration in the family situation, it seems that the teenage Hermann busied himself more and more with collecting plants, beetles, and, in particular, butterflies.[48] These extra-curricular activities took up a lot of Hermann's time and he would play truant from school to add to his collections. He was also writing his first stories during this period, inspired by Turgenev, Dickens, and Hans Christian Andersen.[49]

At school, Hermann became friends with Curt Gitschmann, the son of a successful sculptor and painter. The family, like the Borchardts, was living in Kurfürstenstraße at the time. Curt's father, 'Old Gitschmann', was a friend of the parents of the playwright, Gerhart Hauptmann.[50] Hauptmann, who was born nine years before Hermann, initially set out to be a sculptor and for a time was one of Gitschmann's students.[51] In his essay, 'Der junge Hauptmann und seine Modelle', Hermann recalls that it was Old Gitschmann who gave him a copy of Hauptmann's first, Ibsen-influenced play, *Vor Sonnenaufgang* [Before Sunrise].[52] The social realism of the play had created something of a scandal in Berlin and beyond, and it has come to be seen as a seminal work. Jethro Bithell, for instance, argues that *Vor Sonnenaufgang* 'marks the date when the existence of a new orientation in literature was forced on the consciousness of the nation at large.'[53]

Hermann was not familiar with the play but took Gitschmann's copy of it with him one Sunday in early April 1889 on an outing to some water meadows near Charlottenburg. At the time Hermann was in obsessive pursuit of a rare moth (*Endromis versicolora*) but that day it was conspicuous by its absence. So, remembering the book he had brought with him, Hermann settled down to read, sitting on last year's yellow grass by the foot of a birch that swayed softly against the light-blue spring sky. An hour later when Hermann had finished reading the play, his face was bathed in tears. He seems to have experienced some kind of literary epiphany. The play had an impact on the eighteen-year-old Hermann which he said was greater than any he had experienced before from the printed word. He later recalled that the similarities between his youthful sorrow and the play struck him like a young and bitter early spring.[54] Further evidence of the importance of the play to Hermann comes across in a letter he wrote to Hauptmann in 1921 where he thanks the playwright for the very personal gift — without even knowing it — that he gave him in *Vor Sonnenaufgang*.[55]

Contrary to the expectations for a young man from a reputable family, Georg Hermann did not pursue the Abitur exam, and instead, in 1890, he left school to become an apprentice salesman. In June that year his father died, four months before what would have been his sixtieth birthday. Hermann recalls how on the day that his father died he asked for a book to read, but specified that it should not be his favourite work by the political writer and satirist Ludwig Börne, which he knew by heart.

Hermann published initially under his real name (Georg Borchardt) but in 1897 he adopted the pen name, Georg Hermann. In his preface to the 1911 reissue of *Spielkinder* Hermann says that the official reason he gives for adopting a pen name is that he likes to protect his privacy. But the true reason, he explains, lies in something his mother said that determined him to associate his father's forename with his public persona. Berta had told her three sons, Ludwig, Heinrich and Georg, a few days before her husband's death that it was now down to them to restore their father's name to honour.[56] The name 'Hermann' is, of course, strongly associated with heroism in German culture. The legendary German chieftain Hermann, famous for his victory against the Romans in the Teutoburg Forest, had become a potent symbol of German nationalism. Four years after unification, for instance, he was memorialized in the massive Hermannsdenkmal. But paradoxically for Georg Hermann, in adopting his father's name and so attaching his father's flag to his mast, the connotations were those of bitter failure rather than glorious success.

To a remarkable extent, the three brothers did restore the family's prestige, but for Hermann, his pen name would always attest not only to family loyalty but also to hardships overcome.

Notes to Chapter 1

1. Quoted in Walter Laqueur, *The History of Zionism* (London: Tauris Parke, 2003), p. 27.
2. Today this part of Berlin is the site of a public park, the Marx-Engels Forum.
3. C. G. van Liere, *Georg Hermann: Materialien zur Kenntnis seines Lebens und seines Werkes* (Amsterdam: Rodopi, 1974), p. 9.
4. Paul J. Jacobi, 'Geschichtliche Grundlagen zu Georg Hermanns *Jettchen Gebert*', *Bulletin des Leo Baeck Instituts*, no. 51 (1975), 114–21.
5. Amos Elon, *The Pity of It All — A Portrait of the German-Jewish Epoch 1743–1933* (New York: Picador, 2003), p. 14.
6. Jacobi, 'Geschichtliche Grundlagen zu Georg Hermanns *Jettchen Gebert*', p. 116.
7. Jacob Jacobson (ed.), *Die Judenbürgerbücher der Stadt Berlin 1809–1851: Mit Ergänzungen für die Jahre 1791–1809* (Berlin: De Gruyter, 1962), p. 98
8. See Jacobson, *Die Judenbürgerbücher*, p. 151. See also Steven M. Lowenstein, *The Berlin Jewish Community: Enlightenment, Family and Crisis, 1770–1830* (Oxford: Oxford University Press, 2000), p. 234, footnote 47.
9. Jacobson, *Die Judenbürgerbücher*, p. 151.
10. Georg Hermann, 'Meine Eltern', in *Die Reise nach Massow. Erzählungen und Skizzen* (Berlin: Das Neue Berlin, 1973), pp. 287–91. Here, pp. 290–91.
11. Georg Hermann, 'Die Reise nach Massow', in *Die Reise nach Massow*, pp. 7–18.
12. Ibid., p. 7. Hermann adds that Simon was a man after his own heart.
13. Ibid., p. 8. There is a little old maid in *Jettchen Gebert* who seems to owe something to Simon's wife. We are told she was inseparable from her knitting but that for whom she knitted all the stockings she produced was an inscrutable mystery, and that '...if the stockings she made for Wolfgang turned out too small she always knew of another pair of legs they would fit.' Hermann, *Hetty Geybert*, p. 49.
14. The entry for Samuel Bentheim in *Jüdische Trauungen in Berlin 1759 bis 1813*, ed. by Jacob Jacobson (Berlin: De Gruyter, 2011), p. 332, states only that he was a businessman.
15. Hermann, 'Die Reise', p. 9. The Yiddish word 'kharpe' means a real disgrace.
16. Ibid., p. 9.
17. Today Massow is known as Maszewo and is in Poland. It is about 125 miles east of Berlin.
18. Hermann, 'Die Reise', p. 10. The records show that Jette was actually eighteen when she married Heinrich and that he was twenty-seven-years old. Their graves can still be found today, in the Jewish Cemetery in Schönhauser Allee, Berlin.
19. Ibid., p. 15.

20. Ibid., pp. 15–16.

21. Ibid., p, 18.

22. Georg Hermann, *Unvorhanden und stumm, doch zu Menschen noch reden Briefe aus dem Exil 1933–41 an seine Tochter Hilde*, ed. by Laureen Nussbaum (Mannheim: persona verlag, 1991), pp. 173–74. Hereafter cited as *Unvorhanden und stumm*.

23. Eva subsequently said that Hermann Borchardt's father was a Prussian officer. (Private family recording, 1979).

24. Ibid. Today the town of Schwerin an der Warthe is known as Skwierzyna and is in Poland. At the time of Hermann Borchardt's birth it was part of the Grand Duchy of Posen.

25. Private correspondence, September 2014. I would also like to thank Uri Shani for providing me with additional information about Johanna Casper. Today Jastrow is known as Jastrowie and is in Poland.

26. Hermann, 'Meine Eltern', pp. 287–91.

27. Ibid., p. 287.

28. Ibid., p. 289.

29. Private family recording (1979).

30. Georg Hermann, 'Also — ein Jubiläum', in Hermann, *Die Reise nach Massow*, pp. 292–300. The essay, written in 1926, marked the fiftieth anniversary of Hermann's attendance at the synagogue.

31. Today's Stauffenbergstraße.

32. In a chapter on the Landwehr Canal in *Spazieren in Berlin* (1929), Franz Hessel writes of this enchanting area and 'the chestnut trees that the children of the Berlin west got to know in all seasons; their first and most pleasant botany lesson was the damp abundance of their buds, their flowers like tapers, and the brown fruits loosening themselves from thorny shells.' Franz Hessel, *Walking in Berlin: A Flâneur in the Capital*, trans. by Amanda DeMarco (Melbourne: Scribe, 2016), p. 150.

33. Hermann, 'Also — ein Jubiläum', pp. 295–96.

34. Ibid., p. 296.

35. Bagel-like caraway spiced rolls.

36. Hermann, 'Also — ein Jubiläum', p. 297.

37. Ibid., pp. 297–98.

38. Ibid., p. 299.

39. Ibid., p. 300.

40. Elon, *The Pity of It All*, p. 211. Arthur Schnitzler's father was one of those who lost his life's savings in the crash. See Arthur Schnitzler, *My Youth in Vienna*, trans. Catherine Hutter (London: Weidenfeld and Nicholson, 1971), p. 39.

41. Georg Hermann, 'Im Spiegel', in *Die Reise nach Massow*, pp. 301–09.

42. Thomas Mann, *Buddenbrooks — The Decline of a Family*, trans. by H. T. Lowe-Porter (London: Vintage Classics, 1996), p. 178.

43. Hermann, 'Meine Eltern', p. 287.

44. Hermann, *Hetty Geybert*, p. 247.

45. Hermann, 'Meine Eltern', p. 288.

46. Ibid. pp. 288–89.

47. Hermann, 'Im Spiegel', p. 302.

48. George Rothschild writes about Hermann's enthusiasm for the natural world in 'Mein Großvater Georg Hermann', his preface to Hermann's *Spaziergang in Potsdam* (Berlin: Verlag für Berlin-Brandenburg, 2013), pp. 8–9.

49. Hermann, 'Im Spiegel', p. 301.

50. Walter A. Reichart, 'Review of *Das Letzte Geheimnis: Eine psychologische Studie über die Brüder Gerhart und Carl Hauptmann* by Jean Jofen', *Journal of English and Germanic Philology*, vol. 72, no. 4 (October 1973), 599–603.

51. Gerhart Hauptmann drew upon this experience in his 1912 play, *Peter Brauer*. The eponymous lead character is based upon Old Gitschmann who died in 1903, with the choice of surname (Brewer) apparently meant to suggest his former teacher's fondness for alcohol. See Warren

R. Maurer, 'Gerhart Hauptmann's Character Names', *German Quarterly*, vol. 52, no. 4 (1979), 457–71.

52. Georg Hermann, *Die Zeitlupe und andere Betrachtungen über Menschen und Dinge* (Berlin: DVA, 1928), pp. 54–62. The collection is hereafter cited as *Die Zeitlupe*.

53. Jethro Bithell, *Modern German Literature 1880–1950* (London: Methuen, 1959), p. 1. The play was translated into English by Ludwig Lewisohn. See Lewisohn, *The Dramatic Works of Gerhart Hauptmann*, vol. 1 (London: Secker, 1912), pp. 1–93.

54. Hermann, 'Der junge Hauptmann und seine Modelle', p. 61.

55. The letter is available online: http://digital.staatsbibliothek-berlin.de. (Search under Georg Hermann Borchardt.)

56. Georg Hermann, 'Vorwort zur zweiten Auflage', in Georg Hermann, *Spielkinder* (Berlin: Das Neue Berlin, 1998), pp. 273–79.

CHAPTER 2

❖

Spielkinder

Georg Hermann identified three figures as standing at his literary cradle.[1] The first, as we have seen, was Gerhart Hauptmann. Hermann made the most of their mutual acquaintance with the Gitschmanns and shared with the rising playwright some of his early manuscripts. It was raw and confused stuff, according to Hermann but Hauptmann was not discouraging and recommended he read the novel *Gift* [Poison] by the Norwegian writer, Alexander Kielland.

The second figure was Fritz Mauthner, an Austro-Hungarian novelist and theatre critic. Hermann recounts how, some years after his contact with Hauptmann, feigning a headache, he left work, and went uninvited to Mauthner's house in Wangenheimstraße in Grunewald. Hermann simply knocked on the writer's door and handed him the manuscript of a play that he had written, asking him to read it. Mauthner replied that he could not read the play straight-away but obligingly said to Hermann to go into the garden and then in an hour's time he would invite him inside to read it. As Hermann acknowledges, Mauthner's response was very generous, considering they had never met before. He listened to all five acts of the play and said that it was technically well-constructed, amongst other encouraging observations. The third literary figure was the writer and theatre director Paul Schlenther whom Hermann gave some of his plays in 1892/93. Schlenther's advice was to the point. Hermann should stick to a business career: he faced a bleak future as a writer!

At the time, Hermann was working as an apprentice in a firm manufacturing neckties. Writing was an escape from a business career which was bringing him neither personal satisfaction nor financial reward. Hermann worked from eight in the morning to eight at night and his take home pay of just 60 Mark a month was less than the earnings of a street cleaner. Indeed, most workers earned more in a week than Hermann was earning in a month as an apprentice at the factory.[2] When he started at the necktie business it was unusual in already having its own factory. Hermann had thought that the company might be more progressive than other firms he had read about but he was soon struck by its dehumanising industrial nature. He drew upon his impressions of the factory in his first novel, describing how it is that hundreds of individual beings come together to form a great machine, each carrying out their specific and unvarying mechanical task, their actions like the interlocking gears which keep the whole enterprise going. The speed of the operation and the extent to which the cogs should be oiled is, of course, determined by the factory managers. And yet, Hermann writes, the machine is not built from dead iron but from living human material, individuals each with their own inalienable value, and their own sense of self.[3]

By his own admission, Hermann had little enthusiasm for the world of commerce but he stuck it out at the factory until autumn 1894. The sole thing he claimed to have learned from his apprenticeship was not to jump to conclusions about people based on their ties: 'Geschmack in Krawatten höchst variabel ist, und nicht mit Sicherheit Rückschlüsse erlaubt.' [Taste in ties is highly variable and one can't make inferences with any certainty].[4] Throughout this period, Hermann was writing late into the evening and building up a pile of manuscripts. He wrote and wrote — no sooner sketching out one thing than embarking on the next.[5]

Hermann elected to do his compulsory military service in Bavaria — according to Eva, this was because there was less anti-Semitism at the time in southern Germany. Despite German unification in 1871, unlike other state militias, the Bavarian Army had continued to exist as an independent entity, albeit under the overall command of the Kaiser. Hermann was in the Tenth Company of the Second Bavarian Infantry Regiment — a 'preußischer Spion' [Prussian spy] in the Royal Bavarian Army.[6]

Amongst the family photographs is one of Georg in his soldier's uniform. He looks the part, with his pencil-thin moustache and serious gazing eyes looking out from under an imposing helmet. His tunic would have been blue, the buttons golden and his collar and cuffs red. It seems likely that this was the first time that Hermann spent a prolonged period outside of Berlin. It was in Bavaria that he encountered New Year's Eve fireworks (not at that time a custom in the north) and also the pleasures of the shower-bath. He had, he later wrote, found the solution to the perennial question of what is the loveliest thing in the world — the smile of a woman, the ice-crystals of a hoar frost, art, music, fine wines — *nein*, all pale into insignificance compared to the pleasure of taking a shower.[7] Hermann's army experiences appear to have been reasonably positive. When he was discharged in 1895 he was given a leadership certificate and a testimonial which emphasized both his physical and mental gifts.[8] Hermann's discharge did, however, come earlier than planned because he had contracted pneumonia, and he spent his last weeks in the army convalescing in the mountain resort of Garmisch-Partenkirchen.

It was during this period of recuperation that Hermann completed *Spielkinder*.[9] Even before he fell ill, Hermann had found that he enjoyed a great deal of free time once he started his military service, the like of which he had never known before. In the preface to the second edition of *Spielkinder*, Hermann describes how in the spring of 1896 by a strange set of circumstances, too complicated to unravel, there was a young woman who was kind enough to type up the novel for him. He dictated part of it to her but she also worked from some of Hermann's manuscripts, having to wrestle, he says, with very difficult material. All this she did for no money, and the natural assumption that she was Hermann's girlfriend at the time, he denies, saying that there was no relationship between them which can explain her kindness and support in devoting weeks and weeks to producing a typescript

FIG. 2.1. The Prussian Spy

of the novel. She was like a person who saves someone from drowning by grabbing them by the neck, although in his case, Hermann muses, she had to expend even more energy to effect his rescue.

Back in Berlin in the summer of 1896, Hermann hand-delivered the manuscript to the Fontane publishing house in Lützowstraße. Hermann was a devotee of Theodor Fontane's novels and felt that if anyone was likely to have an appreciation of *Spielkinder*, it was Fontane, although the publishing house was actually run by his son, Friedrich. While he was waiting to hear if Fontane was interested, Hermann tried a number of other publishers. One magazine invited him into their offices to discuss the novel. The editor was willing to serialize it but only if Hermann cut a number of passages which he felt were too candid. At the time, Hermann was out of work and living at home with his mother and his sister Rose who suffered from tuberculosis and was unable to work due to her poor health. The magazine editor was offering him more money than he had earned in a long time but Hermann was not prepared to make the requested cuts and did not take up his offer. One gets the sense of a determined and uncompromising young man. Despite his lack of success in life, Hermann evidently retained a strong self-belief in his writing. His confidence proved to be justified. Fontane opted to publish the novel and it was also serialized as written in *Vorwärts*, the newspaper of the Social Democratic Party (SPD).

Spielkinder charts the life of its protagonist, Georg, from the age of four to twenty-three. The novel's plot draws heavily on Hermann's own childhood and adolescence. In his preface to the second edition, Hermann acknowledges that it is an autobiographical work, although he caveats this by saying that all writing is autobiographical if one considers literature as a mirror of reality.[10] Hermann uses the word 'Spielkinder' in the novel to denote people who do not take their occupation or even their lives seriously. These 'Spielkinder' lack uprightness and strength of character. Geiger, Georg's deluded father in the novel, who always maintains his hopes of regaining his former financial security but never recovers, Georg himself and his friends, Walter and Eugen, as well as the factory workers whose lives are dominated by routine, are all described as 'Spielkinder'.

The novel begins with a depiction of Georg's boyhood in Gründerzeit Berlin before the family is plunged into poverty as a result of Geiger being tricked by his brother-in-law and an associate into buying a piece of worthless land. This failed speculation leaves Geiger with insurmountable debts. The family (as had happened to the Borchardts) is forced to sell its furniture and cut back on servants. Georg's father is driven to try to wheedle money out of anyone he can find and the family becomes increasingly isolated while trying to maintain a façade of bourgeois respectability. The household has to relocate to smaller apartments in less salubrious parts of Berlin and eventually must let go of all its servants. We are told that the family goes without food on a regular basis. Godela Weiss-Sussex, in her study of the novel, suggests that Hermann wants the reader to see Geiger and his family as victims of a cruel society.[11] Hermann himself felt that at the crux of the novel is the anguished cry of youth and there is certainly a strong focus on Georg's suffering: his poverty-stricken childhood, the failures of his weak father and the mind-numbing work he has to do.

Another source of Georg's youthful anguish is the doomed relationship with his first love, Lies. They meet when they are just twelve years old but already Lies has had to learn to be self-sufficient. Her father is a drunkard and her mother has frequent visits from 'gentlemen friends'.[12] Lies is regularly beaten and has to inure herself against the physical cruelty of her parents. Attractive and graceful in her movements, from the point when Lies is thirteen and first kisses Georg, the two constantly find excuses to be together. As Lies matures, she becomes increasingly aware of her physical attractiveness. Georg tells us that she knew exactly how pretty she was and liked to admire herself in the mirror. They drift apart for a time and Georg does not see Lies again until he is sixteen when they meet by chance in the shop where she now works. Lies reawakens his attention with her body. We are told that Georg is infatuated with her intoxicating beauty and that night they make love on a park bench. 'Ich liebte Lies, wie sie mich liebte. Jetzt wußte ich es. Wir gehörten ganz einander, mit Leib und Seele, mit Seele und Leib.' [I loved Lies, how she loved me. Now I knew. We belonged to each other completely, body and soul].[13]

Soon afterwards, Georg's father dies. Geiger's last days, presumably modelled on Hermann's memories of his own father, describe him seated, impassive by a window, smoking but no longer able to read or to enjoy being read to. Once again, Georg and Lies lose touch and it is not until Georg's mother uses her remaining contacts to get her son a job in a shop which turns out to be the same as the one where Lies works that their paths cross again. Lies has now left home and lives in a small apartment where, before long, Georg is spending every evening.

> [...] so denke ich jener ersten Monate unserer Liebe doch stets als der glücklichsten und ungetrübtesten meines Lebens. Ich liebte und wurde geliebt.

> [I always think of those first few months of our love as the happiest and most untroubled of my life. I loved and was loved.][14]

It proves to be a short-lived idyll, in part because of Georg's jealousy of the friendship which exists between Lies and his childhood friend, Eugen. But other factors also undermine the relationship. There is a social gulf between Georg and Lies. Georg's family may have become impoverished and the neighbourhood children he fraternizes with as a youngster may be working class, but his family strives to hang on to its bourgeois credentials. We are told that the Geigers continue to live beyond their means and Georg's mother does her best to keep up appearances, speaking French so that the maids will not understand talk of the family's financial woes.

Lies is dangerous because she has the potential to pull Georg down irrevocably into the ranks of the working class. He acknowledges that he should be looking for a 'respectable' woman and feels guilty about the fact that his mother and sisters bear the brunt of the family's financial ruin. Maintaining bourgeois respectability is crucial, not least because of the associated opportunities. The children must do well and Georg is obliged to seek to marry someone with money. His mother tells him that having money is the summit of earthly bliss.

FIG. 2.2. Hans Baluschek, *Neue Häuser*, 1895 (Märkisches Museum, Berlin).

As the story unfolds, the same things that attracted Georg to Lies, her beauty and sexuality, are the traits he blames for the end of their relationship when she becomes the lover of his friend, Eugen. Not long afterwards, Lies loses her job because of the type of woman she has become in her boss's eyes. Formerly a good worker, he says that Lies is now a corrupt element. She has become a girl who is ripe for Friedrichstraße (i.e. being a prostitute). Despite Georg's bourgeois attempts at 'improving' Lies, her interests remain frivolous and materialistic — fashion, lewd jokes and horse racing. Her descent in the novel is inexorable and by the time Georg next sees her, on his return from two years' military service, Lies has become a prostitute. Initially she is delighted by his return but Georg feels that he cannot even touch Lies now. He tries to find her a better place to live and does so. But when he returns to tell her the good news, Lies has gone. He looks for her for over a month and eventually finds her the night before he must leave for another eight weeks of military service. Lies is ill with tuberculosis and it is to be their final meeting.

Alongside the story of Georg and Lies' relationship, a focus on the depiction of Berlin — one of the primary themes in Hermann's subsequent works — is already evident in *Spielkinder*.[15] The novel presents a multi-faceted picture of the city and Weiss-Sussex suggests that even in his debut novel, Hermann's masterly skill in evoking the atmosphere of particular areas and situations is detectable.[16]

As she shows, Hermann represents the different social levels of city life through the contrasting homes of the leading characters, from the bourgeois apartment of Georg's uncle, to the sordid quarters to which Lies moves and the seedy tenement house in the new suburbs where his friend Walter lives, at the periphery of the city. Weiss-Sussex also highlights the similarities in the lifelessness that permeates Hans Baluschek's paintings of the new suburbs and Hermann's descriptions of them as being enveloped in darkness and a deadly quiet; 'uninhabited and unsafe in their semi-finished state [...] but also drenched in anonymity and desolation.'[17]

It appears that those closest to Hermann had no inkling of the autobiographical nature of the novel as its publication caused a huge family argument. Hermann recalled many years later, 'Mein Roman *Spielkinder* [...] ist autobiographisch [...] und verursacht im Familienkreis eine Explosion. Haß und Boykott folgen.' [My novel *Spielkinder* [...] is autobiographic and caused an explosion within the family circle. Hatred and ostracism ensued].[18] It is perhaps not surprising that family members were deeply upset by what they saw as a brutal and inaccurate public portrayal of the troubles they had endured.

The family furore was probably compounded by the fact that while his mother and older brothers were striving to restore the family's bourgeois credentials, Hermann continued to flounder. Around this time a decision was made that he was not to pursue a career in commerce. Hermann suggests that it was the business world that gave up on him rather than a positive decision on his part, but whatever the prompt, 1896 represented a turning point for Hermann because it was the year that he enrolled at the Friedrich-Wilhelm University (today's Humboldt University of Berlin).

As a part-time student, Hermann studied the History of Art, German Literature and Philosophy over six semesters from 1896 to 1899. He saw journalism as a way of earning his livelihood and hoped his studies would help him learn how to become a literary critic.[19] Typically self-deprecating about his time at university, Hermann said that he studied in the Russian fashion and was forever being distracted by his passion for chess. But it would be wrong to surmise that he did not gain from his time at university. We know, for instance, that Hermann attended lectures given by the sociologist Georg Simmel and his ideas on the impact of the metropolis on the individual city dweller would have connected with Hermann, whose awareness and sensitivity to the changing nature of Berlin, as noted, was already apparent in *Spielkinder*. Hermann also studied under Erich Schmidt who was the professor of German Language and Literature at the university at the time. Schmidt was an advocate of contemporary Naturalist modern literature (sharing, for example, Hermann's enthusiasm for Gerhart Hauptmann) and also counted among his students the writers Alfred Kerr and Arthur Eloesser.

Hermann was most taken with his art studies. Although he always felt he was more of an amateur enthusiast than a bona fide art historian, Hermann had been captivated by visual art from early in life. In the essay 'Im Spiegel' he explains how he is drawn — body and soul — to the mute eloquence of visual art. The love he feels for it is purer than his affection for literature because his nature is

FIG. 2.3. Hermann was a keen chess player throughout his life. This picture is from 1916.

more sensual than cerebral. While many other things in life remain dead to him — nation, family, social ties, trade and commerce — and he never feels part of them and stands alone, like a child who doesn't want to join in with the game and remains outside the circle, in art Hermann says he feels a sense of belonging. Art is something that resonates with him to his core, bringing him an inner warmth and sense of contentment. Indeed, he recalls that during these student years, when he was at his lowest ebb, he would travel fourth class by train to see the Rembrandts in the Herzog Anton Ulrich-Museum in Braunschweig. Only they could give him a sense of reconnection with the world.[20]

It was during one such period of depression, in May 1897, that Georg Hermann took a holiday with friends in Heidelberg. The short trip had a profound impact on him. Writing thirty years later, Hermann explained how the origins of the holiday lay in a friendship he formed in the early 1890s at a Berlin gymnastics club with a young architect, Ludwig Jahn.[21] Jahn was 'der zwar zum Turner sich eignete wie ein Elefant zum Seiltanzen' [as suited to gymnastics as an elephant is to walking the tightrope].[22] But he was a well-educated and artistically gifted man who was on friendly terms with the poets Alfred Mombert and Richard Dehmel as well as other members of the Friedrichshagener Dichterkreis, a group of writers, located in the Berlin suburb of that name, who championed German Naturalism. Jahn and Hermann found that they shared similar interests, and after the architect moved away from Berlin, their friendship was maintained by correspondence. It was as a result of a more downbeat than normal letter from Hermann that Jahn invited him for a visit to his home in Rohrbacher Straße, Heidelberg.

Hermann appears to have thoroughly enjoyed himself, spending time exploring the old towns of the south and, like a good art history student, visiting as many galleries as he could manage. He was struck by how much further the spring was advanced in the softer climes of the Palatinate. Already laburnum, wisteria, lilac, apple trees, hawthorns and chestnuts were in flower. He could enjoy mild moonlit nights when there was a soft breeze quietly drifting down from the green beech tree forests of the mountains and sit outside, drinking Maibowle by lantern light.

The vacation prompted a remarkable change in Hermann's outlook and approach to writing. As with *Vor Sonnenaufgang*, it was something of an epiphany.

> Diese Frühlingstage in Heidelberg — nicht mehr als zwei Wochen, an die sich eine Reise durch die süddeutschen Galerien und alten Städte anschloß [...] sind bestimmend für mein ganzes weiteres schriftstellerisches Schaffen geworden.

> [These spring days in Heidelberg — not more than two weeks — followed by a journey through the southern German galleries and its old towns [...] have shaped all of my subsequent literary work.][23]

Hermann suddenly felt the contrast between the *joie de vivre* of the southern way of life and the stark rigidity of his northern mentality and was ashamed of how as a writer his preoccupation with realism bled all of the colour from life. It was the holiday in Heidelberg which Hermann said gave him the confidence to bring a greater emotional range into his writing. He was immediately inspired to write a number of short stories including 'Tränen' [Tears] and 'Der Wert des Lebens' [The Value of Life], which represented a complete departure from the bleak factual style of his previous efforts. While he had not perhaps yet found his true artistic soul, the connection he felt with the less buttoned-up south had given Hermann the courage to express himself in a new, less spartan way. In recognition of this, when Fontane published *Modelle*, a collection of twenty-one of his short stories and sketches later that year, Hermann dedicated the book to Ludwig Jahn.[24]

While at university, Hermann helped fund his studies by taking odd jobs to supplement whatever income he could earn from writing. These jobs were often drab affairs. In 'Die Zukunftsfrohen', which gives its name to a second collection of sketches published by Fontane in 1898, Hermann paints a poignant portrait of the time he spent during this period working as a temporary statistician for the city council.[25] The story which is related through the narrator's diary entries, begins with a description of the Dickensian ground floor office where he works. There are shelves everywhere which are so high that they reach up to the ceiling. Each is laden with grey boxes which in turn are sub-divided into hundreds of small compartments. Hermann likens them to the cells in a wasp nest. Piles of forms and dossiers, thick with dust, are strewn all over the office. The dust is everywhere. It conquers new areas of the office on a daily basis. Two cobwebbed maps of the city hang on a wall.

The narrator dubs the colleagues with whom he shares this dingy environment the 'Zukunftsfrohen'. Like Trollope's Lady Carbury, their happiness is 'ever in the future, never reached but always coming.'[26] All employed on temporary contracts, the men have been brought together for a few months before they are scattered to the four winds again and must look afresh for new offices where they can find shelter. The Zukunftsfrohen are stylish dressers. Their clothes seem to have been salvaged from some better time and habits from these former days, like maintaining a neatly trimmed beard, still survive. Most of the men have known success in the past and none admit that they have been brought low as a result of their own mistakes. Rather, they believe themselves to be the victims of fate and live in hope of being restored to their former status. One of the Zukunftsfrohen, Herr Lorenz, says that the whole of humanity can be divided into two camps: those who ride in carriages and those who get splashed by them. Lorenz once belonged to the former group but now ranks among the splashed. Conversation in the office is frequently intellectual. The Zukunftsfrohen enjoy discussing complex scientific matters, dropping foreign words into their conversation and spicing their observations with Latin quotes. But this intellectual energy doesn't find its way into the work that they do. Ardent anti-careerists, they work reluctantly and ineffectively, especially on the Monday after payday when almost nothing is done as the Zukunftsfrohen nurse their hangovers.

Alcohol, as in the world of the Krauses in *Vor Sonnenaufgang*, plays a central role in the lives of the Zukunftsfrohen. Their most pressing concern is whether or not they have enough money to buy liquor. For all the chatter and apparent mirth in the office, the narrator comments that there is always a mournful accompanying undertone. Hermann's concern with life's under-achievers and their weaknesses in the face of an indifferent world finds focus in the character of one particular bureau worker, Ernst Lintrov. Lintrov is a keen satirist and able to argue an issue from all sides but he is also a consumptive alcoholic and one day falls seriously ill at work. There is a collection in the office for him and the narrator goes to visit Lintrov with the money at his home in an impoverished quarter of the city. He has assumed his colleague is a bachelor and is surprised when his knock at the door is answered by an attractive, young, heavily pregnant woman, Frau Lintrov. Such is her beauty that he is reminded of a Botticelli Madonna. Lintrov is in bed, very ill. When the narrator returns the following day he witnesses his death. Mausi, his wife, throws herself onto Lintrov's body and screams, a piercing scream which we are told is heard like the echo of a locomotive through the quiet streets at night.

Lintrov's death has only a marginal impact on his former work colleagues. They contribute a wreath for the funeral but his death is quickly passed over. The final day comes when all of the Zukunftsfrohen must leave the bureau. Their contracts have ended. The wave which brought them to the bureau for this transient period is dispersed into droplets and the Zukunftsfrohen are once more scattered to the four winds. Lintrov's child, like the playwright Gotthold Ephraim Lessing's son, we are told, was an exceptionally bright boy. The doctor had to use forceps to prise him out but it was to no avail, the baby died soon afterwards and took his mother with him.[27]

II. KUNST-AUSSTELLUNG
MAI · OCTOBER 1900.

BERLINER
SECESSION

KANTSTR. 12.
NEBEN DEM THEATER DES WESTENS
GEÖFFNET TÄGLICH v. 9 - 7 UHR
EINTRITTSPREIS 1 MK.

FIG. 2.4. Poster advertising the Berlin Secession Exhibition of 1900, by Wilhelm Schulz.

Whatever the shortcomings of his studies, Hermann's university experience does seem to have paved his way into a new career. From 1899 until around 1907, he worked mainly as an art critic for newspapers of the Ullstein publishing house, as well as regularly contributing pieces about art for other journals and periodicals.[28] In 1900 Hermann published a survey of the work of graphic artists featured in the weekly satirical magazine *Simplicissimus*.[29] This was soon followed by a substantial essay *Die deutsche Karikatur im 19. Jahrhundert* [German Caricature in the Nineteenth Century][30] in which Hermann argued the case for a re-evaluation of the place of graphic artists and illustrators in the world of art, pointing out that they tend to be progressive individuals whose work is deeply connected with life. Their art, he suggests, opens our eyes to new areas of aesthetic enjoyment, as well as giving solid form to what might otherwise soon be swept away by the passage of time.

It was a propitious time to be embarking on a career as an art critic. While official art remained dominated by the conservative edicts of the royal academy, the Berlin Secession, which had been founded in May 1898 by sixty-five artists, had breathed new life into the visual arts in Berlin and coincided with the opening of a number of new galleries in the city. Hermann grew close to several members of the Berlin Secession, corresponding with Lovis Corinth, Käthe Kollwitz, Heinrich Zille, and Max Liebermann, its first president. As well as promoting these German artists, Hermann was also an advocate for Munch, Cezanne, Manet, Van Gogh,

Degas and many other artists of the modern trend. The Berlin Secession became, in Peter Paret's words, 'the institutional centre of German Impressionism'.[31] In like fashion, its three most eminent painters, Liebermann, Corinth, and Max Slevogt — dubbed by Cassirer 'the constellation of German Impressionism' — adopted the French Impressionists' pleinair subjects, bright tonality, suppression of detail and quick brushwork.[32]

As an art critic, Hermann championed Impressionism. Beyond technical traits like visible brush strokes and a strong emphasis on the changing qualities of light, Hermann believed that:

> Der tiefere Sinn des Impressionismus liegt [...] sondern einzig und allein in der neuen Stellung, welche durch sie der Kulturmensch, der Städter zu seiner landschaftlichen Umgebung gewonnen. Es ist eine Wandlung in der Struktur des menschlichen Empfindens [...] eine Weltanschauung.

> [The deeper meaning of Impressionism lies [...] solely in the new perspective it has given the man of culture, the city dweller, on his environment. It is a change in the nature of human sensibility, [...] a new world view.][33]

Less concerned with objective verisimilitude than evoking mood and atmosphere, Hermann believed that the Impressionists had managed to get ten steps closer to life than any previous artists.[34] Their works presented often familiar subjects through the prism of the artist's sensibility and in so doing revealed new depths. Berliners who had traversed the Grunewald hundreds of times, Hermann wrote in an article in 1900, discovered that the beauty of its landscape, as revealed in Walter Leistikow's paintings, had remained hidden from them.[35] Hermann regarded Liebermann as 'unbestritten die stärkste Befähigung der heutigen deutschen Kunst' [indisputably the finest talent in contemporary German art].[36] In particular, Hermann admired his sense of nuance and of the inter-relations of colours. He believed that it was Liebermann's temperament and verve, as expressed in his work, which enabled him to render the intensity of life.[37] It is evident that Hermann shared the Impressionists' commitment to depicting atmosphere as perceived by the artist at a given time in a given place, and just as his appreciation for Hans Baluschek's paintings had been reflected in his portrayal of the city's new suburbs in *Spielkinder*, so Hermann's affinity for the approach of the Impressionists came to shape his literary style.

At the same time that Georg Hermann's life was finally taking shape professionally, he met and became engaged to Martha Heynemann. Hermann was a keen tennis player and according to my grandmother they met over a game of tennis and it was love at first sight. Martha's father, Robert, born in Magdeburg in 1839, was a successful businessman. He was eighteen years older than her mother, Elise Heidenreich, who according to Eva had little say in her marriage and can only have been sixteen or seventeen at the time. The couple moved from Magdeburg to Berlin after their wedding and soon had two daughters, Martha (b. 1875) and Paula (b. 1878). But in 1881 Robert died, leaving Elise, still only twenty-four, widowed with two small children. Elise never remarried.

Not a great deal is known about Martha's childhood but a few photographs in the family albums tell the story in outline. The first picture in the Heynemann

FIG. 2.5. Martha Heynemann

insert which my grandmother added to the Borchardt album is of the thickly bearded Robert Heynemann. Then we see Elise, with cropped hair and wearing an elaborate checked dress with billowing leg-of-mutton sleeves, edged with lace and ribbons, holding Martha who is perhaps seven or eight months old. Elise, despite, her outfit, looks little more than a child. There is no hint of a smile in her serious gaze. And then we jump to July 1888, a torn photograph of Elise, Martha and Paula looking out from an open ground floor window. A downcast Elise is leaning forward with her folded arms resting on the sill and next to her is Martha, her hand wrapped around the central frame. Paula, a pert expression on her face, sits on the ledge, her head resting on her sister's curls. Later photos show Martha and Paula in their teens, formal portraits by Albert Meyer, somewhat faded now. In one, Elise stands proudly behind her two daughters, still with her neatly cropped hair but now wearing pince-nez. Elise made sure that her daughters had the appropriate bourgeois accomplishments. Martha, for example, spoke French fluently and from all accounts was a wonderful pianist.

Martha and Georg became engaged in 1900 and were married on 28 March 1901. Her sister Paula married a talented lawyer, Theo Sternberg, the following year. Hermann and Martha set up home in an apartment at Kaiserallee 68 in the southwest suburb of Friedenau.[38] Their first child, Ilse, was born on 3 February 1902. There is just the one picture of Ilse in the Borchardt family album. It shows a chubby looking baby in a long white gown. Tragically, Ilse contracted diphtheria and died on 14 January 1903. Martha was devastated. For the rest of her life she always carried a pair of Ilse's booties in her handbag.

Hermann's grief is evident from private letters and the essay 'Sehnsucht' [Longing] in which he wrote that his heart had been struck by the hardest weight which can fall upon anyone — the loss of a child. Prior to Ilse's illness, Hermann describes in the essay how he had placed two butterfly pupae under glass on a windowsill at home. During the weeks that his daughter was fighting for her young life he entirely forgot about them. It was only after Ilse's death, when the house had become completely quiet and Hermann was pacing up and down as if a prisoner in a solitary cell, that his eyes turned to the glass and there he saw an exquisite swallowtail, rhythmically opening and closing its broad yellow wings with their striped black brush lines, the colour of which is deeper than any Chinese ink. And it was at that moment, Hermann writes, that he broke down and his tears began to fall.[39]

At the time of Ilse's death, Martha was already pregnant with my grandmother, Eva-Maria who was born on 25 September 1903. Unable to continue living in the same apartment where Ilse had died, Hermann and Martha had moved a few doors down to Kaiserallee 108 and it was here that Eva was born. Eva's birth was followed swiftly by the birth of another daughter, Hilde, on 25 August 1904 and then by a third, Elise, on 24 May 1906. A few days after Elise's arrival, Fleischel published *Jettchen Gebert*, the novel which was to make Hermann's name and transform the family's world.

Fig. 2.6. Ilse Borchardt

Notes to Chapter 2

1. Hermann, *Spielkinder*, 'Vorwort zur zweiten Auflage', p. 277.
2. See Gerhard Bry (assisted by Charlotte Boschan), *Wages in Germany, 1871–1945* (Princeton, NJ: Princeton University Press, 1960), pp. 51–79.
3. Georg Hermann, *Spielkinder* (Berlin: Das Neue Berlin, 1998), pp. 150–51.
4. Georg Hermann, 'Die Zeitung', in *Vom gesicherten und ungesicherten Leben* (Berlin: Fleischel, 1915), p. 172.
5. Hermann, *Spielkinder*, 'Vorwort zur zweiten Auflage', p. 273.
6. Georg Hermann, 'Das Schönste auf der Welt', in *Die Reise nach Massow*, pp. 201–05. Here, p. 204.
7. Ibid.
8. Georg Hermann, 'Weltabschied', in *Unvorhanden und stumm*, p. 253.
9. It seems likely that early drafts of the novel were among the stack of manuscripts he had produced during his apprenticeship.
10. But literature is not history, Hermann adds, and the experiences of the soul can lay no claim to be a factual record. Hermann, *Spielkinder*, 'Vorwort zur zweiten Auflage', p. 275.
11. Godela Weiss-Sussex, *Metropolitan Chronicles: Georg Hermann's Berlin Novels 1897–1912* (Stuttgart: Heinz, 2001), p. 51.
12. For more detail about Lies and Georg's relationship, see Catherine Maitland, 'Dora and her Sisters: Control and Rebellion in Hermann and Schnitzler', doctoral thesis (University of North Carolina at Chapel Hill, 2006), pp. 38–47.
13. Hermann, *Spielkinder*, p. 141.
14. Ibid., p. 155
15. Weiss-Sussex, *Metropolitan Chronicles*, pp. 71–104.
16. Ibid., p. 98.
17. Ibid., p. 86.
18. Georg Hermann, *Autobiographisches* (1938) trans. by Hub Nijssen. See ... *Aber ihr Ruf verhallt ins Leere hinein. Der Schriftsteller Georg Hermann*, ed. by Kerstin Schoor (Berlin: Weidler, 1999), pp. 231–33.
19. Hermann, 'Im Spiegel', p. 304.
20. Ibid., p. 305.
21. Georg Hermann, 'Wie ich auf Heidelberg kam', in *Die Zeitlupe*, pp. 186–94.
22. Ibid., p. 187.
23. Ibid., p. 188.
24. Georg Hermann, *Modelle: Ein Skizzenbuch* (Berlin: Fontane, 1897).
25. Georg Hermann, *Die Zukunftsfrohen: Neue Skizzen* (Berlin: Fontane, 1898). Hermann dedicated the collection to his mother. 'Die Zukunftsfrohen' is included in Hermann, *Die Reise nach Massow*, pp. 86–118.
26. Anthony Trollope, *The Way We Live Now* (London: Vintage, 2012), p. 100.
27. Lessing's son died only a few hours after he had been christened. In the famous letter to his friend Johann Eschenberg, Lessing wrote that it was testimony to the child's good sense that he came so unwillingly into the world and then seized the first opportunity of leaving it again. See Hugh Barr Nisbet, *Gotthold Ephraim Lessing: His Life, Works, and Thought* (Oxford: Oxford University Press, 2013), p. 553.
28. For a detailed analysis of Hermann's career as an art critic, see Godela Weiss-Sussex, 'Impressionismus als Weltanschauung. Die Kunstkritik Georg Hermanns', in *Georg Hermann: Deutsch-jüdischer Schriftsteller und Journalist 1871–1943*, ed. by Godela Weiss-Sussex (Tübingen: Niemeyer, 2004), pp. 87–102.
29. 'Der Simplicissimus und seine Zeichner' (Berlin: Die Welt am Montag, 1900).
30. Georg Hermann, *Die deutsche Karikatur im 19. Jahrhundert* (Bielefeld: Velhagen und Klasing, 1901).
31. Peter Paret, *The Berlin Secession: Modernism and Its Enemies in Imperial Germany* (Cambridge, MA: Belknap Press of Harvard University Press, 1980), p. 210.

32. Gert Schiff, 'Review of *The Berlin Secession: Modernism and Its Enemies in Imperial Germany* by Peter Paret', *Art Journal*, vol. 42, no. 4 (1982), p. 357 and p. 359.

33. Georg Hermann, 'Berliner Kunstausstellungen', 1901, quoted in Weiss-Sussex, 'Impressionismus als Weltanschauung', p. 100.

34. Georg Hermann, 'Die Nationalgalerie', *Berliner Morgenpost*, 24 December 1909. Quoted in Godela Weiss-Sussex, 'Naturalist Metaphor of Destruction or Impressionist Panorama? A Re-evaluation of Georg Hermann's Berlin Novel *Kubinke*', *CLS*, vol. 35, no. 4. 1998, fn. 36, p. 378.

35. Georg Hermann, 'Walter Leistikow', *Morgenpost*, 23 November 1900. Quoted in Weiss-Sussex, 'Impressionismus als Weltanschauung', p. 100.

36. Georg Hermann, 'Die Ausstellung der Secession', *Die Gegenwart*, 36 (1909), p. 294. Quoted in Godela Weiss-Sussex, 'Naturalist Metaphor of Destruction or Impressionist Panorama? A Re-evaluation of Georg Hermann's Berlin Novel, *Kubinke*', *CLS*, vol. 35, no. 4, 1998, 356–79, here, p. 370.

37. Georg Hermann, 'Max Liebermann', in *Jüdische Künstler*, ed. by Martin Buber (Berlin: Jüdischer Verlag, 1903), pp. 105–35.

38. Kaiserallee was renamed Bundesallee in 1950.

39. Georg Hermann, 'Sehnsucht', in *Gesammelte Werke*, vol. 5 (Stuttgart: DVA, 1922), pp. 612–18.

CHAPTER 3

❖

Jettchen Gebert

FIG. 3.1. Hermann dedicated *Jettchen Gebert* to Martha.

For his second novel, *Jettchen Gebert*, Georg Hermann again drew upon family history but this time he went back to his grandparents' generation, to Biedermeier Berlin, a period that held a special fascination for him.

Hitherto, the years from 1815 to 1848 had tended to be seen mainly in political terms. Described as the 'Vormärz', the time was characterized as a period of state repression which culminated in the March revolutions of 1848. But gradually from the early 1900s onwards, interest grew in the cultural achievements of the post-Napoleonic years and collectors, such as Hermann, began to acquire Biedermeier furniture and artefacts. In 1901 at the Überbrettl, Berlin's first cabaret, Robert Koppel and Bozena Bradsky, decked out in the fashions of the Biedermeier, had a notable popular success with 'Der lustige Ehemann' [The Merry Husband]. As Peter

Jelavisch notes in his history of Berlin cabaret, 'the number represented a nostalgic looking-back to a supposedly idyllic, cosy, pre-metropolitan age.'[1] Hermann's *Jettchen Gebert* tapped into this wistful mood and played a significant part in the continuing revival of interest in the Biedermeier.

Prior to writing the novel, he immersed himself in a detailed study of the period. This research formed the basis of his anthology, *Das Biedermeier im Spiegel seiner Zeit* [The Biedermeier Reflected in Documents of its Time].[2] *Das Biedermeier* comprises a collection of extracts from a wide variety of contemporary and historical sources including letters, diaries and memoirs. Hermann's introductory essay to the collection presents a rounded portrait of the period, covering both its political character and its culture.[3] He does not underplay the oppressive nature of political life, acknowledging that the years following Napoleon's defeat were marked by poverty for many and that the freedoms which the French had granted, the civil rights and legal equality, were swiftly taken away again as the old establishment reasserted its primacy. The whole period, Hermann argues, was marked by a constant struggle against the government, against the police and state censorship.

One aspect of this repression was that state harassment of universities resumed. Hermann points out that during the Biedermeier simply to have studied at university made you politically suspect in the eyes of the authorities.

> Und wenn wir heute die Geschichte dieser Jahre überblicken, so gibt es kaum einen Mann von Bedeutung, der nicht irgendwie in politische Prozesse verwickelt war und der nicht zum mindesten die Bekanntschaft mit Untersuchungsrichtern und Untersuchungsgefängnissen gemacht hat [...].

> [And if we look over the history of those years today, there is scarcely a man of importance during this period who did not fall foul of the political authorities and not have at least some acquaintance with investigating magistrates and remand centres.][4]

Notably, both Ludwig Börne and Heinrich Heine were driven into exile. But those who left Germany for political reasons were only a small fraction of the emigrants. By the end of the Biedermeier period, annual emigration had reached 200,000 as more and more Germans left to try their luck in America.[5]

Despite the harsh prevailing political and social conditions, Hermann notes that there was a rich cultural life. He pays particular attention to the story-telling of the time. In the same way that his mother would recount tales of her childhood, like her parents' ill-fated journey to Massow, Hermann emphasizes the plethora of anecdotes from the Biedermeier time handed down through the generations in every family. The art of conversation was highly prized; cafés were like political clubs and the bourgeoisie would meet in them to exchange news over coffee and cakes. The tobacconists, which were like small trattorias, Hermann says, served the same purpose for the working classes.

With almost all political valves shut off and the press heavily censored, literature and the theatre assumed greater prominence. Faith in the power of literature and its sphere of influence, Hermann contends, was never so strong or wide again. Among educated people, there was a love of language and many dabbled in poetry

FIG. 3.2. Georg Friedrich Kersting, *Woman Embroidering*, 1817 (National Musueum, Warsaw).

and prose. It was a time when seemingly everyone from doctors, statesmen, military officers, scholars, historians and scientists to the humble letter writer, was captivated by the culture of writing. Hermann continues 'Ebenso kann man sich heute schwer vorstellen, mit welchem Enthusiasmus Börne gelesen wurde und was er der Generation vor uns bedeutete.' [Likewise, one can only imagine today, the enthusiasm with which Börne was read and what he meant to the generation before us].[6] Someone of Börne's ilk who writes mainly about politics and history, Hermann suggests, would nowadays be the preserve of a small, politically savvy coterie but during the Biedermeier his appeal was broad and wide. Readers like Hermann's father were so well acquainted with Börne's works that they knew his books by heart: 'Sie las wohl nicht so viel wie die heutige, aber sie las ihre Lieblingsschriftsteller sehr intensiv, drang in ihr Wesen ein und empfing von ihnen eine ganz bestimmte Geistesrichtung.' [Most likely they did not read as extensively as we do today but they read their favourite writers with such intensity that they absorbed their words into their very being and acquired from them a particular way of thinking].[7]

Just as with music and literature, it was a period, Hermann observes approvingly, when amateur dabbling in fine arts and crafts was widespread and generated very pleasing results. The exquisite quality of the embroidery produced during the Biedermeier, for instance, he suggests, could not be replicated today. Hermann had particular regard for artists such as Adolph Menzel, Franz Krüger, Carl Blechen and Ferdinand Georg Waldmüller who skilfully depicted the simple life of the day — all the comfort, cleanliness and brightness, the seriousness and thoroughness that reflected the intimate life of the times. He took special delight in Biedermeier fashions, the beautiful patterns of the fabrics utilized, the joy in the use of colour and the fine details that adorned handbags, notebooks, watches, trinkets, tie pins, umbrellas and canes, lace scarves and silk shawls.

Hermann acknowledges in *Das Biedermeier* that the revival of interest in the period is tinged with nostalgia. He highlights the contrast between the gathering pace of contemporary modern life and that earlier time when life was simpler and proud traditions of craftsmanship had yet to be usurped by the mass production of the factories.

> ja, daß sich unser Leben immer mehr amerikanisieren und verhastigen wird, [...]. Überhaupt können wir uns doch nicht ganz verhehlen, daß bei unserer Vorliebe für die Biedermeierzeit eine Sentimentalität mitspricht.
>
> [yes, our lives have become increasingly Americanized and hurried. [...]. We cannot entirely conceal the fact that there's a degree of sentimentality in the affection we feel for the Biedermeier.][8]

Hermann certainly adopts an affectionate tone in his portrayal of Biedermeier Berlin in *Jettchen Gebert*. But while his detailed descriptions create a picture of a more personal, quainter world, they are often laden with irony and reflect his awareness — evident in *Das Biedermeier* — of the tensions and frictions of the period and of the repressive political climate. Russell A. Berman has argued that *Jettchen Gebert* presents an 'unbroken spectacle of description' and that Hermann

FIG. 3.3. Hermann and Eva, 1906.

fails to draw attention to social problems. 'Instead the world is dissolved into an impressionistic glow which concerns itself solely with objects of beauty.'[9] Most studies of the novel, however, recognize that Hermann does actually present a more nuanced picture of the period. Serge Niémetz, for example, notes Hermann's intimate understanding of the period and writes that 'la reconstitution méticuleuse de ce monde disparu procure déjà un grand plaisir de lecture. Chaque détail [...] est juste et parlant' [the meticulous recreation of this vanished world gives great pleasure to the reader. Every detail is apposite and resonant].[10]

By his own account, Hermann had been thinking about the book which was to become *Jettchen Gebert* for ten years. He wanted to capture the feel of the period down to the last trouser button, to depict the interiors as he felt one of his favourite writers, the Danish novelist, Jens Peter Jacobsen, had done in *Frau Marie Grubbe* (1876).[11] But after a year of preparation, not a single line of the novel had been written. At this point Hermann received a reminder from his publisher Fleischel which had paid him an advance of 1000 Mark for the novel. Spurred into action, Hermann wrote the first hundred pages which he gave to Arthur Eloesser, the associate editor of the literary supplement of *Vossische Zeitung*. It had been agreed as part of the contract that the novel would be serialized in the paper. Eloesser immediately decided to publish what Hermann had written.[12] According to an account of the episode given by the journalist Fritz Friedländer many years later, the astonished Hermann exclaimed, 'But you don't know how the story continues', to which Eloesser replied, 'If something is well written I am not interested in the plot.' Friedländer says that Hermann told a friend afterwards that it was the most intelligent remark about literature he ever heard.[13]

Jettchen Gebert (1906) and its sequel *Henriette Jacoby* (1908) are set towards the end of the Biedermeier period, covering the years 1839/40, and portray the everyday life of an upper middle-class Jewish family. Jettchen, left an orphan at the age of three by her father's death in the Battle of Ligny in 1815, lives with her Uncle Salomon and his wife, Riekchen. Salomon is an 'honoured and respected merchant'[14] who has run the family's clothing business for over thirty years. It is his brother, the intellectual Jason who introduces the unsuccessful writer, Fritz Kössling, to Jettchen. Kössling is a Doctor of Philosophy, a Christian and from a lower middle class background (his father was a brass founder). The two fall in love but Jettchen's family object to the match and she is pressurized into a hastily arranged marriage with Riekchen's choice of husband, a cousin from her provincial Jacoby side of the family. In despair, Jettchen runs away on her wedding night. *Henriette Jacoby* continues Jettchen's story as, having found sanctuary in Jason's house, she gradually re-establishes her relationship with her family and with Dr Kössling. But finally, believing that the differences that separate her from Kössling cannot be surmounted and that her true love is for Jason, Jettchen takes her own life.

The extent to which the characters in the novel and its events are based in reality has attracted some discussion. Possibly this has been encouraged by Hermann's preface to the novel in which he tells the reader that Henriette Jacoby née Gebert lived from 1812 to 1840 and that her gravestone can be seen in Berlin, together with those of her relatives. My grandmother maintained that there was a real-life Jettchen Gebert but that she was a feistier character than her fictitious namesake and had refused to be pressurized into marrying a man she did not love. Paul J. Jacobi identifies another potential real-life model for Jettchen.[15] It is evident that Hermann raided names in the family tree for his characters — Salomon, Jason, Ferdinand and Moritz, the four brothers in the novel, were all sons of his great-grandparents, Samuel Bentheim (the jeweller) and Hanna Aron. Hermann also used the names of some of their daughters for his characters — Rike, Mine and Henriette, his real-life grandmother. It seems probable that Hermann drew upon the names of his ancestors and stories which he had heard from his mother of the family's past but that, unlike *Spielkinder* which is rooted much more directly in actual events, the Jettchen novels are works of invention.

The most developed character in the books is Jettchen's bachelor uncle, Jason Gebert and the conflict between him and the Jacobys is a central theme. Jason embodies the values of the established, culturally 'westernized' Gebert family, whereas the less assimilated Jacobys, recent arrivals in Berlin from Posen in Prussian-occupied Poland, are portrayed as provincial, philistine and materialistic.[16] According to Kössling, Jason is a 'connoisseur in everything, not only in reading but in whatever appeals to his sense of beauty'.[17] The Enlightenment authors Voltaire, Diderot and Lichtenberg are his spiritual ancestors; Jean Paul, Goethe, Heine and Börne, the writers he most reveres. He is representative of the way that Enlightenment 'high culture' was becoming increasingly valued by the educated upper-middle classes during the period. The idea of *Bildung*, individual self-development and the cultivation of reason and aesthetic taste, which had been espoused by such luminaries as Lessing, Goethe, Schiller and Wilhelm von Humboldt, is close to Jason's heart. George L. Mosse maintains that real life Jewish families which like the fictitious Geberts had been established in Berlin since the last quarter of the eighteenth century, reached for *Bildung* as a way of integrating themselves into German society.[18] On first meeting Kössling, Salomon tells the doctor that at one time all kinds of literary and theatrical people used to like to visit him, writers like Moritz Saphir, Adolf Glassbrenner and Ludwig Rellstab.[19] In days gone by, the Geberts frequented Rahel Varnhagen's famous salon. But their appreciation for 'high culture' has waned. Salomon says he now has nothing intellectual to offer Kössling. According to Jason, the family is on a downward path. These days the food is better than the conversation at a Gebert dinner party.[20]

Jettchen and Kössling are the only characters in the novel who share Jason's aesthetic sensibilities. Jason sees his niece as the family's best hope for the future. He actively seeks to encourage her intellectual and cultural appreciation, lending her books by Mörike, Börne, Thackeray and Balzac (all authors much read by Hermann). But *Tante* Riekchen tells him that he is making Jettchen quite stupid with all his mass of books[21] and complains of what she sees as the pretensions of the Geberts 'exciting themselves over hundreds of things of no concern to anyone: politics, books, theatres and newspapers, matters that didn't affect anybody.'[22] We are told that even Salomon recognizes that his wife has waged war these thirty years against everything that bore the name of Gebert because it was higher, of finer feeling and healthier than the petty, narrow spite that adorned the members of her own family.[23] Jason describes his sisters-in-law as 'cursed little Lithuanian horses' and blames them for the family's decline.[24]

This differentiation Jason makes between Eastern and Western Jews was well entrenched by the time Hermann was writing. As Eric Hobsbawm notes, 'to proclaim that they had left the ghetto, that they had entered civilisation, that they were not like their 'Eastern' neighbours or 'Eastern immigrants' was a dominant theme among German Jews for much of the nineteenth century.'[25] Steven E. Aschheim points out that there was a whole genre of German Jewish Wilhelmine novels featuring the Eastern Jew as the stranger and threat to middle-class respectability and argues that *Jettchen Gebert* is its apogee.[26] In the Jettchen novels, there is even a physical demarcation. Julius Jacoby is described as small and oily. When Jettchen meets him she feels as if she has touched unawares, some live, clammy creature, a frog or a caterpillar.[27] By contrast, everything about Jettchen is touched with proud beauty, her tall stature, her long but not thin face with the high white forehead and her firmly closed mouth. Uncle Eli says that Jettchen's marrying Julius is like putting 'a silken patch on a rag-sack.'[28]

Another thing which separates the Posen and Berlin branches of the family is their degree of religious observance. When Julius's Uncle Naphthali arrives from Benschen (Zbąszyń) and starts offering Salomon Gebert advice on the wedding feast (which he insists must be kosher), Salomon quickly becomes annoyed and echoes Heinrich Levin's dictum, 'Heaven protect us from small towns!'[29] Provincialism and observance of religious ritual are portrayed as going hand-in-hand. The population of Benschen in 1840 was just 1300, compared to Berlin's 300,000, and it is clear that Jettchen, who has lived her whole life in the city, shares her uncle's views.[30] She tells Kössling earlier in the novel, 'I would not like to live anywhere but in Berlin, certainly not in any small town.'[31]

But while there is little evidence of religious practice on the part of the urbanite Geberts, the fact that Kössling is a Christian and not a Jew, is a significant barrier to any relationship with Jettchen. Uncle Eli is the first person to see in Kössling a chance for Jettchen but no sooner has he voiced his thoughts to his wife, Mine, than she responds by saying it will have to be someone different as there is no possibility that Salomon will let Jettchen marry a Christian.[32] Here, at least, the Geberts are not so different from their country cousins. When Jason talks to Kössling about his prospects of marrying Jettchen, he advises him that in addition to all other obstacles — Kössling does not belong to the life of the middle class and Jettchen is so firmly planted in it that she cannot be uprooted, Jettchen spends more on frocks and gloves in a year than Kössling can scrape together for his whole living — beyond these material considerations, is added the fact that Kössling is a Christian. It was illegal to convert to Judaism and there was no civil marriage before 1860 so marriage to Kössling would have required Jettchen to convert. We know that she is already aware from personal experience of the barriers that exist between Jews and Christians — she tells Kössling that Karoline Ceestow, her bosom friend, married a Captain of the Guard and that of course has put an end to any contact between them.[33]

In a key passage in the novel, Jason seeks to explain to Kössling why his Christianity represents so significant a barrier to his prospects with Jettchen:

> You think that we should be broad-minded enough to disregard this outer accident. Perhaps! But then you forget a certain pride, inherent in our family, that we are looked upon here and respected as Jews. If my father had allowed himself and us to be baptized, as he was so often urged to do, we might today have a title and be privy councillors. That we have not done so, nor crept to the Cross, nor in any way sold our convictions, whether for pleasure or profit, is our pride and we would not have it relinquished by our family in the days to come. You can understand that, I am sure![34]

The historian Gordon A. Craig suggests that while Kössling may find it difficult to understand Jason, 'Jewish readers who believed that integration must be based on mutual respect and must not demand sacrifices from one of the parties, would have seen the point, while sympathising with Jettchen.'[35]

When Jason puts forward Kössling's case to his uncle and his brothers, Ferdinand immediately asks, what about his being a Christian? Eli argues that nowadays no one should worry about such foolishness.[36] Jason concurs although we are told that in truth he was of quite another opinion in this matter. Salomon is adamant that Jettchen should not marry a Christian:

> ... although I may privately have the same ideas about religion as Eli, still Jettchen shall never, with our consent, marry a Christian. With our consent never, — you understand. [...] It is no question of a few customs or of being buried at last in Chaussee Street rather than in Hamburg Street, it is not that, but you know just as well as I do why we cling to the Jewish faith and refuse to let it die out in our family.[37]

Ferdinand may have been awarded the title *Kommissionsrat* by the Prussian Court for services rendered in providing the royal household with carriages and be known to the Prussian prince as 'lieber Gebert'[38] but he still maintains that he would rather never see his daughter marry than that she should take a Christian. How Jason can advocate such a thing is beyond his comprehension. He asks Jason if he thinks that their brother, Moritz (Jettchen's father) would have wished it. Jason acknowledges that he would not but argues that by doing everything to make his only child happy, they can do more honour to Moritz's memory than by 'false sentiment and narrow-mindedness.'[39]

Eric Hobsbawm suggests that assimilation did not entail a denial of Jewish identity, even in the very unusual case of conversion but it is clear that the Geberts take a dim view of the latter.[40] Salomon describes the jurist Eduard Gans as a man quite out of the common, 'although he had allowed himself to be baptized.'[41] Gans had been one of the first German Jews to secure a position teaching law at the new University of Berlin, only to lose it when in 1822 the government issued a new royal decree explicitly banning the employment of Jews in universities and the public sector. Conversion enabled him to get a professorship but was seen as an act of treason by his friends. Heine also converted in 1825, describing his baptismal certificate as 'the entrance ticket to European culture'[42] but that did not stop him venting his anger at Gans for 'crawling to the Cross' in his poem 'An einen Abtrünnigen' [To an Apostate].[43] Börne also converted and like Heine, came to regret his decision. In his sixty-third Letter from Paris (1831), he writes,

> In the end I wished someone would give me back the three gold pieces I paid the clergyman for my Christianity. It's been eighteen years since I was baptized and it hasn't helped a bit. Three gold pieces for a tiny corner in the German nut-house! What a foolish waste of money.[44]

In any case, despite their conversion, society continued to regard both Heine and Börne as Jews. Jewishness was, as Heine put it, an incurable disease.[45]

Rather than a residual sense of faith, it is perhaps a shared sense of loyalty to the family's roots and its constancy in rejecting the opportunities conversion would have brought which makes both Salomon and Jason baulk at the idea of Jettchen marrying a Christian. As the historian Marion Kaplan has highlighted, 'feelings, convictions and allegiances lingered long after ritual had waned.'[46] Increasingly the family became the substitute for religious activity, the cornerstone of a more secular version of Judaism. To an extent, *Jettchen Gebert* is a sequence of family get-togethers and the shifting family dynamics, the growing influence of the Jacobys at Jason's expense is charted through the conversations that take place at these gatherings. When Jason prematurely leaves the family's end-of-summer Charlottenburg get-together, for instance, a strange mood falls upon all the Geberts, a depression as after some defeat. In a moment the insipid chatter rises in its many-headed unrestraint; the Jacoby's provincial gossip about nothing at all, triumphs.[47]

Jason comes to see the value of the family when he falls seriously ill with typhoid. Salomon, Ferdinand and Eli are with him all the time and he acknowledges that though he has never been one to set great store by it, the family's support does matter. Making a reference to the splendour of Jettchen's trousseau, Jason tells his niece,

> We two are like wandering children that have come back home — and if we should consider it carefully, what should we do away from it? Nowhere else can we find a room heated for us and so nice and warm and comfortable as those at home.[48]

But such comfort comes at a price. Jettchen's life is circumscribed by family obligations. She tells Kössling that 'amongst us, no one breaks away from his family — no one can do as he likes. Everyone is pushed and poked by all for good as well as ill.'[49] The forces which are exerted over Jettchen are rendered more insidious by their friendly demeanour. She is told by Salomon that in a certain sense she is indebted to her aunt whose dearest wish now is that she should marry Julius. Jettchen feels that she has been eating the bread of Salomon and Riekchen for twenty years and that marrying Julius is the price she has to pay. She tells Kössling, 'Do you understand, Fritz, they handed me the bill. I was twenty years in that house [...] you see, now I must pay for them.'[50]

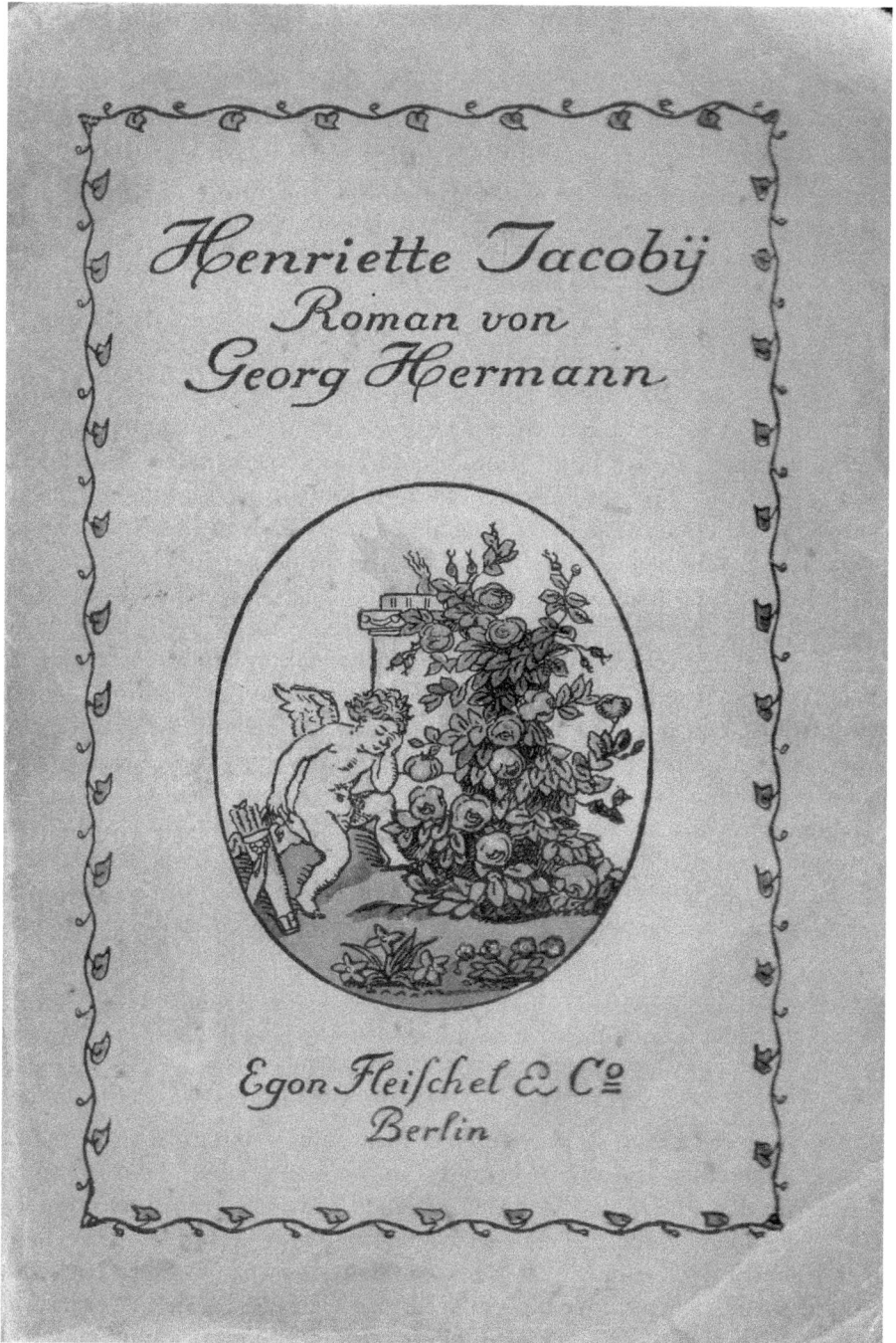

FIG. 3.4. Kurt Tuch's illustration for the original cover of *Henriette Jacoby*

Jettchen's passivity is in part a product of her circumstances but there is also a sense of inevitability which permeates both novels. The leitmotif sentence used throughout, 'Es kam wie es kommen mußte.' [And everything came, as come it must] makes the reader feel that the way in which the novel's characters' lives unfold is as inevitable as the passing of the seasons Hermann depicts.[51] In the end, Fortuna, who brought Kössling and Jettchen together, reveals her true face:

> It was the same Chance as had led [Kössling] to Jettchen when he was in Königstraße with Jason, but then Chance had a tight bandage over her eyes. It was the same Chance as, a few weeks later, brought the two together by themselves in Königstraße and then continued her game out in Charlottenburg; the same Chance as had brought Kössling and Jason together on the Elector's Bridge. By then she had loosened the bandage a little and peeped out under it with secret, stolen glances. But now this Chance had taken off the bandage and showed her true face, a face with stern iron features and eyes blue as tempered steel. And then her name was Fate. Fate that seizes two human beings and welds them together and drags them by their chains to airy heights and to sorrow's deepest depths, Fate that lifts them up and casts them down, that pushes and kneads, that inspires and crushes.[...] It was Fate here [...] silently demanding its fulfilment...[52]

From its first appearance, *Jettchen Gebert* was an enormous popular success. Both the novel and its sequel, *Henriette Jacoby*, were best sellers in Germany. Between 1906 and 1910 on average 8,000 copies of *Jettchen Gebert* were printed annually. The novel was already in its thirty-second impression by 1910 and new editions carried on being published during the war, so that by 1919 it had reached its eighty-fifth impression. It continued to sell well in Germany throughout the 1920s. Shulamit Volkov suggests that *Jettchen Gebert* probably made Hermann the most widely read writer among German Jews before the First World War.[53] In laudatory articles published on the occasion of his sixtieth birthday, Hermann was invariably celebrated as the author of *Jettchen Gebert*.[54] The Jettchen novels also proved popular across Europe. Dutch translations appeared in 1909, there were Swedish versions in 1910, French (1911), Danish (1917), Hungarian (1919 and 1921), Finnish (1920), Russian (1923) and English (1924).[55]

In his introduction to the Hebrew edition of *Jettchen Gebert* which was not published until 1941, the writer and Zionist activist Sammy Gronemann recalls how the original publication of the novel in 1906 had triggered a kind of 'Jettchenmania'. In every place, at every masquerade ball and fancy dress party, *Jettchen Gebert* outfits were *de rigueur*. According to Gronemann, such a phenomenon had not been witnessed since the 'Werther Fever' of the 1770s. Suddenly the seventy-year-old Biedermeier fashions became the *dernier cri* of the first decade of the twentieth century.[56] Indeed, almost no other writer, Gronemann contends, not even Thomas Mann, succeeded in appealing to such a wide and varied circle of readers and in opening the eyes of so many people to a world so far from their own.[57]

Hermann came to be frustrated by the popular reception of the novels which he felt had resulted in a focus on superficial period details and trivial aspects like Eli's penchant for *Mürbekuchen* [shortbread].

Ich platze vor Wut, wenn ich das Wort "Mürbekuchen" höre! Sie haben gar nichts mit dem Sinn des Buches zu tun, sind ein Nebenher, eine Belanglosigkeit, ein Farbenflecken im Zeitkolorit, wie das Rubinglas und die Sinumbralampe.

[I am furious when I hear the word 'Mürbekuchen'! It has nothing to do with the meaning of the book, it is an unimportant detail, a fleck of colour contributing to the period atmosphere, like the ruby glass and the sinumbra lamp.][58]

The novel was, however, a critical as well as a popular success. For instance, Karl Holl in an article about contemporary German literature for the *Modern Language Review* wrote 'Notable among the North German writers is Georg Hermann whose *Jettchen Gebert* is, undoubtedly, one of the best modern German novels.'[59] In his survey of modern German literature, Jethro Bithell concludes his analysis of the novel by saying

Altogether *Jettchen Gebert* must be given high rank as more or less a Jewish classic, and certainly the one Berliner *Roman* of the period which is likely to live. [...] *Jettchen Gebert* succeeds because, over and above its masterly and detailed presentation of the milieu of a given period, it creates vividly individualized characters and handles racial and social problems with inner knowledge and keen insight.[60]

For George L. Mosse, *Jettchen Gebert* is 'the most famous novel of German-Jewish life'.[61] If Lessing's play *Nathan the Wise* came to symbolize Enlightenment liberalism, which aspired to a more perfect toleration, *Jettchen Gebert,* he suggests, drew a picture of assimilation accomplished and of the ideal bourgeois life.

Notes to Chapter 3

1. Peter Jelavich, *Berlin Cabaret* (Cambridge, MA: Harvard University Press, 1993), p. 41.
2. Georg Hermann, *Das Biedermeier im Spiegel seiner Zeit* (Berlin: Bong, 1913).
3. The essay is included in Hermann, *Die Reise nach Massow*, pp. 359–401.
4. Ibid., p. 374.
5. Ibid., p. 379.
6. Ibid., p. 390.
7. Ibid., p. 391.
8. Ibid., p. 366.
9. Russell A. Berman, *The Rise of the Modern German Novel: Crisis and Charisma* (Cambridge, MA: Harvard University Press, 1986), pp. 161–78. Here, p. 163.
10. Serge Niémetz, 'Préface to *Henriette Jacoby*' (Paris: Albin Michel, 2002), p. 12.
11. Hermann, 'Im Spiegel', p. 306.
12. *Jettchen Gebert* was serialized in *Vossische Zeitung* between 7 June and 9 September, 1906. See van Liere, *Georg Hermann: Materialien*, p. 66.
13. Fritz Friedländer, 'Arthur Eloesser: Centenary of his Birth' (London: Association of Jewish Refugees, Information, April 1970), p. 7. Friedländer (1901–1980) was a Social Democratic journalist, teacher and activist of the Centralverein. For more information about his life and works, see the Fritz Friedlaender Collection; AR 7201, in the Leo Baeck Institute.
14. Hermann, *Hetty Geybert*, p. 10.
15. Samuel Gewer's second marriage produced a son called Jacob (b. 1741). Jacob had a daughter named Henriette who was born in 1771. In 1798 she married a man described as 'Jacob von Posen' (1753–1829). Henriette and Jacob von Posen were divorced in 1818. Jacobi speculates

that Hermann took her story as a basis for *Jettchen Gebert* but brought the time period forward by forty years. See Jacobi, 'Geschichtliche Grundlagen zu Georg Hermanns Jettchen Gebert', p. 120. Henriette Meyerstein née Gebert (1847–1915) has been proposed as another possible real-life model for Jettchen. She was the great-great-granddaughter of Daniel Gewer, the younger brother of Samuel. David Arad writes that 'she served the writer Georg Hermann as an example for the character in his novel.' See David Arad, 'Memories of Eduard Meyerstein', *International Association of Jewish Lawyers and Jurists*, no. 22, Winter 1999, 20–22.

16. As Hans Otto Horch points out, Jason is already distinguished from the rest of the family by his Greek first name. See Hans Otto Horch, 'Über Georg Hermann: Plädoyer zur Wiederentdeckung eines bedeutenden Deutsch-Jüdischen Schriftstellers', *Bulletin des Leo Baeck Instituts*, no. 77 (1987), 73–94. Here, p. 86.

17. Hermann, *Hetty Geybert*, p. 183.

18. George L. Mosse, *German Jews beyond Judaism* (Bloomington, IN: Indiana University Press, 1985), p. 3. Rather than *Bildung*, John Ward suggests that Hermann 'champions the work ethic as a vehicle of assimilation' in the Jettchen novels (p. 2) and argues that the Geberts' silk manufacturing company is portrayed as 'a paragon of successful Jewish integration into German public life.' (p. 261). John Ward, *Jews in Business and their Representation in German Literature 1827–1934* (Oxford: Peter Lang, 2010).

19. Hermann, *Hetty Geybert*, p. 50.

20. Ibid., p. 65.

21. Ibid., p. 142.

22. Ibid., p. 138.

23. Ibid., p. 36.

24. Ibid., p. 65.

25. Eric Hobsbawm, 'Homesickness', *LRB*, vol. 15, no. 7, April 1993, p. 21.

26. Steven E. Aschheim, *Brothers and Strangers: The East European Jew in German and German Jewish Consciousness 1700–1923* (Madison, WI: University of Wisconsin, 1982), p. 53.

27. Hermann, *Hetty Geybert*, p. 134.

28. Ibid., p. 334.

29. Ibid., p. 346.

30. See Inge Rippmann, *Vormärz im Biedermeier — Zu Georg Hermanns Doppelroman* Jettchen Gebert *und* Henriette Jacobi, (Bielefeld: Aisthesis, 2014), p. 21.

31. Hermann, *Hetty Geybert*, p. 106.

32. Ibid., p. 126.

33. Ibid., p. 80. As Horch points out, after being able to serve in the War of Liberation, the world of the Prussian military had again become closed to Jews. Horch, 'Über Georg Hermann', p. 89.

34. Ibid., p. 213.

35. Gordon A. Craig, 'Rahel's Jewish Sofa', *New York Review of Books*, 12 May 1988, 41–42.

36. Hermann, *Hetty Geybert*, p. 246.

37. Ibid., pp. 248–49. The Jewish cemetery was in Große Hamburger Straße and the Protestant Dorotheenstadt Cemetery in Chausseestraße.

38. Georg Hermann, *Henriette Jacoby* (Berlin: Das Neue Berlin, 1998), p. 65.

39. Hermann, *Hetty Geybert*, p. 249.

40. Hobsbawm, 'Homesickness', p. 22.

41. Hermann, *Hetty Geybert*, p. 58.

42. See Hugo Bieber, *Heinrich Heine: A Biographical Anthology*, trans. by M. Hadas (Philadelphia: Jewish Publication Society of America, 1956), p. 157.

43. Solomon Liptzin argues that 'there is no doubt that Heine was castigating himself no less than Gans' in the poem. *Germany's Stepchildren* (Cleveland: Meridian, 1961), p. 71.

44. See Mark M. Anderson, 'Ludwig Börne Begins His Career', *Yale Companion to Jewish Writing and Thought in German Culture, 1096–1996*, ed. by Sander L. Gilman and Jack Zipes, (New Haven, CT: Yale University Press, 1997), pp. 129–35. Here, p. 135.

45. Heinrich Heine, 'Das neue israelitische Hospital zu Hamburg' [The New Jewish Hospital in Hamburg], 1841.

46. Marion A. Kaplan, 'Redefining Judaism in Imperial Germany', *Jewish Social Studies New Series*, vol. 9, no. 1 (2002), 12.

47. Hermann, *Hetty Geybert*, p. 317. This shift in ascendency is signalled earlier in the novel when, having failed to persuade Salomon of Kössling's case, Jason leaves the family's previous gathering in Charlottenburg prematurely and Julius takes 'full possession' of his place in the back seat in Ferdinand's carriage (p. 282).

48. Ibid., pp. 352–53.

49. Ibid., p. 115. In *Henriette Jacoby* Kössling remarks on his amazement at how closely knit Jettchen's family is and draws a contrast with his own family. Hermann, *Henriette Jacoby*, p. 256.

50. Hermann, *Hetty Geybert*, p. 361.

51. Weiss-Sussex, *Metropolitan Chronicles*, p. 127. Jethro Bithell argues that in 'ticketing individual characters by recurrent phrases and long passages in which season and weather move in lyric unison with the story', both Thomas Mann and Hermann directly imitated Dickens. Bithell, *Modern German Literature 1880–1950*, p. 318–20. We know from his 'Im Spiegel' essay that Dickens was one of Hermann's favourite authors when he was young. Michel Vanhelleputte argues that Hermann's approach is more subtle and that through his depiction of the city and the different gardens which feature in the novel, he convincingly explores the interaction between the outer world and the personal hinterland of his characters. See Michel Vanelleputte, 'Eine Stadt und dreierlei Garten in Georg Hermanns Roman *Jettchen Gebert* (1906), in *Literarische Mikrokosmen. Begrenzung und Entgrenzung. Festschrift für Ernst Leonardy*, ed. by Christian Drösch, Hubert Roland and Stéphanie Vanasten (Brussels: Peter Lang, 2006), pp. 107–21.

52. Hermann, *Hetty Geybert*, p. 355.

53. *Germans, Jews, and Antisemites: Trials in Emancipation* (Cambridge, MA: Cambridge University Press, 2006), p. 251. Van Liere indicates that 268,000 copies had been sold of the two books in Germany by 1933 (*Georg Hermann: Materialien*, p. 216).

54. Weiss-Sussex, *Metropolitan Chronicles*, p. 105.

55. See van Liere, *Georg Hermann: Materialien*, pp. 78–80. Van Liere states that 35,000 copies of the Danish translation were sold between 1917 and 1921. See p. 224.

56. Sammy Gronemann, preface to Georg Hermann, *Jettchen Gebert*, trans. by Itzhak Schönberg (Tel Aviv: 'Ligvulam' with Bialik Institute, 1941), p. x.

57. Ibid., p. xi.

58. Georg Hermann, 'Was von Büchern übrigbleibt. Ein Zwiegespräch', *UHU*, 2, 1926, p. 49.

59. Karl Holl, 'Review of *Dichtung und Dichter der Zeit. Ein Schilderung der deutschen Literatur der letzten Jahrzehnte* by Albert Soergel and other works', *MLR*, 7, (1912), 416–21. Here p. 420.

60. Bithell, *Modern German Literature 1880–1950*, p. 320.

61. George L. Mosse, *Masses and Man: Nationalist and Fascist Perceptions of Reality* (Detroit, MI: Wayne State University Press, 1987), p. 257.

CHAPTER 4

❖

The Grunewald Years

FIG. 4.1. Trabener Straße 19, Grunewald. The family is on the left hand-side balcony.

The success of *Jettchen Gebert* was life-changing and Georg Hermann found his sudden fame a heady experience. Every day he would receive letters from readers and requests for his photograph. Suddenly he found that he belonged to society. He would be recognized in the street and his opinions were solicited ... moreover, for perhaps the first time in his life, he could now pay his bills on time.[1]

Following its enormous success, Hermann and the family were able to move in 1910 from their home in Friedenau into part of a beautiful villa in Trabener Straße in the elegant suburb of Grunewald. The composer Engelbert Humperdinck lived just across the road at Number 16, where Isadora Duncan had also established her first school of dance in 1904. Eva, Hilde and Liese played with Humperdinck's son and Duncan's daughter.

The move to Grunewald gave the family more space, although Hermann's ever-growing collection of paintings and ornaments quickly filled the rooms. There are

FIG. 4.2. At home, Trabener Straße 19, Grunewald.

FIG. 4.3. Hilde, Elise Heynemann, Liese and Eva, 1907.

some photographs from this time of the elegant interior of the villa. They show how Hermann had recreated the Biedermeier environment of his own childhood — the mahogany tables, the family portraits and wooden display cabinets containing porcelain figurines — but also added new pieces, like the numerous Japanese prints that hang on the walls. In one of the photographs, Hermann is posed reading a letter, while Liese looks through a large album. Martha is playing a grand piano on top of which sits Hermann's carved fifteenth century Madonna. Hilde sits alongside her mother, with her arm around her neck and Eva is glimpsed on the balcony overlooking the blossoming trees in the garden behind. The picture presents a happy domestic scene of the successful writer with his family; his surrounding collection emphasizes his taste and sophistication.

In a talk about her father which Hilde gave many years later, she said that while one could imagine that the family environment would be very disturbing for a writer, for Hermann this was not the case:

> Es ist nicht übertrieben, wenn ich Ihnen erzähle, daß mein Vater *Henriette Jacoby* geschrieben hat, während wir zu dritt, sehr klein noch, eineinhalb-, drei- und vierjährig, auf und unter unserem Vater und seinem Schreibtisch herumgekrabbelt sind. Und wenn meine Mutter, ganz unglücklich über die Wahl unseres Spielplatzes, uns wegholen wollte, waren wir tief entsetzt über diese Zumutung, und der für unsere Begriffe gemütliche Mann auf dem Schreibtischstuhl auch.

> [It is no exaggeration when I tell you that my father wrote *Henriette Jacoby* while the three of us (I was three, my older sister, four and our youngest sister eighteen months) ... crawled all over him and over and under his desk. And if my mother, unhappy about our choice of playground, suggested that we should

go elsewhere, we were mortified and so was the good-natured man on his chair behind the desk.][2]

Hermann himself appears to have been less sanguine about the way the family environment impacted on his writing. Looking back on these years, he complained that he could find peace nowhere at home and that there was a general lack of consideration for his role as the family's breadwinner.[3] From the outset, he seems not to have adjusted easily to his changed circumstances as a married man and then a father of three small girls. Hermann's semi-autobiographical novel *Der kleine Gast* [The Little Guest] published in 1925 charts these early years of his marriage. In it Hermann's alter ego, Fritz Eisner, reflects on how often before his marriage he would be arm-in-arm with a girl, snuggled together. He misses the warmth of that feeling and yearns to rediscover his former sense of unfettered lightness.[4]

The sudden prominence which came with the popular success of *Jettchen Gebert* fuelled Hermann's interest in the place of the writer in society. A short study of Kipling[5] which was followed by the essay collection, *Sehnsucht: Ernste Plaudereien* both reflect a growing concern with the place of literature in society at large[6] and in March 1910 Hermann co-founded with Hans Landsberg the Schutzverband deutscher Schriftsteller [The German Writers' Association]. He was the association's first chairman until 1913.

Hermann's next novel, *Kubinke*, which appeared two years after *Henriette Jacoby*, was set in contemporary Berlin. It tells the tragicomic story of the naïve barber's apprentice Emil Kubinke, following his move from the countryside to Berlin. While making house calls to shave his relatively affluent clientele, Kubinke makes the acquaintance of three servant girls, Hedwig, Emma, and Pauline and promptly falls in love with each.[7] The girls, fun-loving and fast, initiate Kubinke in the ways of the city. Both Hedwig and Emma have flings with Kubinke but it is with Pauline that he finds true love. However, their happiness is short-lived as both Hedwig and Emma, finding themselves expecting, blame their unwanted pregnancies on Kubinke. They take the hapless barber to court where he is convicted and made to pay maintenance for their support. Kubinke subsequently hangs himself out of shame.[8] 'La farce est jouée, tirez le rideau,' writes Hermann.[9]

As in his previous novels, Hermann employs an intrusive narrator, but in *Kubinke*, unlike *Spielkinder*, he does not seek to win our sympathy, nor as in the Jettchen novels does he try to create a sense of complicity with the reader. Instead, Hermann invites us to look at his characters with a degree of detachment. There is a gentle irony in the way he portrays them and the world they inhabit. Emil Kubinke is naïve and gauche, a victim of the big city girls' savvy. Like the daydreamer Kössling and the ill-starred Geiger, he is a weak character, another of life's losers. The girls' thoughts and feelings are sketched rather than being presented to the reader in detail and in this respect Heinrich Zille's cover illustration of the three servants is very apt.

Hermann's affinity with the approach of the Impressionists, so evident in his art criticism, is very apparent in *Kubinke*. Weiss-Sussex in her study of the novel argues that Hermann seeks in the book to capture the immediate impression gained of

FIG. 4.4. Heinrich Zille's illustration for the cover of *Kubinke*.

transitory scenes, to render the sensory impact of what he describes rather than to interpret it for the reader.[10] As she highlights, this passage in which Hermann describes a carefree Sunday mood is illustrative:

Ja, das war mal so ein richtiger Sonntag, ein Tag, der so schön war, so strahlend und ungetrübt von früh an, daß ihn wochentags jeder als eine persönliche Beleidigung empfunden hätte. Die Straßen lagen lang, hell und blank, und das letzte kleine, eingegitterte Bäumchen an der Bordschwelle war mit mindestens zehn grünen neuen Blättchen aufgeputzt. Und die Spatzen waren schon am frühen Morgen so verliebt in die Sonne, daß sie sich beinahe von der Straßenbahn überfahren ließen und erst in der letzten Sekunde zu der Jungfrau mit dem Merkurstab hinaufschwirrten, um dort weiter piepsend, schreiend und flügelschlagend durcheinander zu wirbeln. Und alle Bahnen waren von früh an voll mit geputzten Menschen, und jeder hatte ein Kind auf dem Schoß, und sogar vorn auf der Plattform standen die Liebespaare, ließen sich den Wind um die Nase wehen und lächelten dabei einander an. An den Ecken hatten sich junge Leute in der Sonne postiert und warteten rauchend auf Freunde, um mit ihnen hinauszuziehen; oder andere, mit der Uhr in der Hand, standen da, keineswegs gleichgültig mit der Zigarre, und sie blickten sehnlichst straßauf, straßab nach hellen Kleidern, ob das vielleicht ihr Gang wäre, bis ihnen doch mit einemmal ein frischgewaschenes Sonntagsgesicht unter dem neuen Strohhut entgegenlächelte. [...]

Nirgends ein Arbeitswagen, nirgends ein Geschäftsrad, — der Asphalt so lang und hell und grau, ... und nur die Wallfahrt von geputzten Menschenkindern, und nur in der Sonne diese Bahnen, eine nach der anderen, die hinausstreben, angefüllt bis auf den letzten Platz. Nirgends ist eigentlich Schatten. Gerade von Südosten her fällt das Licht ein; breit wie ein Strom zieht es zwischen den hellen Häuserreihen in den vier Baumlinien dahin, und nur in den Nischen der Fenster liegt so etwas wie Dunkelheit, und nur auf dem Bürgersteig zittert das Widerspiel der ersten grünen Blättchen, und nur wie matte, bläuliche Monde sind in regelrechten Abständen, mitten zwischen den Straßenbahnschienen, die Umrisse der Bogenlampen aus der Höhe hingezeichnet.

[Yes, this was indeed a real Sunday, a day that was so beautiful, so radiant and clear from early on, that on a weekday, everyone would have taken it as a personal insult. The streets lay long, bright and shiny, and every tiny tree, fenced in on the pavement, was dressed up with at least ten new, little, green leaves. And already in the early morning, the sparrows were so in love with the sun that they almost let themselves be run over by the tram and only in the last second whirred up to the (statue of the) virgin with the caduceus, in order there to continue swirling about, chirping, screaming and beating their wings. And from early on, all the trams were full of smartly dressed people, and everyone had a child on their lap, and even out on the platform, the lovers stood, letting the wind blow about them and smiling all the while at one another. On the street corners, young men had taken up their positions in the sun and, smoking, waited for their friends in order to go out with them; or others, watch in hand, stood there, not at all indifferent, with their cigars, and looked yearningly up the street, down the street, for bright dresses, whether that might perhaps be her walk, until at last, suddenly, a freshly washed Sunday face smiled to greet them under a new straw hat. [...]

Not a workman's cart anywhere, nowhere a messenger's cycle — the asphalt so long and bright and grey [...] and only the pilgrimage of well-scrubbed humankind, and only these trams in the sun, one after the other, striving out of town, every last space filled. There is no real shadow anywhere. Straight from the south east, the light is falling in; broad like a stream, it flows along between the bright rows of houses, in the four lines of trees, and only in the corners of the windows lies something like darkness, and only on the pavement, the interplay of the first little green leaves is trembling, and only like faint, blueish moons are the contours of the street lamps drawn from above at regular intervals, right in the middle of the tram tracks.][11]

As Weiss-Sussex observes, 'the impression is given that images have simply been recorded, compiled and presented, unaltered and uninterrupted. [...] visual impressions are simply juxtaposed.'[12]

The medium may be different but there are clear parallels between Hermann's impressionistic approach and that of Max Liebermann, as a later Hermann essay about Liebermann's artistic credo underlines. What matters, he argues in the article, is the way in which the artist represents the quintessence of what he depicts, without one brushstroke too many or too few, capturing the mood or sense of movement in such a way that we have the illusion that what we are seeing is real. The work must always be full of feeling, Hermann states, but never sentimental and it should bear testimony to the unique personality of its maker.[13] Oscar Wilde makes a similar argument in his essay 'The Soul of Man under Socialism' where he writes 'a work of art is the unique result of a unique temperament. Its beauty comes from the fact that the author is what he is.'[14] The subjective and personal nature of artistic creation was something that Hermann stressed repeatedly. In his essay 'Der tote Naturalismus', for example, he writes,

Kein Künstler nämlich, der etwas Gutes, Wertvolles, Bleibendes geschaffen hat, hat eine Sache geschaffen, die ihn nichts anging. [...] Ich will mein Leben in einer Reihe von Kunstwerken darstellen, wenn die Sonne sinkt und wenn der Mond die Wolken vergoldet, will ich die fliehenden Geister festhalten!

[No artist creates something lasting and precious which does not concern his inner self. [...] I want to portray my life in a sequence of works of art so that when the sun sinks and moonbeams gild the clouds, I can still hold on to the fleeting visions!][15]

Kubinke, as was recognized by contemporary reviewers, is above all a novel about Berlin and Hermann shows it to be a fascinating and at times extraordinarily beautiful city.[16] He explores all aspects of the modern metropolis and in particular, the impact on the individual of living in this new urban environment. For Emil Kubinke, used to the slower pace of provincial life, Berlin offers a superabundance of sensory experiences. From the moment of his arrival by train, he finds the city centre overwhelming. But he discovers that the freedom and anonymity of the metropolis does not bring happiness. Instead, he finds, as Hermann's former professor Georg Simmel had argued in his 1903 treatise 'Die Großstädte und das Geistesleben' [The Metropolis and Mental Life] that being in the metropolitan crowd can be a corrosive experience:

The individual becomes a single cog [within] the vast overwhelming organisation of things and forces which gradually take out of his hands everything connected with progress, spirituality and value. [...] Life is composed more and more of [...] impersonal cultural elements [...] which seek to suppress peculiar personal interests [...]. As a result, in order that this most personal element be saved, extremities, peculiarities and individualisations must be produced and they must be over-exaggerated merely to be brought into the awareness even of the individual himself.[17]

Hermann saw the need to adapt to the changed urban environment as inevitable and in *Kubinke* he seeks to understand rather than judge modern metropolitan ways. In an unsent letter to Alfred Kerr, Hermann says that the novel's leitmotif is the withholding of moral judgements.[18] Hermann withholds judgement entirely, as when Kubinke tired of waiting for Pauline decides to go on a flirtatious evening walk with Hedwig, simply because she crosses his path first.[19] Similarly, Hedwig, Emma, and Pauline are not portrayed as victims of the city. They take the opportunities it presents for sexual adventures and, as Weiss-Sussex observes, moral scruples are something they cannot afford and do not have time for.[20]

Although it did not match the enormous success of *Jettchen Gebert* and *Henriette Jacoby*, *Kubinke* did well, selling 17,000 copies, and further cementing Hermann's status as one of Germany's most popular writers. It was turned into a musical comedy, with Georg Zeppler writing the songs but when the show opened in May 1916, almost two years into the First World War, at the Theater des Westens in Berlin, it met with limited success, running for just one week and seemingly never being performed again.[21] Ten years later, a movie adaptation was made, *Kubinke der Portier und die drei Dienstmädchen*.[22]

Georg Hermann's mother, Berta Borchardt, died in November 1910. She was seventy-five and had lived long enough to see the remarkable turnaround in her youngest son's life. A best-selling author, he was now a family man, living in some comfort in affluent Grunewald. With his oldest brother, Ludwig, a renowned Egyptologist leading the excavations of the German Oriental Society, and Heinrich a successful architect, Berta's hopes that her sons would restore the family's honour after their father's bankruptcy and sad decline had been fulfilled. She had been the rock upon which that success had been built. Her determination and ability to keep the family afloat despite its dire financial straits had been well-rewarded.

Hermann's next venture was a two act comedy about Nietzsche, *Der Wüstling oder Die Reise nach Breslau* [The Rake or the Journey to Breslau] which opened together with the Expressionist Carl Sternheim's *Die Cassette* in Berlin in 1911.[23] It seems likely that Hermann had reworked an earlier version of the play written in 1904 which had fallen foul of the censor. It was not a success, and after an initial short run has not been revived since. But Hermann had other projects on the go. There was the publication of the second edition of *Spielkinder* complete with a cover illustration by Max Liebermann and *Aus guter alter Zeit*, the second in a series of eight coffee table books which the publisher and photographer Franz Goerke was to jointly produce with different writers over the next four years. Hermann's volume celebrates German architecture and is full of picturesque photographs of historic buildings for which he provides the commentary.

FIG. 4.5. Max Liebermann's cover illustration for the
second edition of Spielkinder, 1911.

FIG. 4.6. *Um Berlin*

Hermann also provided the introductory text to ten lithographs depicting Berlin's outskirts by the graphic artist and Berlin Secession member, Rudolf Grossmann, in a limited edition book, *Um Berlin*, published by Paul Cassirer in September 1912. In his introduction Hermann writes that exploring the city's suburbs is a journey of sensory discovery, their state of constant flux offering an ever-flowing stream of new experiences.[24]

Hermann's fascination with Berlin's suburbs and the way in which they blended the natural world and the city is also apparent in his fifth novel, *Die Nacht des Doktor Herzfeld* [The Night of Doctor Herzfeld].[25] According to his daughter Hilde, *Die Nacht* evolved from personal experience and it is evident that there is much of Hermann himself in the central character, the Jewish intellectual, collector of books and fine art objects, Dr Alwin Herzfeld.[26] As Laureen Nussbaum observes, Herzfeld shares Hermann's contemplative, highly sensitive but somewhat self-indulgent nature and similarly feels himself to be at the mercy of women.[27] Some of the opinions ascribed to Herzfeld in the novel, such as his admiration for the Realist author Wilhelm Raabe and his views on Nietzsche and Schopenhauer, also accord with Hermann's own. Herzfeld is however more bereft than Hermann. His wife and child are dead and Hermann likens him to a 'schnappender Fisch', a snapping fish, tossed ashore on a wave and cast out of its element.[28]

One of the traits that Herzfeld shares with his creator is an absence of musicality. 'We used to say that my father was as musical as a fish!' my grandmother Eva would tell us and it is a characteristic which he seems to have bestowed on Herzfeld. Dr Herzfeld is so 'rechtschaffen unmusikalisch' that his tone-deaf singing sets his neighbours' teeth on edge.[29] Hermann acknowledged,

> Von Musik verstehe ich nichts. Es ist ein Nachteil in der Geographie meines Lebens, daß kein breiter Weg, nicht einmal, ja kaum ein Schmugglersteig für mich in dieses Land führt.

> [I do not understand anything about music. It is a defect in my personal geography that no broad path, not even a smuggler's track, can take me into that country.][30]

It is indeed a feature of many of Hermann's characters that while they have a strong visual appreciation, music tends not to be important to them.

There is little in the way of action in *Die Nacht*. The plot, in so far as there is one, involves Herzfeld, together with his friend and drinking buddy, Hermann Gutzeit, a failed journalist, spending the night wandering through the streets and cafés of Berlin. As they walk they evaluate their lives, holding on to each other's company to stave off despair as their conversation brings into sharp relief the futility of their existence. Gutzeit contemplates divorce or suicide as means of escape. Following a chance meeting with a prostitute, Lene Held, who infected him with syphilis many years before, Herzfeld is seized with a fit of rage at how he has squandered his life. After the crisis of the night, Gutzeit returns to his wife to continue the masquerade that his existence has become. Herzfeld's mounting despair, in part linked to the guilt he feels about the death of his wife, culminates in a nervous crisis which is heightened by his solitary wandering through unfamiliar parts of Berlin. The novel ends with Herzfeld purged from his despair as a result of a fainting fit from which he awakens, ready to begin again.[31]

Weiss-Sussex suggests that *Die Nacht* stands on the threshold between the traditional and the modern novel.[32] Given that it is in essence a psychological study of individual consciousness, it is perhaps not surprising that Sigmund Freud was among the work's admirers. He wrote to Hermann to say that, after enjoying the 'schmerzhafte[n] Schönheit' [painful beauty] of the novel, he had a lingering feeling of intimacy with the writer.[33] One of the features of *Die Nacht* is Hermann's adoption of a more conversational style. The intrusive narrator of his previous books is absent and instead we view the world of the novel through Herzfeld's mind, complete with stream of consciousness passages and lengthy digressions. Stefan Zweig believed the novel and its sequel to represent Hermann's best work. His advice, however, that Hermann make some hefty cuts (removing between fifty and a hundred pages) is unlikely to have been well received.[34]

A key theme in *Die Nacht* is the relationship between Herzfeld's inner self and the city environment. In the first part of the novel when Herzfeld is wandering with Gutzeit around the Kurfürstendamm area, the city is presented positively. Hermann finds beauty in this part of Berlin not just in its natural features but also in the busy traffic and the locomotives of the express trains. The epicentre of

FIG. 4.7. Paul Hoeniger, *Spittelmarkt*, 1912 (Stadtmuseum, Berlin).

bohemian Berlin at the time was the Café des Westens at Kurfürstendamm 18/19 and Hermann paints a precise picture of the café and its clientele in the novel. It is the haunt of a coterie of bright young things — women who have recently arrived in Berlin from the provinces and now reinvent themselves as glamorous urban sophisticates, and youthful would-be artists. A later essay by Hermann suggests that Herzfeld's attitude of 'mellow ambivalence' to the bohemian reflects the author's own take on that world.[35] Just as when he was a younger man, Hermann was on the fringes rather than being part of the Friedrichshagener Dichterkreis, so he preferred to stay on the edges of bohemian life in Berlin; a detached observer. He remains 'sympathetic and objective and concentrates on what he is a master in; namely, the description of atmosphere.'[36]

Comparatively at home in the cultural centre of West Berlin, Herzfeld feels lost and alienated from the commercial world of the Friedrichstraße district. He tries to find a sense of equilibrium by reference to landmarks that resonate with his cultural frame of reference — the churches and the museum — to anchor himself in his cultural knowledge. But the prayer house (like the synagogue Hermann remembers attending as a child in 'Also — ein Jubiläum') has become a department store and he is unable to find his bearings. Herzfeld becomes increasingly anxious and confused. There are parallels with the displacement Dr Kössling feels during his nocturnal

wanderings in Berlin after he has said goodnight to Jettchen in Charlottenburg.
We are told that,

> as he wandered in more and more distant and unfamiliar streets — he reached
> devious and distant domains of his mind until to end with, here as there, in the
> outer as in his inner world, he no longer had any idea where he was.[37]

Herzfeld's sense of his own insignificance grows as he feels engulfed in the
poverty and stench of the unfamiliar district. Strangely, he is only shaken out of
his personal maelstrom when he encounters a coachman beating his horses.[38] The
two carthorses in their despair turn on each other. At the sight of this Herzfeld
suddenly comes to recognize the need above all else for sympathy with his fellow
human beings who, like him, are victims of a cruel power. Herzfeld takes a cab
back to the Kurfürstendamm and, safely returned to the cultural heart of the city,
his equilibrium is restored.

The crisis that Alwin Herzfeld experiences in *Die Nacht* stems from the
realisation that the cultured persona which he has developed is a façade. Bereft
of genuine human intimacy, Herzfeld has cloaked his true self in the role of the
detached aesthete. Although he would not choose to be isolated and devoid of close
human relationships, he comes to recognize by the end of the novel that it is only
by continuing to play the role he has assumed that he can preserve his individuality
and carry on. To confront his true feelings risks making life unbearable. But as in
Kubinke, Hermann refrains from any judgements. It is enough that Herzfeld has
succeeded in finding a positive way of accommodating to life in the metropolis.

While the rich cultural opportunities offered by the capital are a large part of
what attracts the art-loving Herzfeld to Berlin, he also feels a sense of rootedness
in the city of his birth. Berlin is where he has grown-up; he has lived through its
changes, has an intimate knowledge of its history and feels a connection with it.
At one point in their wanders, Herzfeld tells Gutzeit that he prefers to walk down
a particular street because he remembers it when the trees were no thicker than his
arm and he feels as if somehow he has helped to create it.[39] We are told that while
other cities like Paris and London have their attractions, Herzfeld only feels at home
in Berlin. Everywhere else he is just a spectator, an onlooker. He declares himself
a *Städter* through and through and sees himself as a *Mitspieler*, part of the history of
the city, a player in the team.[40] Again, Herzfeld's feelings mirror those of Hermann.
My grandmother Eva often remarked how, despite his love of nature, her father was
a *Städter* whereas, she preferred the countryside.[41]

Herzfeld strives for individuality, culture and *Bildung*, and one of the primary
reasons why he feels a sense of belonging to Berlin is that it is a seat of German
high culture and learning. George Mosse maintains that, especially after the end of
the nineteenth century, when the original concept of *Bildung* had become distorted
beyond recognition, it became for many Jews synonymous with their Jewishness.[42]
If this is so, then some of what binds Herzfeld to Berlin — his preoccupation with
the cultural opportunities it presents for self-development — may also reinforce
his sense of Jewishness. It is also of note that Herzfeld's identification with Berlin
has become limited to the old west of the city. Whereas that earlier flâneur, Jason

Gebert, glides freely around Biedermeier Berlin, in the fragmented metropolis of the early twentieth century, Herzfeld feels alienated from large parts of his birthplace.

Contemporary critics linked these feelings of alienation to Herzfeld's Jewishness and Hermann himself subsequently wrote that he had sought in the character of his protagonist to portray the type of rootless, deracinated intellectual city Jew with whom he had much in common.[43] But secular and intellectual though he is, Herzfeld is not wholly devoid of religious sensibility. We are told that secretly in an extreme corner of his heart, there remains a place for it. He cherishes a memory of going to the synagogue with his father on feast days, the men with their tangled beards and kippahs and the melodious singsong of the litanies.[44]

Writing in 1941, the author Sammy Gronemann cited Hermann's differentiated portrayal of Herzfeld and Gutzeit as evidence of his ability to capture what sets the Jew apart. They are so close to each other, so similar yet there is an invisible wall between them. According to Gronemann, 'nowhere else in literature can we find such subtle exploration, which hunts every fine nuance and seeks every slight quiver, of that which sets the Jew apart...'[45] Contemporary reviewers, such as Arthur Eloesser similarly assumed that Hermann was seeking through his portrayal of Herzfeld and Gutzeit to delineate differences between Jew and Gentile. Interestingly, as Weiss-Sussex points out, this is not actually the case as both characters are Jewish.[46] In the sequel to the novel, Hermann describes Gutzeit's son Kurt as being of 'Mischblut — die Mutter war Christin.' [mixed blood — the mother was a Christian].[47]

Die Nacht was well received and brought Hermann further success. By 1916 it had sold 11,000 copies, a figure which had doubled by 1930.[48]

★   ★   ★   ★   ★

Before and during these years when Hermann was establishing himself as a leading novelist, his Egyptologist brother, Ludwig Borchardt, had been building a growing reputation in his chosen field. On 6 December 1912, a few months after the publication of *Die Nacht*, Ludwig made the discovery which with he will be forever associated.

Initially he had studied architecture, intending to become an architect, the path which the middle of the three brothers, Heinrich, subsequently took. But Ludwig switched to Egyptology and in 1895, the year that Hermann was completing his military service in Bavaria, he joined the Egyptian Art Department at the Berlin Museum. Under the auspices of the Prussian Academy of Sciences he travelled for the first time to Egypt, carrying out excavations in Aswan.

It was while Ludwig was working for the French-led Egyptian Antiquities Service in Cairo that he first met Emilie Cohen.[49] Mimi, fourteen years younger than Ludwig, was part of an illustrious and affluent family, based in Frankfurt but with connections in the United States. Her wealthy father, Eduard Cohen, was a painter and philanthropist and her maternal grandfather, Abraham Kuhn, was the co-founder of Kuhn, Loeb & Co which by 1885 had developed into one of the leading banks in America.[50]

Wilh. Fechner   BERLIN W.

FIG. 4.8. Ludwig Borchardt.

FIG. 4.9. Mimi Cohen–Borchardt.

It seems that Ludwig continued to court Mimi on his trips back to Germany in the years that followed. Eduard Cohen tended to keep a close eye on Mimi's prospective marriage candidates and in October 1902 he went to listen to a lecture which Ludwig gave in Berlin. The following day he wrote to Mimi, who was in Florence at the time:

> Gestern war der Vortrag von Dr B., der sehr interessant war und für mich mancherlei Neues enthielt, z. B. die Entstehung der Pyramide aus dem einfachen Grabhügel etc. Er sprach sehr gut, hatte wohl Notizen vor sich, die er aber kaum benutzte, und hörte ich beim Herausgehen Stimmen aus dem Publikum, die sehr befriedigt klangen. Der Saal war gedrängt voll, der Kaiser, die Kaiserin und der hier anwesende Kronprinz von Dänemark waren auch da und wurde Dr B. nach der Vorlesung in die kaiserliche Loge gerufen und sprach der Kaiser lange mit ihm.

> [Yesterday was the talk by Dr B. which was very interesting for me and contained many new ideas relating to the development of pyramids from simple burial mounds. He spoke very well, from notes which he used but little, and I heard the remarks of the audience as they were leaving and they were very complimentary. The room was crowded, the Emperor and Empress and the Crown Prince of Denmark were there and after the lecture, Dr B. was called to the imperial box and the Emperor talked with him for a long time.][51]

The couple became officially engaged in December 1902 and were married on 7 June 1903 in Frankfurt. A few weeks after the wedding they left for Egypt. Ludwig was now working as a scientific attaché at the German Consulate General of Egyptology in Cairo and he had bought a house, situated on the Nile island of Zamalek, earlier in the year. In 1907 he founded the German Institute for Egyptian Archaeology in Cairo and two years later began directing an archaeological mission in Amarna, sponsored by the entrepreneur, philanthropist and art patron, James Simon.

Exhuming the workshop studio of the court sculptor Thutmose, Ludwig discovered many carved portraits, including in December 1912 the famous bust of Queen Nefertiti. Ludwig's brief diary entry recording the find says, 'Suddenly we had in our hands the most living Egyptian work of art. You cannot describe it in words; you must see it.' He later wrote that the perfect symmetry of the bust endows Nefertiti with an aura of peace, making her 'the epitome of tranquillity and harmony.'[52]

How the bust ended up in Germany and continues to remain on display in the Neues Museum in Berlin is a matter of ongoing controversy. The story of its export has grown in the telling and Ludwig is often portrayed as having tricked the authorities so that it could be smuggled out of Egypt. Under the terms of the concession, all finds had to be split evenly between the French-run museum service and the excavator. The authorities had first pickings but although the bust was at the top of the exchange list, the museum inspector, Gustave Lefebvre, did not choose it. *Der Spiegel* in 2009 claimed to have found new evidence that the authorities had been manipulated in a 'secret' document written in 1924 by the then secretary of the German Oriental Society. The secretary had been present at the meeting to

FIG. 4.10. The Nefertiti bust (Neues Museum, Berlin)

divide up the spoils of the dig and records in the document that Ludwig 'wanted to save the bust for us' and so presented an unflattering photograph of it.[53] The bust was given to James Simon, the principal backer of the excavation and became part of his private collection until 1920 when Simon donated it to the Neues Museum. Four years later it went on public display. The public reaction to the bust was immediate and enthusiastic. Its appeal continues undiminished today.[54]

Notes to Chapter 4

1. Hermann, 'Im Spiegel', p. 307.
2. *Unvorhanden und stumm*, p. 11.
3. Georg Hermann, 'Rückblick zum Fünfzigsten', in *Gesammelte Werke*, vol. 5 (Stuttgart: DVA), 1922, pp. 423–54. Here, p. 431.
4. Georg Hermann, *Der kleine Gast* (Berlin: Das Neue Berlin), 1999, p. 155.
5. Georg Hermann, *Rudyard Kipling: Eine Studie* (Berlin: Vita Deutsches Verlagshaus, 1909).
6. See for instance the essays 'Über die Würde' and 'Über Bücher'. Georg Hermann, *Sehnsucht. Ernste Plaudereien* (Berlin: Fleischel, 1909).
7. Hermann took the names of the family's real-life nanny, Hedwig (Quandt) and their two live-in servants.
8. Weiss-Sussex, *Metropolitan Chronicles*, p. 170.
9. Supposedly the last words of Rabelais. Georg Hermann, *Kubinke* (Berlin: Das Neue Berlin, 1997), p. 382.
10. Weiss-Sussex, *Metropolitan Chronicles*, p. 187.
11. Hermann, *Kubinke*, pp. 155–56. This translation is by Weiss-Sussex and is taken from her article 'Naturalist Metaphor', p. 376.
12. Weiss-Sussex, *Metropolitan Chronicles*, p. 193.

13. Georg Hermann, 'Holland und Liebermann', *Central-Verein-Zeitung*, Berlin, no. 1, 4 January 1934.
14. Oscar Wilde, *Plays, Prose Writings and Poems* (London: David Campbell, 1991), p. 371.
15. Georg Hermann, 'Der tote Naturalismus', in *Vom gesicherten und ungesicherten Leben* (Berlin: Fleischel, 1915), p. 64.
16. See Weiss-Sussex, *Metropolitan Chronicles*, pp. 210–21.
17. Georg Simmel, 'The Metropolis and Mental Life' (1903), reprinted in *The Blackwell City Reader*, ed. by Gary Bridge and Sophie Watson (Oxford: John Wiley and Sons, 2010), p. 110.
18. Weiss-Sussex, *Metropolitan Chronicles*, pp. 241–44. The letter is dated 18 October 1910 and is in the George Hermann Collection (GHC) in the Leo Baeck Institute (LBI): GHC; AR 7074; Box 7, Folder 25, 403/855. Hermann cites Kerr's review of Georg Hirschfeld's 1899 comedy *Pauline*, in particular his observations about the amorality of Berlin servant girls. I finally handed a copy of the letter to Kerr's daughter, the children's writer, Judith Kerr, at a book festival, 102 years after it was written.
19. Weiss-Sussex, *Metropolitan Chronicles*, p. 187.
20. Ibid., p. 241.
21. van Liere, *Georg Hermann: Materialien*, p. 77.
22. Directed by Carl Boese who was one of the most commercially successful German film directors of the time, the movie starred Werner Fuetterer as Kubinke. The three servants were played by Erika Glässner, Käte Haack and Hilde Maroff.
23. For a synopsis of the play see Richard Frank Krummel, *Nietzsche und der deutsche Geist: Ausbreitung und Wirkung des Nietzscheschen Werkes im deutschen Sprachraum vom Todesjahr bis zum Ende des Ersten Weltkrieges: ein Schrifttumsverzeichnis der Jahre 1901–1918* (Berlin: De Gruyter, 2006), p. 549.
24. Rudolf Großmann, *Um Berlin*, Zehn Original Lithographien. Text: Georg Hermann (Berlin: Cassirer, 1912).
25. Georg Hermann, *Die Nacht des Doktor Herzfeld*, (Berlin: Fleischel, 1912). Subsequent references are to the edition of the novel published by Das Neue Berlin in 1998.
26. *Unvorhanden und stumm*, p. 15.
27. Laureen Nussbaum, 'Georg Hermann Attacks the Special Issue of *Der Jude*', in *The Yale Companion to Jewish Writing and Thought in German Culture, 1096–1996*, ed. by Sander L. Gilman and Jack Zipes (New Haven, CT: Yale University Press, 1997), p. 451.
28. Hermann, *Die Nacht des Doktor Herzfeld*, p. 201.
29. Hans Scholz, 'Georg Hermann und die Berliner Dichtung', in *Rosenemil* (Munich: Süddeutscher Verlag, 1962), p. 352.
30. Georg Hermann, 'Vorwort zu *Ruths schwere Stunde*' (Berlin: Das Neue Berlin, 2001), p. 5.
31. This summary is taken from Weiss-Sussex, *Metropolitan Chronicles*, p. 247.
32. Ibid., p. 263.
33. Sigmund Freud, letter to Georg Hermann, 1 February 1936, GHC; AR 7074; Box 1, Folder 1, LBI, 161/991.
34. Stefan Zweig, letter to Georg Hermann, 23 July 1921, GHC; AR 7074; Box 1; Folder 4, LBI, 610/991.
35. Weiss-Sussex, *Metropolitan Chronicles*, p. 288.
36. Ibid., p. 289.
37. Hermann, *Hetty Geybert*, p. 207.
38. This episode in the novel may be a nod to the incident said to have triggered Friedrich Nietzsche's mental breakdown. In Turin in 1889, on seeing a horse being flogged, Nietzsche became enraged and tried to intervene before collapsing to the ground.
39. Hermann, *Die Nacht des Doktor Herzfeld*, p. 28.
40. Ibid., p. 20
41. Herzfeld's rootedness in the city reflects the increasing urbanisation of the Jewish population across Germany. In the year of Hermann's birth, 1871, only thirty per cent of Jews lived in big cities. By 1910 (two years before *Die Nacht des Doktor Herzfeld* was published) that figure had risen to seventy per cent. See Kaplan, 'Redefining Judaism in Imperial Germany', p. 6.

42. George L Mosse, *German Jews beyond Judaism* (Bloomington, IN: Indiana University Press, 1985), p. 4.
43. Georg Hermann, 'Der deutsche Jude und das Großstadtproblem', *c*. 1926–32, GHC; AR 7074; Box 5, Folder 6, LBI, p. 4. Godela Weiss-Sussex has pointed out that a reference in the article indicates it must have been published in *Central-Verein-Zeitung* in the 1930s. See Weiss-Sussex, *Metropolitan Chronicles*, p. 304.
44. Hermann, *Die Nacht des Doktor Herzfeld*, p. 227.
45. Gronemann, preface to Georg Hermann, *Jettchen Gebert*, p. x. Gronemann suggests that Hermann explores this invisible wall — a wall over which one cannot jump — in the relationships between Jettchen and Dr Kössling and Heinrich Schön jun. and Hannchen Mühlensiefen.
46. Weiss-Sussex, *Metropolitan Chronicles*, p. 305.
47. Georg Hermann, *Schnee* (Berlin: Das Neue Berlin, 1997), p. 318. Quoted in Weiss-Sussex, *Metropolitan Chronicles*, p. 305.
48. van Liere, *Georg Hermann: Materialien*, p. 216.
49. All of these details about the courtship between Ludwig and Emilie and the quotations from family letters are taken from Cilli Kasper-Holtkotte's essay, 'Vom Main an den Nil. Zur Geschichte der Familie Cohen in Frankfurt und des Ehepaares Borchardt in Kairo', in *Sahure. Tod und Leben eines großen Pharao. Eine Ausstellung der Liebighaus Skulpturensammlung*, ed. by V. Brinkmann (Frankfurt a.M.: Liebighaus, 2010), pp. 122–41.
50. Kuhn, Loeb & Co merged with Lehman Brothers in 1977.
51. Kasper-Holtkotte, 'Vom Main an den Nil', p. 129.
52. Ludwig Borchardt, 'Porträts der Königin Nofretete. Aus den Grabungen 1912/13 in Tell El-Amarna' (1923), quoted in Joyce A. Tyldesley, *Nefertiti: Egypt's Sun Queen* (London: Penguin, 1998), p. 198.
53. 'Archaeological Controversy: Did Germany Cheat to Get Bust of Nefertiti?', *Der Spiegel*, 10 February 2009.
54. The exhibition 'In the Light of Amarna. 100 Years of the Nefertiti Discovery' was at the Neues Museum from July 2012 to April 2013.

CHAPTER 5

❖

War

With *Jettchen Gebert* still popular, seven years after its publication, Hermann was commissioned to adapt it for the stage. First performed in Frankfurt in May 1913, the play proved to be a notable success, running until April the following year. Many hundreds of performances were given across Germany and Austria and productions were also staged in Prague and Zurich.[1] When the play was performed at the Fledermaus Theater in Berlin, some of the Biedermeier furniture from the family home in Grunewald was used in its staging, another example of the way in which Hermann's real life intersected with his literary world.

The popularity of *Jettchen Gebert* notwithstanding, Hermann still insists in his 'Im Spiegel' essay of 1914 that he remains a dabbler in everything and can evidence no real development. While on the surface he may appear reconciled to the bourgeois life — the greying author in his comfortable Grunewald villa — Hermann still feels a deep-seated need for self-reflection. The passage of years has failed to bring him greater self-understanding. He quotes Friedrich Hebbel's dictum: 'Je länger man auf der Welt ist, desto weniger versteht man, wozu man es ist.' [The longer you are in the world, the less you understand what for].[2]

Eva was ten years old when the First World War broke out. On being told by her father that there was going to be a war she apparently replied, 'War? But I thought that was like witchcraft, something from the past'. The news of the outbreak of hostilities was met with frenzied patriotic enthusiasm in Germany and German writers and artists were almost unanimous in welcoming the conflict. Thomas Mann saw it as an opportunity to cleanse one's soul. For Stefan George, it was a sacred liberating spring and Leo Baeck, while acknowledging that war in general was evil, felt that this one 'allows us to sense how the life of the fatherland is ours and how its conscience resonates in our own.'[3]

The Central Association of German Citizens of Jewish Faith called upon its members to serve the fatherland beyond the call of duty. Jewish intellectuals were as gung-ho about the war as anyone. 'It was,' the historian Amos Elon writes, 'their worst hour since the unification of Germany in 1870.'[4] During the first week of the war Freud said that he could not wait to see German troops march triumphantly into Paris.[5] The philosopher Hermann Cohen believed that his finest ideals would be realized in the war. Martin Buber celebrated the war as a liberating shared experience and argued that Germany was merely acting in self-defence.

Elon suggests that 'long devoted to the cult of *Bildung*, many Jewish intellectuals convinced themselves that the superiority of German *Kultur* justified the German cause.'[6] Emil Ludwig, Arnold Zweig, Alfred Kerr, Julius Bab, Rudolf Borchardt and Ernst Lissauer, for instance, all welcomed and supported the war. Lissauer's poem, *Haßgesang gegen England* [Hymn of Hate against England] was adopted as part of Germany's official war propaganda. The Manifesto of the Ninety-Three, organized in November 1914 at the War Ministry's instigation by the playwright Ludwig Fulda denounced all criticism of Germany as poisonous lies and celebrated the way German militarism had ensured the preservation of German culture. It stated 'we shall carry on this war to the end as a civilized nation, to whom the legacy of a Goethe, a Beethoven and a Kant is just as sacred as its own hearths and homes.' Amongst the signatories were a number of Nobel Prize laureates such as Paul Ehrlich, Philipp Lenard and Gerhart Hauptmann as well as Max Liebermann, and the Hermanns' Grunewald neighbour, Engelbert Humperdinck.

Stefan Zweig in his memoir *The World of Yesterday* recalls the mood surrounding the general mobilisation in Vienna at the outbreak of the war:

> Parades formed in the streets, suddenly there were banners, streamers, music everywhere. The young recruits marched along in triumph, their faces bright because they, ordinary people who passed entirely unnoticed in everyday life, were being cheered and applauded. To be perfectly honest, I must admit that there was something fine, inspiring, even seductive in that first mass outburst of feeling. It was difficult to resist it.[7]

Only a very small number of German writers did resist it and keep their distance from the warmongers. Heinrich Mann was one and Georg Hermann another. A committed pacifist, he opposed the war from the outset and came to see the patriotic enthusiasm with which it was greeted as a tidal wave of madness, a relapse into barbarism.[8] Everybody was expected to join the chorus of approval:

> Zuerst wurde die Frage an jeden gestellt: Wie stehst du zu diesem heiligen Krieg? Bejahst du ihn oder verneinst du ihn innerlich? Das heißt, bist du von heute auf morgen irrsinnig geworden, oder hast du dir deine fünf Sinne und dein Menschentum gesund bewahrt? Wenn du ihn aber — was wir annehmen — bejahst, so erhebe deine Stimme für ihn.

> [First the question was put to everyone, how do you feel about this holy war? Do you proclaim your support or are you inwardly against it? That is, have you overnight gone insane or are your five senses and your humanity intact? If you endorse the war — as we assume — then raise your voice for it.][9]

It was difficult to oppose the war publicly; anti-war writings were banned by the censor. When the Communist Karl Liebknecht spoke up in the Reichstag and voted against the war budget, his speech was struck from the official record.[10]

Hermann was quick to recognize that August 1914 was a turning point and that the war was fuelling a rising tide of anti-Semitism in Germany. The solidarity of the early months of the conflict had proved illusionary. By August 1916 Walther Rathenau was writing to his friend the journalist Wilhelm Schwaner that the more Jews were killed in the war, the more persistent would be their opponents' complaints that the Jews did nothing but sit behind the frontlines, profiteering.[11] The number of Jews killed on the battlefield numbered 3000 by that autumn and 7000 had been decorated but the War Minister, Wild von Hohenborn, nonetheless commissioned a statistical survey ('Nachweisung der beim Heere befindlichen wehrpflichtigen Juden') to ascertain the proportion of Jews in the army serving on the frontline. The results of the count which showed that the figure was 80% were never officially released. In total about 10,000 German Jews volunteered for duty and over 100,000 served during the war. Some 78% saw front-line service; 12,000 died in battle and 30,000 received decorations.[12] Hermann was not among those who served. Being under the age of forty-five, he was called up but after being examined by three military doctors, he was categorized as unfit.[13]

In some ways the experience of Jewish-German soldiers in the First World War foreshadowed that of black soldiers in the US military in the 1940s. In an essay marking the thirtieth anniversary of his novel *Invisible Man*, Ralph Ellison describes how originally he had imagined his central character as a black pilot serving in the US Airforce:

> My [Negro] pilot was prepared to make the ultimate wartime sacrifice that most governments demand of their able bodied citizens, but his government was one that regarded his life as of lesser value than the lives of the whites making the same sacrifice.[14]

Just as black American soldiers were to find in the Second World War that their lives were less valuable to the state for which they were fighting, so the First World War demonstrated that the sacrifice of Jewish German soldiers counted for less with the German authorities. The *Judenzählung* gave the lie to the Kaiser's talk in the early days of the war that differences of religion, political affiliation and ethnic origin no longer mattered.

As Hermann understood, the war which in those heady days of August 1914 was purportedly unifying all Germans in their shared devotion to the fatherland, to Goethe, Beethoven and other titans of German high culture, actually effected a decisive change in the development of the German-Jewish relationship. He came to see 1914 as the moment when the schism began. Some later commentators, notably Gershom Scholem, have questioned this correlation between the war and anti-Semitism, arguing that the love affair between Germans and Jews was always one-sided and unreciprocated. However, most agree that the war and its aftermath did result in a transformation in German Jewish attitudes. Eva Reichmann, for example, while acknowledging that German anti-Semitism had a long pre-history, argues that the First World War was the crucial turning point and that the latent germs of anti-Semitism had been revitalized by the post-war crisis.[15] The nationalist conception of Germany which was fostered by the war was defined not by shared cultural heritage, not by inclusivity, but by exclusion. In Toni Morrison's memorable phrase, 'all paradises, all utopias are designed by who is not there, by the people who are not allowed in.'[16] The result was that, as the historian, Michael Brenner notes, 'most significantly, liberal Jews like the writer Georg Hermann had their belief in successful assimilation shattered.'[17]

Hermann's response to the war pervades his 1915 collection of essays, *Vom gesicherten und ungesicherten Leben* [On Secure and Insecure Life].[18] In the treatise which gives its name to the collection, Hermann argues that just as the Earth is divided into the northern and southern hemispheres so the human world is split between the secure and the insecure. There is more than a suggestion of this polarity already in *Jettchen Gebert*. Dr Kössling's first impression of Solomon and Riekchen Gebert is that they live in a different world from him, quite without any points of contact. They accept life as a fact and are 'insultingly content'.[19] The frustration and anxiety of life that drives Kössling forward is unknown to them. Like Solomon and Riekchen, secure people, Hermann maintains, are always sure of themselves and of their position in the world. Accordingly, they are the elements upon which the state rests.[20] They have an unconscious self-belief which cannot be shaken and provides protection from life's vicissitudes. Their eyes lack that flicker of uncertainty, that undertone of anxiety which is ever-present in those of the insecure.

For Hermann the insecure life offers richer creative possibilities and he believes it is the source of all that is precious and great. There is no people in the world as insecure as the Jews, he writes, but the absence of the inhibiting conventions of a nation and the trappings of statehood have meant that the Jew has been at the forefront of finding new ways of doing things since the old ones are invariably closed to him. Hermann describes the Social Democrats (SPD) as the natural party of the insecure but he expresses concern at the way it has endorsed the war and argues that it would be deeply regrettable if it should become a nationalist party and betray its fundamental principles.[21] Surely, Hermann writes, we will move beyond our current conception of the state as something which can command the slaughter of its citizens. He denies that he is an anarchist, a dreamer of a new social order. He is simply someone who prizes human life above all else and yet today finds that it is being frittered away by the million, as if it is worthless. Hermann's internationalist credentials shine through in the essay. He quotes Walt Whitman and Oscar Wilde and makes reference to George Bernard Shaw (a prominent opponent of the war), Balzac, and Maupassant, amongst others. The subtext is clear. Hermann remains receptive to what writers from the so-called enemy nations have to say. His theme transcends national boundaries.

Another article in the collection, 'Erinnerungen an...' [Memories of...] further underlines Hermann's concern at the appalling human cost of the war.[22] In the opening section of the essay, he recalls happy days spent exploring the meadows and forests of Finkenkrug, a district of Falkensee, a town west of Berlin. Hermann explains that he has been making the pilgrimage from Berlin to Finkenkrug every spring for the last thirty years, chasing butterflies and admiring the young birches coming into leaf, the anemones and the liverwort. But now these cherished memories have been tarnished by the war and the friends he has lost to it. He poses the question 'I yearn for Finkenkrug but who would I go there with now?'

Hermann recalls that the first visit he made in 1885 was a school trip. But now, as their lives are cut short by the war, 'Ich habe die Nachrufe für meine Mitschüler jetzt gelesen.' [I read the obituaries for my former classmates].[23] A few years afterwards, he started taking his girlfriends to Finkenkrug for romantic strolls in the forest. He recalls one spring day when he was there with two other young men, a lady and her two daughters. High water levels had transformed the meadows into vast lakes. As the evening sun was about to go down the sky acquired that strange fluorescence unique to spring. A deer emerged from the woods, and scared, it leapt ahead of them, backlit against the setting sun. Hermann remembers the delight he felt, remarking that when three young men are with two lovely young women they tend to have a reason to be particularly enthralled by the things of the world. With a jolt he realizes that seventeen years have passed since that evening. Of his two companions, one is interned a thousand miles away and the other is missing in action, following a failed offensive in which sixty-two men died. His thoughts turn to a young doctor with whom he could go to Finkenkrug but he has been shot in the head in the war. He thinks of another acquaintance. They used to work on the same newspaper but never found the time to go together. Now he has all the time in the world: he rests with so many others in Flanders. Hermann yearns to go once more to Finkenkrug in the spring but he fears that his heart would break if he were to go there alone.

Hermann's most outspoken criticism of the war comes in another treatise from the same collection, *Weltliteratur oder Literatur für den Hausgebrauch?* [World Literature or Literature for Domestic Consumption?].[24] In the essay Hermann argues that good literature has always been international and he celebrates the way in which literature from abroad has enriched Germany. The country might now require a 'national economy' but Hermann sees no reason for a similarly parochial approach to the arts — arguing that we impoverish ourselves if we boycott foreign literature. Instead, he argues, we should pay heed to writers who have meaningful things to say to us whether they are Russian, German or British.

Hermann laments the way German intellectuals have embraced the war so indiscriminately and in so doing side-lined completely consideration of every other social ill. He argues persuasively that reducing poverty, improving public health, and making progress in areas such as agriculture and transportation, will be far more significant to mankind in the long run than transient shifts in the balance of political power. But rather than focusing on how to lift the condition of the masses and to improve their educational opportunities, Hermann protests that Europe is now further removed from such matters than in the days of Nebuchadnezzar. It has gone speeding off, like a comet, in the opposite direction from such concerns. And yet no one seems to recognize the madness of the war and the wasted human potential it represents.

Instead, everywhere Hermann encounters the same desire to justify the hostilities. He cites the clergy who appear to have no difficulty in reconciling their faith with the conflict, and references Thomas Mann, and other public figures like Wilhelm Bölsche, who had stressed the war's moral necessity. Should we return to cannibalism, Hermann says, no doubt the cognoscenti will prove to us that it is a moral affair, well-grounded in nature, as evidenced by the habits of wolves, sharks and wild hogs.

He argues that the quality of literature a country produces is actually in inverse proportion to its political power — sentiments which could hardly have been more out of step with the bellicose mood of the time. German literature, he contends, flourished in the days before unification and Italian art likewise thrived when the region was politically weak and fragmented. Hermann concludes the essay with a passionate defence of the importance and universal nature of contemporary literature which, he argues, transcends notions of nationality:

> Die Literatur, in der wir heute leben und atmen, ist (wie die Kunst) eine Sache, die jenseits von Krieg und Frieden ist, ein internationaler Pakt der Geister, immer neue, schönere, erklärendere Formen für das Leben zu finden.[...] Wir vergessen ganz, welcher Nationalität diese Dinge angehören ... für uns haben sie alle nur ein Vaterland in der modernen Seele.

> [The literature that we live and breathe today (like art) is a thing beyond war and peace, it is an international Pact of the Mind, finding new, ever finer ways of interpreting life. We completely forget what nationality these works belong to ... for us they all have only one fatherland in the modern soul.][25]

In 1917 Hermann sent a copy of *Vom gesicherten und ungesicherten Leben* to the German Secretary of Cultural Affairs, highlighting 'Weltliteratur oder Literatur für den Hausgebrauch?' and suggesting that Germany would do well to encourage her best writers to build bridges, first to neutral nations and subsequently to present foes.[26]

The nature of literature and the purpose of the serious writer are themes which feature recurrently in the collection. In the autobiographical essay 'Die Unstetheit des Schriftstellers' [The Restlessness of the Writer] Hermann notes that in the great organisation of life and the state, the man of letters occupies a prominent position and yet he has no official status.[27] The literary man would like to do pleasant things like travelling and reading and to immerse himself in wine, women and music but ultimately all of this leaves him unfulfilled since he cannot stop questioning the meaning of this existence, this society in which he is confined. He is consumed with the attempt through writing to give shape and permanence to his transient life. Consequently, a part of the writer, Hermann insists, is always on the outside looking in. He cites a passage in Maupassant's story *Sur L'eau* (1888) describing how the writer, even at the funeral of a loved one, still cannot help but notice a thousand details. Hermann maintains that while writers may be good spouses and fathers, entertaining companions, none of this touches the core of their being. They belong neither to wife, family or society.

Given the success of *Jettchen Gebert* on the stage, it was only natural that Hermann should also adapt its sequel *Henriette Jacoby*. The play opened at the Kleine Theater in Berlin on 18 November 1915. Agnes Straub, who went on to be a successful film actress, played Henriette and the adaptation, like its predecessor, did well.[28] Productions were staged in Strasbourg, Munich, Leipzig, Breslau, Dusseldorf and Stuttgart, no doubt helping to fuel the continuing demand for the novels.

Hermann returned to the Biedermeier for his sixth novel, *Heinrich Schön jun.*, but this time the setting is Potsdam rather than Berlin.[29] Heinrich's widowed father,

Eduard, has married a significantly younger woman, Antonie Armstein. She is twenty-three, he is fifty-seven, and Antonie has much more in common with her stepson, Heinrich. They fall in love but eventually Antonie leaves her husband, not for Heinrich but for his friend, Maltitz.

The Schöns have made their money from property. Heinrich's grandfather, Samuel, was a developer and since his success the family has ranked among Potsdam's bourgeoisie, although now its fortunes are in steady decline. Eduard represents the traditional unchanging values associated with the older generation, as do the family's friends, the Mühlensiefens whose attractive daughter Hannchen is Heinrich's fiancée. She is the same age as Antonie but Heinrich decides that she belongs to the provinces (always a negative in a Hermann novel). She reads low-brow books, lacks initiative and is not intellectual. Heinrich adopts a patronising attitude towards Hannchen, repeatedly referring to her as a child, and believes that with his influence she will develop. In a similar way, his father mistakenly thinks that he can mould Antonie.

Antonie, Maltitz and Heinrich form the younger generation, at odds with the established social norms. Antonie, in particular, seems to have been imported from the early twentieth century. She represents the new generation of women from the middle classes: self-sufficient, educated and no longer content to uphold a constraining social order.[30] Antonie's directness challenges the way that women are expected to behave. After she has left him, Eduard compares Antonie to a comet, an uncontrollable force of nature. His one regret is that he transgressed the laws of bourgeois sense by marrying such a 'junges, seltsames Wesen' [young, strange creature].[31] Rather in the way that Jettchen Gebert perceives her marriage as a business transaction, it is clear that Antonie's marriage to Eduard was largely about securing her family's financial future. Heinrich feels that she was purchased by his father like a voucher for a dozen new scarves. For all her unconventionality, Antonie is a complicit if reluctant partner in the transaction.

In contrast to Hannchen, Antonie reads Goethe and Schiller and shares Heinrich's interests in literature and philosophy. Her reading habits, we learn, have been cultivated by Jason Gebert, who she says oversaw her first steps as a *mensch* (i.e. a decent person, someone with integrity). Although less physically attractive than Hannchen, she is a woman of greater depth and charm. Heinrich is entranced by both her body and her mind. But Hannchen and Antonie are not the only women in Heinrich's life. He is also sleeping with a nineteen-year-old working class girl, referred to only by her surname, Wulkow.

Maitland notes that in their central scene, when Heinrich and Antonie take a boat trip together during which they acknowledge their feelings for one another, Heinrich's relationship with Wulkow is mirrored but in reverse. It is Antonie who suggests the outing; she asks Heinrich not to invite Hannchen as he had intended, and it is she who takes control in the boat. When Heinrich admits his feelings for her, it is Antonie who prolongs their embrace. Feeling increasingly guilty at betraying his father and Hannchen, Heinrich takes flight. He asks his father to break off his engagement and departs for Rio, pretending that it is because of the gossip about him and Wulkow. But unlike Jettchen Gebert, Antonie is not the passive victim of others' decisions. She does not remain in a loveless match with Eduard; instead she also leaves, not to join Heinrich but instead to go to Vienna with the lively Maltitz.

Although *Heinrich Schön jun.* did not prove as popular as Hermann's earlier Biedermeier novels, the book was another commercial success. By 1919, 24,000 copies had been sold, out-stripping sales of both *Kubinke* and *Die Nacht des Doktor Herzfeld*.[32] For Sammy Gronemann, *Heinrich Schön jun.* again demonstrated Hermann's great artistic skill in describing and evoking a milieu, his magical ability to bring bygone times and places vividly before the reader's eyes.[33] Four years after its publication, Hermann dramatized the novel as *Frau Antonie*. It premiered at the Frankfurt Playhouse but was not a success and the play seems to have disappeared without trace, never to be performed again.

Notes to Chapter 5

1. van Liere, *Georg Hermann: Materialien*, p. 68. Lotte Lenya, then seventeen years old, played Rosalie Jacoby in the Pfauen Theater's production in 1914/15, her first performance under the direction of Ricard Révy.
2. Hermann, 'Im Spiegel', p. 309.
3. Quoted by Elon, *The Pity of It All*, p. 305.
4. Ibid., p. 318.
5. Ibid.
6. Ibid., p. 321.
7. Stefan Zweig, *The World of Yesterday*, trans. by Anthea Bell (London: Pushkin Press, 2009), pp. 245–46.
8. Mark H. Gelber, 'Georg Hermann's Late Assessment of German-Jewish and Aryan-German Writers', *Monatsheft* 82, 1 (1990), 6–16. Here p. 9.
9. Georg Hermann, 'Weltabschied', in *Unvorhanden und stumm*, p. 233.
10. Elon, *The Pity of It All*, p. 328.
11. Ibid., p. 338.
12. Bryan Mark Rigg, *Hitler's Jewish Soldiers* (Lawrence, KS: University Press of Kansas, 2002), p. 72.
13. Hermann, 'Rückblick zum Fünfzigsten', p. 441.
14. Ralph Ellison, *Invisible Man* (London: Penguin Modern Classics), 2001, p. xxx.
15. See Tim Grady, *The German-Jewish Soldiers of the First World War in History and Memory* (Liverpool: Liverpool University Press, 2012), pp. 201–02.
16. Toni Morrison, *Conversations*, ed. by Carolyn C. Denard (Jackson, MS: University Press of Mississippi, 2008), p. 156.
17. Michael Brenner, *The Renaissance of Jewish Culture in Weimar Germany* (New Haven, CT: Yale University Press, 1996), p. 32.
18. Hermann, *Vom gesicherten und ungesicherten Leben. Ernste Plaudereien* (Berlin: Fleischel, 1915).
19. Hermann, *Hetty Geybert*, p. 52.
20. Weiss-Sussex, *Metropolitan Chronicles*, p. 135.
21. This was a very live issue. Already by the time of the publication of *Vom gesicherten und ungesicherten Leben*, a growing minority of SPD deputies was no longer willing to support the continued provision of war loans and in March 1916 the party (which had been the largest in the Reichstag at the outbreak of the war) split.
22. 'Erinnerungen an...', in Hermann, *Die Reise nach Massow*, pp. 317–34.
23. Ibid., p. 328.
24. Georg Hermann, 'Weltliteratur oder Literatur für den Hausgebrauch?', in *Vom gesicherten und ungesicherten Leben*, p. 67–106.

25. Ibid., p. 103.
26. See Laureen Nussbaum, 'A Sampling of Georg Hermann's Letters about German Literature', in Weiss-Sussex (ed.), *Georg Hermann: Deutsch-jüdischer Schriftsteller und Journalist 1871–1943*, p. 75.
27. Georg Hermann, 'Die Unstetheit des Schriftstellers', *Gesammelte Werke*, vol. 5 (Stuttgart: DVA, 1922), pp. 600–11.
28. Frieda Brock played Aunt Riekchen; Alice Toming, Hannchen Gebert; Robert Forsch, Salomon Gebert; Lupu Pick, Uncle Eli; and Fritz Beckmann played Ferdinand Gebert.
29. Georg Hermann, *Heinrich Schön jun.* (Berlin: Fleischel, 1915). Subsequent references are to the edition of the novel published by Das Neue Berlin in 1998.
30. Maitland, 'Dora and her Sisters', p. 80.
31. Hermann, *Heinrich Schön jun.*, p. 384.
32. van Liere, *Georg Hermann: Materialien*, p. 216.
33. Gronemann, preface to Georg Hermann, *Jettchen Gebert*, p. xiii.

CHAPTER 6

❖

Separation

In the summer of 1914 Hermann took a lease on a house in Neckargemünd, a village ten miles upriver from Heidelberg, located at the confluence between the Neckar and the river Elsenz. The house, very similar in design to the villa in Trabener Straße, had been owned since 1901 by his old friend, Ludwig Jahn, who had first opened Hermann's eyes to the attractions of southern Germany.

Many years later, Hermann wrote about the move in the essay 'Wie ich auf Heidelberg kam' [How I Hit upon Heidelberg]:

> Kurz, ich war um 1914 reichlich berlinmüde und wäre froh gewesen, es eine Anzahl von Monaten im Jahre nicht zu sehen ... auch ohne persönliche Gründe. Also ich mietete jenes Neckargemünder Haus als zweites, als Tuskulum[I]; und alsbald brach der Krieg aus und kehrte das Unterste zuoberst. In diesem Augenblick aber dachte die Welt und Deutschland an sehr andere Dinge, als Bücher zu lesen und Bücher zu kaufen; und ich fürchtete, den Verpflichtungen, die mir zwei Wohnungen auferlegten, nicht mehr gerecht werden zu können. Ich tat das, was niemand tat — die anderen blieben einfach die Miete schuldig! — , ich gab, wie ich dachte, vorübergehend meine Berliner Wohnung auf. Und in diesem Augenblick schnappte hinter mir die Rattenfalle zu. Es war natürlich unnötig gewesen. Man las im Kriege zehnmal soviel Bücher wie heute...
>
> [All in all around 1914, I was rather tired of Berlin and would have been happy not to see it for several months a year [...] even without any personal reasons. So I rented the aforementioned house in Neckargemünd as a second residence, like as in Tusculum. Soon the war broke out and turned everything upside down. In that moment, Germany and the rest of the world was preoccupied with very different things from reading and buying books and I feared that I would not be able to meet the expense of having two homes. I did what nobody else did — the others just fell behind with their rent payments! — I gave up my Berlin apartment (temporarily, so I thought). And at that moment the rat trap snapped shut behind me. It turned out to be unnecessary, of course. People read ten times more books during the war than they do today...][2]

The family home in Grunewald was finally vacated in March 1915 for the Neckargemünd house (Poststraße 2). In October 1914 Jahn had accepted a professorship in Thuringia and moved to Hildburghausen, more than a hundred miles from Neckargemünd. Presumably he now wanted permanent tenants and Hermann took the opportunity. Hermann made inquiries about buying the house in December 1918 and a sales contract was drawn up in February the following year.

Fig. 6.1. Poststraße 2, Neckargemünd.

The price was 36,000 Mark. Hermann paid 12,500 of this in cash and borrowed the balance from the Catholic Foundation in Karlsruhe and the Heidelberger Building Society.[3]

Although Martha and the girls lived permanently at the new house, Hermann continued to split his time during the war between Berlin and Neckargemünd and in fact seems to have spent more time in the capital. While Hermann emphasizes his disenchantment with Berlin and the need to tighten his purse as key factors in the move, Eva always said that he anticipated there would be food shortages in Berlin as a result of the war. Liese's health was fragile and that was another reason for wanting to move away from the city. Hermann was proved correct. Britain's naval blockade, exacerbated by a combination of bad harvests and maladministration resulted in food shortages which reached critical levels in urban areas from the winter of 1916 onwards. The family was certainly better off in Heidelberg but with Hermann spending so much of his time in Berlin, the change also offered him greater independence which may have been another factor in the move. Hermann's only new publication in 1916 came in February that year and was another collection of short fictional pieces, *Der Guckkasten — Altes und Neues* [The Peepshow: Old and New Items].[4] Dedicated to Hermann's friends in the battlefield, it was in fact more old than new, with only three of the sixteen stories not already available.

FIG. 6.2. Dagny Servaes as Eminé in the Berlin production of *Mein Nachbar Ameise*.

Buoyed perhaps by the success of the adaptations of the Jettchen novels, Hermann turned his hand again to writing for the stage. In the preface to *Mein Nachbar Ameise* [My Neighbour Ant], a period drama set in spring 1760 in the Potsdam of Frederick the Great, Hermann acknowledges that he is perhaps transgressing one of the laws of the theatre by putting the material of a novella on the stage. But he argues that dramatizing the story means that the craft of the novelist in evoking the feel and texture of the period can be replaced by the visual spectacle of the stage. Instead of having to write the long descriptions which with a thousand details would have been needed to support the bare bones of the story, here, Hermann maintains, the actors, the staging and everything that the audience sees does the job for him.[5]

But he was mistaken. The play, which opened at the Lessingtheater in Berlin on 12 September 1917, did not prove successful and closed just nine days later. It does not appear to have ever been restaged. Van Liere suggests that *Mein Nachbar Ameise* was no worse than the adaptations of the Jettchen novels but the difference was that as they had already captured a place in the public's affections there was a ready audience. The critic Paul Schlenther, for instance, writing about the play, *Henriette Jacoby* in *Berliner Tageblatt* in November 1915 had commented on the appeal of seeing Hermann's familiar story and characters given new scope on the stage.[6] But Hermann's new play lacked his normal story-telling fluency and it received only negative notices.

Hermann must have been discouraged by the failure of *Mein Nachbar Ameise* — he was never to try his hand again at writing an original play. But, as ever, he had other projects on the go. The year 1917 also saw the publication of a new novel, *Einen Sommer lang* [For One Summer].[7] Hermann took his title from a poem by the German lyric poet Detlev von Liliencron. He quotes its opening stanza at the start of the story, setting the wistful bucolic mood which characterizes the whole novel:

> Zwischen Feld und Hecken | führt ein schmaler Gang;
> süßes, seliges Verstecken | einen Sommer lang.
>
> [Between the field and the hedges | A narrow passage leads;
> A sweet, blissful hiding place | For one summer.][8]

Set in 1899, Hermann portrays in the novel what, in the context of the war, now seemed like another world; a lost age of stability. The plot is minimal. In place of action, there is a stultifying stillness. The novel tells of the summer courtship between Fritz Eisner and Ännchen Lindenberg and between Eginhard Meyer and Ännchen's younger sister, Hannchen. But from the outset it is clear that the young people are meant for one another, just like the other matched pairs in the novel: Lucie and Johannes Hansen; Selma and Wilhelm Klein; and Emmchen Liebmann and Paul Gumpert. The setting is Potsdam again, the holiday house that Frau Lindenberg, the mother of Annchen and Hannchen, has rented for the summer.

In some ways *Einen Sommer lang* represents a return to the approach of *Spielkinder* as Hermann presents a fictionalized version of his own life experiences. The character of the writer, Fritz Eisner, stands for the author. There are also obvious parallels between Frau Lindenberg and Elise Heynemann, Hermann's mother-in-

FIG. 6.3. Theo Sternberg (Hermann's brother-in-law).

FIG. 6.4. Robert (Lulu) with his mother Paula and her sister-in-law, Edith Sternberg.

law. Like Elise, Frau Lindenberg was pressurized into a marriage with a man far older than herself, and left a widow only a few years after giving birth to two girls. She is presented as being old before her time, intellectually narrow and provincial.[9] Materially orientated, in her world 'das Pfund Suppenfleisch kommt zuerst' [the pound of boiled meat comes first].[10] Frau Lindenberg's two daughters, Ännchen and Hannchen are evidently based upon Martha and Paula.

Fritz and Ännchen get engaged on 15 March and at the same time Hannchen becomes secretly engaged to Eginhard Meyer. Hermann suggests in the novel that so interwoven are the two sister's lives that once one is engaged, the other feels she must be too. As portrayed in the novel, in real life, Paula married just one year after her sister. She and her husband, Theodor Sternberg, had a son, Robert, who was born the same year as Eva. Theo was an academic and taught law and ethics at the University of Lausanne, where the family lived. The cousins seem to have had plenty of contact. Eva's photograph albums contain many pictures of Robert or 'Lulu' as he was known as a little boy. She was very close to her *Tante* Paula.

But Paula's marriage proved to be unhappy. She suffered from tuberculosis and had to spend extended periods at a sanatorium in Davos. In her absence Theo took a mistress. Whether it was to escape the failing marriage or as a result of family censure, Theo went to live in Japan when Robert was still a boy. By 1913 he was a professor of German law at the Imperial University of Tokyo. He remained in Japan throughout the war and in time made it his second home. He and Paula, although separated, did not divorce and Theo continued to support her and Robert financially.[11]

Among Eva's boxes of old photos, which unlike the pictures of Robert Sternberg never made it into albums, is a formal picture postcard of a group of around twenty people. Half of the men are wearing military uniforms. Other, more elderly men, sit in chairs along the front row. Some hold their canes in one hand and in the other, large drinking glasses.

The women in the picture are plainly dressed apart from an attractive young woman at the far left. She is wearing a patterned skirt and a bow blouse and in contrast to her sombre faced companions she appears to be on the verge of a smile. A short straight line has been pencilled above her head. On the reverse of the card the photographer's name is printed (Fritz Schumann) and the location, Bad Kissingen. That is why the men are holding their drinking glasses so prominently. This is a group of people who have come to the health resort to partake of its healing mineral waters. On the back of the card are just two words — 'Arrivederci! Ali'.

'Ali' is the young woman at the left of the picture and the recipient of the card was Hermann who had gone to Bad Kissingen for health reasons, possibly linked to what made him unfit for military service. Hermann and Ali found more to occupy themselves than simply taking the curative waters and it appears that Hermann was completely smitten. 'Ali' was Paula Ali Wiesenfelder. Born in Bamberg in 1894, she was twenty-three years younger than Hermann. It appears that the relationship was no casual fling. According to Eva, her father wanted to marry Paula but the affair was smoothed over and Martha and Hermann's marriage survived the episode. Paula married the artist and art historian, Arthur Galliner in 1922.[12]

FIG. 6.5. Frau Galiner, Bad Kissingen.

The affair with Frau Galiner was not Hermann's only extramarital relationship. There are seven letters in the Georg Hermann Collection in the Leo Baeck Institute which chart his relationship with Gertrud Cassel between June 1915 and January 1918. Trude was just twenty-one when they met and a post-graduate student.[13] In one of Trude's letters to Hermann, dated 20 March 1917, she writes about the deep sense of togetherness she feels with him and her delight at the secret hours they spend together between evening and morning.[14] In a fragment of a letter written later that summer, Trude expresses her longing for Hermann. An autographed copy of *Mein Nachbar Ameise* with a dedication to Trude Cassel is in the LBI's collection. Possibly the relationship ended before Hermann gave it to Trude and it remained with his papers or she returned it.

Whether Hermann had been having relationships with other women from earlier in the marriage isn't clear. From his own account, Hermann found monogamy a challenge. He felt himself to be, like a number of his male protagonists, powerless to resist the physical attractions of the opposite sex. Eva maintained that because of his literary success, women chased after him. They wanted to be with the famous author, she said. He certainly seems to have exerted a strong pull on women.

Whatever marital problems Hermann and Martha had experienced before 1914 were exacerbated by the family's move to Neckargemünd. Looking back on this period in 1921, Hermann writes that he spent most of the four years of the war in Berlin while his wife and children were in Neckargemünd, so that increasingly they had been living apart.[15] Occasionally he would go south but when he did so, he would soon flee back to Berlin. There he had a peripatetic existence, sometimes staying at guest-houses or furnished rooms or squatting in other people's homes.

FIG. 6.6. Gertrud Cassel.

FIG. 6.7. Lotte Samter, 1918.

He would stay out late in restaurants and cafés, wining and dining with friends. Constantly, the talk was about women. It was suddenly like being a bachelor again but without, Hermann writes, the advantages. And all this time he was consumed with a nameless hunger, yearning to forget his misery and wishing that once again he was holding somebody in his arms.

After their wedding in March 1901, Martha spent most of the first five years of the marriage being pregnant. She had given birth to four girls between February 1902 and May 1906. So far as we know, she did not fall pregnant again until 1917 when she was in her early forties. Tragically, the baby, a boy, arrived prematurely and was still-born.[16]

It seems probable that at this time Hermann had already begun a relationship with Lotte Samter, who worked on the editorial staff at Ullstein, one of the largest publishing companies in Germany. Since *Spielkinder* all of Hermann's novels had been published by Fleischel but *Einen Sommer lang* was the first he published with Ullstein and it is likely that Lotte worked with him on it. The writer Elisabeth Castonier recalls in her memoirs that Kurt Korff, who was editor-in-chief at Ullstein, complained that each time Hermann visited the publisher's offices, he would 'kidnap' one of the company's secretaries. Hermann, apparently unable to remember their names, would refer to them as 'Vögelchen' [little birds].[17]

Lotte was twenty-one; Hermann, forty-six. Like the fictional Jacobys, Lotte's family came from Posen where her father, Samuel (1845–1919) ran a successful business. In 1878 he had married Jenny Schottländer (1858–1893) and together they had six children. Two years after Jenny's death, Samuel married Klara Landsberg (1861–1923). Lotte was the only child from this second marriage. The Samters were an affluent and accomplished family — one of Lotte's half-brothers, Artur, was a leading socialist barrister — and Lotte, educated and very attractive, epitomised the new breed of contemporary independent-minded women which Hermann had portrayed, albeit anachronistically, in the character of Antonie Arnstein.

Eva acquired her first camera about the time that the family moved to Neckar-gemünd and from this point onwards there are many photographs documenting her Heidelberg days. One of her albums contains forty-eight pockets full of negatives from the years 1915 to 1928. Amongst these negatives, there are a handful of Lotte taken with the family in Schwäbisch Hall around 1918. Whether or not Martha and the girls were aware of the relationship at this time is not clear but the photos seem to capture the awkwardness of the day. In one picture, Lotte stands between Hermann and another man. Lotte's eyes are turned to Hermann. Martha is looking down, no flicker of a smile on her face.

Hermann's adultery became obvious when Lotte fell pregnant in autumn 1918, effectively signalling the end of his marriage to Martha. Ludwig and Else were outraged by their brother's behaviour and virtually disowned him. Once again, Hermann was acting in a way that compromised the family's hard won bourgeois respectability and it is unclear during this period what financial provision, if any, he made for Martha and the three girls. Some of the family's friends cut all ties with Hermann and it is interesting to note that three years later he felt the need to

FIG. 6.8. Martha, Hermann, Lotte, unknown, 1918.

publish a private paper for his friends setting out in detail his version of events. In it he paints a dim picture of the marriage. Hermann complains that no consideration was made for his needs as the family's breadwinner. Although the family home had ten rooms, there was no space where he could find peace. The children, he says, were never made attentive to the fact that their father had an occupation and were never quiet. The house was overrun with a constant stream of visitors, people who Hermann found intellectually inferior, and yet he was isolated from the friends with whom he corresponded. Everything was invariably regarded as more important than his work.

Unhappy in the marriage, Hermann sought the company of other women. Yet however beautiful they were, and often, he writes, they were not, it always ended painfully. As an escape from his misery, Hermann says, he focused more and more on his growing collection of paintings, sculpture and antiquities. He surrounded himself with artefacts to an extent where his collection swelled to the proportions of a small museum. And now these objects, he writes, have become entwined with his existence. Indeed, he attributes the fact that he was able to endure the unhappiness of his marriage to the succour he gained from his collection.[18]

There is evident self-justification in what Hermann writes and we only have his account. Martha's voice is unheard. But it does appear that the family home was far from tranquil. Hedwig Quandt, the children's nanny who had moved with the family from Berlin to Neckargemünd, told my mother many years later, 'You simply cannot imagine the chaos of that household!'[19]

During these months when Hermann and Martha's marriage was unravelling, the imminence of Germany's defeat in the war was becoming increasingly apparent. Social unrest which began at the end of October 1918 with sailors' revolts in the naval ports of Wilhelmshaven and in Kiel in the first days of November, rapidly spread across the country. On 9 November both the SPD deputy chairman, Philipp Scheidemann, and a few hours later Karl Liebknecht, declared a new republic in Berlin. The following day the Kaiser went into exile in the Netherlands. By this time, Hermann was splitting his time between Berlin and Munich where he and Lotte had settled. He welcomed the November Revolution in Berlin but was in Munich when it occurred and so did not experience it first-hand.

The day before the republic was declared, the movie version of *Jettchen Gebert* had opened in Berlin at the Union Theater Kurfürstendamm.[20] The film was made by the Richard Oswald Production Company. Mechtildis Thein, who enjoyed a brief but busy cinema career, played Jettchen in the film and Conrad Veidt played Dr. Kössling. Veidt was one of Oswald's regular actors and became a leading star of German silent cinema.[21] Sadly there are no surviving copies of the film. All that remains are some stills, which suggest that, in the best traditions of silent movie making, *Jettchen Gebert* did not stint on the melodrama. The following month the sequel *Henriette Jacoby* premiered in Berlin at the Union Theater Nollendorfplatz. Both films had been shot over the summer using the same cast.

Contemporary reviews of the movies were positive. The correspondent of *Der Film (Berlin)* commented on Oswald's skilful adaptation and sensitive direction, remarking that the film of *Jettchen Gebert* was closer to the novel than the stage play. The reviewer in *Der Kinematograph* expressed similar sentiments: 'one must judge this masterpiece by the highest standards as in both conception and execution, it ranks well above other productions.' They congratulated Oswald on capturing the charm and grace of the novel and on the wonderfully composed interior scenes.[22] Another reviewer who must also have seen *Jettchen Gebert* at its first showing at the Schadow-Lichtspiele in Düsseldorf in October 1918, asserted that even Georg Hermann could not have aroused deeper or truer feelings![23]

Hermann did not publish any new works in 1918 but he had of course been writing and 1919 saw the publication of his wartime notes, *Randbemerkungen (1914–17)* [Marginalia].[24] A collection of Hermann's observations on the first three years of the war, the book is also interspersed with quotations from writers such as Goethe, Whitman, Fontane, Stendhal, Nietzsche and Shaw. My grandmother would often talk about this book of her father's. I have her well-thumbed copy which is inscribed 'Meinen lieben Busibiben, Peps' (Hermann was always known in the family as 'Peps'). All of Eva's books have homemade paper bookmarks on pages which she found of special interest and in addition she has annotated many of her father's observations where she found them particularly pertinent.

In the preface to the book, dated December 1918, Hermann describes its genesis. It is not the product of time spent at his desk, he writes. Rather, most of it was composed while he was on the move, travelling on trains, sat in restaurants or first thing in the morning when he would wake to find thoughts of the war buzzing around in his head. These are jottings, scribbled down in old notebooks and on crumpled scraps of paper, in the margins of old art exhibition catalogues. He was motivated to keep scribbling by the thought that perhaps fifty or more years from now people would wonder at how the war could have happened. Was there no-one who at least inwardly did not embrace it? He wants the personal satisfaction of being able to testify for himself from the first hour of the war, to prove for posterity his innocence. It is a characteristic motivation. Hermann's acute awareness of the corrosive effects of the passage of time makes him want to put on record his opposition to the war, something which otherwise could be lost and never known or understood. Typically, at the same time that Hermann is experiencing the war he is contemplating how it will be viewed historically and what light his observations might shed on its future interpretation.

Very soon, in the first few months of the war, Hermann developed the idea that all of the thoughts he was jotting down would form the material for a book or at least an extended essay. He mulled over what its title should be — 'Der Bankerott des alten Staatsgedankens' [The Bankruptcy of the Old Idea of the State] perhaps or alternatively 'Staat oder Gesellschaft?' [State or Society?]. Conscious of his isolation, he wanted to write the essay because every professional commentator in all the newspapers, magazines and books, proclaimed the opposite to what he was feeling and believed. Hermann underlines the importance to him of being able to set out his own independent thoughts, his own truths. He argues that the mathematical proof that a teacher draws on the blackboard may be wrong for the student, even if the teacher is right. 'Der, den wir selbst gefunden haben, ist für uns richtig — auch wenn er falsch sein sollte.' [The one we discovered ourselves is right for us, even if it should be wrong].[25]

But now, Hermann no longer feels the need to write the essay he had originally intended, not least because he thinks there is merit in the aphoristic form of *Randbemerkungen*. He has not gone back and edited what he wrote at the time. The book shows the ebb and flow of his thoughts during the first three years of the war and this gives it an immediacy. It reflects the spontaneous untidy way in which ideas and feelings flit through our minds and dominate our lives. Lives which, after all, Hermann writes (and perhaps he was thinking of his own affairs here) are not well-structured books.

Georg Hermann's sense during the early months of the war that the world had been turned upside down is clear in *Randbemerkungen*. In one entry he writes,

> Wenn uns jemand gesagt hätte, daß am 1. August 1914 der Begriff der Kultur in Europa suspendiert werden würde, Harakiri begehen würde, daß Millionen und aber Millionen Leute, weggerissen aus der Arbeit, dem Fortschreiten der Welt, würden, daß Kunst, Literatur, Wissenschaft, Handel, alles, alles plötzlich dem einen systematischen Mord hinten angesetzt werden sollte, wenn uns jemand das gesagt hätte, dem hätten wir als Verleumder an der Menschheit ins Gesicht gespuckt. Nun — und wenn uns heute, Ende 1915, jemand sagt, daß das geschehen ist, dass mit diesem Datum, mit dem 1. August 1914, Europa auf ungewisse Zeit jegliche Kultur zum Tempel hinaus gesagt hat, um an seiner Stelle den blanken Mord zu proklamieren, nun dann spucken wir dem Mann gleichfalls ins Gesicht ... als Verleumder des "heiligen" Krieges.

> [If someone had told us that on 1 August 1914, the concept of culture would be suspended in Europe, would commit hara-kiri, that millions and millions of people would be torn away from their work, from the progress of the world, that art would suddenly become secondary to systematic murder, if someone had said that, we would have spat in his face, deeming him a detractor of humanity. But now, when today, at the end of 1915, someone says that this has happened, that on that date of 1 August 1914, Europe chased any kind of culture out of the temple in order to replace it with bald murder, then we spit in the face of this man as a denigrator [...] of the "holy" war.][26]

Hermann's over-riding feeling in August 1914 was one of mortification. He saw the war as a terrible indictment of mankind and believed that everyone should feel ashamed of it. 'Ob wir als Sieger oder als Besiegte aus diesem Krieg hervorgehen, dieser Krieg, der Krieg wird immer das Beschämendste und Traurigste, Wahnsinnigste meines Lebens bleiben.' [Whether we emerge victorious or vanquished from this war, it will always remain the most shameful and sorrowful, the most insane event of my life].[27]

Hermann's sense of shame soon developed into anger at those who were responsible for the war. How those leaders who had instigated it could go on living, given the horrors that they had unleashed defied his understanding.[28] It was only too easy for the Kaiser to talk about heroism when it was other people's children being killed on the front.[29] Hermann records that initially he felt some sense of brotherly feeling with his co-nationals; a greater affinity with the loss of German soldiers than their French or Russian counterparts.[30] But now that on a daily basis he sees the French and Russian soldiers taken captive, he finds that he feels the same emotions directed to them as the German soldiers — affection, pity and sadness. His feelings are universal. 'Jeder Krieg ist ein Bruderkrieg.' [Every war is a civil war].[31] All of the soldiers who have been on the front, regardless of nationality, have the same haunted look in their eyes, 'etwas auf dem Grund der Augen, wie solche, die ein Gespenst gesehen.'[32]

Hermann's *Randbemerkungen* show his sense of injustice and anger at the double standards applied to the war. He contrasts the reaction to the deaths of the 1198 people aboard RMS *Lusitania* when she was torpedoed by a German U-boat in May 1915 with the loss of 1500 lives in the sinking of the *Titanic*, three years before. The loss of the *Titanic*, seen as the result of a natural disaster, was regarded as a tragedy whereas the sinking of the *Lusitania* is universally regarded within Germany as a necessary and just act. Hermann compares the public jubilation at the news of the sinking of HMS *Cressy* to his own reaction: 'Ach Gott!' sagt ich.'[33] The preciousness of life is indeed a persistent theme in Hermann's *Randbemerkungen*. He regards the mindless destruction of life brought about by the war as wholly reprehensible. 'All unsere Kultur geht auf Achtung, Erhaltung des Lebens aus jede Erfindung, jede Neuschöpfung.' [All our culture is predicated on respect for, and the preservation of, life — every invention, every new creation].[34]

As Hermann's wartime diary continues he becomes progressively more radical, embittered and subversive.[35] He records the shifting public mood as the initial euphoria wears off. War fatigue sets in and increasingly people see the continuing conflict as a madness. In one entry, Hermann writes 'An diesem Krieg interessieren mich nur die Revolutionen, die er im Gefolge haben wird. [What interests me in this war are the revolutions which must surely follow it].[36] Hermann's growing antipathy towards the state emerges as a key theme. He writes 'Jedes Volk hat nur einen Feind: seine eigene Regierung' [Every nation has only one enemy: its own government].[37] After three years of the conflict, he forecasts, with obvious satisfaction, that the war, intended to reinforce and perpetuate autocracy and mammon, serves only to destroy them and instead, to strengthen internationalism.[38] Hermann describes himself as a 'dissident of nationality' and says that the concept of the nation state is something that the human mind must overcome. For him, the 'fatherland' is not about notions of statehood or territory; he can feel at home in any country where he speaks the language, where there are beautiful women, flowers and art, a good library, a chess board, pleasant and cultivated society and where the climate is healthy and agreeable and the landscape attractive.[39]

Initially Hermann does not seek to explain this lack of nationalism in terms of ethnicity, writing that he has never busied himself with *Volkspsychologie* and that for the individual, there are no peoples, only individual humans. They have good or bad attributes.[40] But by autumn 1916, when the *Judenzählung* was launched, his position has changed.[41] For the first time he equates his alienation from the war and his antipathy to nationalism with his Jewishness. In this entry, which interestingly is one of those highlighted by Eva, her father writes,

> Ich gehöre als Jude einer zu alten Rasse an, um den Massensuggestionen zu verfallen, Worte wie Volk, Krieg, Staat sind für mich farb- und klanglos. Für mich haben nur die Worte Mensch und Leben Klang, aber einen Klang von einer Hoheit und Fülle, den zu empfinden die andern Rassen anscheinend noch zu jung sind.

> [As a Jew I belong to a race that is too old to succumb to mass suggestion. For me words like *Volk*, *Krieg*, and *Staat* are colourless and have no resonance. For me only the words *Mensch* and *Leben* ring true with a sound of majesty and fullness which the other races apparently are still too young to perceive.][42]

Hermann writes that 'Es gibt nur einen Stamm von Weltbürgern bis heute — und das sind die Juden.' [To this day, there is only one strain of world citizen — and that is the Jew].[43] It appears that the war has led him to believe that Jews possess a different kind of political psyche.

Most of the entries in *Randbemerkungen* are very short but Hermann devotes seven pages to the way in which the state has assumed the right to commit murder through the mechanism of war.[44] Previously, we were wont to speak of murder as the act of one individual against another, Hermann writes. But even if one ignores the human and moral cost of war, purely in business terms, the price outweighs any benefits, regardless of whether you are ultimately victorious.[45] Hermann's frustration at the vast sums of money being poured into the conflict is a recurrent theme in the diary entries. Just think, he writes of what benefits could have been brought to the country and its people, both socially and culturally, had even a fraction of the sums squandered on the war been better spent.[46]

It is clear that Hermann was not persuaded by the German government's portrayal of the war as a legitimate act of self-defence in the face of Russian mobilisation. He underlines the traditions of Imperial Prussian war-mongering and its historic lack of diplomatic acumen.[47] Hermann is also very conscious of the way opponents of the war are being stifled. For instance, in one entry he makes reference to how the Hamburg branch of the German Peace Society was being prevented from holding a planned meeting for fear that it should spread its secret manifesto against the war.[48] Karl Liebknecht was one of the most prominent anti-war figures, and in another entry, Hermann writes about his imprisonment for high treason, drawing parallels with Lucian of Samosata's exposure of the mystic, Alexander of Abonoteichus.[49]

By the time that Hermann's *Randbemerkungen* were published Liebknecht was already dead, murdered by the rightist Freikorps following the failed Spartacist uprising in January 1919. Hermann later reflected upon Liebknecht's life in one of the essays in his 1928 collection, *Die Zeitlupe und andere Betrachtungen über Menschen und Dinge*.[50] In it he explains how he once played tennis with Liebknecht's future wife, Julia Paradies. She seems to have made quite an impression on the younger Hermann. He remembers her summer-freckled skin, fiery red hair and open, genuine nature. He recalls subsequently hearing that she had married a promising lawyer but she slips from his world and it is only fifteen years after those fondly remembered games of tennis, that he meets Julia again. She complains to him about the political passions of her husband but their conversation is cut short when Hermann is whisked away to play a game of chess in which he becomes completely engrossed. Later he looks up from the chessboard to see a pale man at the door who seems to carry the noise and atmosphere of public debate about him. Hermann is struck by the serious expression in the man's eyes and a sense of foreboding which he feels hangs about him. Hermann's only other encounter with Liebknecht was when he came across him by chance in Berlin when he was on his way to the west of the city. He was astonished to find Königstraße packed with people, surrounding a lorry which was being driven slowly between them. There was no military cordon and no sign of the police intervening. Liebknecht was speaking and the power of his words resounded in the street. In that instance, Hermann says he felt for the first time with unshakable certainty, 'Zusammenbruch! Revolution!!'

In early February 1919 Hermann finally bought the house in Neckargemünd. The girls were settled in Heidelberg and the purchase would probably have been welcomed by Martha. Hermann and Lotte in the meantime continued to live in Munich, where things were far from secure. Surprisingly, Bavaria had been at the forefront of the revolutionary movement. The former journalist, Kurt Eisner, soon after his release from nine months in Stadelheim Prison, had roused 50,000 workers to strike in Munich on 9 November 1918 in protest against the war. By evening that same day Ludwig III, the Bavarian king had fled and armed soldiers were patrolling the streets in support of Eisner and his revolutionaries. A Bavarian democratic socialist republic was declared and Eisner appointed prime minister.

But Eisner's public insistence that Germany had played a central role in provoking the war fuelled a growing hate campaign against him. On 21 February 1919 he was murdered by a nationalist aristocrat, Anton Arco-Valley. Initially sentenced to death, Arco-Valley's sentence was commuted to ten years in prison; the state prosecutor apparently convinced that he had been motivated by a deeply rooted love of the fatherland.[51] Following Eisner's death, a succession of short-lived administrations struggled to maintain public order until in May right wing paramilitary White Guards joined forces with troops sent by the Berlin government and put a bloody end to Bavaria's socialist republic.

In the preface to *Randbemerkungen* Hermann claimed to have put aside the notion of producing a treatise based upon his wartime reflections. But in July 1919, six days after Lotte had given birth in Munich to their daughter, Ursula, his article 'Zur Frage der Westjuden' [On the Question of the Western Jews] appeared in *Neue jüdische Monatshefte*.[52] The publication of this 'surprisingly frank'[53] essay so soon after the bold anti-war *Randbemerkungen* represented another controversial foray into public debate.

Hermann begins the essay by stating that although he runs the risk of being misunderstood, he feels that he must give expression to feelings which he believes are shared by many thousands of German Jews. As German Jews, he argues, they have felt the same mental and spiritual disappointments that he himself has suffered since 1914:

> Man wird mich fragen, woher ich das Weiß? Wie ich das festgestellt habe? Etwa durch Umfrage? Durch Gespräche? Durch schriftliche Äußerungen? Durch nichts von alledem. Ich weiß es daher, weil (5 + 3 + 4 — 2) x (3) : (2) (3) 5 ist.

Und; weil es immer und ewig unter den gleichen Umständen ergeben muss, weil die Summe gleicher Faktoren — in den gleichen Relationen stets das gleiche Endresultat zeiligen muss. Und die deutschen Juden gewisser Gruppen und Schichtungen sind — soweit sie auch scheinbar voneinander differieren mögen, als Wesenseinheiten immer aus den gleichen seelischen Faktoren zusammengesetzt....

[I will be asked, how do I know this? How did I determine this? Through questionnaires? Through conversations with others? Through reading literature? No, through none of the above. I know it because $(5 + 3 + 4 — 2) \times (3): (2) (3) = 5$. And because it will always and forever give the same result under the same conditions because the same factors in the same relation to one another must always yield the same end result. And the German Jews of different groupings and social stratification — irrespective of how different from one another they might appear — are always, as a consubstantiality, made up of the same *seelisch* factors...][54]

Hermann writes that, like many thousands of German Jews (or as is now said, 'German citizens of the Jewish faith') he has abstained completely from religious observance, for as long as he can remember. But he has always felt himself to be racially a Jew, a typical Western Jew. He acknowledges that in identifying himself as a Western Jew he is drawing a circle that shuts out the still 'unzivilisierten Ostjuden'. He has, he says, always felt a rather violent aversion to the Eastern Jews (no great surprise perhaps to readers of the *Jettchen* novels).

He regarded himself as a typical assimilated Western Jew, living in the lap of the Germans thankful for the gifts of their language and culture. His Jewishness he felt as little more than an 'aftertaste', a 'sprinkling of salt' or a 'psychological accent'. Like his many brothers he felt that as a German Jew he not only lived amongst the Germans but lived with them. He believed himself to be both a German and a Jew but not to the same extent. He was first a German and he retained his connection to his Jewish roots mainly from a sense of respect for his ancestors, in the same way that one feels an attachment for a cherished family heirloom and would not willingly become separated from it.

But in the last five years, Hermann says he has experienced a strong spiritual conversion. He has become much more conscious of his Jewishness and now dwells on it daily — but not outwardly. Unlike Heine, he cannot say that after his wanderings, he has returned to his God.[55] Hermann is still not religious but he does feel a profound sense of displacement. Now he believes that the Jew is not German and never has been completely. He likens the relationship to that between a man and a woman who, though they might live together in the same household, eat together, sleep together, and believe that they know one another inside out, remain always alone, their souls never touching. The war has demonstrated the incompatibility of *Deutschtum* and *Judentum* and Hermann says that he now recognizes that the German Jew has always had two homelands, an ancient imaginary Heimat, and a kind of *pays d'amitié*.

Even within thoroughly assimilated Western Jews this duality existed, unbeknown to us, Herman writes. And the balance between our sense of being a German and being Jewish changed slowly over the course of the last five years with each fresh disappointment we experienced. Whether they wanted to or not, German Jews found that they had to reflect more on their Jewishness because from year to year the war demonstrated the differences that separated them from their compatriots.

> Wir haben eine große Enttäuschung am Deutschen erlebt und wir erleben sie noch heute jede Stunde. Lasst mich offen ein hartes Wort sagen, wozu es verschweigen und vertuschen?! Die Deutschen haben sich als schlechte Siegelbewahrer des Menschentums bewährt. Und was schlimmer ist, sie bewähren sich noch heute als schlechte Siegelbewahrer des Menschentums ... ja heute im Unglück mehr denn je.

> [We have experienced a severe disappointment in the German people and we continue to experience it every hour today. Let me be frank, why hide it and cover it up? The Germans have proved themselves to be poor guardians of humanity. And worse, they are still today poor guardians of humanity ... yes, now more so than ever.][56]

This disappointment has made assimilated Jews like himself, Herman contends, much more racially conscious. As Aschheim points out, Hermann's essay reflects the extent to which the Right had succeeded in forcing political discourse into its own frame of reference. 'Through their actions, anti-Semites had pushed liberals like Georg Hermann into acknowledging German-Jewish incompatibility.'[57]

Passing over the fact that the war fever in 1914 seems to have gripped all Germans indiscriminately, Hermann speculates that Jews, because they have been stateless for so long, have less affinity for the trappings of nationhood. Whereas most Germans are preoccupied with power, subjugation, strength and militarism, Jews are more focused on the future and orientated towards ethics and the needs of mankind as a whole. Jewish capitalists such as Walther Rathenau, Albert Ballin, James Simon and Jacob Schiff, Hermann argues, evince a social conscience and concern with the future of humanity, which is not matched by their non-Jewish counterparts, Hugo Stinnes, August Thyssen, and Henckel von Donnersmarck. He ascribes Rathenau's unwillingness to accept things as they are and his wish to work towards developing a better future, directly to his racial heritage. And for Hermann, Jewish socialists such as Luxemburg and Eisner better represent the ancient human soul of the Jewish tribe than any religious revival could do.

The crucial point, Hermann repeats, is that today the Western Jew finds himself in a world that has been completely reconfigured. He has been expelled from the psychological domain he took to be his *Heimat* and in his soul he now yearns for a new home where he can find repose. That might suggest that the Zionists are right, that the future depends on securing Jewish nationhood, but Hermann says that he continues to be strongly opposed to Zionism, at least as concerns Western Jews. There may be merit in seeking a secure home for the beleaguered Eastern Jews — a spiritual centre where the Jews of the world can be — but only as an expedient, a temporary throwback. For Western Jews like himself, however, Hermann argues that Zionism holds no great attraction and he is left with that feeling of loneliness that comes when all of a sudden you no longer understand the milieu in which you live. Hermann's Zion is the future of humanity, unconstrained by nationalism and the trappings of state, and he concludes the essay with the assertion that the continual striving towards a more humane future is today stronger in Western Jewry than in any other race in Europe.

'Zur Frage der Westjuden' marks a significant turning point in both Hermann's sense of himself and of his view of the society in which he was living. As Ritchie Robertson observes, with anti-Semitism becoming increasingly respectable after 1914, a gulf was threatening to open up between how the German Jews saw themselves and how the non-Jews perceived them.[58] For the rest of his life Hermann maintained that 1914 marked the starting point in the development of this schism.

Although he makes no explicit reference to anti-Semitism when he refers to the changes that have taken place within Germany over the past five years, its resurgence would have reinforced Hermann's sense of his Jewishness and fostered the ethnic pride expressed in the article. This questioning of the logic of assimilation was accompanied, not surprisingly, by an attempt to reconnect to a hidden or repressed Jewish heritage — a Jewishness defined, Noah Strote argues, primarily in terms of psychological particularity.[59] Assimilated Jews like Hermann did not begin observing the laws of *kashrut* or reading the Torah as a result of the war but they did change the way they spoke about their Jewishness, particularly as it impacted on their world view.[60]

Hermann's article provoked a number of letters from the readers of *Neue jüdische Monatshefte*. One ex-soldier, Julius Simon, praised Hermann for making public something which he believed most German Jews had only felt comfortable talking about privately. Simon wrote that, like Hermann, he believed himself to be above all German despite his attachment to Judaism. But in the trenches he came to realize that an abyss separates Germans from Jews, a division in outlooks on life, in ways of feeling and thinking, and in their positions on the moral and intellectual questions of life.[61] Felix A. Theilhaber took issue with Hermann's assertions about the still uncivilized Eastern Jews and a statement in the article that he had sought to show the divide between them and the Western Jews through the conflict between the Geberts and the Jacobys. Theilhaber comments on the superficiality of Hermann's portrayal of the Jacobys and refutes the idea that they are in any way representative of Eastern Jewry. They might not collect fine porcelain but that doesn't mean they are any less noble of heart.[62]

Notes to Chapter 6

1. Hermann was very conscious of the fact that Heidelberg had been part of the Roman Empire, hence the reference to Tusculum, the Roman city in the Alban hills which was famous for its luxury country villas.
2. Hermann, 'Wie ich auf Heidelberg kam', pp. 191–92.
3. See Gheorge Stanomir, 'Georg Hermann und das Haus Poststraße 2', *Neckargemünder Jahrbuch*, vol. 5 (Stadt Neckargemünd, 1993), 85–105.
4. Georg Hermann, *Der Guckkasten — Altes und Neues* (Berlin: Fleischel, 1916).
5. Georg Hermann, *Mein Nachbar Ameise* (Berlin: Fleischel, 1917).
6. van Liere, *Georg Hermann: Materialien*, p. 43.
7. Georg Hermann, *Einen Sommer lang* (Berlin: Ullstein, 1917). Subsequent references are to the

edition of the novel published by Das Neue Berlin in 1999. *Einen Sommer lang* proved to be the first instalment in a series of five linked novels published between 1917 and 1934. The novels span the period from 1899 to 1923 and Hermann came to call the pentalogy, *Die Kette* [The Chain]. He had used the metaphor previously in the preface to *Jettchen Gebert* where he writes of the chains we wear, 'so inextricably interwoven of the iron rings and golden links of happiness and sorrow'. See Hermann, *Hetty Geybert*, p. 10.

8. The poem was first published in Liliencron's 1892 collection *Neue Gedichte*. Hermann misquotes the first line which is actually 'Zwischen Roggenfeld und Hecken' [Between the rye field and hedges].

9. Hermann, *Einen Sommer lang*, p. 41.

10. Georg Hermann, *Der kleine Gast* (Berlin: Das Neue Berlin, 1999), p. 381.

11. For more information about Theo Sternberg see Anna Bartels-Ishikawa's biography, *Theodor Sternberg — einer der Begründer des Freirechts in Deutschland und Japan* (Berlin: Duncker & Humblot, 1998) and also her book, *Post im Schatten des Hakenkreuzes. Das Schicksal der jüdischen Familie Sternberg in ihren Briefen von Berlin nach Tokyo in der Zeit von 1910 bis 1950* (Berlin: Duncker & Humblot, 2000).

12. Private family recording, 1979.

13. Trude completed a doctorate from the University of Greifswald and subsequently worked as a librarian in Berlin. In 1921/22 she had an affair with the Expressionist poet Gottfried Benn. Trude and Benn maintained an extensive correspondence, long after the end of their relationship. See Gottfried Benn, *Absinth schlürft man mit Strohhalm, Lyrik mit Rotstift. Ausgewählte Briefe 1904–1956*, ed. by Holger Hoff (Göttingen: Wallstein, 2017).

14. Letter from Trude Cassel to Georg Hermann, GHC; AR 7074; Box 7; Folder 26, LBI, 500/855. I am grateful to Professor Dr. Stephan Kraft for his analysis of Trude's letters to Hermann (private correspondence).

15. See Hermann, 'Rückblick zum Fünfzigsten', pp. 431–32.

16. van Liere, *Georg Hermann: Materialien*, p. 44.

17. Elisabeth Castonier, *Stürmisch bis heiter. Memoiren einer Außenseiterin* (Munich: Deutscher Taschenbuch Verlag, 1967), p. 83.

18. Hermann, 'Rückblick zum Fünfzigsten', p. 433.

19. Hedwig died at the age of ninety-three in September 1984. After the Second World War she lived in East Germany. According to Eva, Hedwig had the ability to get on with all people. She never married.

20. The first dedicated standalone cinema in Germany was opened in Mannheim in 1906, the year *Jettchen Gebert* was published. By 1910 there were already over a thousand cinemas across the country. See Stephen Brockmann, *A Critical History of German Film* (New York: Camden House, 2010), p. 18.

21. Veidt left Germany in 1933. His best-known Hollywood role is Major Heinrich Strasser in *Casablanca* (1942).

22. *Der Kinematograph*, No. 615; 16 October 1918, quoted in John T. Soister, *Conrad Veidt on Screen: A Comprehensive Illustrated Filmology* (Jefferson, NC: McFarland, 2002), p. 54.

23. Unknown source, ibid., p. 52.

24. Georg Hermann, *Randbemerkungen 1914–17* (Berlin: Fleischel, 1919).

25. Ibid., p. 3.

26. Ibid., pp. 38–39.

27. Ibid., pp. 8–9.

28. Ibid., p. 39.

29. Ibid., p. 14.

30. See Laureen Nussbaum, 'Wenn Deutschland die ganze Welt gewänne, nichts könnte den Kummer dieses Krieges gutmachen: Georg Hermanns *Randbemerkungen (1914–1917)*', in Schoor (ed.), *Der Schriftsteller Georg Hermann*, p. 158.

31. Hermann, *Randbemerkungen*, p. 130.

32. Ibid., p. 26.

33. Ibid., p. 62.

34. Ibid., p. 15.
35. Nussbaum, 'Georg Hermanns *Randbemerkungen*', p. 158.
36. Hermann, *Randbemerkungen*, p. 138. Eva highlighted this statement in red and wrote underneath 'und sie kamen!'
37. Ibid., p. 145.
38. Ibid., p. 156.
39. Ibid., p. 146.
40. Ibid., p. 12.
41. Noah B. Strote, 'The Birth of the "Psychological Jew" in the Age of Ethnic Pride', *New German Critique* 115, vol. 39, no. 1 (2012), 211.
42. Hermann, *Randbemerkungen*, p. 151.
43. Ibid., p. 147. Another entry that Eva has marked in red pen.
44. Nussbaum, 'Georg Hermanns *Randbemerkungen*', p. 160.
45. Hermann, *Randbemerkungen*, p. 70.
46. Nussbaum, 'Georg Hermanns *Randbemerkungen*', p. 161. Nussbaum cites references to this issue on pages 33, 75 and 150 of Hermann, *Randbemerkungen*.
47. Hermann, *Randbemerkungen*, p. 47.
48. Nussbaum, 'Georg Hermanns *Randbemerkungen*', p. 162.
49. Hermann, *Randbemerkungen*, p. 88.
50. Hermann, 'Liebknecht', in *Die Zeitlupe*, pp. 31–36.
51. Elon, *The Pity of It All*, p. 350.
52. Georg Hermann, 'Zur Frage der Westjuden', *Neue jüdische Monatsheft*, 10 July 1919, pp. 400–05.
53. Aschheim, *Brothers and Strangers*, p. 216.
54. Hermann, 'Zur Frage der Westjuden', p. 400. The translation is by Noah Strote.
55. In Heine's afterword to *Romanzero* (1851) he says that he has returned to God after a period of atheism.
56. Ibid., p. 404.
57. Aschheim, *Brothers and Strangers*, p. 216.
58. Ritchie Robertson, 'Cultural Stereotypes and Social Anxiety in Georg Hermann's *Jettchen Gebert*', in Weiss-Sussex (ed.), *Georg Hermann: Deutsch-jüdischer Schriftsteller und Journalist 1871–1943*, p. 6.
59. Strote, 'The Birth of the "Psychological Jew"', p. 202.
60. Ibid., p. 211.
61. Ibid., pp. 215–16.
62. Felix A. Theilhaber, 'Open Letter to Mr. Georg Hermann', in *Neue Jüdische Monatsheft* 22, 25 August 1919, 482–85. Theilhaber (1884–1956) was a leading dermatologist. In 1913 he founded the Society for Sexual Reformation in Berlin. He wrote numerous books in support of birth control and against the criminalisation of abortion and homosexuality.

CHAPTER 7

❖

Life with Lotte

In the new Germany of the Weimar Republic, Jews were finally equal not just in theory but in practice. More than a century after the official emancipation, Judaism was put on the same footing as other faiths and long-standing barriers which had largely excluded Jews from positions in government and the higher echelons of the judiciary and public administration were removed. There is an irony that just at the time Hermann was expressing his loss of faith in assimilation, politically Jews were participating in public life as never before. There were twenty-four Jewish deputies in the Reichstag and between 1919 and 1924 six served as senior cabinet ministers.[1]

German universities finally opened up their faculties at all levels. Eva, who had excelled at school, was one of the beneficiaries. She enrolled at Heidelberg University in 1921. Like her father, she had a fascination with the natural world and chose to read zoology. The year before, in March 1920, Hermann and Martha had finally divorced. He and Lotte married in Munich on 9 June 1920, by which time their daughter Usche was fast approaching her first birthday. Lotte and Hermann appear to have done much travelling during the early years of their relationship. They usually did not take Usche along on their travels and by her own account she spent most of the first two years of her life with a wet-nurse in Munich.

In summer 1920 Hermann and Lotte stayed with friends in Bloemendaal. A sign perhaps of the better relations with Martha is that they took Liese with them on the trip. Now fourteen, her health continued to be fragile, in part due to under-nourishment during the war, and it was hoped that a prolonged stay in the Netherlands would help her to regain strength.[2] It is likely that Hermann and Lotte's travels included a visit to England during this period. Hermann recorded his impressions in an unpublished article, 'England... Stichworte' [England... Keywords].[3] After a turbulent crossing from Boulogne, Hermann seems to have formed a positive impression of the country. Everything struck him as very tidy and well-ordered — the little houses, the fields and cricket pitches. The English he found to be discrete and never asked personal questions unlike in Germany where, he writes, within five minutes everybody wants to poke their fat fingers into the deepest recesses of one's soul. His only complaint appears to have been how little known Goethe is to the English.

Further evidence of a rapprochement with Martha and the girls is suggested by Hermann's move back to Heidelberg, in the summer of 1921. Together with Lotte

FIG. 7.1. Lotte and Usche.

and Usche he took up residence in Schlierbach just three miles from Neckargemünd. The house they rented (Mittlere Aue 6 — today's Maisenbachweg) was in a modern development, mainly comprising three- and four-roomed apartments. Their neighbours were junior government officials in the main and, according to Hermann, many were saddled with debts and struggling to make their way in life. On the whole recently married couples, they did not have any children and Hermann found it wonderfully quiet.[4]

The establishment of better relations with Martha and the girls and the resumption of his life in Heidelberg coincided with a more productive period for Hermann. After a four year gap, he published a new novel, *Schnee* [Snow].[5] A sequel to *Die Nacht des Doktor Herzfeld* (1912) the plot of *Schnee* encompasses two nights and one day in late November 1916. The novel's motto 'Da ist's denn wieder, wie die Sterne wollten' [So back it comes, what's written in the stars] is taken from Goethe's poem 'Urworte. Orphisch'.[6] It sets the fatalistic tone of the opening description of a late November evening in Berlin, when rain and snow clouds reinforce a pervasive sense of despair. As Andrea Dortmann highlights in her analysis of *Schnee*, the reader is made aware that the snow is not an incidental adornment to the story about to unfold but fundamental to it.[7] There are times and conditions in the heavens, in the atmosphere, we are told, for memories, for love and desire, for being born, for death and for suicide. Had it not been for these low-hanging clouds on a dull wet day in late November, this story might have been quite different.

Herzfeld remembers his own childhood when he believed that he could control the falling snowflakes with his mind, making them fall slowly or quickly (rather as the novelist controls the fate of his characters) but now as a fifty-year-old he is no longer able to conjure up the old childhood magic. While he can still appreciate the beauty of the snow, it is the snow which controls him rather than vice versa.[8] Like the soldiers in the battlefields, the snow falls in masses. One young man on his way to war tells Herzfeld that everyone falls, his entire generation will be obliterated. The lives of the soldiers falling in the trenches, their bodies blown to bits by shells have no more meaning than the snow which falls from the sky and turns in puddles to dirt over which everyone tramples.

The war is all-consuming. From the moment he wakes up to the time he goes asleep, Herzfeld cannot get the eternal buzzing of the shells out of his ears. It is the constant oppressive accompaniment to everything he says, reads, thinks and does. Sometimes he feels like running through the streets, the theatres and across the squares — every place where people are gathered — like King Lear, roaring and shaking his fists.[9] And the worst of it for Herzfeld is that the war has left him feeling that everything is pointless. The world of art and culture to which he has devoted his life and which has become the crutch upon which he depends cannot withstand the brutality and stupidity of nationalism and war. Herzfeld's Berlin home (rather like Hermann's Heidelberg retreat) is replete with art treasures and books and has become his fortress against the madness of the external world. It is a place to which he has been able to withdraw but now those treasures and books appear to him to be mere trifles, playthings far too flimsy to predicate a whole life on. As Saul Bellow once observed, to think continually of nothing but aggression and defence, terrorism and war, shrinks art to nothing and endangers even the more ordinary kinds of aesthetic experience.[10] For Herzfeld, the quest for knowledge and culture, for *Bildung*, has proved to be vacuous and he is left devoid of hope.

Preoccupied though he is in his Berlin apartment with reflections on the senselessness of the war, Herzfeld is not unconscious of the trains passing by his window and he is suddenly seized with an urge to get away on one of them. His yearning fixes on a tangible goal, to take himself somewhere else. Herzfeld is grabbed by a longing to see the silvery cool, untarnished snow of the mountains of Bavaria and to visit his holiday home in Garmisch. Although Herzfeld questions what this sudden madness is that is driving him to make the journey, he is powerless to resist. He brings a volume of Goethe's poems with him to read on the train and opening a page at random, Herzfeld hits upon the stanza from which the novel's motto is taken, 'Ananke, Nötigung' [Necessity]. As is his habit, he turns the lines of the poem over and over in his head. Herzfeld's sense of his own agency has been

FIG. 7.2. The holiday home in Garmisch which the family rented between 1912 and 1915.

found to be illusionary and so there is a particular resonance for him in the poem with its implication that although we may seem free there are actually boundaries, limits and laws that are divinely decreed and determined. Herzfeld feels that he must resign himself to what Ananke, the primeval goddess of fate, intends.

But before reaching Garmisch, Herzfeld attempts one last stab at happiness by calling on his former lover, Rehchen, in Munich. He fantasizes about snatching her away from her new husband. Hermann appears to have based the character of Rehchen on his former lover, Gertrud Cassel. Rehchen's rushed departure from Herzfeld and Berlin, and a scene in which she sits in her lover's armchair, dressed in her pyjamas, mirror Hermann's own experiences as recorded in Trude Cassel's letters.[11] Weiss-Sussex has established that a whole passage of one of Trude's letters is reproduced in *Schnee* as the work of Rehchen, further underlining Hilde's observation that the Herzfeld novels are based on her father's personal experiences.[12]

Herzfeld's fragile hopes of happiness are shattered when he learns that Rehchen is pregnant and after parting from her, he experiences a mental and emotional breakdown. While witnessing the recruitment of young soldiers at the train station, on resuming his journey, he collapses in uncontrollable tears, sobs that almost choke him. Finally arriving in Garmisch, Herzfeld takes a nocturnal woodland walk. He has the illusion that Rehchen is walking by his side. After falling asleep on a park bench, he wakes and has a second hallucination that he is with his dead young friend, Kurt. Dortmann suggests that the evocation of Rehchen, the still living woman and Kurt, his deceased friend, signals Herzfeld's transitional position between the living and the dead and his slipping away into the latter sphere.[13] In his final moments before he freezes to death on the bench, Herzfeld looks up at the glorious incandescent stars which float in the deep blue of the night sky. He has always wished that at his death his gaze should rest on the stars above as he chooses a place for his soul to inhabit. It is with this image in his mind of the stars and the glow of the snow that Herzfeld takes leave from '... Diese wundervollste und wahnsinnigste aller Welten!!!' [this most wonderful and maddest of all worlds].[14]

Schnee sold around 15,000 copies.[15] Arthur Schnitzler was among its readers. In his diary entry for 1 August 1921 he wrote, 'Nm. Schnee von Hermann ausgelesen; feines Buch, doch manchmal gar zu salopp. Jüdischer Fontane (*cum grano*). [Read *Schnee* by Hermann; fine book, but sometimes too loose. Jewish Fontane (*cum grano*)].[16]

In October 1921 Hermann turned fifty. Always prone to self-reflection, the prospect of that milestone triggered a bout of personal stock-taking, similar to *Im Spiegel*. Written in August 1921 'Rückblick zum Fünfzigsten' [Reminiscences on Reaching Fifty] finds Hermann in a downbeat mood and, as ever, struggling to live in the moment.[17] At fifty, he muses, one knows with certainty that the larger portion of one's existence has passed. Looking back on the way his life has turned out, Hermann reflects that, although he began writing when he was fourteen, he had never thought that it would be his sole purpose in life. He speculates that by now, had he become a banker, he would probably be enjoying a secure and comfortable existence. Instead, he has been dogged by financial worries and following the breakdown of his first marriage and his re-marriage, he finds himself needing to support two families. Hermann emphasizes his sense of isolation. He is without many of his prized possessions, separated from the three girls from his first marriage, without contact with relatives and former friends. The loose bonds that linked him to his brothers and sister, who he says have never forgiven him his literary success, have been torn asunder by their reaction to his divorce. But he doesn't suffer too much, he says, and quotes Ibsen, 'Here in the world of trolls, we say "to thine own self be all-sufficient".'[18] Moreover, Hermann acknowledges that he is not somebody to whom it is easy to get close. He is a contradictory mixture, sometimes open but at other times reticent and tends to become evasive if people want to get intimate, or when situations are difficult. He describes himself as a born onlooker.

Hermann's list of grievances continues. There are the friends he has given copies of his new books who have never taken the trouble to thank him; other acquaintances who have borrowed and never returned books from his library; and the way in which he has been exploited and denied due royalties. Hermann gives a particularly piquant example of the general lack of reciprocity he has found in his dealings with his fellow men. He describes how in Munich in 1919 he helped a revolutionary soldier to evade capture by giving him one of his best suits and a warm coat. The solider changed out of his tattered uniform and into Hermann's clothes and was able to escape the government forces pursuing him. Sometime later, when things had quietened down, Hermann found out the man's address and wrote to him to request the return of his suit and coat. The former revolutionary responded that he would do so when Hermann gave him back his old uniform; otherwise he was content to leave things as they were. Hermann reflects that the experience afforded him a salutary insight into human nature, much better than any he could have gained from even the wisest philosopher.

The first thirty-five years of his life, Hermann writes, were not materially comfortable. But then, with the success of *Jettchen Gebert* he enjoyed ten years of relative prosperity. In the last five years, however, he has again been preoccupied with financial concerns. The poor state of his affairs has come to be reflected in the shabbiness of his clothes. There is a sense for Hermann that life has come full circle:

> Und wenn ich mit fünfzehn Jahren mein Tagebuch begann: "Ich war heute auf der Eisbahn. Ich wäre gern mit Lieschen H. gelaufen. Aber meine Stiefel waren so zerrissen, das ich mich nicht an sie herantraute," so könnte ich heute mit fünfzig es ähnlich beginnen.

> [As I began my diary when I was fifteen: "I was on the ice-rink today. I would have liked to have gone skating with Lieschen H. But my boots are so tattered that I daren't approach her," so I could start my diary today at fifty.][19]

Hermann accepts that it could have been different had he capitalized on the success of *Jettchen Gebert* and written what was expected of him. But rather than being governed by commercial considerations, he has chosen to write only what he has wanted to write, to experiment. But as a writer, that is not the way to grow rich, he grumbles, especially given the changing tastes in contemporary German society. Today the literary writer's words no longer resonate. It is as if he is speaking into a void, stumbling along in semi-darkness on a path which comes to an abrupt end and leaves him stranded.

Hermann admits that this balance sheet he is drawing up may appear exceedingly negative and bitter; that he is looking back with disproportionate resentment at the people he has known and the life he has led. Yet, he has not even broached the subject of his thoughts on the world at large. He quotes Voltaire's comment: 'Nous laisserons ce monde-ci aussi sot, aussi méchant que nous l'avons trouvé en y arrivant.' [We shall leave this world as foolish and as wicked as we found it on our arrival].[20] But it's not true, Hermann writes. For his generation, the world they are leaving has become so mean and base that it is not the same as the one into which they first came.

Despite the relentlessly gloomy tone of his reflections, Hermann argues he is neither angry nor despairing. Citing Aristotle's observation that those who become eminent in philosophy, poetry or the arts tend to be of an atrabilious temperament, Hermann says it is only natural that artists should tend towards melancholia. What upsets him more than his lack of financial security is that as a consequence of his divorce he can no longer guide the intellectual development of Eva, Hilde and Liese and now must watch with his hands tied as they slip slowly away from him, spiritually.

Hermann had already written about his Judaism in terms of race in 'Zur Frage der Westjuden' and he emphasizes its importance to him again in 'Rückblick zum Fünfzigsten', writing 'ich gehöre einer sehr alten Rasse durch Geburt' [I belong to a very old race by birth].[21] And while he feels that the religious rites of Judaism are an encumbrance today, he appreciates the qualities of his racial brothers and refutes with all the energy at his disposal any assertions of their inferiority. He recognizes that some are cultured and some are not but he takes pride in the fact that all of his ancestors, both men and women, going back over 3500 years, have been able to read and write.

Hermann ascribes to his Jewishness an inherited attitude towards the world which is at his very core. On the one hand, it has given him a certain degree of independence and distance, made him less susceptible to dogma. On the other, and in spite of everything and all his disappointments, his Jewishness has given him an absolute belief in the preciousness of life in all its forms and in the human being as the most complex manifestation of a mysterious life-force. In one or two thousand years he hopes the preoccupation with 'difference' which besets the current age will be a thing of the past as all peoples will have acquired the same longevity as today's Jews.

Hermann observes that he has managed to be just as bourgeois in his habits as a writer as if he had been a bank director, albeit he's not smoking '10 Mark' cigars. He claims that he has always been something of a home-bird. Never attracted to the Bohemian lifestyle, Hermann prefers to spend his evenings not in salons, boudoirs, hotels, bars or cafés but instead comfortably at home in the sitting room with a good book, his children gathered close by, and in sight of pieces from his art collection. It is a description which conjures up a picture of contented domesticity, similar to the Biedermeier interior views of a painter like Eduard Gaertner or indeed the pre-war interior photographs of Hermann, Martha and the girls in their Grunewald home. Although Hermann states that he does not yearn for the kind of secure existence he might now be enjoying had he followed a different path, he does wish that he were in a better position financially at this point in his life, not so much for his own sake as for his two families. Cerberus, the hound of Hades, Hermann jokes, had only three heads but he has seven mouths to supply with honey cake and he quotes Ecclesiastes 7. 11: 'Wisdom along with an inheritance is good'.

Hermann's need to take stock was perhaps reinforced by the landmark of the publication in 1922 of his *Gesammelte Werke* in five volumes.[22] Lotte worked closely with him on their preparation. The first volume contained the two Jettchen novels; the second combined *Spielkinder* and *Kubinke;* the third brought together Hermann's play *Mein Nachbar Ameise, Heinrich Schön jun.* and *Einen Sommer lang* and the fourth, the two Herzfeld novels. The fifth volume comprised forty-six of Hermann's short prose pieces drawn mainly from *Modelle* (1897), *Die Zukunftsfrohen* (1898), *Aus dem letzten Hause* (1900), *Sehnsucht* (1909), *Vom gesicherten und ungesicherten Leben* (1915) and *Kleine Erlebnisse* (1919).[23] Hermann's *Randbemerkungen* was the only notable exclusion from the collected works.

Two weeks after his fiftieth birthday Hermann began a weekly column 'Brieven over Duitsche literatuur' [Letters about German Literature] for the liberal Dutch newspaper *Algemeen Handelsblad*. The French writer and theatre critic Edmond Sée had also been asked to contribute a weekly column about literary events in his country, and a number of British writers, including Ernest Percival Rhys, shared the task for the UK. This kind of cultural exchange appealed deeply to Hermann given his strong belief in the role of the arts in promoting mutual understanding between nations. Altogether Hermann wrote 221 columns over the next four and a half years for the Saturday edition of the paper and they offer an interesting insight into the breadth of his reading and range of his literary interests.[24] The letters were most likely translated into Dutch by Alice van Nahuys who during the 1920s translated eight Hermann novels for his Dutch publisher, Querido.

Nussbaum's analysis of a sample of Hermann's articles gives a flavour of the approach Hermann took and the topics he covered.[25] One of his first columns focused on the German literature of the last years of the war, much of it produced in Switzerland by refugee writers. Hermann praises the writers' anti-war sentiments and their willingness to participate in the developments of the world, the state and society. He does not necessarily subscribe to political activism on the part of writers but he does believe that,

> [...] writers are the virtual leaders of the people, and true world history is not the political history, nor the genealogy of the dynasties and sequence of wars, but rather the history of culture and of philosophical stance.[26]

Hermann focused again on the social role of writers in an April 1924 column, '*De betekenis van het boek*' [The Importance of the Book]. In it, he argues that society sees itself reflected in its literature and in this way is made conscious of itself. Thus, Hermann argues, the writer serves as the conscience of his country and of his time. He suggests that despite their cultural differences, great writers are,

> psychologically always left of centre [...] they dream of a more advanced mankind, a happier world, of peace and of a better social order [...] and what is more: [the writer] is the bridge from country to country, the most solid, reliable and accessible one we have and, at this moment, possibly the only one.[27]

There can be no such thing as 'patriotic art' or 'patriotic science'. The arts and the sciences belong to the whole world and they can only prosper through free interchange based on mutual respect.

Although Hermann's weekly columns focused mainly on recent German fiction, in December 1923, April 1925 and January 1926, he celebrated the availability at long last of important foreign literature in German translation. Fractured international ties are being reconnected, he writes, as fairly complete German editions of the works of Zola, Balzac, Rolland and Proust were starting to appear. He draws attention to new translations of D. H. Lawrence, John Galsworthy, Upton Sinclair, Eugene O'Neill, Sinclair Lewis and H. G. Wells 'whose humane and sensible political words at times managed to reach us during the war, much to our joy.'[28] Hermann similarly welcomes translations of works by Russian writers such as Ilya Ehrenburg and Ivan Shmelev, as well as of Scandinavians such as Georg Brandes.

In a review of seven books of poetry in April 1922, Hermann argues that no poetry has yet been able to render the tempo of the big cities, the speed of traffic, the unscrupulous wild chase after sex and wealth. Possibly, only cabaret songs can approximate modern life, he muses. In December the following year, he devotes a third of his column to books recently published by the Jüdische Verlag in Berlin. He attributes the appeal of the 'illusion of Zionism' to the rise in anti-Semitism triggered by the war. The large influx of Eastern European Jews displaced as a result of the conflict, he suggests, has also kindled a stronger awareness of the Jewish heritage and this increased consciousness is being mirrored in recent literature. But Hermann says in reviewing some novels focused on the life and dilemmas of Eastern European Jewry, that he feels little kinship with their characters. Western Jews, he argues, face very different problems as their development has become part of the history of the modern soul.

In an October 1925 column Hermann considered the poor quality of Germany's literary magazines. In the article, he argues that most Germans are too cranky, too opinionated and party bound to foster cultural magazines, and rues the fact that 'the democratic, free expression of opinion, the civilized exchange of viewpoints with people of a different persuasion, is unknown in Germany.'[29] He felt much more positive about the journalism of his friend, the Czech Communist, Egon Erwin Kisch, the self-styled 'Rasende Reporter' [Racing Reporter]. Kisch and others of his ilk, Hermann felt were making a worthwhile contribution to public debate.

One of the benefits for Hermann of his column in *Algemeen Handelsblad* was that he was paid in Dutch currency. Already by the end of the war, the Mark had lost forty per cent of its pre-war value of twenty-five American cents but it remained relatively stable until the summer of 1921 when the Allied Powers' demands for reparation payments, the 'London Ultimatum', triggered an increasingly rapid devaluation. By the time that Hermann was starting his *Algemeen Handelsblad* column in October of that year, the Mark had fallen in value to less than a third of a cent. Amongst the family's collection of coins are a number of German ones from this period. They include a 200 Mark coin from 1923, by which time the dollar was worth 4.2 billion Mark. Made from aluminium, the coin is almost weightless and I remember as a child being fascinated by the idea that this real money weighed no more than my plastic toy coins.

The hyperinflation exacerbated the instability and political violence which had characterized the Weimar Republic from the outset. For many the new regime became synonymous with economic distress. The post-war support for republican parties like the SPD and the German Democratic Party (DDP) started to wane as voters, especially members of the middle classes whose savings had been wiped out, switched allegiance to right wing anti-republican conservatives and nationalists. Extremists continued to wage a calculated campaign of assassinations and other terrorist acts against significant and symbolic figures within the fledgling Weimar government, further plaguing the new republic. One of the highest profile victims of this campaign was Walther Rathenau, Germany's Foreign Minister. Rathenau was gunned down on his way to the ministry on 24 June 1922 by members of the ultra-nationalist Organisation Consul. Plots against Rathenau's life had been so numerous that the police had advised him to carry a pistol at all times and the threats made against him were frequently anti-Semitic. From the outset of his short-lived tenure as Foreign Minister, bands of German students had chanted 'Knallt ab den Walther Rathenau! Die Gott-verfluchte Judensau!' [Strike down Walther Rathenau! The goddamn Jewish swine!][30]

Rathenau's murder, in the words of Amos Elon 'symbolized the crisis of assimilation'.[31] On the day of the assassination, Hermann was in the Netherlands.[32] He had escaped inflation-ridden Germany and was spending a pleasant Saturday enjoying the sights of the Dutch countryside, the canals and pasturelands, the children in their clogs. Stopping in a magnificent old city, he soaked up the afternoon life in the main streets, observing the well-dressed locals going about their business and reflecting on his affection for the character of the country and its people. But then, on his return to his friends' house, came his host — 'did you hear that Foreign Minister Rathenau was murdered this morning?!' He does not tell him the details of what has happened but '... von der Minute an war ich nicht mehr in Holland, sondern ich war in Deutschland! Rathenau ermordert!' [... from that minute I was no longer in Holland, I was in Germany! Rathenau murdered!].[33] Clearly shaken by the news, Hermann characteristically gave expression to what he felt by writing it down that evening. Hermann was not personally acquainted with Walther Rathenau (although the two had exchanged a number of letters) but the Foreign Minister was someone he respected and Hermann recognized the significance of the assassination.

An impression of Hermann and Lotte's life together at this time emerges from the reminiscences of Frieda Hirsch. The daughter of Moses Goldberg, a co-owner of the Strauss & Co. Bank, Frieda and her paediatrician husband, Albert, lived in a tree-lined avenue in Heidelberg, across the road from another doctor and his family, the Braunschweigs. Usche who started school in Heidelberg played with their children and the families became close. Although the Hirschs were both committed Zionists, this difference did not prevent a friendship forming.[34] Frieda recalls that Hermann and Lotte had moved from Munich to Schlierbach to be nearer to Eva, Hilde and Liese. He was much attached to the girls, she writes, and always worried a great deal about them. Hermann called his large house 'das ideale Wohnmuseum' [the ideal living museum] but in truth, Hirsch writes, it was more a museum than a family home, so full was it with furniture, books and ornaments. She recalls the display cases with their porcelain figures, the finely polished crystal bowls, the glasses and the cups. Daguerreotypes (like those mentioned in *Jettchen Gebert*) hung on the walls and elegant wooden Biedermeier bookcases housed a treasure-trove of rare first editions and classical works. Hermann's bedroom, according to Hirsch, was so crammed with antiques that there was scarcely air to breathe, yet he was very happy living in this way and loved every individual piece in his collection. Sometimes, Hirsch remembers, he would stroke a precious carafe as if it was a beloved child.

Hirsch recalls Lotte as being very beautiful; slim with dark hair and dreamy jet-black eyes. She understood Hermann and managed to overcome the incongruity between museum and family home with good humour and practical sense. Hirsch

FIGS. 7.3, 7.4. Pieces from Hermann's collection.

writes that she and her husband Albert spent many enjoyable hours at this *Traumhaus* [dream house], drinking good wines and eating gourmet food from the finest porcelain plates. Hermann would regale them with stories. He had a remarkable memory and would recall tales from his days as a journalist, and quote whole pages from novels, letters and poems. All kinds of educational and political subjects were discussed. It also seems that Hermann and Lotte were keen gardeners. They succeeded in growing artichokes which at the time were something of a rarity. Hirsch recollects that an invitation to an artichoke meal chez Borchardts was a special treat — there would be real butter and everything would be seasoned with Hermann's lively conversation.

Frieda Hirsch's memories of the house accord with those of Usche who in later life recalled that as a child growing up, her father's collection belonged to the family's everyday life. Living in a home with Riemenschneider sculptures, Ming porcelain and Biedermeier furniture seemed entirely normal and natural.[35]

During this period when he was living in Schlierbach, Hermann was working on a sequel to *Einen Sommer lang*. Published in 1925, *Der kleine Gast* [The Little Guest] is dedicated to Eva, Hilde and Liese, and opens with a misquotation from one of Rilke's *Sonnets to Orpheus* which had been published two years before:

'Ist die Jugend, die vielversprechliche, | In den Wurzeln endlich still?'

[Is youth, so full of promise | In the roots, silent at last?][36]

The setting has moved from the bucolic Potsdam of 1899 to the pulsating metropolis of Berlin. It is a time before the war, Hermann writes, when those who now sleep on the seabed or in the soil of Flanders or the chalky clay of Champagne, or God knows where else, played childhood games in the park. Hermann does not actually specify the year but instead sets out in eighteen mostly one-sentence paragraphs which all begin with the word 'Als', sundry events that took place in 1904. The list includes the Battle of Port Arthur; the publication of Wilhelm Busch's *Zu guter Letzt* [Last but not Least]; the premiere of Leoncavallo's 'Der Roland von Berlin' at the Städtische Oper; the death of the writer Peter Hille; the victory of Thaddaeus Robl in the annual cycle race for the 'Goldene Rad' von Friedenau; the rise of the actor Ferdinand Bonn and the fall of the 'Dreschflegelgraf' (Count Walter Pückler-Muskau).

Peter Sprengel, in an essay about the novel, highlights this reference to Count Pückler who from 1899 onwards was prominent in the anti-Semitic movement.[37] His populist harangues were distinguished for their 'extreme vulgarity of language' in the words of the 1906 *Jewish Encyclopedia*:

> In all his addresses, mostly delivered in Berlin, he has advised the most violent measures against the Jews — breaking into their stores, plundering, whipping, driving them from their homes, killing them. From his constant repetition of 'beat the Jews,' 'crack their skulls,' 'kick them out,' 'thrash them,' and similar rowdyisms, he has received the cognomen *Dreschgraf* [the thrashing count].[38]

As Hermann writes, Pückler was on the way down by 1904. He was imprisoned for a spell and then, not long after a particularly frenzied speech in Berlin in

September 1906, was admitted to a mental asylum where he saw out his days.[39] Although Hermann often downplayed the extent of anti-Semitism in Wilhelmine Germany, the allusions to Pückler in the novel show that he did recognize it as a facet of life before the war. Its effects are felt by some of Eisner's friends. We learn, for instance, that the gifted radiologist Dr Julius Spanier, who comes from an old Sephardic family, would long ago have had a full professorship had he deigned to be baptized.[40] Spanier is said to be descended from the physician Ephraim Bueno whose portrait was painted by Rembrandt. It is an ancestry of which Spanier is very conscious, and, like Hermann, to which he feels a deep loyalty.[41]

The novel continues the story of Fritz Eisner, Hermann's alter ego, charting his fragile hopes in the early years of his marriage to Ännchen and how already the relationship is floundering. Eisner is working upon a book about the Biedermeier, just as Hermann was working on *Jettchen Gebert* at this time. He wants his Biedermeier novel to be like a symphony complete with Andante, Allegro and Rondo movements, to create an account of the times and the people from a bygone epoch. For Eisner (and one suspects, Hermann) novels are precious time capsules:

> Alles, was wir nämlich über ein Land wissen, danken wir seinen Romanen, und was es selbst über sich selbst weiß, verdankt es ihnen ebenfalls. Sie sind das einzige, in dem das Leben sich dauernd bewahrt. Wie von Registriermaschinen werden die letzten und feinsten Seelenschwingungen eines Stammes, einer Epoche von ihnen aufgezeichnet. Das einfache, vorüberfließende, tägliche Dasein mit all seinen hunderttausend kaum deutbaren Nuancen wird in ihm zum Rang der Historie erhoben.
>
> [...] Ein Tolstoi, Dostojewski, Fontane, Hamsun, Flaubert — was ist denn ihr eigentlicher Sinn? Nicht, daß sie Ausnahmemenschen sind, sondern daß sie das feinste Sprachrohr der Massenseele ihres Volkes, ihres Landes, ihrer Zeit sind...
>
> [Everything that we know about a country, is thanks to its novels, and what that country knows about itself, it also owes to them. It is only in novels that life is constantly captured and preserved. They are like recording machines which catch the finest, most sensitive *Seelenschwingungen* [soul vibrations] of a people and their time. In this way novels elevate the simple, fleeting stuff of daily life, with all its myriad barely interpretable nuances to the ranks of history. [...]
>
> A Tolstoy, Dostoevsky, Fontane, Hamsun, Flaubert — what is their real significance? It is not that they are exceptional people, but that they are the finest spokesmen of the collective soul of their people, their country, their epoch...][42]

Dora is the little guest of the novel's title, Ännchen and Fritz's daughter who contracts pneumonia and dies after a short illness before her first birthday. Hermann had already written about the death of his and Martha's first child, Ilse, in his essay 'Sehnsucht'[43] and clearly in writing a novel about this period of his life, her loss must have been uppermost in his mind. The novel further underlines the fact that, however painful the personal or family experience, Hermann would always draw upon it in his work. Just one example of this in the novel is when Frau Eisner tells her son that she has had to wait until her sixty-eighth year to become a grandmother and now she fears that she must give the child back again, just as she herself had to do with her little Mariannchen forty years ago.[44] Hermann's mother, Berta, was about this age when Ilse was born and her daughter, Marianne, died in 1869 when just a few days old.

Once again, the city of Berlin, in all its different guises, is at the centre of the novel. The U-Bahn opened in 1902 (two years before the novel's setting) and Hermann likens the new subway cars crawling up in the darkness to Nollendorfplatz to fireflies; the trains are luminous beads of light. By 1900 the number of telephone customers in Berlin had grown to 130,000 and the telephone plays a conspicuous role in *Der kleine Gast*. Much of the dialogue takes place over the telephone and when Dora's health starts to give some cause for concern, Eisner takes comfort from the fact that he can be contacted in his office by phone. But Hermann suggests that despite the connectivity provided by the telephones now scattered all over the city, Berliners are actually becoming more rather than less isolated.

An extended description of a shopping trip Eisner takes to the Wertheim department store on Leipziger Platz offers Hermann a chance to show another facet of the changes taking place in turn of the century Berlin.[45] He describes department stores as 'Brennpunkte des Lebens' [focal points of life][46] and he shows them to be a natural and life enhancing environment for a sophisticated urbanite like Eisner. He is enthralled by the visual delight of the abundant colourful displays of merchandise but is not, however, enticed into buying anything. Ever the detached observer, Eisner's approach to shopping is more akin to that of the museum visitor than the consumer. He wistfully contemplates the displays of lingerie, jewellery and brass beds not as potential purchases but as seductive emblems of lives that once were open to him.[47]

The transformation of Berlin into a modern metropolis is the central theme in a preface that Hermann wrote to a new edition of Felix Eberty's *Jugenderinnerungen eines alten Berliners* [Childhood Memories of an Old Berliner].[48] Eberty (1812–1884) was a lawyer, amateur astronomer and writer, whose memoirs of his youth in Biedermeier Berlin had originally been published in 1878. As the author of the Jettchen novels, Hermann was a natural choice to write the preface to the new edition.

Hermann maintains in his introduction that such has been the pace of change within his own lifetime that it is impossible for those born since 1878 to imagine the world of Berliners like Eberty. Berlin has gone from being a provincial town, to an imperial capital and city, to now striding in seven-league boots to become a world city on a par with London, Paris, Vienna and New York. He feels lucky to have been able to witness such a transformation but it is clear from the preface that Hermann is ambivalent about the changes that have reshaped Berlin. Modern developments like electric railways, cars, giant armies and the massive Krupp Works have forced upon life an unnatural speed, he writes. Moreover, the inhabitants of the modern city have come to appear as if they have been punched out by machines by the thousand rather like the cut-price sheet metal toys you can buy in department stores. Looking back, Hermann feels that too much was sacrificed on the altar of modernisation:

Wir hatten uns zivilisiert, scheinbar um uns zu entkultivieren. Für jedes neue Stück Zivilisation, das in unser Dasein trat, gaben wir im Tausch ein Stück Kultur fort. Wir waren wie die Neger, die ihr edles Elfenbein, Gummi und Goldstaub für Glasperlen, bedruckte Kattunfetzen und alte Gewehre weggaben. Ich weiß nicht, wie ich dahin kam, dass ich das fand. Aber plötzlich kam mir zum Bewußtsein, daß unsere Väter und Großväter, Mütter und Großmütter noch etwas besessen hatten, unverlierbar mit ihnen verwachsen, was wir nicht mehr hatten.

[In our rush to civilize ourselves, it seems, we let go of our culture. For each new piece of civilisation that entered our life we gave away a piece of our culture in exchange. We were like the Negroes who exchanged their noble ivory, rubber and gold dust for glass beads, bits of calico and old rifles [...]. Thus I came to realize that our fathers and grandfathers, mothers and grandmothers still possessed something as an integral part of their existence which we have lost.]⁴⁹

Might it have been possible to achieve the technological gains of recent decades, Hermann ponders, without squandering the richer cultural life to which Eberty's book bears testimony? In just two or three generations, the *Seelenkultur* [culture of the soul] our parents and grandparents enjoyed has disappeared. Modern day Berlin with its elevated railways and department stores, wine palaces and pulsating traffic, continues to encroach on the remains of the Berlin of yesteryear. Beautiful old buildings and landmarks succumb daily to the pickaxe to make way for bland new utilitarian structures. And all the achievements of civilisation, Hermann concludes, cannot prevent the growing cultural impoverishment of our lives.

Notes to Chapter 7

1. Elon, *The Pity of It All*, p. 358.
2. Laureen Nussbaum, 'Verliebt in Holland: ein wichtiges und wechselndes Verhältnis in Georg Hermanns reiferen Jahren', in *Interbellum und Exil*, ed. by Sjaak Onderdelinden (Amsterdam: Rodopi, 1991), p. 181.
3. Georg Hermann, 'England... Stichworte von Georg Hermann', *c.* 1920s (the article is undated but it is clear from the text that the trip took place after 1918), GHC; AR 7074; Box 6; Folder 25, LBI.
4. Georg Hermann, 'Was wäre wenn?', *Die Weltbühne*, 17 November 1929.
5. Georg Hermann, *Schnee* (Stuttgart: DVA, 1921). The novel is dedicated to Lotte. Subsequent references to the novel are to the edition published by Das Neue Berlin in 1997.
6. The poem is included in Goethe, *Selected Poetry*, ed. by David Luke (London: Penguin, 2005), p. 193.
7. Andrea Dortmann, *Winter Facets: Traces and Tropes of the Cold* (Oxford: Peter Lang, 2007). See pp. 139–49 for Dortmann's analysis of *Schnee*. The reference here is from p. 139.
8. Ibid., p. 142.
9. Hermann, *Schnee*, p. 279.
10. Saul Bellow, *To Jerusalem and Back: A Personal Account*, (Harmondsworth: Penguin, 1976), p. 94.
11. Weiss-Sussex, *Metropolitan Chronicles*, p. 251. The letter is actually dated 20 March 1917 (not 1914) and so the parallel with *Schnee* is even closer.
12. *Unvorhanden und stumm*, p. 15.
13. Dortmann, *Winter Facets*, p. 146.

14. Hermann, *Schnee*, p. 582.
15. van Liere, *Georg Hermann: Materialien*, p. 216.
16. Arthur Schnitzler, *Tagebuch 1920–1922*, ed. by Werner Welzig (Vienna: Österreichische Akademie der Wissenschaften). Entry for 1 August 1921 (1921: V31-VIII 4, p. 211).
17. Hermann, 'Rückblick zum Fünfzigsten', pp. 423–54.
18. Henrik Ibsen, *Peer Gynt*, Act 2 (1876).
19. Hermann, 'Rückblick zum Fünfzigsten', p. 440. In Hermann's essay 'Meine Eltern' he makes reference to this diary entry again but there the girl's name is Grete. Hermann, 'Meine Eltern', in Hermann, *Die Reise nach Massow*, p. 288.
20. Voltaire, *Œuvres complètes de Voltaire*, (ed.) by Louis Moland, 50 vols (Paris: Garnier, 1877–83). Here, vol. 40, p. 332.
21. Hermann, 'Rückblick zum Fünfzigsten', p. 448.
22. Georg Hermann, *Gesammelte Werke* (Stuttgart: DVA, 1922).
23. For full details see van Liere's listing, *Georg Hermann: Materialien*, pp. 62–63.
24. van Liere (pp. 90–94) includes a list of the authors covered in each of Hermann's letters in his bibliography of Georg Hermann's works. The original German versions of the letters are not amongst the papers in the Georg Hermann Collection in the LBI and are probably lost.
25. Nussbaum, 'A Sampling of Georg Hermann's Letters about German Literature'.
26. Column of 5 November, 1921. Ibid., p. 75.
27. Column of 19 April 1924. Ibid., p. 76.
28. Column of 16 January 1926. Ibid., p. 78.
29. Column of 18 October 1924. Ibid., p. 85.
30. Carole Fink, 'The Murder of Walther Rathenau', *Judaism* 44.3 (1995), 259–69.
31. Elon, *The Pity of It All*, p. 370.
32. Georg Hermann, 'Rathenau', in *Die Zeitlupe*, pp. 41–48.
33. Ibid., p. 44.
34. Frieda Hirsch, 'Von Heidelberg nach Haifa. Lebenserinnerungen einer Zionistin 1918–1933', in *Erinnertes Leben: Autobiographische Texte zur jüdischen Geschichte Heidelbergs*, ed. by Norbert Giovannini and Frank Moraw (Heidelberg: Wunderhorn, 1998), pp. 37–39.
35. Shulamith Ben-Dror, 'Erinnerungen an eine unbehelligte Existenz', in Giovannini and Moraw (eds), *Erinnertes Leben*, pp. 61–64.
36. I am grateful to Laureen Nussbaum for her translation of these lines. Hermann must have quoted the verse from memory as it differs from Rilke's original: 'Ist die Kindheit, die tiefe, versprechliche, | in den Wurzeln — später — still?'. The sonnets were a response to the death at the age of just nineteen of Wera Ouckama Knoop, a friend since childhood of Rilke's daughter.
37. Peter Sprengel, 'Der Dreschflegelgraf. Antisemitismus als Tendenz der Epoche in Georg Hermanns *Der kleine Gast*', in Schoor (ed.), *Der Schriftsteller Georg Hermann*, pp. 189–95.
38. Gotthard Deutsch and S. Mannheimer, entry for 'Pückler-Muskau, Walter, Count', *Jewish Encyclopedia* (New York: Funk and Wagnalls, 1906), p. 266.
39. Subsequently, as Sprengel points out, Pückler was lauded by the likes of Philipp Stauff, one of the co-founders in 1912 of the *Germanenorden* (Germanic or Teutonic Order). Its symbol was the swastika and it espoused ideologies of Nordic racial superiority and anti-Semitism.
40. Hermann, *Der kleine Gast*, p. 200.
41. Horch, 'Über Georg Hermann', p. 81.
42. Hermann, *Der kleine Gast*, p. 323.
43. Georg Hermann, 'Sehnsucht', in *Sehnsucht. Ernste Plaudereien* (Berlin: Fleischel, 1909). Reprinted in volume 5 of Hermann's *Gesammelte Werke* (Stuttgart: DVA, 1922), pp. 612–19.
44. Hermann, *Der kleine Gast*, p. 570.
45. The first of the Wertheim department stores to open was in Stralsund. The architect for the building was Hermann's brother, Heinrich Borchardt, who was a student of Alfred Messel. See van Liere, *Georg Hermann: Materialien*, p. 15.
46. Hermann, *Der kleine Gast*, p. 39.
47. For a detailed analysis of this aspect of *Der kleine Gast*, see Godela Weiss-Sussex, 'Confronting

Stereotypes: Department Store Novels by German-Jewish Authors 1916–1925', in Godela Weiss-Sussex and Ulrike Zitzlsperger (eds), *Konsum und Imagination. Tales of Commerce and Imagination* (Oxford: Peter Lang, 2015), pp. 89–106.
48. Georg Hermann, preface to Felix Eberty's *Jugenderinnerungen eines alten Berliners* (Berlin: Verlag für Kulturpolitik, 1925), pp. 5–16.
49. Ibid., pp. 11–14.

CHAPTER 8

❖

Der doppelte Spiegel

On 4 February 1926 Lotte died from a kidney ailment from which she had been suffering since the autumn. Usche was just six years old. Many years later, she recalled,

> I remember one morning in February 1926 going to my parents' bedroom, and there on the bedcover was something dark coloured, like spilt chocolate sauce. I felt that something was wrong but my father jokingly said, 'Your mother had too much chocolate last night.' Soon after this an ambulance arrived and my mother left the house. She died not long after...[1]

Lotte was only twenty-nine years old. She was buried on the evening of 6 February in the Jewish part of the large cemetery above Heidelberg known as the Bergfriedhof, in the same grave where her mother, Clara, had been buried three years before. On Lotte's gravestone Hermann had the words 'Die herrlichsten Gottesgeschenke werden zuerst zurückgefordert' [God's most precious gifts are the first to be claimed back] inscribed. Hermann gave the eulogy at the funeral and his speech was subsequently printed in *Jüdische-Liberalen Zeitung*.[2]

Although consumed with grief, Hermann told the mourners that he felt he must speak at the service. Lotte had bestowed on him the greatest happiness and ultimate fulfilment of his ageing life. But she had always had premonitions that their time together would be short and that they must make the most of it. How often she would quote Confucius's adage, 'Leuchtende Tage, nicht weinen, dass sie vorüber, sondern lächeln, dass sie gewesen.' [Bright days — do not weep that they are passed — smile that they have been].

Hermann chose to hold the ceremony at the unusual time of seven o'clock in the evening because he wanted it to take place when the stars were visible in the night sky; in particular, when the Pleiades could be seen, high above the faded treetops, shining like diamonds. For, he explained, it was on an August night, seven years ago, that a couple stepped out onto the small wooden balcony of a guesthouse in the Brandenburg lakelands. That night, the rain-soaked alders swayed heavily and the sky was misty. Only the seven luminous stars of the Pleiades, hanging very low in the sky, were visible; their twinkling reflections caught in the ripples of the dark water of the lake. Many times afterwards he and Lotte would look up into the night sky, see their seven stars and remember that first evening together.

Had he known in 1918 that each of those stars would represent but a year of their time together, Hermann told the mourners, he would still have unconditionally chosen to be with Lotte, despite the bitter price paid for such happiness. Yet Lotte never lost her sense that their time together would be short. A thousand times, he had heard from her lips the lines: 'Hastig entschwinden die Tage des Lebens... Die Himmlischen wollen unser Verderben, die Götter, sie graben uns selber das Grab.' [Quickly slip away, the days of our lives ... the heavenly gods seek our ruin and dig our graves themselves].[3] Even when they were together in beautiful Taormina, those words were still on her lips. And now, after only seven years together, Lotte was gone. Gone, though there was not yet a single grey hair amongst her ebony curls. How could it be one so young, still in the bloom of life should be buried in the ground? Burial befits those who are aged, their bodies and minds spent. Beauty such as Lotte's should not be lost to the world.

Almost everyone who had spoken to him since Lotte's death, Hermann said, had talked about her vitality and how clever she was — the cleverest woman in Heidelberg, the most intelligent they ever met. Often we characterize women in ethereal terms, we liken their gracefulness to nymphs and to goddesses like Psyche and Hebe. Rarely do we call a woman a *Feuergeist* [a fiery spirit] but that is what Hermann says he often called Lotte. Articulate, knowledgeable and wise, Lotte was equal to any discussion. To Hermann, she was like Aphrodite and Pallas Athene, sprung from the head of Zeus. She embodied beauty, humanity and wisdom in equal measure. Her marvellous eyes, now forever closed, gave expression to the wonderful spirit that sparkled within.

Hermann never imagined that he would enjoy such happiness as he has experienced with Lotte but now she was returning to the primordial elements whence she came, leaving him with only memories of what had been: 'O, unsere leuchtenden Tage, nicht weinen, weil sie vergangen.'

★　★　★　★　★

Soon after the funeral, Hermann went away to the Netherlands. In his essay 'Amsterdam', which was written in March 1926 and dedicated to Lotte, Hermann professes his love for the tidy, sparkling clean and democratic Holland; adding that over the years, as tensions had grown worse in Germany, he and Lotte had often toyed with the idea of moving to the country where they had almost more friends than in Germany.[4] A book entitled *Holland, Rembrandt und Amsterdam* was published later in the year, which brought together this essay on the Dutch capital with an earlier article Hermann had written about Holland in 1920 and two pieces about Rembrandt, one from 1906 and the other written in July 1925. The essay about Holland gives Hermann's personal observations on the country's landscape, its houses, streets, shops and milk-wagons. He maintains that very little has changed in Holland during the preceding 350 years and that the wealth of Dutch painting to be found in the country's museums, is a natural continuation of the beauty and inner sense of Dutch life: the essence of Holland, as it was and as it is, realized on canvas.[5]

In the essays about Rembrandt, Hermann argues that his art marks the first striking departure from the classical beauty revived by the Renaissance. He writes

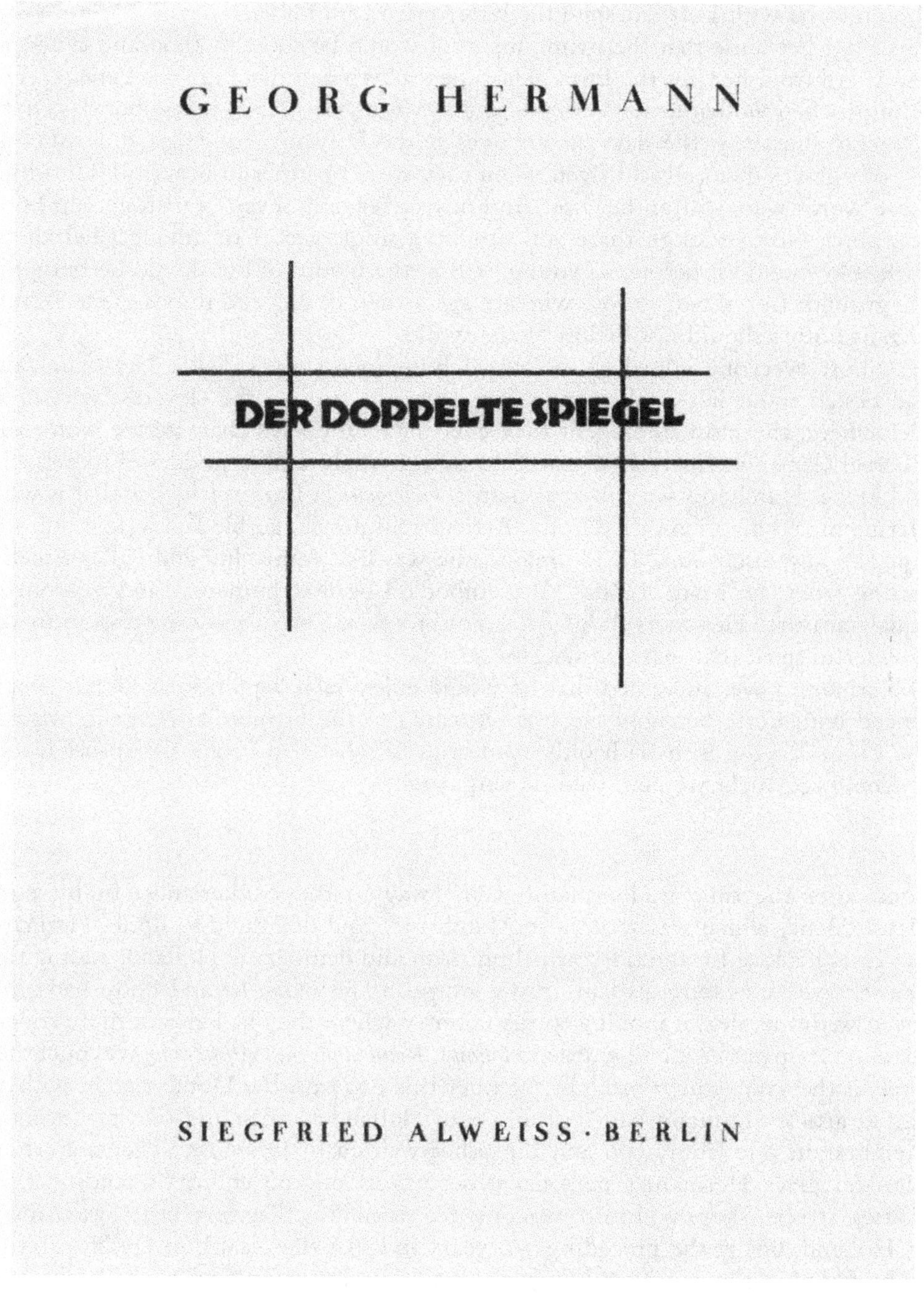

FIG. 8.1. Der doppelte Spiegel.

that it was Rembrandt who created 'the harmony of the disharmonic', evidencing an inward perception which never leaves him and around which everything crystallizes — form, colour and structure. The sculptor Arnold Rönnebeck, in a review of the book, concluded that Hermann was showing us Rembrandt from a new angle, seen from the standpoint of national and individual psychology and environment.[6]

In late 1925 Martin Buber's monthly magazine *Der Jude* had published a special issue under the title 'Antisemitismus und jüdisches Volkstum' [Anti-Semitism and Jewish National Characteristics]. A number of non-Jewish writers were asked to contribute their views on the subject. Hermann had been appalled by what he read in the magazine and in June 1926 he published a strident rebuttal, a ninety-one-page booklet *Der doppelte Spiegel* [The Double Mirror].[7] Hermann had used the motif of the mirror twice before: as the title of his autobiographic essay, 'Im Spiegel' and for his Biedermeier anthology, *Das Biedermeier im Spiegel seiner Zeit*. But whereas previously Hermann was using it to denote an attempt to capture reality, here the double mirror distorts the appearance of what it reflects, like the magic mirror in Hans Christian Andersen's *The Snow Queen*.

Following *Randbemerkungen* and his 'Zur Frage der Westjuden' essay, *Der doppelte Spiegel* shows the further development of Hermann's thinking and also the pace with which social norms were changing in Weimar Germany. In a letter to Solomon Liptzin written in 1939 Hermann recalls that as he read the special issue of *Der Jude* he had his head in his hands:

> "Um Himmelswillen!" sagte ich mir. "Was geht vor? Wenn es in den Hirnen dieser zur ersten geistigen Gilde Deutschlands zählender Menschen schon so aussieht, wie muß es dazu in dem hirnlosen pommerschen Viehknecht, dem dicken Kleinbürger, dem Münchener Strizzi und dem oberbayerischen Holzhacker erst aussehen?! Das kann doch nicht mal die Phantasie eines Höllenbreughel sich ausmalen!"

> ["For heaven's sake!" I said to myself, "If this is what goes on in the brains of the intellectual elite of Germany, what will it be like with the brainless Pomeranian cattleman, the fat petit-bourgeois, the Munich pimp and the woodcutter of Upper Bavaria? Even the hellish imagination of a Breughel cannot depict that!"][8]

In his letter to Liptzin, Hermann writes that his response was first published in a leading Jewish periodical, although he does not name the journal. The paper's editor accused Hermann of exaggeration, however, and made so many changes and cuts that the essay was completely toothless as a result, according to Hermann.

The full unabridged version of *Der doppelte Spiegel*, which was subsequently published by Siegfried Alweiss, opens with Hermann's reflection that in 1914, he could have said with certainty what was true, what was false, black or white, right or wrong. But now he feels at a loss with regard to all ethical and aesthetic, religious and political matters. He reads every day how those who commit crimes get off with impunity.[9] He had believed in the sanctity of human life and always assumed that that with the passage of time it would only come to be valued even more. But now the basest lies are treated with respect and human lives are regarded as disposable. What an individual person would never believe, thousands swear to be true without any apparent misgivings.

Today even the simplest things which previously Hermann could take for granted, like his parentage, his race and nationality, have been rendered insecure. He was fortunate to be born in 1871, just after German unification, into a cultured family, albeit that his branch was impoverished. But it was this combination of poverty and cultural awareness which shaped him. A failure at school, unsuited to every normal job, he escaped into writing. He counted himself fortunate to be German. He loved the German language. He did not live on the fringes but rather in the centre of Berlin and he also had the good fortune to be a Jew, just as Fontane had the good fortune of being born in Prussia into a French-speaking (Huguenot) family.[10]

Hermann notes that before 1914 some things were taboo — conversion and marriage to a Christian, but in those days the distinction was between Jews and Christians, not Jews and Germans. In a later, unpublished essay from c. 1932 entitled 'Die Juden in der deutschen Kultur', Hermann writes that for him German and Jewish culture were intertwined before the war. It was quite straight-forward to identify oneself as being both Jewish and German. It was the war which created the sense of a double identity. Hermann likens it to the fable of the centipede and the toad. Something which before was self-evident and unconscious — a sense of being both Jewish and German — had been disrupted by the war.[11]

When Hermann was growing up, Jews accepted that some higher military and civil service careers were unavailable to them. One could take that as evidence of being second class citizens but in Hermann's view Jews were never too enamoured with honours and high office. The exclusion of Jews from scientific careers was more significant, a loss not so much for the Jews as for science. But in all other areas of life it did not signify; nobody was overly conscious about to which religion or race a person belonged. Both Schnitzler and Stefan George were important in German literature; it was not significant that one was Jewish and the other a Christian.

Hermann acknowledges the wave of anti-Semitism at the turn of the century but argues that figures like Count Pückler-Muskau, Karl Lueger and Johann Sigl were not taken too seriously.[12] More significant was the subsequent over-estimation of the Jews. It was true that there were many capable and valuable people amongst us, Hermann writes — scholars, inventors, politicians, writers, actors, painters, musicians, doctors, lawyers, philosophers, innovative businessmen and industrialists — but just as with any group of people, in reality, all human types were represented among the Jews.

The year before the publication of *Der doppelte Spiegel*, Hermann had been asked by *Jüdisch-liberale Zeitung* to set out briefly the importance of his Jewishness, both to himself and his work. In his response he makes a similar point about the diversity of Jewish identity, questioning the assumption that there is a shared understanding of what it means to be Jewish, a spiritual unity which is common to all those who practise the Jewish faith or are children of the Jewish race 'sofern von solcher zu sprechen' [so far as one can speak of such]. In reality he points out, it is not so. The

Jewish tree, he writes, like the old pear tree in his neighbour's garden, has split into many branches which differ widely.[13]

Before 1914, Hermann argues in *Der doppelte Spiegel*, he knew where he stood. He had definite opinions on subjects like Zionism and the position of the Eastern Jews and he maintained an elevated opinion of the German people in part predicated on his love of German literature. Hermann likens his sense of his Jewishness to old goblets which have been in the family for a long time and are only brought out on special occasions; they would never be used every day. There was an awareness of Judaism being a broad-minded religion which unlike its younger, more popular siblings, never seeks to impose itself on others. But all religions, he suggests, are like rivers which spring from the same source. The water is the same everywhere, even the mysterious force that drives it. Only the riverbanks are different. For sure, he writes, it does not matter to which religion you belong; whatever their different guises, all religions seek to satisfy the same human need.

But Hermann would have chosen no other religion than the one allotted to him by chance. And even if in later life religious practise plays no part in a person's life, Hermann believes that the associated impressions formed at an early age tend to stick:

> ... haben natürlich diese Dinge, wie alle religiösen Dinge, wenn sie von früh an gepflegt werden, eine außerordentliche Einprägsamkeit, und man behält sie, auch ohne einen genauen Sinn mit ihnen zu verbinden; selbst wenn sie aufgehört haben, im Leben ei ne Rolle zu spielen über Jahrzehnte hinaus.

> [... of course, these things, like all religious things, if they are cultivated from an early age, have an extraordinary memorability, and they stay with you, become associated with you, even without an exact understanding, or having ceased to play a role in your life for decades.][14]

Hermann would have chosen to have been born at no other time, and wished for no other nationality. He would not even have chosen to spend his youth anywhere other than Berlin. He was born at just the right moment and could live unburdened, a child of his race, his generation, his country, his language, his birthplace and the milieu in which he grew up.

Before the war Hermann was convinced that civilisation, despite inevitable setbacks, was fundamentally on an upward trajectory and that the lot of humanity would improve over time. But after twelve disastrous years for Europe and far beyond its borders, he has no such faith in the future. Now his only conviction is that in this world

> die Summe der Dummheit, der Einsichtslosigkeit, anscheinend immer die gleiche bleiben muss, und dass wie in zwei miteinander verbundenen Gefäßen der Wasserspiegel stets bestrebt ist, die gleiche Höhe zu halten, sich gerade so wohl auch menschlicher Wahnwitz und menschliche Einsicht zu einander verhalten müssen. Das heißt: jeder Zuwachs an Vernunft und Einsicht lässt auf der andern Seite auch die Dummheit steigen.

> [the sum of stupidity and irrationality, it seems, must be constant, and in the same way that water always seeks to maintain an equal level in two connected

vessels, so are human delusion and human understanding related. Hence every increase in reason on the one hand is matched by a commensurate rise in stupidity on the other.][15]

Hermann cites his amazement that his German compatriots could have learned so little from their defeat in the war. He likens them to his pet terrier who cannot pass any mutt, no matter how miserable, on the street without barking and getting into a wild rage. Injured, after an encounter with a bulldog, he returns home, his ears in shreds, cuts all over his body and with bloodied fur. He spends a wretched week, not eating and only drinking a little but slowly he recovers and begins to limp around the house. Now, you think he will learn something from his experience and become more reasonable. But no, the first time he is back outside in the garden and insulted the same way by one of his canine pals, he responds like a madman, even wilder and louder than before, and is soon embroiled in another bloody brawl.

Out of the experience of the war, a new and virulent anti-Semitism sprang up, which Hermann argues, originated with frustrated army officers and Munich right-wingers. The infantrymen who slept next to Jewish soldiers in the trenches saw in them only comrades but non-Jewish officers, Hermann writes, began to hate them when they showed their military capability. He recalls in Munich, in the aftermath of Germany's defeat, reading a newspaper in which one article maintained that all Jewish painters and musicians were devoid of merit, all Jewish scholars charlatans, and the likes of Simmel, Bergson, Einstein, Ehrlich, Traube, Königsberger and dozens of others, completely insignificant. Elsewhere in the paper it was stated that Jewish university lecturers should be removed from their posts as unfit to teach science to pure-bred German students; that the Chief Rabbi of Bytom in Upper Silesia (Max Kopfstein) had been arrested for raping and killing three women, and how in the basement of a synagogue in Breslau a secret bacon factory had been discovered — in their disgusting greed, the Jews would even desecrate their temples to make a quick buck. At the time, Hermann, said to himself that the accusations were ghastly but he did not think that such a rag would have any influence. However, soon he came to realize that the editors of the paper were much more in tune with the psychology of the Germans and the mood on the ground than he was.[16]

Hermann explains that it was only when he was reading the obituaries of the victims taken hostage and shot by the Red Army in Munich in April 1919 that he discovered that six were members of the Thule Society and first saw a sign which has subsequently become of great importance — the swastika.[17] Hermann was amazed to find the swastika being used as a symbol of the noble blond German. As a collector of East Asian artefacts, he was familiar with it as part of the ornamentation on Japanese swords and Indian bronzes and recognized it as a sacred symbol in both Hinduism and Buddhism.

It was at this time, Hermann writes, that it became clear to him who was organising the campaign. The revolution was not yet over and the threat of the guillotine was still present. The manufactured whipping up of anti-Semitism amongst the lower classes across Germany was no more than a skilful political manoeuvre on the part of those who feared that their heads would be on the block.

Over a thousand of the supporters of the Munich council government were killed and around 700 men and women were arrested and summarily executed by the victorious Freikorps in the bloodbath which took place in Munich in May 1919. Hermann cites the case of Gustav Landauer who was brutally battered to death by the counter-revolutionaries and argues that the most deep-seated brutality was exhibited not by the ordinary soldiers but by the upper classes and the supposedly educated.[18] Yet, despite the defeat of the communists in Bavaria and the slow re-assertion of the old order across Germany, there remained the danger that the counter-revolution could be undone by the forces of the left. A whipping boy had to be created to divert the disgruntled masses and who better than the Jew who had served the purpose on similar occasions for centuries past.

And who were these Jews, the objects of this anti-Semitism, Hermann asks. Wherever you looked in Germany before 1914 the Jews were long-established in the country. Beyond religion, there was hardly anything to distinguish them from their Christian compatriots. The German Jew was a good citizen like everyone else. Neither an angel nor a devil, he did his civic duties, paid his taxes. Perhaps the one thing that distinguished him was that he was 'in deutsche Kunst und deutsche Kultur war er ohne Zweifel verliebter, als die andern Deutschen' [more infatuated with German art and culture than other Germans].[19]

It is true that the war precipitated an influx of East European Jews. Yet these people were actually, Hermann argues, the descendants of German Jews who had been driven out in their droves in the Middle Ages from the Rhine and from Franconia, and so in a sense were returnees rather than immigrants. Moreover, the number seeking asylum was very small relative to the country's population. Hermann points out that in more advanced countries like Switzerland, England, the Netherlands and America granting asylum to refugees is a fundamental right and failure to do so seen as an offence against humanity. Echoing the words he used in his 1919 article 'Zur Frage der Westjuden' Hermann concludes that the experience of the war and the subsequent tide of anti-Semitism has left many Jewish intellectuals feeling '[...] daß der Deutsche die gewaltigste Enttäuschung seines Lebens war.' [that the German was the most formidable disappointment of his life].[20]

In the second half of *Der doppelte Spiegel* Hermann concentrates on refuting the misconceptions of four of the contributors to *Der Jude* — Oscar Schmitz, Otto Flake, Wilhelm Michel and Wolfgang Schumann.[21] He feels the need to respond out of a sense of profound sadness and dejection. If such thoughts had nestled themselves in the minds of intelligent, progressive writers, 'deren Menschlichkeit über allem Zweifel erhaben ist' [whose humaneness is beyond any doubt] Hermann shuddered to think what was going on in other people's heads.[22]

He takes issue with Wolfgang Schumann's suggestion that their excessive ambition has led to Jews in Germany pushing themselves forward into positions of prominence in all walks of the nation's life. Hermann points out that Jews are fully entitled under the constitution to participate in public life. Why should Max Liebermann not be president of the Prussian Academy of Arts? Has he usurped the position? Is he only to be allowed to be active as an art teacher? Should Einstein be teaching maths in a primary school? Should old Schnitzler go back to being a doctor again, or perhaps, better, a medical assistant?

Hermann bemoans the fact that his own profile is so high — his works have been translated into Dutch, Swedish, Finnish, English, French, Italian, Hungarian, and Russian. But being Jewish, should he be representing German literature abroad or is that task the preserve of writers like Hans von Wolzogen, Artur Dinter and Adolf Bartels?[23] And what is worse, Hermann writes, together with his fellow Jew, the writer Hans Landsberg and the half-Jewish journalist, Robert Breuer, he founded the Schutzverband deutscher Schriftsteller, even having the audacity to act as its first chairman! But in the same way, he says that Rathenau accepted his ministerial posts, Hermann was not motivated by overweening ego but rather by belief in the cause and a sense that he could make a contribution. Further ammunition against him, Hermann continues, is that each week he writes a long essay on new German books in a foreign newspaper. It is often a tedious and unprofitable exercise but he has received a letter from a foreign diplomat to say that it serves an important purpose, helping to repair Germany's tattered relations with other European states. Hermann's own misdemeanours are compounded, he says, by those of his brother, Ludwig, who today is one of the leading German Egyptologists, certainly not regarded as a German-Jewish Egyptologist. He is in fact one of the leading European Egyptologists. But in future Ludwig should take heed of Wolfgang Schumann and if he comes across Amenhotep or Queen Tiye in his excavations, he had best leave them there for others to unearth.

Concluding, Hermann takes issue with the notion that the German people act as the host nation of the German Jews. He emphasizes the fact that the Jews are long-established across the whole of the country:

> ... wo wir in Deutschland hinsehen, waren die Juden alteingesessen und durchaus und seit langem schon von Königsberg bis zum Bodensee, aufs engste mit ihrer speziellen Heimat verwurzelt. Typisch ist ja, daß gerade sie oft die besten Kenner und die feinsten Schilderer und Deuter ihrer Heimat sind. Wenigstens ist das sowohl Arthur Schnitzler für Wien, wie Georg Hermann für Berlin oft nachgesagt worden.

> [... wherever we look in Germany, the Jews have been well-established and deeply rooted in their special homeland, from Konigsberg to Lake Constance. Typically, they tend to be the best connoisseurs and the finest portrayers and interpreters of their *Heimat*. At least that is what has often been claimed for both Arthur Schnitzler as regards Vienna and Georg Hermann with respect to Berlin.][24]

Hermann sought to have the following addendum inserted before the final paragraph of *Der doppelte Spiegel*:

> Und das wäre schade, da es sich ja um nichts weniger als das Wohl und Wehe von 600,000 deutschen Brüdern und um die geistige Gesundung von 60,000,000 deutschen Brüdern dreht.

> [And what is at stake, is nothing less than the well-being of 600,000 German brethren and the spiritual recovery of 60,000,000 German brethren.][25]

As Nussbaum points out, by his use of the words 'deutschen Brüdern', Hermann was emphasizing that he still thought in terms of Jewish Germans rather than German Jews.[26]

But Hermann's warning about the state of the nation went unheard. Why did what Nussbaum describes as Hermann's 'righteous indignation and almost prophetic insight' go so unheeded?[27] Hermann subsequently came to believe that *Der doppelte Spiegel* may have been deliberately prevented from circulating in the normal way.[28] Another explanation of its lack of impact could be that by 1926 Germany was experiencing its most stable and prosperous period since the war. After the protracted chaos of the early years of the Weimar Republic, the country was now re-establishing itself. The Dawes Plan had softened the impact of reparation payments on the economy and Germany's admittance to the League of Nations as the fifth permanent member of the League Council, further suggested (to some, at least) the restoration of its pre-war prestige.

There was no new Hermann novel in 1926 but he did publish *Spaziergang in Potsdam* [Strolling in Potsdam] a guide to the city which held such a special place in his affections and which he regarded as an enclave of the south.[29] Hermann's text was accompanied by drawings by Paul Scheurich.[30] He wrote it at home in the greenery of the Odenwald, nearly 400 miles away from Potsdam, relying upon his memory, supplemented by a wide assortment of books.

Hermann makes it clear that *Spaziergang* is not intended to be a conventional guide. Rather it is a book of remembrance, akin, he says, to George Moore's *Memoirs of My Dead Life*.[31] It is his personal take on Potsdam; what it has meant to him in the past. He adopts a conversational style, as if taking the reader on an unhurried idiosyncratic saunter around the city, seeking to capture the essence of what he characterizes as a rococo town. Franz Hessel wrote of *Spaziergang in Potsdam* that,

> wherever Hermann leads us, he serenely practices what he himself calls the "peripatetic study of style". [...] Arm-in-arm with this guide, you'll be well equipped to wander the streets of the city with their happy vistas and obstructions, to live among all of the vases, garlands, flutes and lyres, the coats of arms and sphinxes of the architectural sculptures, which "even [have] cupids patching nets on the roof peaks in the district where the fishers live".[32]

Just as in his portrayals of Berlin, Hermann emphasizes the multifaceted nature of Potsdam. At one and the same time, it is the royal city, the military town, the seat of bureaucracy and the home of its citizens. But he also highlights the unusual extent to which Potsdam has been designed and built by princes according to a plan. Frederick the Great 'determined the overall form of the city as if he had always had its entirety before his mind's eye.'[33] Hermann asks whether the current generation has the right to change the harmonious order of the city which has evolved over centuries, and considers the threat that its beauty could be irrevocably lost from the world. He is unimpressed, for instance, by the modern commercial signage which has been bolted across the historic facades of the buildings in the city centre. But he feels confident that whatever the government, so valued are the historical sites of

Potsdam and Sanssouci, Frederick the Great's summer palace, that they will always be treasured.

Hermann ruminates that it is unlikely that one person, ever again, will be able to create a palace on the scale of Sanssouci, to turn into reality such a dream. For all its charm and beauty, he recognizes that Frederick's summer retreat is testimony to his absolute power. At the time Hermann was writing, the *Fridericus Rex* films which glorified Prussian history and in particular the military accomplishments of Old Fritz, were proving enormously popular.[34] But it is clear from *Spaziergang* that Hermann had no time for the idealisation of Frederick the Great or Prussian military might more generally. Absolutism holds no appeal for him and he says that he cannot even rattle off the genealogy of the Prussian kings. It seems likely that in choosing to celebrate the French influence that shaped Potsdam, Hermann deliberately takes a swipe in *Spaziergang* at those narrow polemicists who sought to denigrate French culture as superficial and frivolous when compared to its German counterpart.[35]

Hermann notes that it is community buildings rather than palaces which represent the challenge for city planners of the future — railway stations, department stores, skyscrapers, courts, administrative buildings, hospitals, hotels, theatres and so on. The new open spaces will need to be designed for the masses, providing sports fields and swimming pools. Given this, only very little can be learnt from Sanssouci. By contrast, he says that the city of Potsdam offers an inexhaustible but untapped wealth of ideas relevant to the future tasks of urban planning — indeed, it is an irony that Potsdam, so often viewed as a remnant from the past, is actually very much alive for the present.[36]

★   ★   ★   ★   ★

Hermann loved Italy. It was a country that he returned to many times. Freud, who was also a frequent visitor, acknowledged in a letter to Hermann written in 1936 that 'Für mich wie für Sie [...] wohnt die Schönheit in Italien und am Mittelmeer.' [For me, as well as for you [...] beauty resides in Italy and around the Mediterranean Sea].[37] Hermann wrote articles about his experiences exploring Italy in 1912 in *Berliner Zeitung am Mittag* and *Central-Verein-Zeitung*, and in 1924 he took Eva and Hilde on a holiday there. Eva had completed her degree and was about to begin a doctorate at Amsterdam University. She would often talk to us about this trip, explaining how her father seemed to have friends everywhere they stayed and recalling his indefatigable appetite for seeing the sights. She recollected that once, faced with yet another visit to a museum, both she and Hilde had gone on strike and said 'No more!' In particular, Eva remembered their stay in Fiesole, where one of her father's friends, on learning that she was twenty-one kissed her hand and cried, 'Oh! To be twenty-one again!'[38]

Mussolini's Italy in the summer of 1926 provides the setting for *Tränen um Modesta Zamboni* [Tears for Modesta Zamboni], the first novel that Hermann published after Lotte's death, and like *Spaziergang in Potsdam*, dedicated to her memory.[39] All of his previous nine novels had been set predominantly in Berlin or Potsdam, so the

Fig. 8.2. Eva, Hermann and Hilde in Italy, 1924

FIG. 8.3. Paul Rosié's cover illustration for the 1977 edition of *Modesta Zamboni*

new book represented something of a departure for Hermann. A romantic fantasy, the novel explores the identity crisis of a married German art historian, Wilhelm Schmidt, and his relationship with a younger Italian widow, Modesta Zamboni. Described by van Liere as Hermann's most light-footed work,[40] the novel conveys both Hermann's love and appreciation of Italian art (the book contains a great deal about the painting, sculpture and architecture of northern Italy) and his dismay at the country's fascist government. Modesta, for whom Schmidt leaves his wife and child, shares some of the traits of Antonie Armstein (and perhaps Lotte). As well as being beautiful, she is confident, well-educated and determined; while Schmidt shares Dr Herzfeld's sense of art as a surrogate for the deeper things in life.

The novel received mixed reviews and van Liere estimates that it sold only 10,000 copies, relatively low for a Georg Hermann book.[41] *Zamboni* was followed quickly by another novel, *Träume der Ellen Stein* [Ellen Stein's Dreams].[42] The eponymous Ellen Stein is a spinster living in Berlin, subtenant of one Herr Brenneisen who embodies many of the negative aspects of contemporary Berlin which concerned Hermann. We are told that Ellen is not yet forty, although gaunt and with her hair, which she wears in a bun, greying, she appears much older. Ellen's suitors died in the war, one from typhus in a distant hospital on the eastern front, another missing in action in the Pinsk Marshes, and a third in the first days of the fighting in August 1914. Her niece Ruth, to whom she is very close, visits with her fiancé, Fred Meirowitz, one late November evening and the visit rekindles Ellen's memories of her own youth. That night, she dreams of the different lives she might have led, had she married each of the three men who had courted her, one of whom bears a certain similarity to Meirowitz.

As originally conceived, Hermann planned that Ellen would poison herself that same night. However, he changed his mind and the first edition of the novel has a happier ending. Ellen's suicide is prevented by a timely visit from Ruth, who tells her aunt that she has broken-off her engagement and the story concludes with the two women planning a trip to Italy. In his commentary on the novel, van Liere argues that Ellen's suicide does not make sense in terms of her character, the broader plot and the overall structure of the book. The happier ending, he suggests, is more coherent and satisfying.[43] Marianne Gerards indicates that Hermann may have changed the ending because of a possible adaptation.[44] It is the case that Hermann adapted the novel for the stage, that same year, but although the play was published separately, it does not appear to have ever been performed in Germany. Hilde offered another explanation, telling van Liere that her father made the change to the novel's ending at the insistence of his daughters.[45]

In any event, Hermann subsequently changed his mind again and a revised edition was published in which Ellen Stein does succeed in taking her own life. Hermann added an epilogue dated 10 April 1929 to explain the new ending. He states that he has made the change not because the world at large had been displeased with the novel's denouement but because he personally was dis-satisfied with it. Never previously has he changed any of his published works. Quoting Fontane, he says that he relies on his instincts. 'Wer rechnet, ist immer in Gefahr, sich zu verrechnen. Die dumme Kuh trifft immer das richtige Gras.' [If one chooses to calculate, one runs the risk of miscalculating. The stupid cow always finds the right grass].[46] It was for reasons of expediency that he had been persuaded to give the book a more conciliatory ending, even though, he felt, this had detracted from its gravity and undermined its ultimate meaning.

Hermann's pacifism is again a strong current in the novel and Sophie Court in her review of the book noted that *Träume der Ellen Stein* was 'an indictment of war and its ruthless fashion of taking away men in their prime, among them geniuses whose death has probably stopped the progress of humanity in one direction or another.'[47] Edlef Koeppen reviewed the novel for *Die literarische Welt*. Koeppen, who led the literary department at *Funk-Stunde AG Berlin*, Germany's first radio station, had served in the army during the war and suffered both physically from a lung contusion and mentally as a result of his wartime experiences. In a positive review of the novel, he wished that more of Hermann's books could find their way into as many homes as possible, as an antidote to the rising tide of anti-Semitism.[48]

While the appetite for Hermann's new works within Germany appears to have been on the wane,[49] the 1920s saw new Dutch translations of the Herzfeld novels, *Einen Sommer lang*, *Der kleine Gast* and *Tränen um Modesta Zamboni*. Six of Hermann's novels were published in translation in Russia during the decade, including *Modesta Zamboni*. In the preface to the latter, it was suggested that the novel represented a remarkable example of the conversion of a bourgeois writer to the side of the proletariat.[50]

Between 1924 and 1928 five impressions of the English translation of *Jettchen Gebert* were published. It garnered some positive reviews. The *Bookman* proclaimed the Gebert family to be the German counterparts of Galsworthy's Forsytes and described the novel as 'a fascinating book of the Germany of a century ago'.[51] A reviewer in the *Christian Science Monitor* detected similarities with the English writer Arnold Bennett:

> George Hermann who might be called the German Arnold Bennett has laid the scene of this novel in the Berlin of a hundred years ago, a Berlin which in many ways was a small town where the stream of life flowed slowly and calmly. In this old-world milieu, depicted with fidelity to life down to every little detail of dress and furniture, the author shows us the lovely figure of Hetty Geybert, an orphan girl who has been brought up by her uncle, a well-to-do Jewish silk mercer, and his wife.
>
> Hetty's love story with a young Christian is full of a delicate charm all its own. The characters of Hetty's many uncles and aunts stand out clearly against the picturesque background. They are all typical of their time, race and social standing: and before the reader finishes the book, they will all have become his good friends.
>
> Strange to say, it is little known outside Germany that "Hetty Geybert" is only the first part of a novel, the sequel of which "Henrietta Jacoby" is if anything an even finer work of art in its mellow tones and its mature view of life. George Hermann has also written several novels the scenes of which are laid in modern Berlin, the best known of which are "Dr. Herzfeld" and "Snow". The hero of both is a literary man with interests and fads which presumably are also the interests and hobbies of the author. It is to be hoped that

in the course of time the English-speaking public will be given an opportunity
of becoming acquainted with the complete work of George Hermann.[52]

To Hermann's disappointment, *Hetty Geybert* does not appear to have met with a
great deal of success in either Britain or America. In March 1927 he sent a speculative letter and a copy of the book to Arnold Bennett whom he hoped would be
able to engender renewed interest in the novel:

> Dear Sir!
>
> I have commissioned my publisher to send you a copy of my novel *Hetty
> Geybert*. This translation appeared rather a long time ago in England and then
> in America but did not have the success according its success in Germany and
> other European countries, especially Scandinavia and Holland.
>
> In Germany it belongs to the permanency of literature and in Holland it
> is read in schools. Perhaps it was published too soon after the war, having no
> success, although it was criticized most favourably. I am doubly upset about the
> fact, because by this book I wanted to make my way in English countries for
> others, such like *Dr. Herzfeld*, which have pacifist and nation-reconciliatory
> ideas.
>
> *Hetty Geybert* is without its sequel *Henriette Jacoby* scarcely to be understood
> in its depth. As I am of the opinion that my way of writing ought to be
> understood by English people, the main part of my readers belonging to the
> people of the German idiom (although I also found friends in France, Italy,
> Hungary and Russia), I request you once more, to have the great kindness to
> try to get the book the estimation by the English readers, thanks to you and the
> prominent and notable place that is at your disposal. [...][53]

Hermann also sent a copy of the novel via the publishers, Stanley Unwin to John
Galsworthy. Galsworthy, who was in France at the time, wrote to thank Hermann
and said that on his return to England he would read it with interest.[54] Aside
from the financial benefits of achieving success in Britain and America, as he sets
out in the letter to Bennett, Hermann continued to want to help foster mutual
understanding across nations. It is not clear if either Bennett or Galsworthy read the
book or responded and despite Hermann's efforts *Hetty Geybert* failed to establish
his name amongst English speaking readers.

The novel did however gain a new lease of life the following year as a musical.
Back in 1916 the composer Leo Blech had asked Hermann to write the libretto
for an opera but the project did not get off the ground. Now with music by the
prolific Walter Kollo and lyrics by Willy Wolff and Martin Zickel, a musical
version of the novel opened on 22 December 1928 in Berlin at the New Theatre
on Nollendorfplatz. It was to prove a huge commercial success, being seen by over
20,000 people, and further cemented *Jettchen Gebert* in public consciousness at that
time.[55]

The musical opens with Salomon and Riekchen hosting a traditional Sabbath
dinner. Uncle Jason has brought Dr Kössling along with him, and the doctor and
Jettchen are instantly smitten. They ask Jason to make their case to Salomon. But
Salomon says that his niece cannot marry Kössling because of the latter's low social
position, strained financial circumstances and in particular, his religion. Moreover,
it is already planned that Jettchen should marry her cousin, Julius Jacoby, an

ambitious businessman from the provinces. The engagement to Julius goes ahead but on her wedding day Jettchen disappears after the marriage ceremony. However, it then transpires that Jettchen has been dreaming and it is actually still the night of the Sabbath dinner! She and Kössling affirm their love for one another and although Jettchen feels obliged to her uncle and aunt, she determines to make her own choice and opts for an uncertain life with Kössling. As Jettchen leaves her uncle and aunt's house, hand in hand with Kössling, the curtain falls and love triumphs.

Notes to Chapter 8

1. Shulamith Ben-Dror, 'Recollections 1919–44', Center for Jewish History Digital Collections, PID: 411295; Call Number: ME 1312. MM III 6. The pages are unnumbered.
2. Georg Hermann, 'In Memoriam Lotte Hermann-Borchardt' (Berlin: Verlag der Jüdische-Liberalen Zeitung, 1926).
3. In Hermann's novel *Eine Zeit stirbt* (1934), Ruth Block (who is modelled on Lotte Samter) sings the first part of the line, 'Hastig entschwinden die Tage des Lebens...' before Fritz Eisner stops her by saying she should sing something else. Georg Hermann, *Eine Zeit stirbt* (Berlin: Das Neue Berlin, 2001), p. 355. Hermann attributes the verse to Pushkin but I have not been able to confirm this.
4. Nussbaum, 'Georg Hermann Attacks the Special Issue of *Der Jude*', p. 449. These Dutch friends included the writers Siegfried and Hilde van Praag, Hermann's publisher, Emanuel Querido and the musicians Peter van Anrooy, Karel Mengelberg and Willem Andriessen. See Laureen Nussbaum, 'Verliebt in Holland', p. 183.
5. Arnold Rönnebeck, 'Books in German', *Books Abroad*, vol. 3, no. 3 (July 1929), Board of Regents of the University of Oklahoma, p. 280.
6. Ibid.
7. Georg Hermann, *Der doppelte Spiegel* (Berlin: Alweiss, 1926). Hereafter cited as *Der doppelte Spiegel*.
8. Gelber, 'Georg Hermann's Late Assessment of German-Jewish and Aryan-German Writers', p. 10.
9. According to E. J. Gumbel's calculations, between 1918 and 1922 in only 27 of 354 cases were rightist murderers punished, while leftist assassins were punished in 17 of 22 cases. See E. J. Gumbel, *Vier Jahre politischer Mord* (Berlin-Fichtenau: Verlag Gesellschaft und Erziehung, 1922), p. 81.
10. Almost a hundred years before, Ludwig Börne expressed similar sentiments in the seventy-fourth of his 'Letters from Paris', stating 'I know how to appreciate the unearned fortune of being both a German and a Jew.' See Anderson, 'Ludwig Börne Begins His Career', p. 130.
11. 'Die Juden in der deutschen Kultur', GHC; AR 7074; Box 5; Folder 68, LBI.
12. Hermann does appear to often understate the extent of anti-Semitism before 1914 and this may partly explain why he regards the war as so significant a turning point. Gert Mattenklott has highlighted the disparity between Hermann's recollections of the pre-war period with those of Herzl and Nordau. See his essay, 'Der doppelte Spiegel. Georg Hermann über Juden in Deutschland (vor 1933)', in Weiss-Sussex (ed.), *Georg Hermann: Deutsch-jüdischer Schriftsteller und Journalist*, p. 134. It is hard to sustain, for example, the argument that Lueger was a marginal political figure. Mayor of Vienna from 1897 to 1910, his administration actively pursued discriminatory practices against Jews.
13. 'Das Jüdische in meinem Wesen und Schaffen', *Jüdisch-liberale Zeitung*, no. 42, vol. 5, Berlin, 16 October 1925, p. 1.
14. *Der doppelte Spiegel*, p. 37.
15. Ibid., p. 21.
16. The paper Hermann mentions was probably *Münchener Beobachter* which in 1920 became the official Nazi organ, *Völkischer Beobachter*.

17. Established towards the end of the war, Thule-Gesellschaft [Thule Society] named itself after Iceland which was believed to be the location of ultimate Aryan purity. It used the Aryan swastika to denote its racial objectives. The Thule-Gesellschaft owned *Münchener Beobachter*. See Roland V. Layton, Jr, 'Der Völkische Beobachter 1920–1933: The Nazi Party Newspaper in the Weimar Era', *Central European History*, vol. 3, no. 4 (December, 1970), pp. 353–82.

18. Landauer was briefly Commissioner of Enlightenment and Public Instruction in the Bavarian Soviet Republic. His brutal murder is described in Solomon Liptzin's *Germany's Stepchildren* (New York: Meridian, 1961), pp. 237–38.

19. *Der doppelte Spiegel*, p. 43.

20. Quoted by Nussbaum, 'Georg Hermann Attacks the Special Issue of *Der Jude*', p. 449.

21. Oscar Schmitz was a popular writer and member of the Munich Bohème. Otto Flake, another successful writer, was one of the eighty-eight German writers who signed a public vow of allegiance to Hitler in 1933. The writer Wilhelm Michel worked for many years for the weekly magazine *Die Weltbühne*. Wolfgang Schumann was another writer and journalist.

22. *Der doppelte Spiegel*, p. 54. Quoted in Nussbaum, 'Georg Hermann Attacks the Special Issue of *Der Jude*', p. 449.

23. Hans von Wolzogen is best known as Wagner's biographer. Dinter wrote the 1917 anti-Semitic bestseller *Die Sünde wider das Blut* [The Sin against the Blood]. Bartels' rabidly anti-Semitic history of German literature published in 1897 had been re-discovered after the First World War. Hitler personally awarded Bartels the Adlerschild medal, the Third Reich's highest civilian honour, in 1937.

24. *Der doppelte Spiegel*, pp. 41–42. Joseph Roth, writing in 1933 makes a related point: 'The great gain to German literature from Jewish writers is the theme of the city. Jews have discovered and written about the urban scene and the spiritual landscape of the city dweller. They have revealed the whole diversity of urban civilization.' Joseph Roth, 'The Auto-da-Fé of the Mind', trans. by Michael Hofmann, in *What I Saw: Reports from Berlin 1920–1933* (New York: Norton, 2004), p. 215.

25. *Der doppelte Spiegel*, p. 92–93.

26. Nussbaum, 'Georg Hermann Attacks the Special Issue of *Der Jude*', p. 449.

27. Ibid., p. 448.

28. See Gelber, 'Georg Hermann's Late Assessment of German-Jewish and Aryan-German Writers', p. 10.

29. Georg Hermann, *Spaziergang in Potsdam* (Berlin: Rembrandtverlag, 1926).

30. Hermann may have been unaware that before the war Scheurich had illustrated an anti-Semitic treatise on the supposed Judaisation of the Berlin theatre world. He went on to become an esteemed artist in the Third Reich.

31. A collection of reminiscences published in 1906.

32. Franz Hessel, *Walking in Berlin*, trans. by Amanda DeMarco (Melbourne: Scribe, 2016), p. 258.

33. Ibid.

34. For more about the nature and popular appeal of the 'Fridericus Rex' films see Katherine Roper's article 'Fridericus Films in Weimar Society: Potsdamismus in a Democracy', *German Studies Review*, vol. 26, no. 3 (October 2003), 493–514.

35. See Lothar Müller, 'Franz Hessel und Georg Hermann: Zwei Spaziergänger im Berlin der Neuen Sachlichkeit', in Schoor (ed.), *Der Schriftsteller Georg Hermann*, p. 127.

36. Ibid., p. 128.

37. Letter from Sigmund Freud dated 28 February 1936, GHC; AR 7074; Box 1; Folder 1, LBI, 159/991.

38. Many years later, she wrote a poem about that evening, 'Sudden Memory of Fiesole', see Eva Rothschild, *Talking To Myself and Collected Poems 1919–78* (Charleston: CreateSpace, 2012), p. 111.

39. Georg Hermann, *Tränen um Modesta Zamboni* (Stuttgart: DVA, 1927).

40. van Liere, *Georg Hermann: Materialien*, p. 173.

41. Ibid., p. 216.

42. Hermann, *Träume der Ellen Stein* (Stuttgart: DVA, 1928).

43. van Liere, *Georg Hermann: Materialien*, pp. 171–73.

44. Marianne Gerards, 'Naar aanleiding van Georg Hermann's *Träume der Ellen Stein*', in *Groote Nederland*, 32, I, 1934, pp. 71–80 and pp. 167–76.

45. van Liere, *Georg Hermann: Materialien*, p. 171.

46. Ibid. In his introduction to the 1941 Hebrew edition of *Jettchen Gebert*, Sammy Gronemann emphasizes the instinctive nature of Hermann's writing, suggesting that he does not fully comprehend his own works, and walks as if moonstruck, with eyes closed, yet never stumbling. (Gronemann, preface to Georg Hermann, *Jettchen Gebert*, p. xiii.) Hermann's heavily annotated manuscripts in the Georg Hermann Collection in the Leo Baeck Institute present a rather different picture.

47. Sophie R. A. Court, 'Review of *Träume der Ellen Stein* by Georg Hermann' in *Books Abroad*, vol. 4, no. 2 (April 1930), 140–41.

48. *Die literarische Welt* 5 (1929), no. 10, 6, quoted by Horch, 'Über Georg Hermann', p. 91.

49. van Liere estimates sales of 8,000 for *Träume der Ellen Stein*, see *Georg Hermann: Materialien*, p. 216.

50. Bernhard Kaufhold, 'Nachwort to *Tränen um Modesta Zamboni*' (Berlin: Das Neue Berlin, 1977), p. 296.

51. *The Bookman's Guide to Fiction* (London: Hodder & Stoughton, 1924).

52. *Christian Science Monitor*, Boston, 27 August 1924.

53. GHC; AR 7074; Box 7; Folder 24, 277/855, LBI.

54. GHC; AR 7074; Box 1; Folder 1, LBI.

55. See Erik Levi, *Music in the Third Reich* (London: Palgrave MacMillan, 1994), p. 57.

CHAPTER 9

❖

Neckargemünd

In January 1928 Hermann and Usche moved back to Neckargemünd. Exactly what precipitated the return to Poststraße 2 is not clear; possibly there were financial reasons. At the same time, Martha moved out of the house to Rottmannstraße 30 in Heidelberg-Handschuhsheim, a modern residential area. By now Hermann had been living permanently in the Neckar Valley since 1921 and he had become increasingly fond of Heidelberg and the Palatinate more generally. This affection comes across clearly in a piece he wrote at the time for the Berlin weekly *Die Dame*.[1] While there is not much in the way of great art in the area and the region is not as wealthy as some other parts of Germany, where else in the country, Hermann asks, can you find such wonderful vistas, forests and rivers? There might be no grand hotels but there are fine traditional old inns, offering comfort, tasty food and good wines. The area is still imbued with the spirit of previous settlers, the Romans whose villas once nestled in the slopes, Charlemagne whose confidant, Einhard, built a basilica in Michelstadt and the various princes with their palaces and churches, grand gardens and parks.[2] For Hermann there is always something to see and discover and importantly for all its historical charm, the area, he writes, has not become dead and detached from the present but remains full of life.

Blessed with a mild climate, the whole area from Odenwald to the Rhine Valley is planted with orchards. Hermann describes travelling the mountain road in mid-April when the fruit trees are in blossom and the hillsides are a riot of pink and silver. He writes of the attractions of Schwetzingen's asparagus market and how around Darmstadt, there are almond and chestnut trees, as abundant as those of Lombardy. Every year, the small towns dotted about the landscape harvest hundreds of thousands of cherries. In Seeheim apricot trees grow by the streets and in the summer it can be unbearably hot but just a few moments away in the mountains there is the cool shade of the dense beech forests.

Eva would often talk of the house in Neckargemünd and her life in Heidelberg. Like her father, she emphasized the Roman legacy which she equated with southern Germany being more cultured than the north. 'We enjoyed a very good cultural life, living in Heidelberg', she would say. The family's home in Neckargemünd was semi-detached. Their neighbour was a Catholic jurist whom Eva would recall with a smile was named Weihrauch [incense]. The garden was, like the whole region, very fertile and had plum trees and damsons, as well as three different types of apple tree (one for eating directly, one for storing and one for making wine). Herr

FIG. 9.1. Hermann with Usche, 1928.

Weihrauch had a beautiful peach tree. Every year some of the peaches would fall over into the Borchardt's garden: 'My father would always say, I will give you the peaches back but Weihrauch would say, no, by law they belong to you!'[3] From the house they could stroll down to the Neckar where the family kept a punt. Sometimes they would sail down the river to Heidelberg, being pulled in by a *Schlepper* [tug] when they reached the town. At other times, Eva would go with her sisters and friends on long hikes into the mountains, always accompanied by the family's beloved dog, Teddi.[4] The sisters travelled by train to school in Heidelberg and she remembered how they would call to the train driver to wait for their friends who came from Schönau who they would often see on the bridge, running to catch the same train.[5]

After completing her PhD in Amsterdam, Eva returned to Germany in 1929 to take up a research post at Städtische Krankenanstalten [Municipal Hospital] in Mannheim.[6] On 17 April 1930 she married Siegfried (Ipi) Rothschild. According to Eva, the first time that Siegfried saw her, he said, 'that is the girl I am going to marry!' Then she would add, 'Mind you, I liked him, too'. Siegfried was eight years older. A chemist, his studies had been interrupted by the war but he had also gone on to complete a PhD and had worked at Städtische Untersuchungsamt [Municipal Research Office] in Mannheim in 1926/27. By the time he and Eva wed, he was running his own laboratory. Their first home was at Schlierbacher Landstraße 29. On 8 May 1931, my mother, Beate, was born; Georg Hermann's first grandchild.

FIG. 9.2. Eva with Teddi, summer 1919

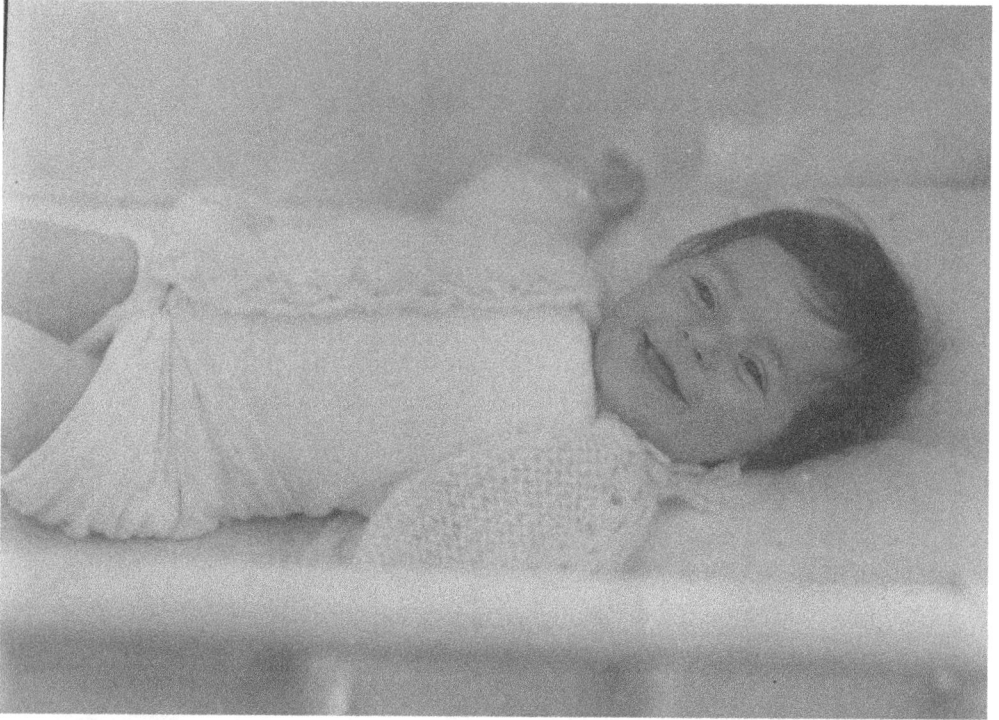

FIG. 9.3. Beate Rothschild, November 1931.

Although Hermann had stopped writing his column for *Algemeen Handelsblad* in May 1926, not long after Lotte's death, he continued to be active as a journalist. From January 1927 he wrote pieces on a regular basis for *Central-Verein-Zeitung* under the banner '*Passanten*' [Passers-by]. In one of these articles, 'Großstadt oder Kleinstadt?' published in June that year, Hermann drew upon his experience of living in Heidelberg to explore the differences between the way of life for Jews in large cities and their experience in the countryside. In the big cities, the Jews live on a 'selbstgewählten Insel' [self-selected island], he argues, or are banished to this island, perhaps without even knowing it. In southern Germany, it is different.

> Hier, vor allem in den kleinen Städten, lebt der deutsche Jude noch vollkommen in der Volksgemeinschaft spricht bis in letzte ihre Sprache, geht mit jeder Färbung ihres Dialektes mit und unterscheidet sich außerhalb seiner Religionsübungen, nicht nennenswert von ihnen. Er genießt genau die gleiche bürgerliche Achtung.
>
> [Here, especially in the small towns, the German Jew still lives entirely within the *Volksgemeinschaft* (community of the people), speaks its language down to the last details, follows each hue of its dialect, and, apart from his religious practices, does not distinguish himself from it in any way worth mentioning. He also enjoys the same civic respect.][7]

But Hermann argues that this close community with the *Volksganzen* [totality of the community] forces the Jews in rural areas to behave differently. He quotes an acquaintance who told him of his constant fear of attracting attention within the wider society. Growing up, the son of the only Jewish family in a small vineyard community along the Rhine, many things were forbidden to him that would have been permitted to young Jewish people in a large city. His father adamantly insisted that the family should not attract attention in any way. His mother was not allowed to wear any jewellery; and even though Hermann's acquaintance had more intellectual interests, he was not allowed to exclude himself from any kind of sporting activities. 'Ich fühlte wohl, daß ich unter einer doppelten Kontrolle lebte, der der Allgemeinheit und der meines Elternhauses.' [I felt that I was living under double control, that of the community and that of my parents' home].[8]

Hermann's *Central-Verein-Zeitung* articles (although not 'Großstadt oder Kleinstadt?') formed the bulk of the thirty-one pieces collected in 1928's *Die Zeitlupe und andere Betrachtungen über Menschen und Dinge* [Slow Motion and other Observations about People and Things]. Together with the autobiographical articles previously mentioned and those about political figures such as Rathenau and Liebknecht, the collection includes vignettes about the artists Menzel and Corinth, the actor, Alexander Moissi, and writers such as Raabe, Hauptmann, Else Lasker-Schüler, Hedwig Dohm, Georg Brandes and Dostoevsky. In his reflections on the latter, Hermann notes that the Russian writer is often regarded within Germany as the epitome of culture, soul and profundity.[9] He does not dispute his psychological depth and acknowledges that he explored the human soul more intensely than writers before him but for Hermann, Dostoevsky is a dish which he keeps trying but can never really enjoy.

In a positive review of *Die Zeitlupe* for the international literary quarterly *Books Abroad*, Kathrine Malterud comments on Hermann's incisive characterisations of public figures, which she notes are often drawn from personal recollection. She continues, 'His reflections are shot through with the seasoned wisdom and sympathy of a man with a richly lived life to look back on. They have a distinguished grace, a light and sure touch, particularly in the short biographical essays.'[10]

In one of the longer pieces in the collection, *Die Politisierung der Schriftsteller* [The Politicisation of Writers][11] Hermann argues that the political soul of German journalism has failed; first under the pressure of the war and even more so in the years that have ensued, despite the greater freedom available. Every point of principle has become subservient to party interests. Increasingly a career in journalism has come to be perceived as a springboard to party and government office, to influence and material gain. Hermann regrets this lack of engagement because he believes that the independence of the writer means he is peculiarly well-placed to contribute to public discourse. He is less materialistic and does not have the vested interests of an industrialist, trembling in case his shares should take a tumble or of the worker fighting for higher wages. The fundamental issues with which he grapples are impervious to forms of government and different social structures. His subject is human nature and emotional development. What would we know and understand about the ancient Greeks, Hermann asks, if we had only a chronology of the battles they fought? It is the poems, plays and philosophical treatises they have bequeathed that reveal their inner world.

He cites the way in which the great writers of Britain and France — Shaw, Wells, Galsworthy, France and Rolland — have engaged in public life and sought to influence and shape the political process. But where are their German counterparts, he asks? Within Germany, Hermann argues, politics has become professionalized. There is an exclusive political community which believes that it alone has the practical answers to Germany's problems. But these populist practical politicians have become blinkered. Hermann quotes Jean-Paul's aphorism 'Jeder Fachmann ist in seinem Fach ein Esel' [Every expert in his field is like an ass]. This stubbornness on the part of professional politicians, Hermann concludes, means that it is absolutely necessary for the non-specialist, the writer, to get a word in, assuming he has something to say.

Hermann himself continued to have plenty to say and the following year he published *Vorschläge eines Schriftstellers* [A Writer's Suggestions], a collection of eighteen political treatises.[12] As with *Die Zeitlupe*, the collection shows the breadth of Hermann's interests. Among other subjects, there are essays about the regulation and sale of food; Wilson's Fourteen Points and the case for co-existence and co-operation across Europe; the need to increase the availability of subsidized housing; and suggestions on how to improve support for prisoners after they are released to ensure their rehabilitation is successful.[13]

In the foreword to *Vorschläge eines Schriftstellers*, Hermann argues that there is a commonly held view in Germany that the writer inhabits a kind of cloud-cuckoo-land, out of touch with the realities of the world. He is not to be taken too seriously, he is still too much the child to be engaged in serious matters. Rather, let him ponder the heavens, pick flowers and chase butterflies. But the writer, Hermann says, is neither child nor dreamer — he is capable of seeing reality with at least as much clarity as others do. He is just as adept at identifying what needs to change.

Hermann shared his father's admiration for Ludwig Börne, and it seems likely that he saw his journalism in that tradition. Like Börne, Hermann was convinced that writing meant intervention in the human world of governments, prisons, censors and newspapers — not an attempt to rise above it or portray it as something more beautiful than it really is.[14] A staunch opponent of the repressive authoritarianism of German political life in the Biedermeier, Börne's political outlook chimed with Hermann's own views. He described Goethe's lines (spoken by Mephistopheles) in *Faust*: 'You must rule and conquer, or be subservient and lose, suffer or triumph, be the anvil or the hammer' as 'a disgusting libel of human nature'. But the Germans, he observed, 'cannot do without giving orders and obeying them, and it is hard to tell which gives them the most pleasure.'[15]

Börne contended that 'to become better than they are, most writers would not require more intelligence but more character.'[16] Hermann certainly demonstrated plenty of character in continuing to seek to engage in public discourse and to advocate the case for pacifism and disarmament at a time when German society was becoming increasingly polarized. As previously evidenced by *Randbemerkungen*, 'Zur Frage der Westjuden', and *Der doppelte Spiegel*, he was not afraid to put his head above the parapet. In his foreword to *Vorschläge eines Schriftstellers*, Hermann emphasizes that all he seeks to do is put ideas and observations forward for discussion. An individual's life is short and the development of government and society takes time, and, like the Echternach Procession, often entails seven steps forward, six steps back (if not six steps forward, seven steps back). But it should not be the sole preserve of party politicians to debate matters of public concern. Although Hermann has no delusions about the likely impact of his suggestions, he does at least hope to explode the German myth that writers are impractical dreamers who have no contribution to make to matters of state.

Eva treasured her copy of her father's *Vorschläge eines Schriftstellers*, and a number of the essays are heavily annotated with her comments and observations. She believed the articles showed Hermann's prescience and underlined the copyright date (1929) in the inside page. One of the essays she re-read many times was 'Die Generation von heute und morgen: Das Desinteressement vom Buch' [The Generation of Today and Tomorrow: Disinterest in the Book], an illuminating survey of the ways in which Hermann felt that German society was changing.[17] He writes that each generation follows its own path, just as a river determines its twisting course and he feels no sympathy for those who chunter on about how things were back in their day. But having said this, Hermann bemoans the prevailing 'spotlight' culture in Germany where all of the focus is on new books. These attract a blaze of interest but it only lasts a few weeks and then they sink into the same oblivion in which all other books deemed to be 'not of the moment' reside. It is the same in the theatre, Hermann contends — a show is the centre of interest for a brief period of time but then disappears completely. Increasingly, theatres find themselves having to put on revues and other lighter fare to attract audiences.

What is it that has changed? Hermann asks. Why is it that people no longer have room in their lives for the riches that the arts have to offer? They read and they go to the theatre not to be challenged but to relax and forget. The explanation, he suggests, has its roots in the change in the mood of the times, a transformation which began in August 1914 and which he argues has eroded the role of the family in providing the secure environment in which an appreciation for the spiritual and cultural dimensions of life was traditionally fostered. Instead, there is a pre-occupation with all forms of physical activity — sport, hiking etc. which is so consuming that it leaves no space for spiritual and cultural pursuits. Today's generation is concerned with being physically healthy but does not want to be overtaxed mentally.

Radio, cinema and the profusion of magazines and newspapers have resulted in a reduced attention span — all offer a more instant hit than reading a serious book. But the core of the change runs deeper and is located in the break-up of the institution of the family and the home as the fulcrum of people's lives. The old roundtable, around which everyone sat, Hermann says, was once the symbol of the family. Illuminated by the secluded light of a kerosene lamp, there the household would sit chatting, reading together, telling stories and passing down family traditions from old to young. Hermann quotes an old teacher friend of his who says that now his students bring nothing to the classroom from their home life. Assumptions about what they will know are no longer valid. Heine and Goethe

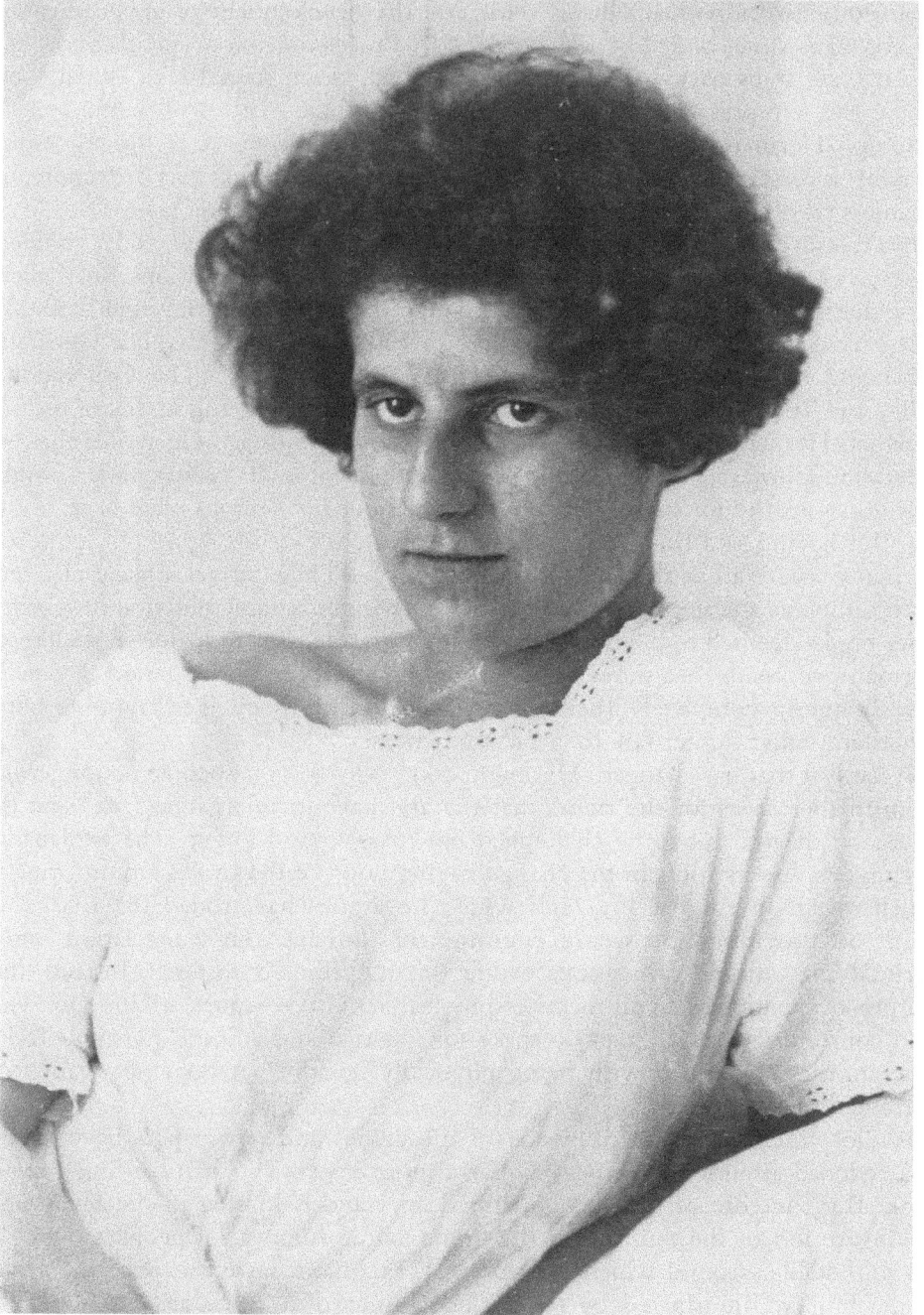

FIG. 9.4. Hilde Borchardt.

have not penetrated their lives.

Hermann does not believe that this will be a permanent state of affairs. Rivers make turns, he says, and the time will come again when the book is a formative experience for the young. But he concludes that 'der fortschreitenden Amerikanisierung unseres Lebens' [the progressive Americanisation of our lives][18] which Hermann equates with the marginalisation of culture, means that the struggle between the current and previous generations has rarely been as acute as at the present time.

In another essay, 'Die Kinder der Geschiedenen' [The Children of the Divorced], Hermann considers the increasing incidence of divorce.[19] He questions the legal requirement to prove one partner guilty in divorce cases since normally, he argues, both husband and wife are implicated when a marriage goes wrong. We know that the separation from his three daughters during the immediate aftermath of his affair with Lotte was something Hermann felt deeply and he argues in the essay that the welfare of the children in divorce cases should be separated from the issue of identifying who is the guilty partner. Rather, he recommends an approach which gives greater discretion to the divorcing parents to work out an arrangement which minimizes the damage done to the children. The impact of divorce on the couple's children is indeed his chief concern. The parents are already adults but their children's lives are ahead of them. Hermann advocates a study to consider the longer term effects on children of divorces. Do they become more cynical, more suspicious and have a more nervous disposition? Do they achieve less academically? He writes that he is firmly convinced that the children of divorced couples always suffer a severe trauma which affects their lives. In part because of the way that the financial settlements associated with divorces are legally prescribed, they suffer downwards social mobility and unless they are resilient, Hermann argues, they are likely to achieve little in later life.

In 'Meine Generation', Hermann's thoughts turn to his generation's growing alienation from contemporary German society.[20] He explains that he has become increasingly aware of the passing of people born around the same time as him: his generation, his people — writers, journalists, artists, scholars, even politicians and diplomats — some of whom were good friends.[21] Whereas in the days of the monarchy, figures like Moltke, Bismarck, Menzel, Fontane and Mommsen continued to be active and influential well into their seventies, the ranks of Hermann's generation are thinning out.[22]

He recalls going to a festival in rural Franconia twenty years ago. He was struck by the unchanging nature of the people's way of life. The families appeared the same as in Dürer's engravings from the 1500s. The same demarcation exists between old and young in such communities but there is not the equivalent gap between the generations which, Hermann argues, is a feature of modern urban existence, where we live in the context of a constantly shifting social culture. Growing old is one of the facts of life that must be accepted, but the deeper tragedy for Hermann's generation is that the environment in which they now find themselves has changed so much as to leave them feeling completely uprooted.

He and his contemporaries, Hermann writes, are the products of the more secure pre-war world in which there was a shared faith in humanity.[23] Now they are faced with the challenge of reworking their lives every day. But more than this, Hermann argues, what is prematurely squeezing the life out of his generation is their sense of impotence. It does not matter how they act, what they say or do, they cannot change a thing. Their voice is never heard. Hermann's generation feels that it is stumbling in a quagmire, with every step they risk sinking to the depths. Whatever as individuals they may have achieved before 1914 now counts for nothing.

It is true, Hermann writes, that he and his generation do not wish to kowtow in front of every new skyscraper and are not filled with enthusiasm by the fact that thousands of cars now race through the streets. Scale of itself does not impress Hermann and his contemporaries. He alludes to Usche coming home from school radiantly happy and saying 'now we are counting with four zeros'. But she does not know, Hermann writes, that the world has long been credited with four zeros. For Hermann and his contemporaries, a boxer is merely a man who inflicts physical violence and no national hero. 'Vor die Wahl gestellt zwischen Nietzsche und Breitensträter ziehen wir Nietzsche vor.' [Faced with a choice between Nietzsche and Breitensträter we prefer Nietzsche].[24]And all of the film divas with their professional beauty are only a pale reflection of the attractions of Empress Eugenie, as painted by Winterhalter.

People of Hermann's generation fail to see why they should worship either the USA or the Soviet Union. Regarding the USSR, Hermann relates how he recently attended a talk at which the speaker applauded the innovation that was taking place in the Soviet states:

> "Verzeihen Sie", sagte ich, "wollen Sie mir eine Frage beantworten? Ist der Gemeinschaftssinn des Russen gewachsen? Ist der neue russische Mensch sichtlich besser zu seinen Mitmenschen geworden, als er es bei uns ist oder dort vorher war? Kurz: ist durch diese Umwälzung eine Änderung in der seelischen Struktur jedes einzelnen Russen eingetreten? Oder gilt auch noch dort wie überall: *homo homini lupus?*" 'Hm', sagte der Professor, diese Frage könnte er noch nicht bejahend beantworten. Dazu wäre die Bewegung noch von zu kurzer Dauer. "Schade", meinte ich, "denn das wäre das einzige gewesen, was mich den Kaufpreis einer hohen zerschlagenen Kultur der russischen Bourgeoisie und seines Adels und ihrer schönen Literatur hätte verschmerzen lassen."

> ["Forgive me," I asked, "but can you say if the sense of community among Russians has grown since the revolution. Does the new Russian treat his fellow citizen better than he did before? Has the new system of government effected any change in the mental outlook of the Russian people, or is it still there, as everywhere, that man is a wolf to man?" "Hmm," the professor replied, he could not yet answer this question in the affirmative. "Too bad," I responded, "because only that would have compensated for the loss of the high culture of the battered Russian bourgeoisie and their beautiful literature."][25]

On Hermann's balance sheet, skyscrapers and movies, the wild tangle of megacities, the submersion of the individual into groupthink, the 'All that Jazz' of Americanism and the cabaret of *Der blaue Vogel* do not compensate for the loss of old Europe's cultural treasures built up over two thousand years and for the abandonment of ethics and values going back even further. Perhaps, Hermann ponders, the war deprived the subsequent generation of those who would have been its standard bearers. He says standard bearers [Fahnenträger] rather than leaders [Führer] because the latter is a word he hates: it carries the stench of the military armband, of 'standing to attention' and subordination.

A belief in the primacy of culture, inherent in the concept of *Bildung* and, as evidenced by essays such as 'Meine Generation', so important a part of Hermann's outlook on life, had been linked positively with integration since the days of Moses Mendelssohn. But now the attachment of Hermann and other like-minded intellectuals to *Bildung* served only to alienate them still further from popular culture and popular politics. Hermann's growing sense of isolation was something he shared with Stefan Zweig. Already in 1925 when he was only in his early forties, Zweig was writing in a letter to his friend, the biographer Emil Ludwig, 'Sometimes I feel that we who possess an encyclopaedic knowledge, men who passionately work at extending their *Bildung*, are already a kind of fossil.'[26]

1929, the year when *Vorschläge eines Schriftstellers* first appeared, was a turning point for the Weimar Republic. It marked the end of the period of relative economic stability which had seen national income increase by twenty-five per cent between 1925 and 1928.[27] Much of that growth had been a result of the Dawes Plan which had enabled the government to borrow from US banks, with German assets, such as the railways and many industries, providing the collateral. But this growing dependence on American finance partly explains why the Wall Street Crash of October 1929 had such a devastating impact on the German economy. By the end of the year around 1.5 million Germans were out of work and twelve months later the figure was over three million.

The slump, of course, gave Hitler his opportunity. In the September 1930 elections, the NSDAP increased its representation in the Reichstag from twelve to 107 seats and became the second largest party, winning eighteen per cent of the total votes. Only the SPD polled more than its 6.4 million votes. In Hermann's beloved Heidelberg the Nazi vote doubled, from fourteen to twenty-nine per cent, and in municipal elections two months later, the Nazis won a plurality with more than a third of the vote.[28] The schism which Hermann had first written about ten years earlier was now becoming manifest.

Against this backdrop, Hermann continued to produce new novels. First came *November achtzehn*, the third instalment of *Die Kette*.[29] Revisiting Hermann's alter-ego Fritz Eisner's life, thirteen years on from *Der kleine Gast*, the novel is set during the days of the 1918 revolution in Berlin. Somehow, however, the revolution itself is never centre-stage. The sound of gunfire is generally in the distance and mentioned only in passing. Eisner observes the revolution and sympathizes with the rebellious soldiers but he does not become actively involved in it. Hermann was an admirer of Flaubert and there are parallels with Eisner's tangential relationship with the events of the revolution and how Frédéric Moreau experiences the 1848 French revolution in *L'Éducation sentimentale* (1869). During the tumultuous days in Paris, Flaubert's anti-hero also invariably fails to realize what is going on or only arrives in the aftermath of events.

November achtzehn focuses on Eisner's personal response to the situation and his relationship with his young girlfriend, Ruth Block, who is modelled on Lotte. Late on the evening of 8 November 1918, at his Grunewald home, Ruth tells Eisner that she is pregnant. Although there have been signs of her troubled state, Eisner has overlooked them. That night Ruth attempts to kill herself with a knife. Eisner intervenes to stop her. After the dramatic events of the night, they both end up sleeping late into the morning of the following day and it is only when one of Eisner's journalist friends telephones him that he learns of the revolution that is taking place in the city. Thus, at the crucial period of the uprising, Eisner is at home, just outside Berlin, and on the periphery of events. He and Ruth do then go into the city to see what is happening and the novel explores Eisner's sense of disorientation and ambivalent feelings towards the events unfolding in the capital. The book ends with Ruth and Eisner boarding a train to Munich.

Although caught up in the urgency and turmoil of the events of November 1918, Eisner (like Hermann) feels that his Jewishness means he views what is happening within a much larger historical timeframe. True, we are told, he may have been born in 1871 which makes him forty-seven years old but that is merely like the date on a house, above the door. The structure of the house has been adapted and modernized but its foundations go back 3,500 years to the time of Amenhotep.

Eisner places the revolution in the rather more recent context of the 1848 uprisings, commenting that now we finally have the republic which we might have had for the past seventy years. One of the characters in the novel, the eighty-five year old Marianne, a member of Eisner's circle, was an eye-witness to those events from 1848. Hermann appears to have based Marianne on the influential salonnière, Mimi von Schleinitz (1842–1912). It is at Marianne's literary salon, we are told, that Richard Wagner met his future wife, Cosima, for whom she left her husband Hans von Bülow. Marianne is the real deal — she is appalled to learn that Ruth has not read *Don Quixote* and when Eisner asks if it was the translation by Ludwig Tieck that Marianne read, she is astonished at the suggestion. 'Ach Gott [...] die Menschen kommen doch immer weiter herunter. Man soll ein Buch in einer Übersetzung lesen.' [Ach God! What are people coming to! That someone would read a book in translation].[30] With her extensive library containing books in five different languages, Marianne represents the old world of European culture, the world of Heine and Börne, of 'Young Germany'.

The gap between Marianne and the younger generation is mirrored in that between Eisner and his nephew, Lulu. Hermann did, of course, have a real-life nephew, Robert Sternberg (his sister-in-law, Paula's son) whose nick-name was Lulu; another instance of how his real world is interwoven with that of Fritz Eisner. In 1918, the real-life Lulu was fifteen years old. In the novel he is two years older and already a committed socialist. When Eisner tells Lulu about how he has come to love this thing called culture, Lulu claims his uncle's passion for collecting fine art is bourgeois decadence. Eisner has no future if he does not serve the socialist cause, according to Lulu, and in any case, artworks should be in public ownership not the playthings of private collectors.[31]

The novel also explores what the new post-war world ushered in by the revolution means for Eisner and Ruth. As Frank Degler observes, because Eisner only learns second-hand via the telephone of the revolution and the reader does not experience it, the transition from the old to the new world has an almost magical quality.[32] It is perhaps something of a conjuring trick. Hermann is writing ten years after the revolution and in the knowledge of its failure. Hindsight does perhaps permeate Eisner's observation that after going into hiding during the first days of the revolution, creeping into their mouse holes, the old privileged elite, slowly emerged and looked around at what was going on. They soon realized that the crowds on the streets did not know what they wanted and so, having been submerged for a moment, just like corks under water, these rulers of yore resurfaced. And how quickly, Eisner reflects, has it become apparent that they will not be pushed down again.[33]

When he finally goes into Berlin Eisner is almost like a sightseer in his hometown. The red flags which have appeared all over the city, including on the Brandenburg Gate, make a pretty sight and everywhere there are women and children waving them. He thinks that he could package up his observations into a nice feature article capturing the mood and atmosphere of the city. He is not wholly a spectator, however. On two occasions before Eisner and Ruth leave Berlin, he goes to the Reichstag, seeking to find a way that he can be involved in the revolution, in support of his political and social ideals. But he finds that the parliament building is like a military camp and is also alienated by the menacing presence of the revolutionary guard's massive trucks which patrol the streets, carrying soldiers armed with machine guns.

Eisner is aware of a different ambience in Berlin. On the trams, for instance, nobody feels obliged to follow the official regulations. No-one rides in the third class carriages because they don't see why they should have to sit on a hard seat anymore. The old rules and signs are no longer observed. But the aesthete Eisner is repelled by the noise and dirt of the revolution. Rather like Jason Gebert retreating into the safety of his private library, Eisner seeks refuge in the pleasure he finds in his porcelain figurines. Ruth's observation that he loves things more than people, is perhaps borne out by the way that Eisner, when caught up in the turmoil of the crowds on Berlin's streets, turns to his friend, Paul Gumpert, and asks him about the latest picture which he has purchased. That is a matter, he tells Gumpert, that is of greater import than the events of the revolution which are merely the stuff of day to day history. The painting is something that will endure and continue to be important to humanity forever.

Franz Hessel wrote a positive review of the novel in *Die literarische Welt,* describing it as Hermann's most mature work.[34] But it appears from the figures in van Liere's biography that Deutsche Verlags-Anstalt (DVA) published only one thousand copies of the book; the lowest print run of any Hermann novel to date; half even of the first edition of *Spielkinder* back in 1897. It is no wonder that Hermann was ruminating on the changing nature and increasingly illiberal book market. But twenty-four years had elapsed since the publication of *Jettchen Gebert* and his pacifist cosmopolitan sentiments were more and more out of kilter with the patriotic mood of the times. DVA, which insisted on cuts amounting to sixty pages from *November achtzehn* probably viewed the novel as a poor commercial prospect.[35] His publisher's approach must have reinforced Hermann's growing sense that his was a voice which people no longer wanted to hear. But, if he ever saw it, Hermann would have been heartened by Johannes Malthaner's positive review of the novel in *Books Abroad*:

> Better than many big books with official data, G. Hermann's novel gives a graphic picture of the situation in Germany, especially Berlin, just before and during the revolution of 1918. Like mosaic, the little scenes and everyday happenings offer in their totality a vivid picture of the weariness of the people, the rotten social stratum of the newly rich, the suffering of the poor, and the hopelessness of the gigantic struggle. One feels that behind the dull uneventful life of these people hovers always like a horrible monster the threat of war, growing suddenly more menacing now and then in a short scene like a flash of lightning.[36]

Hermann's second novel of 1930, *Grenadier Wordelmann*, was published by Ullstein but they also only saw fit to print a thousand copies. Despite his enormous success in the past, Hermann was now being treated as a minor writer.

Based upon old court records and set in 1780, in the last years of the reign of Frederick the Great, *Wordelmann* tells the story of the ageing farmer, Christian Friedrich Schmitzdorff's attempt to marry his young stepdaughter, Sophie. When Schmitzdorff is refused permission by the local pastor on the grounds that it would constitute incest (although they are unrelated by blood), he decides to seek the king's consent to the marriage. An ex-soldier who served in the Seven Years War (1756–63), Schmitzdorff has an inviolable trust in 'Old Fritz' and goes to Potsdam to seek a royal dispensation. There, he meets the manipulative Grenadier Wordelmann, who offers to help him but only for his own and his comrades' entertainment on an otherwise dull day. Wordelmann and his cronies organize a sham wedding for the ex-soldier and his bride. But what starts as a joke soon loses its harmless character and things end tragically for Schmitzdorff.

Hermann makes it clear in the novel's motto that his sympathies rest with society's victims: 'In diesem Augenblick reißt an der Wasserstelle ein Löwe eine Antilope nieder. Andere sehen den Löwen, ich, solange ich denken kann, nur die Antilope.' [At the moment when the lion attacks an antelope drinking at a watering hole and rips into its flesh, others see the lion but for as long as I can remember, I have seen only the antelope].[37] Like Emil Kubinke, Schmitzdorff is one of Hermann's little men, prey to the machinations of the predatory behaviour of others. His tale reflects the unchanging pattern of human existence:

> Wir glauben immer, daß die Geschichte die Welt ändert. Aber sie ändert sie nicht. Meer und Land bleiben Meer und Land in immer gleichen, kaum gegeneinander verschobenen Grenzen. Und so wenig, wie sich Meer und Land ändern, ändert sich in ihren Grundformen die menschliche Seele. Ihre Jahreszeiten und Farben wechseln nur. Aber dieser Wechsel bleibt sich gleich in ewiger Wiederkehr.

> [We always believe that history reshapes the world. But it is not so. The sea and land remain the sea and the land, their respective boundaries hardly shifting.

And as little as the sea and land alter, so it is with the human soul. Only the seasons and the colours vary but these changes recur eternally.][38]

Typically, Hermann does not shy away from portraying the authoritarian nature of Fredrick the Great's rule, the narrow-mindedness of the military officers and Prussia's cultural backwardness, while also rendering Potsdam's architectural treasures, the townhouses, taverns, parks and the quiet beauty of the surrounding landscape. Herbert Scheffler, in a review of the novel, described *Grenadier Wordelmann* as a 'genuinely sympathetic work' and suggested that the author 'employs history not as the actual impulse of action but as the foundation of mood.'[39]

Hermann sent an advance copy of the book to Max Liebermann. The artist wrote back to say he had read it with great delight, particularly the descriptions of Potsdam. 'Ich kenne nichts schöneres, als die Promenade vom neuen Palais zum Obelisken durch den Park von Sanssouci' [I know of nothing more beautiful than the promenade from the new palace to the obelisk...].[40] Liebermann goes on to explain that some weeks before he had attended a tea party hosted by the Secretary for Cultural Affairs on the occasion of the opening of the newly decorated picture gallery in Sanssouci:

> Ich mußte von Herzen den Geschmack Friedrichs — der als Mensch mir wenig sympathisch ist — bewundern; was mir alles bei Lektüre Ihres Buches wieder eingefallen ist. Das Milieu, in dem die Geschichte spielt, haben Sie wundervoll wiederzugeben verstanden; die Soldaten studiert, wie sie Menzel studiert hat, im Grunde eine greuliche Bande. Oder ist es mein Semitenblut, daß ich sie nicht leiden kann?
>
> [I could not help admiring Friedrich's taste — although I find him hardly sympathetic as a person — from the bottom of my heart; all that came back to me while reading your book. You certainly know how to describe the milieu in which the story is set wonderfully; you studied the soldiers in the same way as Menzel; basically they are a dreadful lot. Or is it just my Semitic blood that makes me dislike them?][41]

The day before, Hermann had received a handwritten letter from Thomas Mann. Hermann must have been in touch to express his agreement with a speech (*Address to the Germans: An Appeal to Reason*) that Mann had made earlier in the month in Berlin. Horrified by the massive gains achieved by the Nazis in the September national elections, Mann had spoken out against the movement. Like Hermann, Mann viewed the threat of National Socialism within a cultural context:

> [Militant nationalism's] fanatical love of the fatherland appears chiefly as hatred [...] of everything that makes for the good name and intellectual renown of Germany in the world today. More and more it looks as though the chief goal were [...] the return of the German to the conception that radical nationalism has of him. But can a people old and ripe and highly cultured [...] with a long emotional and intellectual experience behind it, a people who possess a classical literature that is lofty and cosmopolitan, a romantic literature of the profoundest and most subtle, who have Goethe, Schopenhauer, Nietzsche [...] can such a people conform, even after ten thousand banishing and purificatory executions, to the wish image of a primitive, pure-blooded, blue-eyed simplicity, artless in mind and heart, which smiles and submits and clicks its heels together?[42]

Also like Hermann, Mann sees the rise of National Socialism — 'a wave of anomalous barbarism, of primitive popular vulgarity' — as symptomatic of the way that society has changed:

> The fantastic development, the triumphs and catastrophes of our technical progress, our sensational sports records, the frantic overpayment and adoration bestowed upon our "stars", the prize-fights with million-mark purses and hordes of spectators — all these make up the composite picture of our time, together with the decline and disappearance of stern civilising conceptions such as culture, mind, art, ideas. Like boys let out of school, humanity seems to have run away from the humanitarian, idealistic nineteenth century, from whose morality [...] our time represents a wide and wild reaction. Everything is possible, everything permitted as a weapon against human decency...[43]

Although he spoke on behalf of the Social Democrats, Mann writes to Hermann that he does not wish to commit himself in any way to party politics. Rather, he says,

> I embrace everything opposed to National Socialism, even the Catholic Church and Communism, which after all somehow seems to stand for justice and happiness. But revolutionary reaction, this shrill, impertinently yelling put-down of every free thought, I hate from the bottom of my heart...![44]

Notes to Chapter 9

1. Georg Hermann, 'Am Neckar und Am Maine: Eine Autoreise', in *Die Dame*, May 1928, 2–7.
2. Judging from the family photo albums, Michelstadt appears to have been a regular outing for the Borchardts.
3. Private family recording, December 1991.
4. There are many pictures of Teddi amongst the family albums. He was a stray dog that Hermann found, shortly after the family had moved to Neckargemünd. When Teddi died, Hermann wrote a six page obituary: 'Nachruf für Teddi', GHC; AR 7074; Box 5; Folder 74; LBI. 'Teddichen was everything to us!' Eva used to say.
5. Something of the warmth of Eva's memories of those days comes across in her poem, 'Neckargemünd'. See Rothschild, *Talking To Myself*, p. 121.
6. Eva's doctorate was a study of heteromorphic regeneration in *Dixippus morosus* [stick insects].
7. Quoted by Michael Wildt, *Hitler's Volksgemeinschaft and the Dynamics of Racial Exclusion: Violence against Jews in Provincial Germany*, trans. by Bernard W. Heise (New York: Berghahn, 2012), p. 58. Hermann's article is in the 3 June 1927 edition, p. 1–2. Here p. 2.
8. Ibid., pp. 58–59.
9. *Die Zeitlupe*, pp. 78–83.
10. Kathrine Malterud, '*Die Zeitlupe und andere Betrachtungen über Menschen und Dinge* by George Hermann', in *Books Abroad*, vol. 3, no. 3, July 1929 (University of Oklahoma), pp. 305–06.
11. *Die Zeitlupe*, pp. 165–76.
12. Georg Hermann, *Vorschläge eines Schriftstellers* (Baden Baden: Merlin-Verlag, 1929).
13. Hermann was also among a number of writers including Bertolt Brecht who called for reform of Germany's abortion laws. See his essay, 'Was Wäre, Wenn (§218)' in *Die Weltbühne 25, II* (1929), 444–48.
14. Anderson, 'Ludwig Börne Begins His Career', p. 133.
15. Ibid., p. 132.
16. Ludwig Börne, 'How to Become an Original Writer in Three Days', trans. by Leland de la Durantaye, *Harvard Review*, 31, December 2006, 63–70.
17. Hermann, *Vorschläge eines Schriftstellers*, pp. 225–36.
18. Ibid. Here, p. 236. Eva has underlined these words in her copy of *Vorschläge eines Schriftstellers*.

19. Ibid., pp. 95–111.
20. Ibid., pp. 209–21.
21. Ibid. Here, p. 209.
22. Hermann's argument is somewhat undermined, however, by the fact that Hindenburg was already seventy-eight years old when elected to the presidency of the republic in 1925, three years older than Bismarck had been when he was forced to resign by Wilhelm II.
23. Although ten years his junior, Stefan Zweig shared Hermann's sentiments. He describes the time of his childhood and youth before the First World War as a 'Golden Age of Security'. Stefan Zweig, *The World of Yesterday*, trans. by Anthea Bell (London: Pushkin Press, 2009), p. 23.
24. Hans Breitensträter was a heavyweight boxer who achieved great popularity in Germany after the war. Unlike Britain and America where boxing had been established since at least the 1850s, it only existed on the margins of German society before 1914. A number of local laws and police prohibitions banned or sharply restricted the sport throughout most of Wilhelmine Germany. See Erik N. Jenson, *Body by Weimar: Athletes, Gender and German Modernity* (Oxford: Oxford University Press, 2014), p. 53.
25. Hermann, *Vorschläge eines Schriftstellers*, p. 219.
26. Quoted in George L. Mosse, *German Jews beyond Judaism* (Bloomington: Indiana University Press, 1985), pp. 32–33.
27. Dieter Petzina, 'Germany and the Great Depression', *Journal of Contemporary History*, vol. 4, no. 4 (1969), 59.
28. Arthur David Brenner, *Emil J. Gumbel: Weimar German Pacifist and Professor* (Boston: Brill, 2001), p. 115.
29. Georg Hermann, *November achtzehn* (Stuttgart: DVA, 1930). Subsequent references to the novel are to the edition published by Das Neue Berlin in 2000.
30. See Hermann, *November achtzehn*, p. 309.
31. Ibid., p. 97.
32. Frank Degler, 'Die verschlafene Revolution in Georg Hermanns *November achtzehn* (1930) in Kontext des Romanzyklus Kette', in *Friede, Freiheit, Brot! Romane zur deutschen Novemberrevolution*, ed. by Ulrich Kittstein and Regine Zeller (Amsterdam: Rodopi, 2009), pp. 197–219.
33. Hermann, *November achtzehn*, p. 320. With time, the extent to which the events of November 1918 brought about any real change has come to be questioned. For instance, Eric Hobsbawm describes the Weimar Republic as 'little more than the defeated empire minus the Kaiser'. See Hobsbawm, *Age of Extremes*, p. 128.
34. Franz Hessel: 'Georg Hermann *November achtzehn*' in *Die literarische Welt*, 7 July 1932, 5.
35. Hermann wrote in a letter to Hilde in July 1933 that these cuts had deprived *November achtzehn* of its original sharp edges. See *Unvorhanden und stumm*, pp. 30–31.
36. Johannes Malthaner, '*November achtzehn* by Georg Hermann', *Books Abroad*, vol. 5, no. 2, April 1931 (University of Oklahoma), 155.
37. Georg Hermann, *Grenadier Wordelmann* (Berlin: Das Neue Berlin, 1970), p. 5.
38. Ibid.
39. Herbert Scheffler, 'Recent Historical Fiction in Germany', *Books Abroad*, vol. 7, no. 3, July 1933 (University of Oklahoma), 277–80.
40. Handwritten letter from Max Liebermann to Georg Hermann dated 30 October 1930. The letter and this English translation appear in *Jettchen Geberts Kinder*, ed. by Fred Grubel and Eberhard Roters (Leo Baeck Institute of New York, 1985), pp. 167–68.
41. Ibid.
42. Thomas Mann's 'Appell an die Vernunft' was first published in *Berliner Tageblatt* (18 October 1930). These excerpts are taken from the translation in *The Weimar Republic Sourcebook*, ed. by Anton Kaes, Martin Jay and Edward Dimendberg (Oakland, CA: University of California Press, 1994), pp. 150–59.
43. Ibid.
44. Thomas Mann, letter to Georg Hermann dated 29 October 1930. See Grubel, *Jettchen Geberts Kinder*, pp. 166–67.

CHAPTER 10

❖

Flight

In July 1931, Hermann left Neckargemünd and went back to live in Berlin. Exactly what precipitated the return north is not clear but Usche later said that it was mainly because her father believed it would be easier to find work in the capital.

He took an apartment in the Künstlerkolonie Berlin (Berlin artists' colony) in Laubenheimer Straße, Wilmersdorf. The colony had been established in 1927 at the initiative of the Schutzverband deutscher Schriftsteller, the writers' association which Hermann had co-founded in 1910. The association provided twenty-five per cent of the funding for the scheme. The rest of the money came from the German Stage Workers' Cooperative. The aim was to provide cheap and comfortable living space for artists and writers. Comprising three blocks of flats, the colony soon acquired the nickname 'Hungerburg'. It was home to mainly left-wing intellectuals and artists and they formed a 'red block' within what was a predominately nationalist and increasingly pro-Nazi area. Colony residents were regularly subject to intimidation and eventually formed a self-protection group.

Usche followed her father to Berlin later in the year and some months afterwards, Martha and Liese also came from Heidelberg to join them. Hilde lived with her boyfriend, Werner Lippmann in the flat below. Many years later, Usche recalled the apartment blocks as being

> dreadful, many storeys high, and with cramped rooms ... like those austere buildings that one sees in Russia and China. [...] In Berlin, nobody knew each other and everyone was always rushing about. Probably, Peps did also not feel at home, but he needed to be there for his work as a writer. Additionally, as we entered 1932, the first dark clouds of what was to come were already forming, and this was more obvious in Berlin. In a sense, my Holocaust memories began then, because of the atmosphere during this period.[1]

That it was a very different Berlin to which Hermann had returned was demonstrated just a month after he came back to the city. Rosh Hashanah began on the evening of 12 September in 1931, and as dusk fell large numbers of Stormtroopers (out of uniform) started to gather on the Kurfürstendamm. It was later estimated that there were about 1200 of them. Crying 'Deutschland Erwache' [Germany Awake] and 'Juda Verrecke' [Perish Judah] they started wildly attacking passers-by. The riot was left to continue for over two hours before the Berlin police eventually arrived, by which time the SA men had attacked around thirty to forty people whom they believed were Jewish.[2] All of this thuggish violence took place in those same streets where before the war Hermann's Dr Herzfeld had frequented the Café des Westens and its surrounds and found his inner equilibrium restored by its cultural buzz.

In October, Hermann's sixtieth birthday was the occasion for a number of laudatory articles. They included Arthur Galliner's 'Ein Besuch bei Georg Hermann' in *Israelitisches Familienblatt* and Karl Escher's 'Georg Hermann zum Sechzigsten'. Weiss-Sussex highlights how these appreciations of Hermann, like those published on his fiftieth birthday, emphasized his attachment to his native Berlin as a determining factor in his work.[3] Hermann's birthday also appears not to have gone unnoticed by the Nazis. In a subsequent letter to Hilde, Hermann recalls, '"Eines schönen Tages wird die Schildkröte schon zuschnappen" schrieben sie mir schon am Sechzigsten im *Völkischen Beobachter*.' ["One fine day the turtle shall snap" they wrote about me on my sixtieth birthday in *Völkischer Beobachter*].[4] As Nussbaum emphasizes, it was precisely because Hermann had spoken out so many times and in no uncertain terms that he received death threats from 1931 onwards.[5]

In November that year, Hermann gave a lecture about Berlin at the Fontane evening of the city's *Gesellschaft der Bibliophilen* (Society of Bibliophiles). Subsequently, three hundred copies of the talk were privately printed by Arthur Scholem.[6] Hermann's lecture evidences his enduring fascination with the city and its inhabitants. It is true that he has an abiding affection for the city — 'ich liebe Berlin ... das kann ich ja nur schwer abstreiten.' [I love Berlin ... I can hardly deny that].[7] But he likens his feelings to the kind of love-hate relationship which is usual with a lifelong friend or close relative. It is not beautiful and it lacks the cosy intimacy of the Berlin of his youth, but he still finds it a stimulating environment. His imagination is always sparked as he walks amongst Berlin's streets and its green spaces. It is like a riddle that can never be entirely understood. Berlin's mantle, Hermann told his audience, shimmers in a thousand colours. In places it is scuffed and worn out; elsewhere it is made of old brocade; here, heavy velvet and over there, cheap Krefeld silk. The east of the city is far from the west and the south distant from the north. They are like cities in themselves. Every street, every hub is an island to itself — centres of commerce, power, learning. In one part there is beauty; in another; ugliness: cheek by jowl, wealth and poverty; vice and virtue; busy thoroughfares chock-a-block with people and menacing empty dark backstreets.[8]

Hermann's hopes that being back in Berlin would enable him to pick up more journalistic work initially proved to be well-founded. During September he had spent three weeks in Spain and he wrote about his travels in *Central-Verein-Zeitung* as well as in *Die Dame*.[9] Other articles appeared in the paper — a review of a Heine biography and of a new collection of Kurt Tucholsky's essays. Although the work with *Central-Verein-Zeitung* appears to have tailed off in 1932, Hermann continued to carry out speaking engagements. In March at an event in Berlin to mark the centenary of Goethe's death, for instance, he gave a talk about the great writer.[10] Forty years later, Fritz Friedlander who was present, recalled the event in an article for the London Association of Jewish Refugees.[11] For Hermann, Friedlander remembers, Goethe was not so much the egocentric Olympian as a man of social responsibility. He recalls him highlighting Goethe's reference to the contrast between the reality of the starving textile workers in Apolda and the lofty verses of King Thoas he was grappling with while writing *Iphigenie auf Tauris*: 'Here in Apolda my play is not getting written at all; damn it all, King Thoas is supposed to speak as if the textile workers in Apolda were not starving'.[12] At a time of ever-growing social polarisation, Hermann also mentioned in the talk Goethe's openness and willingness to take the best from different worlds, relating how Goethe liked to combine Brandenburg turnips with sweet chestnuts from the south — they might grow far apart but it is in combination that they taste best.[13]

We catch an interesting glimpse of Hermann at this time through the eyes of the writer Sammy Gronemann. In his July 1941 preface to the Hebrew edition of *Jettchen Gebert*, Gronemann remembers Hermann's characteristic intervention at a meeting of the German PEN Club which took place in Berlin towards the end of 1932.[14] The President, Alfred Kerr, had made a fiery speech about the need for the club to stand firm against an attempted infiltration by pro-Nazi elements. Everyone present supported Kerr with the sole exception of Hermann, who argued the opposite, that the club's doors should be open to Nazi writers. Let them get to know us, Hermann maintained, and they will come to acknowledge their mistakes and change their ways.[15]

It is not surprising that Hermann found himself isolated among members of the club. Such idealism on his part probably felt increasingly removed from the Berlin of 1932. The federal elections at the end of July had seen the Nazis make massive gains. With 230 seats, they had a lead of almost a hundred over their nearest rivals, the SPD. An astonishing 13.7 million people had voted for Hitler, 37% of the electorate. Even in Berlin where the Nazis had always lagged behind, they more than doubled their votes in that summer's elections. Von Papen's minority administration stumbled on but government was at a stalemate. Daily street battles raged between the Nazis and the Communists. Further elections were held in November. Again the Nazis emerged as the single biggest party although they lost thirty-four seats and were unable to form a government coalition in the Reichstag. In December von Papen did his deal with Hitler, Hindenburg gave his presidential blessing, and we come to that winter afternoon in January 1933 etched forever in the mind of Eric Hobsbawm, when on his way home from school he saw the headline announcing that Hitler was now Chancellor of Germany.

The political climate meant that publishers could no longer handle Hermann's manuscripts, as evidenced by Ullstein's short letter to Hermann dated 8 February 1933: 'Lieber Georg Hermann — ich schicke Ihnen das Exposé des Rosenemil-Romans zurück. Dass wir einen Vorvertrag nicht machen können, sagt ich Ihnen bereits — zu unserer aller Leidwesen.' [Dear Georg Hermann — I am returning the synopsis of the *Rosenemil* novel. As I previously mentioned, much to our regret, we cannot offer you a preliminary contract].[16]

But more than just Hermann's future prospects as a writer were at risk. When the Reichstag went up in flames on 27 February all of the fundamental rights guaranteed in the German constitution were suspended. Summary arrests could

FIG. 10.1. Mies Blomsma, Hermann and friends, summer 1931.

be made and the Nazis' opponents placed in 'protective custody' in concentration camps. Some 100,000 people were arrested in Prussia alone, among them Hermann's friend Egon Erwin Kisch.[17]

Hermann's daughter Hilde had been an active member of the Communist Party (KPD) for some time and had already left Berlin the previous year for Copenhagen where she took a job as a housekeeper. Her decision to leave was motivated partly by a desire to escape the anti-Semitism of Germany but also by a wish to break away from her father. Eva, living with her husband and daughter in Heidelberg had established her own independent life and Hilde felt that only by moving away could she do likewise. In her recollections, Usche remembers that the nannies that she had when living in Heidelberg usually ended up in her father's bed: 'even those that did not live-in were often asked to come over in the middle of the night!'[18]

Hilde found the fact that her father would bring his girlfriends back to the flat in Laubenheimer Straße very difficult and it was another factor in her decision to move to Copenhagen.[19]

Through friends in the KPD which had its spies in the NSDAP, Hilde learned that Hermann's name was among those on a list of prominent people the Nazis intended to arrest and send to special concentration camps. In the week after the Reichstag fire, members of the Nazi Party made a house check on his Laubenheimer Straße flat. He and his Dutch girlfriend, Mies Blomsma happened to be in Hildesheim, where he had gone to give another talk.[20] He only learned of the visit the following morning when he phoned home and spoke to Martha. In a letter to Hilde dated 13 March 1933, Hermann tells her,

> Da ich doch bei den Idioten sowieso auf der schwarzen Liste stehe [...] so sagt ich mir, ich habe keine Lust den Märtyrer zu spielen und ging, wie ich ging und stand, mit Mies nach Holland, zu Queridos, statt nach Berlin zurück.

> [Since I am already on the idiots' blacklist [...] I say to myself, I have no desire to play the martyr and so instead of returning to Berlin, I went with Mies to Holland, to Querido's.][21]

Usche later recalled,

> When Peps did not come home to Berlin on that Sunday Liese, Mu and I did not know what was going on. Only being a child I was not really aware of the significance of the [March] elections, although the tension that existed was apparent to me. There was a menacing unpleasant atmosphere in Berlin at the time. Liese then had the intuition to ring-up Querido. He answered her call saying, "Yes, your father is here" and I remember Liese fainted next to the phone when she heard the news.[22]

In his 13 March letter to Hilde, Hermann writes that as a well-known left-leaning pacifist Jew, he can't see that he has any prospect of making a living in the new Germany. But there is a house he can rent in Laren for only seventy-five Mark, he will still be able to do some work for Ullstein and can focus on writing his novels in peace, which would be impossible in Germany. He plans to keep the house in Neckargemünd but wants to give up the 'teuer und scheußlich' [expensive and horrible] apartment in Berlin.[23] He goes on to say that there's probably no need to discuss political matters; Hilde will be reading the newspapers. 'Mit diesem Deutschland ist nicht anzufangen.' [With this Germany nothing can be done].[24]

The family's sense that Hermann had escaped just in time must have been reinforced when on 15 March the police mounted a large scale operation in which the Künstlerkolonie in Laubenheimer Platz was sealed off and fourteen people arrested. Kurt Tucholsky's apartment was searched and the account of the raid in *Schöneberg-Friedenauer Lokal-Anzeiger* states that the search for KPD related material was particularly fruitful in Laubenheimer Straße.[25]

In 1933 there was little hindrance to the free movement of people across the German border into the Netherlands. It was relatively easy for Hermann to arrive as a 'visitor' and stay on as the police made few efforts to make sure that such visitors left the country at the end of their stay. Martha, Liese and Usche joined him shortly

FIG. 10.2. Emanuel Querido, at home, 1928/29.

afterwards in Amsterdam, just four of around 4,000 German-Jews who fled to the Netherlands in 1933.[26] Hermann was only one of many authors who left. In fact by the end of March nearly all of Germany's leading writers had gone. The Nazi press was triumphant and celebrated the departure of the hated *Zivilisationsliteraten*.[27]

Events continued to move fast in Germany. On 1 April the Nazis carried out a nationwide boycott, targeting Jewish businesses and professionals, supposedly in reprisal for false atrocity stories that German Jews, assisted by foreign journalists were circulating about the new government. SA men stood menacingly in front of Jewish-owned department stores and shops, and outside the offices of Jewish doctors and lawyers. The Star of David was daubed in yellow and black across thousands of doors and windows, with accompanying anti-Semitic slogans. A week later, Jews were expelled from the National Academy and from government positions, schools, research institutes and universities.

In the aftermath of these events, Hermann penned a stinging rebuke of the German people, entitled *J'accuse* which was translated into French and English:[28]

> We, the German Jews, and Jews all over the world, reproach the German people that they did not act immediately when Hitler and his followers, ten and more years ago, took recourse to anti-Semitism in its vilest form, and turned it into a party platform in order to win over the musty and blockheaded peasantry, as well as the vapid middle classes to its political purposes...
>
> When they began to chant their slogan, 'Juda verrecke!'[29] in the streets...
>
> When they began — without precedent — to desecrate systematically and in different ways Jewish cemeteries...
>
> When they smashed the windows of the synagogues after they had desecrated them with swastikas...
>
> When bands of hooligans sang in the streets songs like, "Rathenau, die Gott-verfluchte Juden-sau"...
>
> When, with songs like "Wetzt die langen Messer auf dem Bürgersteig, laßt die Messer flutschen in den Judenleib" — they fantasized about future pogroms.
>
> When German courts of justice, newspapers like *Völkischer Beobachter*, that even in its first issue demanded that the Jewish professors should be banished from the universities and at the same time published atrocity tales about rabbis who had practised rapine and secret slaughter houses in the basements of synagogues where pigs were butchered...
>
> When the German "impartial" courts of justice gave these newspapers and the dozens of vile sheets with which the villages were flooded, liberty to libel, so that each edition could launch the dirtiest slanders against the German Jews, against the Jewish population...
>
> What I reproach the Germans with, what *we* reproach the Germans with, is that in those times:
>
> When the term "Government of Jews" was applied to every government, even when it contained not a single Jew of any political creed whatsoever...
>
> When "Jewish treason", "Jewish murder" and a thousand similar expressions desecrated the German language...
>
> When in thousands of meetings paid for by the great landowners, captains of industry and other moneyed people, the most unbelievable libels against German Jews were uttered, against a mere handful of people, one in every

hundred and ten — against these same Jews who had, faithfully, together with those who now shouted, "Juda verrecke!" in their faces, only a few years ago — the stumps of the wounded Jewish soldiers, hardly healed, the earth over the graves of 12,000 Jewish soldiers of the German Army not yet dry — who had given their dearest possessions, their sons, brothers and fathers. These Jewish soldiers fought shoulder to shoulder for the same objectives with the men who now demand ten times a day their death and destruction, who now begrudge them even the air that they breathe, the ground that they live upon, the fatherland for which they had lived, striven and shed their blood — who carry in their processions bundles of rags representing Jews, the noose around the neck, dangling from the gallows, and, if this were not enough, solemnly burn them...

What I reproach the Germans with, and what we, Jews, *must* reproach them with, is not so much this blackguardly agitation against the Jews, with which demagogues of the worst sort play upon the instincts of the rabble — not simply the hateful purpose of sowing the wind so that the storm may be reaped...

But our severest reproach against the sixty million fellow Germans who did not take part in that agitation and were not caught, befuddled and robbed of their judgement by the same, is that they did not cry out with sixty million voices:

"We do not suffer in our country such a crime against civilisation! To a man we denounce this campaign of hate! We denounce these forgers of lies! We declare that anti-Semitism in whichever form, is not worthy of Germany! And we are ashamed that it leads to such revolting excesses! We declare that our fellow Jewish countryman who for almost twenty centuries has resided in this land, has done his duty to the state as well as anyone, and therefore enjoys the same rights as we do, and should be protected against slander and against discrimination in the state — and we declare that we should protect him with the complete power of the machinery of the state against vilification and against the incitement of the base instincts of the rabble by those without conscience, the architects of Germany's grave."

These are the words, this is the clear pronouncement that we, Jews, had expected from the better portion of the German people: that calls itself the people of poets and thinkers, and cannot find words enough to praise itself as the highest civilized nation of the present time.

Where were these German voices against this defamation of civilisation known as anti-Semitism heard? Where are they heard today?

Nowhere. [...]

They should have publicly declared:

This hatred of the Jews is not justified in present day Germany. It emanates from the weakness, from the cowardice, from the hankering for a counterweight to the feelings of inferiority, ever-present in Germany. These feelings accentuated by the lost war — which could not be spun into a victory — because it focused the hatred and the contempt of the whole world on the German people — have attained enormous proportions, and are now to be effaced at any price. Therefore the war is said to have been the work of, not the Germans, but of the Jews; and peace was likewise of their making. And the revolution, evaporated as it is, is likewise, for the sake of this effacement, ascribed to the Jews who used it to stab the victorious German heroes in the back. In this way, one Jew has been made consistently responsible for the fate of 110 fellow Germans.

They should have publicly declared —

The German Jews do not, as you claim, enjoy some kind of hospitality on German soil. No more are they a foreign tribe. For as they are settled on this soil for nearly two thousand years, this soil has become their fatherland, at least so long as one may call a country, with which one's thinking and feeling has grown together, one's fatherland. [...]

They should have publicly declared —

Jewry in Germany is numerically insignificant and is diminishing. Less than one per cent of the population [...] so that even if the Jew were of a different nature, any harmful influence of whatever kind on the masses of the people would be impossible.[30] For many generations — for German history is a summary of battles — the Jews have given their blood for their country and sacrificed their lives for Germany. This simple fact ought to be enough to denounce anti-Semitism as repellent ingratitude on the part of German citizens against those whose homes harbour 12,000 shrouded portraits of fathers and brothers.

They should have publicly declared —

A great many German Jews, known all over the world simply as Germans, have contributed names of universal renown to Germany's cultural growth. Jews they were who have built up the largest undertakings, such as the electrical industries and the biggest shipping companies. Germany owes the manufacturing of nitrogen (alas, also that of poisonous gases) and chemical dyes, which have made Germany wealthy, to Jews. That syphilis is no longer one of the world's scourges, and can be recognized and cured is due to the discoveries of German Jews. The greatest German painter, the most important German architect, the only names known abroad, are again those of German Jews.[31] [...]

Nearly all the names of German authors, famous all over the world, for the last twenty or thirty years, are of Jewish origin. They are appreciated abroad for what they are, viz. German artists. How little they differ from them is proved by the fact that German Jews have, by their enthusiastic advocacy of the works of Christian Germans, from Goethe and Schopenhauer, to Hauptmann and Thomas Mann, fostered the recognition of these writers. [...]

Wise men, like Bismarck, have therefore recognized the mission of the German Jews to be among the non-Jewish Germany, like the glass of champagne at the meal.[32]

They should have publicly declared —

We recognize in the insignificant number of Jews [...] a useful and respectable component of the German people, and declare that this unjustifiable, senseless and furious incitement, this tactic to divert attention from the real questions of the present times, which has been engineered against them as German fellow citizens and countrymen is as much unfounded as an offence against civilisation, and we brand it as a disgrace to the people of Germany.

The Germans, even the better and the best of them, instead of speaking in this way, have quietly tolerated this campaign of anti-Semitism in which the vilest methods were deployed, even if they did not approve of it — tolerated it as if they had no concern with it, and therefore had no reason to be ashamed of it. Where are the German protests against this disgrace to civilisation? Where today are the men who dare to disclaim it?

It is therefore that we denounce the Germans.

We, German Jews, and with us Jews all over the world, and we are convinced that we have all civilized nations with us in this — we do not crave, but demand from the German government, whatever kind it may happen to be, that the German Jew should retain his rights without detriment.

That all defamation to which the present government has incited the people, shall end.

That all danger to property, profession, body and life shall be averted; and that those who do not submit to this shall be treated as unmercifully as the present government now acts where it should not.

That the Jews within the realm of Germany shall be guaranteed equal rights and equal opportunities as are assured to the non-Jews, rights and opportunities to which they are constitutionally entitled and which they have acquired by dint of what they have done for Germany in times of peace and war.

We demand that all the Jews who have been banished from scientific institutions, hospitals, schools, universities etc., shall be reinstated in the offices they filled, on account of their skill, their usefulness and not on account of their Jewish origin. Not simply on motives of justice, not simply in their own interest, but in the interests of the progress of science.

There is no German Jew who does not wish that Germany will at last be delivered from the hunger, the unemployment and the desperation of the greatest part of the people.

And there is no German Jew, no matter to which political party he belongs [...] who cares which government will bring this about, as long as it does so. [...]

Neither are there any German Jews at home or abroad who believe in atrocity tales of children's hands being chopped off and eyes being put out or who invent and spread such tales — of the kind as, for instance, Herr Streicher's invents and relates in *Der Stürmer*, tales about Jews with long beards and longer knives who slaughter Christian girls in dark woods, or — like those of *Völkischer Beobachter* — of butchers' wives violated by rabbis. [...]

Suffice it is, that even today, a minister, whose office is not based upon the confidence of the people but at any rate on that of a president who has recently been elected by Jews and social democrats, and whose duty it is to uphold the rights of all citizens [...] broadcasts his reply to a request for protection, saying that his police do not exist for the protection of Jewish criminals, traitors and deceivers, thereby turning them into outlaws.

Suffice it is, that after fourteen years of vituperation for the amusement of the rabble and for giving employment to 60,000 SA men, a trial boycott of Jewish businesses is being enacted. [...]

We, German Jews, and with us Jews all over the world, yea, even civilized humanity as a whole, do not implore, but demand, in the name of our rights, in the name of our blood shed for the fatherland, in the name of what we have done for Germany, in the name of our twenty centuries old union with the German fatherland. And therewith we only do what every decent German ought to have done ten years ago. We demand —

That an end shall be made to anti-Semitism, of this disgrace to civilisation which has assumed the most despicable form.

An end to this!

That the government itself put a stop to it, even if it did sow the wind, in order to reap the storm.

As Jews we feel insulted, vituperated, hindered, endangered, limited in breathing life's air and in life's sphere. All this we could bear. The history of

Jewry has taught us to bear and overcome such things without impairing our human dignity. But as Germans we are ashamed — and this is worst — as every decent German now ought to be ashamed, ought to have been ashamed from the hour that the earth over the graves of our young Jewish brothers in Flanders, in Russia, on the slopes of the alps, in the Vosges, in the Balkans and in the Sinai, had not yet dried, that the stumps of young Jewish brothers, had not yet healed in their bandages and even then the hydra of blind Jew-hatred had raised its poisonous, horrible head, which ought not only to have been cut off but which should have immediately been burned to the very roots.

Notes to Chapter 10

1. Ben-Dror, 'Recollections 1919–44'.
2. Benjamin Carter Helt, *Burning the Reichstag — An Investigation into the Third Reich's Enduring Mystery* (Oxford: Oxford University Press, 2014), p. 52.
3. Weiss-Sussex, *Metropolitan Chronicles*, p. 18. For the newspaper articles, see GHC; AR 7074; Box 8; Folder 32, LBI.
4. Letter to Hilde dated 13 March 1933, *Unvorhanden und stumm*, p. 19.
5. Nussbaum, 'Georg Hermann Attacks the Special Issue of *Der Jude*', p. 452.
6. Georg Hermann, 'Pro Berlin', 1931. Reprinted in Hermann, *Die Reise nach Massow*, pp. 355–58.
7. Ibid., p. 357.
8. Ibid., pp. 357–58.
9. According to Eva her father was told on this trip, 'it is just as well that De Rivera (Spain's dictatorial prime minister from 1923 until 1930) is dead, otherwise everyone would think you were him!' One of the family's theories about Hermann Borchardt's father was that he was a Spanish soldier.
10. Hermann, 'Warum Goethe?', March 1932, GHC; AR 7074; Box 5; Folder 37; LBI.
11. Fritz Friedlander, 'The Author of Jettchen Gebert: Centenary of Georg Hermann's Birth' (London: Association of Jewish Refugees, October 1971), p. 7.
12. This translation is taken from Burkhard Henke, Susanne Kord and Simon Richter's (eds) *Unwrapping Goethe's Weimar: Essays in Cultural Studies and Local Knowledge* (London: Camden House, 2000), p. 299. The quotation comes from Goethe's 6 March 1779 letter to Charlotte von Stein. It is worth noting, however, that in a postcard to his daughter, Hilde (27 September 1939), Hermann writes that this reference to the starving textile workers in Apolda is the only example he has come across where Goethe utters a word of 'sozialer Tendenz'. *Unvorhanden und stumm*, p. 183.
13. Hermann, 'Warum Goethe'. Goethe made the observation in a letter to Carl F. Zelter dated 16 December, 1829.
14. The German branch of the Poets, Essayists and Novelists Club had been established in 1924.
15. Gronemann, preface to Georg Hermann, *Jettchen Gebert*, pp. xv–xvi. If one agrees with Arthur Miller's characterisation of the purpose of the PEN Club as being 'to apply the universalist tradition of literature to the melting down of those geographical and psychological barriers of nationalism for whose perpetuation humanity has always spent its noblest courage, and its most ferocious savagery' (Arthur Miller, *Collected Essays 1944–2000* (London: Methuen, 2000), p. 251), then Hermann's inclusive stance, albeit naïve, was entirely in keeping with the club's ideals.
16. A copy of Ullstein's letter is accessible online at jmberlin.de.
17. Martin Kitchen, *A History of Modern Germany 1800 to the Present* (Oxford: Wiley-Blackwell, 2012), p. 236.
18. Ben-Dror, 'Recollections 1919–44'.
19. *Unvorhanden und stumm*, p. 266.
20. Mies Blomsma (1905–1940) was a successful book illustrator. There are a number of letters from Mies to Hermann in his archive: GHC; AR 7074; Box 8; Folder 1, LBI.

21. Letter to Hilde, 13 March 1933, *Unvorhanden und stumm*, pp. 19–22. Emanuel Querido, Hermann's Dutch publisher, was a family friend. According to Eva, he and his wife had wanted her to marry their son.

22. Ben-Dror, 'Recollections 1919–44'. Usche dated her father's flight to Amsterdam as taking place on 1 January 1933. However, it is clear from his letter to Hilde that he left in early March. If as Usche remembered it was a Sunday, then the date would have been either 5 or 12 March. The elections mentioned by Usche were those which took place on 5 March 1933. They were marked by widespread intimidation. The NSDAP gained ninety-two seats, polling over seventeen million votes but still lacked an overall majority. Nineteen days later the Reichstag approved the Enabling Act which put an end to the last vestiges of parliamentary rule.

23. Letter to Hilde, 13 March 1933, *Unvorhanden und stumm*, p. 21.

24. Ibid., p. 22.

25. *Schöneberg-Friedenauer Lokal-Anzeiger*, 16 March 1933. See Hermann Ebling, *Friedenau erzählt 1914 bis 1933* (Berlin: Friedenauer Brücke, 2008), pp. 336–37.

26. Bob Moore, 'Jewish Refugees in the Netherlands 1933–40', *Leo Baeck Institute Year Book XXIX*, 1984, 76. Amos Elon states that a total of 50,000 Jews left Germany in 1933 but the basis for this figure is not altogether clear. See Elon, *The Pity of It All*, p. 399. The US Holocaust Memorial Museum gives a figure of 37,000.

27. Other writers who left Germany in or around March 1933 include Theodor Adorno, Hannah Arendt, Bertolt Brecht, Alfred Döblin, Lion Feuchtwanger, Hermann Kesten, Else Lasker-Schüler, Heinrich and Thomas Mann, Erich Maria Remarque, Joseph Roth, Ernst Toller and Arnold Zweig.

28. Georg Hermann, *J'accuse*, 1933, GHC; AR 7074: Box 5, Folder 67, LBI. Only parts of the original German version have been published. Laureen Nussbaum and I have made a number of minor wording changes to the English translation reproduced here.

29. The German verb *verrecken* is generally used for animals only.

30. According to the census of 16 June 1933, the Jewish population of Germany was approximately 505,000 people out of a total population of 67 million, or somewhat less than 0.75 per cent. (US Holocaust Memorial Museum website.)

31. Hermann probably has in mind here Albert Ballin, the general director of the Hamburg-Amerikanische Packetfahrt-Actien-Gesellschaft (HAPAG), one of the world's largest shipping companies; Emil Rathenau, the founder of Allgemeine Elektricitäts-Gesellschaft (AEG); Fritz Haber who received the Nobel Prize in Chemistry in 1918 for his invention of the Haber-Bosch process, a method used in industry to synthesize ammonia from nitrogen gas and hydrogen gas; Paul Ehrlich who developed the first effective medicinal treatment for syphilis; Max Liebermann and Alfred Messel.

32. In an interview in the last year of his life Bismarck suggested that the presence of Jews in Germany added a certain *mousseux*, a champagne like sparkle to an otherwise dull society. See George Huppert, *Comrade Huppert: A Poet in Stalin's World* (Bloomington, IN: Indiana University Press, 2016), p. 40.

PART II

❖

1933–1943

CHAPTER 11

❖

Hilversum

Even before his appointment as Minister for Public Enlightenment and Propaganda on 13 March 1933, Goebbels set about purging the Schutzverband deutscher Schriftsteller, the writers' association which Hermann had co-founded in 1910. Eight members of the old committee were forced out, all communists and pacifists were excluded and the racial background of every member examined. The *Gleichschaltung* of the writers' association was quick and total.[1]

Soon afterwards, Goebbels commissioned the Association of German Librarians to produce a blacklist to be used to cleanse the country's libraries. Wolfgang Herrmann, a librarian who had joined the Nazi Party in 1931, produced a list of 131 authors.[2] They included Bertolt Brecht, Max Brod, Alfred Döblin, Lion Feuchtwanger, Georg Fink, Maxim Gorky, Ernest Hemingway, Erich Kästner, Gina Kaus, Alfred Kerr, Eva Leidmann, Emil Ludwig, Heinrich Mann, Robert Neumann, Erich Maria Remarque, Arthur Schnitzler, Anna Seghers, Upton Sinclair, Ernst Toller, Kurt Tucholsky, Jakob Wassermann, Arnold Zweig and Stefan Zweig. Hermann was on the list, sandwiched between Ernest Hemingway and Leo Hirsch, with three of his novels highlighted: *Kubinke, Die Nacht des Doktor Herzfeld* and *Schnee*.

This list-making was the precursor for the book-burning ceremonies which took place across German university towns on 10 May 1933. Hermann's books, along with those of other writers on the list were doused in paraffin and set aflame. The greatest number of books were burned in Berlin — 10,000 from the Hirschfeld Institute alone — but all of the events followed a similar pattern and they took place in Bonn, Braunschweig, Breslau, Cologne, Darmstadt, Dresden, Erlangen, Frankfurt, Giessen, Göttingen, Greifswald, Halle-Wittenberg, Hamburg, Hanover, Münden, Kaiserslautern, Karlsruhe, Kiel, Königsberg, Mannheim, Marburg, Munich, Münster, Nuremberg, Rostock, Worms and Würzburg. For good measure, there were two book burnings in Heidelberg's University Square — the first eleven days after my mother had celebrated her second birthday in nearby Ziegelhausen — and then another on 17 June at which von Ribbentrop spoke.[3] The burning was preceded by a torchlight procession through the town in which Nazi Stormtroopers and Stahlhelm members were supported by the students' duelling corps.

In the aftermath of these events, Joseph Roth wrote,

> Very few observers anywhere in the world seem to have understood what the Third Reich's burning of books, the expulsion of Jewish writers, and all

its other crazy assaults on the intellect actually mean. The technical apotheosis of the barbarians, the terrible march of the mechanized orangutans, armed with hand grenades, poison gas, ammonia, and nitro-glycerine, with gas masks and airplanes, the return of the spiritual (if not the actual) descendants of the Cimbri and Teutoni — all this means far more than the threatened and terrorized world seems to realize: it must be understood. Let me say it loud and clear: the European mind is capitulating. It is capitulating out of weakness, out of sloth, out of apathy, out of lack of imagination (it will be the task of some future generation to establish the reasons for this disgraceful capitulation).

Now, as the smoke of our burned books rises into the sky, we German writers of Jewish descent must acknowledge above all that we have been defeated. Let us, who were fighting on the front line, under the banner of the European mind, let us fulfil the noblest duty of the defeated warrior: let us concede our defeat. Yes, we have been beaten.[4]

In these first months of exile, Hermann was far from feeling himself defeated. In an unpublished essay 'Wiedersehen mit Holland' [Reunion with Holland] written during this period, he sounds upbeat, writing of his positive impressions of his new home. The people, if not elegant in their attire, are always well-dressed, all available land has been put to productive use, there is a calm atmosphere and unlike in Germany it's understood that the state exists for the benefit of the individual not the individual for the state.[5]

Despite Ullstein's rejection of the synopsis for *Rosenemil*, Hermann appears initially to have remained confident that they would continue to print his works and that Querido would follow suit with Dutch translations. But he was to be disappointed in these expectations. Ullstein had been 'Aryanized' and was not willing to publish Hermann's manuscripts of the last two novels in the *Die Kette* series.[6] Querido had not published translations of either *Grenadier Wordelmann* or *November achtzehn* and was not interested in producing translations of the new novels. There was, however, soon some better news. Not long after arriving in the Netherlands, Hermann spent an evening at the Amsterdam home of his friend, the Dutch novelist, Siegfried van Praag. A call from there was sufficient to get a representative from the Allert de Lange publishing house to come around and that same evening it committed to publishing in the Netherlands some of Hermann's novels in their original German.[7]

In his memoirs, the publisher Fritz Landshoff credits Hermann with inspiring both Querido and Gérard de Lange to publish the new works of banned German writers more generally. He indicates that it was Hermann who came up with the idea:

Neben Emanuel Querido zeigte auch der niederländische Verleger Gérard de Lange Interesse, verbotene deutsche Literatur herauszugeben, und offenbar waren beide von Georg Hermann (Georg Borchardt) angeregt worden. [...] Obgleich er, ein grundgütiger, äußerst gemütlicher Herr, keinerlei Aufhebens davon machte, halte ich es für erwiesen, daß er den beiden Verlegern den ersten Anstoß gegeben hat.

[In addition to Emanuel Querido, the Dutch publisher Gérard de Lange showed interest in publishing banned German literature, and apparently both were inspired by Georg Hermann (Georg Borchardt). [...] Although he, a very

FIG. 11.1. Mies Blomsma's drawing of Joseph Roth, Paris, 1938.
(Literatuurmuseum, Den Haag). Roth has written at the bottom:
'That's really me; nasty, soused, but clever.'

good natured gentleman, made no fuss about it, I consider it proven that it was
Hermann who gave the two publishers the initial prompt.][8]

Around this time Hermann published an essay in German in the Dutch literary
journal, *De Stem* [The Voice].[9] 'Die Bilanz des Vorkriegsmenschen' explores a
familiar Hermann theme: the contrast between pre- and post-war man, his values
and his way of life. It reflects the same sense of frustration apparent in Joseph Roth's
essay at the lack of response outside of Germany to the treatment of the Jews and
the triumph of barbarianism over culture.

Hermann reiterates that for the pre-war man, a belief in the development of
mankind, although not a religion as such, was associated with a similar kind of
intensity and devotion, and gave meaning to his life. He observed ethical norms of
behaviour, seeking to be a respectable citizen and to be perceived as a gentleman.
Above all, pre-war man believed in the sanctity and inviolability of life. Indeed,
it would have been quite beyond his comprehension that this fundamental belief
should cease to be upheld; that the poor instead of being helped should be vilified
and that art and science should become politicized. War, rather than being
glorified, was regarded as a relic from the past. Pacifism was not seen as something
reprehensible. It has only been since 1914, Hermann contends, that the Boeotians
have overcome the Athenians; that the barbarians have triumphed, burning books,
perverting science and effecting a victory of primitivism over an urban culture that
had been developing for the past two thousand years.

The war brought about a new type of hatred. Previously, the king had never
hated his subjects or the state its citizens but now there was a new perverted
hatred from top to bottom, and its object was the tiny Jewish minority. It became
impossible to obtain justice in the courts. All of the aspirations that pre-war man
had held for the next generation and what it might achieve were shattered by
the war. The family which had been the cornerstone of the pre-war man's world
became increasingly dysfunctional. There was a loss of faith in high culture, sexual
mores changed and love was devalued. The individual became nothing and political
discourse polarized.

Hermann writes that before the war the Jew saw himself from 1 to 10 as a
Mensch, a citizen of the world, from 11 to 20 as a child of his native Germany, its
language and landscape, and only 21st as a Jew. But this changed in the face of the
new virulent form of anti-Semitism in Germany which has now become a state-
driven pogrom impacting on Jews' ability to participate in the economy, stopping
them from taking part in the sciences and medicine, the administration of justice,
literature and education, as well as political life. What he objects to most, Hermann
writes, is not how Hitler and his backers have exploited historic anti-Semitism for
their own political ends but the abject way in which the German people have gone
along with it. Here he includes verbatim the first section of his *J'accuse* essay on the
Nazi persecution of Jews in Germany over the preceding ten years and the lack of
German voices raised against it.[10]

Hermann concludes the essay on a personal note. His banknotes are now
obsolete, his coinage withdrawn from circulation and his goods publicly burned in

the market. His cherished gold bars of humanity — respect for the lives of others and trust in the truth — have vanished without trace. Everything has gone up in smoke. Quoting Ibsen, he writes, 'What you see tonight is a deposed king standing amid the ashes of his burnt-out palace.'[11]

But at least Hermann was reunited with his art collection. By late August he was able to tell Hilde that now all of his good things were in the house in Laren and appeared to even better effect than they had done in the Grunewald villa.[12] That summer he went on a holiday with Mies Blomsma to Lugano. He decided that Usche (now fourteen) should join them. In her recollections, she recalls how her father and Mies would go on amorous walks together, and she would tag along, some steps behind.

> Peps simply had no idea of what was appropriate for me as a child, and really was very egocentric, but he also wanted to give me a good education, and felt that I should see something of the world. However, when they were in museums I just wanted to sit down and "watch the world go by" and I said that I would not budge from where I was. Peps was personally offended by this. He simply had no idea of the things that a child liked to do.[13]

Hermann's personal life continued to be complicated. He and Mies separated that autumn and it appears that Hermann formed a new relationship with Bertel Gold-schmidt, the Berlin friend who had brought Usche to Amsterdam.[14]

Meantime, back in Germany on 13 October, Eva and Siegfried represented Hermann in a case brought by the government which was seeking 'Pfändung auf Grund eines Arrestes' [seizure on the basis of an arrest] of the Neckargemünd house.[15] At the end of January 1934 Siegfried wrote to his father-in-law, in part to update him on the position regarding the enforced sale of the house but more, it seems, to explain why he, Eva and little Beate were still in Germany rather than overseas:

> Lieber Peps! Von der plötzlichen Änderung unserer Pläne hast Du ja schon gehört. Wir wollen Dir heute einiges von den Gründen schreiben. Die verschiedenen Auskünfte, die wir in Bezug auf den Labor-Plan erhielten, waren alle sehr reserviert und wir hatten den Eindruck, dass wir auf besondere Unterstützung kaum zu rechnen hätten. [...] Außerdem hätte ich meinen Ruhegehalt nach längerem Aufenthalt im Ausland vielleicht entzogen bekommen, bei einem Kollegen, der nach Palästina ging war dies jedenfalls so, und wir hätten dann gar nichts mehr gehabt. [...] Überhaupt ist es sehr enttäuschend wie wenig auf die Hilfe der Judenschaft zu rechnen ist. Man ist absolut auf sich angewiesen.

> [Dear Peps! About the sudden change of our plans you will have already heard. I wanted to let you know some of the reasons. It has been very hard to get adequate information about the arrangements regarding the lab and we had the impression that we could not count on any special financial support. [...] Besides, there was also a risk that my pension would be revoked due to a lengthy stay abroad and then we would be left with nothing. This has happened to a colleague who went to Palestine. [...] In general, it is very disappointing how little help one can expect from one's fellow Jews. One is wholly reliant upon oneself.][16]

Siegfried explains that he is still looking at options abroad and in the last ten days has learned of an opportunity to teach chemistry in Lima. For these reasons he believes it is better to wait in Germany rather than leaving now for Holland without anything being settled and then to have to move again. He explains that in mid-February he will be going to Berlin to find out about potential opportunities there. Regarding the Neckargemünd house, there is no particular news — the broker says that the sale will be arranged in the spring. Siegfried adds that he is trying to sort out how to get Hermann's books to him in a way that won't be too expensive. No easy task, one imagines.

A letter Hermann wrote to Hilde the following month suggests that he remained unconvinced about Eva and Siegfried's decision to stay in Ziegelhausen. He does not understand why they do not go to Berlin. What they are doing now, he writes, makes no sense. He still has friends in Berlin who would be able to help them.[17] About his own affairs he tells Hilde that although he has worked for a long time as a journalist in Germany, in the Netherlands it is not something he can pursue, partly for lack of opportunities but also because it doesn't pay well. So instead, he is concentrating on novels and the possibility of reprints and translations. Usche, he informs Hilde, is now receiving some regular money from Lotte's relatives in Posen which will help with her education.

In the same letter, Hermann was able to update Hilde on the positive progress he had made in finding publishers for the final two novels in *Die Kette*. Both had been in manuscript for some time, a reflection of the difficulties besetting writers like Hermann in getting their work published in Germany. Hermann's *Ruths schwere Stunde* (Ruth's Difficult Hour) became the first book to be published by Allert de Lange's new German language branch.[18] Following on from *November achtzehn*, the novel finds Ruth and Fritz Eisner in Munich, some months after their departure from Berlin. Ruth is now heavily pregnant. Eisner's first wife will still not agree to a divorce and so the couple are continuing to cohabitate. They do not have their own apartment and are removed from their Berlin circle of friends. Ruth is estranged from her mother. It feels as if everything is against them in Munich. Not only is Eisner a Jew, but he is also a writer which immediately makes him a suspect figure. Moreover, he is 'living in sin' with a woman twenty-five years his junior who is carrying his child. Still worse, he's a Prussian!

Inevitably, the difficult circumstances put a strain on Eisner and Ruth's relationship. After his failed marriage to Ännchen, Eisner is full of hope that in Ruth he has found an equal partner, someone who has work of her own, who shares his intellectual interests and is politically committed. He feels that they are physically compatible in a way that he and Ännchen were not. They live life at the same tempo. Eisner loves to feel Ruth next to him, to feel the closeness of her breath and her smile. But typically the egocentric Eisner thinks of Ruth more in terms of how she augments himself rather than as a person in her own right.[19] He projects onto Ruth his notions of strong redemptive femininity which, after the male stupidity of the war, he believes offers fresh hope. The new women, Eisner maintains, will be the leaders of tomorrow. But Ruth is preoccupied with her difficult pregnancy and has little time to contemplate the grandiose goals that Eisner is envisaging for womankind in the new republic. In her more down-to-earth way, she suspects that these great plans will not amount to anything.

Eisner is cocooned in his own reveries about what has become of his life and continues to be inattentive to Ruth's needs. She again attempts suicide, soon after giving birth to Maud; this time by taking an overdose of tablets. Ruth says bitterly that Eisner would be happy to be rid of her. The fraught nature of their relationship is exacerbated by the fact that the baby (Maud) is taken away and placed in a children's home because of the still unresolved divorce proceedings. In the midst of all this turmoil, Eisner's refuge is his desk. It continues to be at the core of his existence. He delights in being a writer and finds comfort in the trappings of his bourgeois life, like the purple aster in his button-hole, which give him a sense of equilibrium. But things work out for Eisner and Ruth. Unexpectedly, Ännchen agrees to a divorce and they are able to get married. Maud is retrieved from the foundling hospital and Ruth's mother forgives her daughter.

As well as developing the troubled relationship between Ruth and Eisner and showing how their initial passion fades, the novel also portrays the changing times in which their lives are playing out. The rise in anti-Semitism and its increasingly intimidating nature is a key theme in the novel. Paul Gumpert and Wilhelm Klein discuss the anti-Semitic bullying which has become part of everyday life. The urinals are covered in anti-Semitic graffiti, daubed with skulls and slogans like 'Tod den Juden' [Death to the Jews]. Gumpert tells Klein,

> Mein Nachbar, mit dem ich tausend Jahr und länger zusammengelebt habe, will mich plötzlich totschlagen, weil ich für ihn der Jude bin, und weil er behauptet, daß ich kein Deutscher für ihn bin. Der Pole und der Franzose will mich totschlagen, weil ich ein Deutscher für ihn bin. Der Russe will mich totschlagen, weil er mich für einen hoffnungslosen Bourgeois hält, für eine blutsaugende Kapitalsbestie. Und alle haben sich gegen mich verschworen. Wissen Sie, es ist kein reines Vergnügen, zwischen Leuten dieser Art leben zu müssen?

> [My neighbour with whom I have lived a thousand years suddenly wants to kill me because he sees me as a Jew and claims that I cannot be a German. The Poles and the French want to kill me because they regard me as a German. The Russians want to kill me because they see me as an irremediable bourgeois capitalist. I feel as if everyone has conspired against me. Tell me, where's the pleasure in living among people of this kind?][20]

It is recognized that anti-Semitism poses a real threat and cannot be dismissed as the 'socialism of fools'. By chance, Eisner witnesses an armed attack on the Jewish banker, Landshut. The novel highlights the connivance of the police with the perpetrators of such acts. As a result of the rising tide of anti-Semitism, the characters in the novel start to become more conscious of their Jewishness. Eisner, who previously has always seen himself as a citizen of the world, suddenly finds himself increasingly in discussions about the Jewish question and racial origins. Both Ruth and Eisner emphasize their connection and sense of loyalty to the rich history of the Jews, traced back over the centuries.

As with the three previous books in the series, a feature of *Ruths schwere Stunde* is the way that it celebrates art and culture in the broadest sense. Music, the visual arts and literature are discussed endlessly. For Eisner, literature is ultimately what really matters and his conversation and reflections are sprinkled with literary references. When he visits Ruth in the hospital after she has given birth to Maud and is suffering the trauma of being separated from her baby, he brings with him armfuls of books by writers killed in the war. As ever, Eisner is self-absorbed and detached, happier wool-gathering than confronting difficult truths. He notes that in the year he has been living with Ruth, aside from a few articles, he has produced nothing in the way of new works; nothing at all. But by the end of the novel, his muse has returned and he is sat at his beloved desk, writing away for hour after hour. Ruth is calling him to come to bed but he keeps on writing into the night. It appears that Eisner is working on *Schnee* as he describes to Ruth its protagonist's death in the freezing snow. Ruth is pleased that he is writing again but wryly observes 'Na endlich mal 'was anderes! Auf die Todesart warst du bisher in deinen Romanen noch nicht verfallen.' [Finally something different! That's a mode of death, you've not yet had in your novels].[21]

Eine Zeit stirbt [The Death of an Epoch] the final volume of the pentalogy was actually published before *Ruths schwere Stunde* by the Jüdische Buch-Vereinigung in Berlin.[22] It was the last of Hermann's novels to be published in Germany and the first book to be published by the recently established Jewish Book Association.

Back in May 1933 Julius Bab had written to Hermann to explain his involvement with the organisation of a Kulturbund deutscher Juden (Cultural Association of German Jews) and to invite Hermann to be on its honorary committee.[23] Max Liebermann, Ernst Cassirer, Jakob Wassermann, Max Reinhardt and Franz Oppenheimer were also to be on the committee. Hermann wrote back to accept and suggested the Kulturbund set up a book association. At the time, Bab was not impressed by the idea:

> Was Ihre Frage nach der Buchgemeinschaft betrifft, so finde ich sie (verzeihen Sie das harte Wort) einfach naiv. Natürlich hat man auch dort gleichgeschaltet. Ich bin nicht mehr tätig und "Goethes Leben in seinen Briefen" darf nicht mehr vertrieben werden, weil so einer mit ganz falscher Abstammung wie ich, sie herausgegeben hat. Daß man dort also das Buch eines so durchaus unarischen Mannes wie Sie verlegen wird ist eine Idee, auf die man wirklich bloß in Holland kommen kann.

> [Regarding your question concerning a book association, I find it (please excuse the harsh word) naïve. Naturally *Gleichschaltung* has been enforced in that field, too. I am out of work, and my *Goethe's Life in his Letters* may not be sold anymore because someone like me with this completely wrong origin edited it. To believe that they will publish a book here by a thoroughly "Un-Aryan" person like you is an idea that one can probably only come up with in Holland.][24]

But something must have caused a change of heart because five months later he informed Hermann that a book association for German Jews was now going to be established. Bab suggested that it should be launched with one of Hermann's novels. The following month the formation of the Buchgesellschaft der Deutschen Juden (German Jewish Book Association) was announced in the Cultural League's monthly journal. For one Mark a month, members were eligible to receive four books a year, together with a list of titles that 'due to their particular interest for Jews are no longer available in public bookshops.' The association was launched in 1934 with *Eine Zeit stirbt*.[25] Although he was now on the books of Allert de Lange, Hermann did not believe that handing over the imprint rights to the Jüdische Buch-Vereinigung breached his contract with his Dutch publisher and does not appear to have consulted them. Not surprisingly, Allert de Lange was very annoyed when it learned what had happened and relations between Hermann and the publishing house quickly soured.[26]

Ironically, after all of this trouble, Leo Hirsch in his review for the *Central-Verein-Zeitung* queried the choice of *Eine Zeit stirbt* as the first publication of the newly founded association. He did not regard it as a contemporary Jewish novel complaining, 'vom jüdischen Glauben kommt nicht ein Wort darin vor.' [there is not a mention of the Jewish faith].[27] An anonymous review in the previous edition of the paper similarly commented that 'Georg Hermann behandelt in diesem Roman nicht eigentlich jüdische Probleme ...' [Georg Hermann does not really deal with Jewish problems in this novel].[28] Alec Randall in a review of the novel for the *TLS*, however, acknowledged that 'there are political implications here which would presumably make this novel impossible in Germany today, but individual problems such as those here studied will hardly cease to furnish material for novelists.'[29]

Eine Zeit stirbt picks up Eisner's story four years after the end of *Ruths schwere Stunde*. It is 1923, the peak of the inflation period, and Eisner is living with Ruth and their child, Maud, in the countryside outside of Heidelberg. The traumatic period of the break-up of Eisner's first marriage, the lengthy struggle for a divorce and Ruth's two suicide attempts are behind them but the economic crisis has shaken Germany's social fabric. Some of Eisner's neighbours, especially those who are retired, have barely enough money for life's essentials. Eisner is insulated from the worst of the effects of the hyperinflation because he is writing regular articles for a Danish newspaper and being paid in dollars. He manages to maintain his former wife, Ännchen and their daughters, as well as keeping his new family afloat.

Hermann's affection for the Neckar Valley shines through in the novel in his descriptions of the landscape. He characterizes it is an area where time seems to stand still and there are long monologues in which Hermann expresses his affection for the valley's natural charms. But Ruth does not share Eisner's enthusiasm for country life. She finds the people provincial and uninspiring and worries that it is not a stimulating environment for little Maud. As in the previous novels, it is only belatedly that Eisner recognizes her unhappiness and reluctantly agrees to return to Berlin, as she desires and so that she can resume her career. He would have preferred to remain in Heidelberg, to stay in one place with his collection, and regrets being on the move again. For the last ten years he feels that he has been trundling backwards and forwards like a parcel that never finds its addressee.

Back in Berlin, Eisner quickly makes contact with old friends but he is shocked by how much the city has changed since 1918. The polarisation between the rich and the poor is highlighted in the great wealth that the businessman Dr Groß has accumulated. Eisner knew of him thirty years ago when he was an up and coming young man. Now he is rich and powerful and while Eisner admires his luxurious villa and wonderful collections, he wonders at the contrast with the ruined impoverished lives of so many others. For several years, Dr Groß has been living with Lu, Dr Spanier's attractive and witty wife.

While Dr Groß's fortunes have risen, those of Eisner's long-standing friend Paul Gumpert have tumbled. Once very wealthy, Gumpert's textile business is now on the brink of bankruptcy and he is compelled to sell-off many pieces from his considerable art collection, including his Tiepolos. Gumpert is also separated from his wife and lives with the much younger actress, Joli, but has no plans to get a divorce.

Eisner, Gumpert, Spanier and Groß are all collectors but it is their appreciation of art and literature rather than the act of ownership which is fundamental to their lives. German and European arts and letters more generally is their culture and they, and the other characters in the novel, have a shared devotion to it. Dehmel, Rilke and Fontane are objects of worship. Gumpert is a Heine devotee; Ruth and Eisner share a deep appreciation for Goethe's poetry. This ardour for literature is not something that embellishes their lives, nor a way of showing their educated bourgeois credentials. It is more fundamental than that. But this cultural edifice, this devotion to *Bildung* which once seemed impregnable is increasingly emblematic of a time that has passed. Hermann shows that 'it is not only the currency that has lost its value; the ideals and the raison d'être of writers like Fritz Eisner and many Jews of his generation have also been devalued.'[30] The war, its aftermath and the economic crisis have effected changes which these *Bildungsbürger* have been unable to surmount. Gumpert's suicide note reveals that he has been driven to take his own life by an overwhelming sense of displacement. He is not afraid of being poor but he feels that he simply cannot go on living in the present day godless world of war, hatred, corruption and insanity. It is a world which has inverted all the values he holds most precious and smashed them to smithereens.

The novel ends with Ruth's death. Her earlier suicide attempts, unlike those of her mother and older sister, may have been foiled but, like Lotte's, her life is still destined to end prematurely; the victim of haemorrhaging caused by an incurable kidney disease. Eisner's daughter, Hänse, tells him he must be thankful for the seven years that he had with Ruth and try not to be unhappy but Eisner responds that it is like telling the River Neckar it should not flow. He recalls with Fränze, his oldest daughter, his first night with Ruth. He was the first man she had ever slept with. Their love began with blood and through blood they have waded since — Maud's bloody birth — and now in a sea of blood our love is lost, he tells her. Ruth is likened to a shining star on the horizon, destined to never reach her zenith. Eisner says, ' wie lange wird es dauern [...] dann wird sie eben nur noch ein Märchen sein: es war einmal eine schöne junge kluge Frau.' [how long will it take [...] before it is just a fairy tale: once upon a time there was a beautiful and clever young woman].[31]

The scientific Fränze likens Ruth to an intermediary between a time that is yet to come and a time that is dying, who like all transitional forms, was unable to endure.[32] At the novel's conclusion Eisner's one hope is that Fränze and his other daughters will be able to cope better than his own generation because they are not encumbered with the memories and aspirations of an enlightened bourgeoisie, whose time has gone forever.[33]

This sense that it is not just Ruth's passing but the passing of an era, and that both her true self and her world will be forgotten, lies at the heart of the last two volumes of *Die Kette*. In his preface to *Ruths schwere Stunde* Hermann writes that while it is true that in one form or another, all novels begin with 'once upon a time' there is no such similarity in how they conclude. There are stories which lead nowhere. They just evaporate like gas, leaving no trace. They have no lasting presence and no future. Like the steep steps leading to a Buddhist temple in the mountains of Japan, there are many stages and the arduous climb takes one higher and higher but at the summit there is no building, just the blue sky stretching on and on.

But perhaps, Hermann writes, continuing with his allegory, there is an old metal mirror at the summit, kept in a plain lacquered shrine. When you look into it the reflection you see of yourself is so perfect that you hardly know what is you and what is the reflection. Reality and image flow into one another. And that is all you find in this last windswept and isolated outpost — no present, no memory, no more laughter, and what's worse, no tears. Once the mirror is restored to its shrine, so your picture within it will be erased; lost to the eye, like wispy clouds in the blue sky which drift for a moment before being caught in a shaft of sunlight and then disperse into a rainbow of iridescent fragments.[34]

The novels in *The Chain* are evidently semi-autobiographic and there are close parallels between Fritz Eisner's story and Hermann's own. Hermann, however, stresses in the preface to *Eine Zeit stirbt* that although the characters who feature in the novels may seem familiar, they are no more real than those figures who people our dreams. He acknowledges that there is perhaps only one Fritz Eisner but he is also in every one of us. There are hundreds of Lus, Doctor Spaniers, Ännchens and Hannchens, among us, Paul Gumperts, Jolis and Ruths. And yet their lives and the period covered by the novels, Hermann writes, will in ten or twenty years be quite forgotten. There is something in him that rebels against the thought that no more should survive of this world which he has experienced than the delicate imprint of a blade of grass. It was for the same reasons, Hermann writes, that he once asked himself whether it was right that his grandparents' generation should suffer the injustice of sinking into nothingness and which led him in *Jettchen Gebert* to try to capture something of their times.[35] Already in 1934, Hermann realized that the world he had depicted in *Die Kette* from 1899 to 1923 was as much a period piece as his portrayal of Biedermeier Berlin.

In August 1934 Hilde married. Her Danish husband, Henning Aschenberg, was gay and the marriage was purely to enable Hilde to acquire Danish nationality.[36] Hermann wrote from Laren to give Hilde his best wishes (she did not let on about the purely transactional nature of the marriage) and to make suggestions about some of the things still in the house in Neckargemünd that she could make use of in her new apartment. In an interesting aside at the end of the letter — possibly a response to Hilde intimating that she was considering becoming a writer — Hermann observes 'Schreiben ist nur eine Sache des *sang froid* und der Entschlußkraft' [Writing is just a matter of *sang froid* and determination].[37]

Increasingly, Hermann needed to draw upon his reserves of both qualities. In October he moved from Laren to a quiet residential area on the edge of nearby Hilversum (Siriusstraat 59). The new apartment was comfortable and well-equipped he told Hilde, and had a princely five rooms.[38] The rent was only forty guilders per month. There were electric light fixtures, carpets and even a Louis XVI mirror, all of which Hermann could take over from the former tenants. Moreover, as it was closer to her school, Usche was now able to come home for lunch. But despite their new accommodation, Hermann tells Hilde that he is not particularly happy in Holland. There are no opportunities with the newspapers and there is a general lack of willingness to help emigrants. The people are very friendly when you are a visitor but look less kindly on those forced to live amongst them permanently.

Eight days after Hermann's letter to Hilde, the forced sale of the house in Neckargemünd took place. It was acquired by a Mannheim estate agent for 9,500 Mark (about a quarter of the cost of the house when Hermann bought it in 1919). Hermann's proceeds from the sale were to be 6,000 Mark but it is unclear whether this money which was paid by the purchasers into a Neckargemünd savings bank was ever passed on to him.[39] Aside from the financial aspects of the sale and the intimidating circumstances surrounding it, the loss of the house which had been a cornerstone of the family's life for twenty years, must have had a symbolic dimension for Hermann. His affection for his old home in the Neckar Valley comes across in a description in *Ruths schwere Stunde* of Fritz Eisner returning to it on a sunny July day after a period of absence.[40] He paints a picture of the forested mountains clearly delineated against the blue sky, the expansive valley through which the beautiful grey-green River Neckar, tinged with the red and yellow loam of the earth, flows so fast that the small boats upon it skitter and swirl. And there is the house. The time has come when it needs re-decorating. The outside walls need re-plastering and painting; the woodwork should be renewed and the garden awaits the shears of the gardener. Yet the trees are so heavy with fruit that they need supporting. Eisner enters the house, goes through the musty, half-dark rooms and opens up the shutters.

Notes to Chapter 11

1. J. M. Ritchie, 'The Nazi Book-Burning', *MLR*, vol. 83, no. 3 (July 1988), 634.
2. Leonidas E. Hill, 'The Nazi Attack on "Un-German" Literature 1933–1945', in *The Holocaust and the Book: Destruction and Preservation*, ed. by Jonathan Rose (Amherst, MA: University of Massachusetts Press, 2001), p. 12.
3. Ritchie, 'The Nazi Book-Burning', p. 640.
4. Joseph Roth, 'The Auto-da-Fé of the Mind'. Roth's essay was first published in the Paris bi-monthly journal *Cahiers Juifs* in September 1933. This English translation is by Michael Hofmann. The essay is included in Roth's *What I Saw* (London: Norton, 2004), pp. 207–17. Roth states that the Jews are the 'only legitimate German representatives' of European culture

and in a long discourse about the contribution made by Jews to German literature, he describes Hermann (p. 213) as a 'plain and truthful novelist of the petit bourgeoisie'.

5. Nussbaum, 'Verliebt in Holland', p. 183.

6. Nussbaum, 'Georg Hermann Attacks the Special Issue of *Der Jude*', p. 452.

7. van Liere, *Georg Hermann: Materialien*, pp. 49–50.

8. Fritz H. Landshoff, *Amsterdam, Keizersgracht 333. Querido Verlag — Erinnerungen eines Verlegers. Mit Briefen und Dokumenten* (Berlin: Aufbau-Verlag, 1991), p. 70. I am very grateful to Lisette Buchholz for making me aware of this reference.

9. Georg Hermann, 'Die Bilanz des Vorkriegsmenschen', *De Stem*, XIII (1933), 739–60 and 839–63; reprinted in Schoor (ed.), *Der Schriftsteller Georg Hermann*, pp. 235–82.

10. See the reprint of the essay in Schoor (ed.), *Der Schriftsteller Georg Hermann*, pp. 279–81.

11. Henrik Ibsen, *Rosmersholm*, 1887. The line is spoken by Ulrik Brendel in Act IV of the play.

12. Letter to Hilde, 23 August 1933, *Unvorhanden und stumm*, pp. 27–28. Quoted in Nussbaum, 'Verliebt in Holland', p. 184.

13. Ben-Dror, 'Recollections 1919–44'.

14. Georg Hermann, postcard to Hilde, November 1933, *Unvorhanden und stumm*, p. 32.

15. See Gheorge Stanomir, 'Georg Hermann und das Haus Poststraße 2', in *Neckargemünd Jahrbuch*, vol. 5, Stadt Neckargemünd (1993), pp. 85–105.

16. Letter from Dr Siegfried Rothschild dated 28 January 1934, GHC; AR 7074: Box 8; Folder 3, LBI, 358/840.

17. Letter to Hilde, February 1934, *Unvorhanden und stumm*, p. 34.

18. Georg Hermann, *Ruths schwere Stunde* (Amsterdam: de Lange, 1934).

19. See Inge Stephan, 'Nachwort zu *Ruths schwere Stunde*' (Berlin: Das Neue Berlin, 2001), pp. 321–33.

20. Hermann, *Ruths schwere Stunde*, p. 132.

21. Ibid., p. 312.

22. Hermann, *Eine Zeit stirbt* (Berlin: Jüdische Buch-Vereinigung, 1934).

23. Julius Bab letter to Georg Hermann, dated 31 May 1933. See Grubel, *Jettchen Geberts Kinder*, pp. 168–70.

24. Ibid., 3 July 1933, p. 171.

25. By 1935 the Jewish Book Association had 9,000 members. When it was forced to close down in August 1938, it had published nineteen works. Van Liere (*Georg Hermann: Materialien*, p. 216) indicates that between 5,000 and 7,000 copies of *Eine Zeit stirbt* were sold.

26. Schoor (ed.), *Der Schriftsteller Georg Hermann*, pp. 41–42.

27. Leo Hirsch, 'Der neue Georg Hermann: *Eine Zeit stirbt*', *Central-Verein-Zeitung*, no. 12, 22 March 1934, p. 13.

28. *Central-Verein-Zeitung*, no. 11, 15 March 1934, p. 14.

29. Sir Alec Walter George Randall, 'Wandering Germans and the Bread of Banishment', *TLS*, 25 January 1936:70. Randall describes Hermann as 'the realist portrayer of German city life.'

30. Nussbaum, 'Georg Hermann Attacks the Special Issue of *Der Jude*', p. 452.

31. Hermann, *Eine Zeit stirbt*, p. 417.

32. Rebecca West's observation — 'It is a thankless task to be the perfect embodiment of a transition period.' — springs to mind. See Molly F. Deakin, *Rebecca West* (New York: Twayne, 1980), p. 75.

33. Nussbaum, 'Georg Hermann Attacks the Special Issue of *Der Jude*', p. 452.

34. Hermann, *Ruths schwere Stunde*, pp. 5–7.

35. Hermann, *Eine Zeit stirbt*, p. 8.

36. Hilde and Aschenberg were divorced within nine months. During that period she met Villum Hansen, an architect. Hilde and Villum married in 1937.

37. Letter to Hilde, 22 August 1934, *Unvorhanden und stumm*, p. 41.

38. Letter to Hilde, 22 October 1934, Ibid., p. 42.

39. See Stanomir, 'Georg Hermann und das Haus Poststraße 2', 85–105.

40. Hermann, *Ruths schwere Stunde*, pp. 288–89.

CHAPTER 12

❖

Weltabschied

In spring 1935, Georg Hermann wrote an essay 'Weltabschied' [A Farewell to the World] which he marked 'Für meine Kinder bestimmt' [Intended for my children].[1] Conscious that he was now in his sixty-fourth year and not in the best of health, Hermann wanted, while he was still able, to set out his reflections on life. Like his earlier autobiographical essays, 'Weltabschied' is partly an exercise in personal stock-taking but Hermann goes beyond that, setting out his most intimate beliefs and concerns. Indeed, as a considered statement of Hermann's opinions, 'Weltabschied' is a key text, fundamental to an understanding of his world view.

Hermann had previously reflected in the preface to *Eine Zeit stirbt* how the world only exists for us in terms of our individual capacity to appreciate and project ourselves into it. In the introduction to 'Weltabschied' he develops this same thought, writing that when we die, as we vanish from the world, so the world vanishes from us. Every individual should have, he suggests, at least once in their lives, the right to set down for others the truths they have discovered. They should be able to do so for posterity, so that those they leave behind might better know what the individual really thought and felt. The prospect of his impending death, is not something about which Hermann is sanguine. He takes some comfort from the fact that part of him lives on through his children but that cannot overcome his natural affection and love of life, his appreciation for the beauty of the natural world and the wisdom of the centuries which, he says, shines a beam of light into our spiritual darkness. Hermann's appreciation of the natural world is not that of the aesthete — he loves to understand the scientific basis of life and believes humans differ from other living creatures far less than we are inclined to think. But, he suggests that most human of traits, our thirst for knowledge, makes him grateful to exist as a human being rather than say, a buttercup, a pine tree, a cholera bacterium or an antelope.

Notwithstanding what he describes as a very inferior intellectual talent, Hermann has been able to share his sense of the world with millions of people through his writing. When you read, he argues, you are indirectly taking the pulse of another unique human being. And only a handful of people get the opportunity to express their uniqueness in this way. 'Es ist eine Lotterie [...]. Ich habe gewiß nicht den Hauptgewinn gezogen, vielleicht nur einen ganz kleinen Treffer [...], aber [...] eine Niete habe ich in dieser Lotterie nicht erwischt. Und das ist immerhin etwas.' [It is

FIG. 12.1. Georg Hermann.

a lottery [...]. I have certainly not won the main prize but I have perhaps secured a small hit and not drawn a complete blank. And after all that's something].[2]

Hermann remains amazed at what a gifted creature man is and cites the technological achievements which since his boyhood have transformed the lives of the masses and brought great benefits. Much hard human and animal labour which for millennia was simply the way of things has now been eliminated through gas and electric power, he reflects. But despite these positive observations, it would be quite mistaken, Hermann continues, to believe that he sees life as some kind of perfect golden idyll. We cannot understand the meaning of life any more than we understand its necessity and purpose. It doesn't operate in terms of man-made concepts like meaning and purpose. For all we know, he writes, life may come into being anywhere in the universe under similar conditions and may indeed have been created already a hundred times and vanished a hundred times.

But to be born a human being is a fortunate accident. It is undeniably a good vantage point from which to experience the entire system, Hermann writes. Consciousness may only be a short gift, a transitory ray of light between two infinite points of darkness but it is a unique gift and not to be spurned. The life that we have inside of us is as old as life itself. This life has never paused for a second. Even without our awareness from the first point of darkness inside the womb, we can hear sounds. Only in the second soundless darkness of death are we enveloped entirely.

Hermann's thoughts then turn to the present day state of the world. He writes,

> In welch eine wahnsinnige Welt bin ich durch meine Geburt hineingeraten, und welch eine zehnmal wahnsinnigere Welt verläßt man! Eine Welt, in der sich der Kampf zwischen Staat und Mensch bis zur permanenten Explosion gesteigert hat. Eine Welt, in der nicht nur die Staaten unter sich in der Form des Krieges den Kampf bis aufs Messer proklamierten, in Form von Handel und Zöllen den Raub, sondern eine Welt, in der der Einzelmensch keinen intensiveren, mitleidsloseren und gefährlicheren Feind hat [...].

> [Truly, I was born into a mad world and yet the world I am leaving is ten times more crazy and deluded. It is a world in which the struggle between the state and the individual has escalated to a status of permanent explosion. A world in which states have not only proclaimed a struggle to the knife in the form of war, plunder in the form of trade and tariffs, but a world in which the state is the most intense, most pitiless and most dangerous enemy of the individual person.][3]

It is a world which, like Chronos, devours its own children. The size of the army, Hermann laments, is steadily increased and improvements in artillery, aeroplanes, poison gas, submarines, air squadrons and other instruments of death and destruction, are prioritized, time and again, over improving the living conditions of the state's citizens. It is a world in which the official propaganda of the government has long since supplanted every truth and transgressed all values and reason. The state today, Hermann writes, no longer exists for the benefit of its citizens. Rather, they exist for the purposes of the state.

Rearmament in the context of a permanent atmosphere of mutual hostility must inevitably result in violence and war. It is certain, Hermann argues, that the whole civilized world, mesmerized by military regalia and tales of heroism, will succumb to the lunacy of war. The present day preparation for war, he writes, is what the psychoanalysts describe as a 'ständige seelische Bereitschaft zum Mord' [constant mental readiness for murder].[4]

The Siamese twin of modern man, Hermann continues, is the Stone Age mentality of the obstructive war-mongering state which, bereft of understanding, still pays homage to the primitive notion that wars reward the winner.[5] There is surely no-one, Hermann argues, who doesn't believe that pursuing the path to war is wrong-headed. Likewise, there is surely no-one who is unconvinced that the anti-peace actions taken by states, like currency measures, the imposition of tariffs and quotas and the prioritisation of the armaments industry, are the wrong policies to take and have led, time and again, to war and social collapse within the states that follow them. It seems almost impossible to Hermann that there should not be leaders in Europe and America with the insight to look past these ancient ways and to pioneer a new approach that reaches beyond the individual state to humanity's common and supranational interests.

Hermann accepts that it is not possible through friendly persuasion to stop plague bacilli from spreading the plague. One has to find a radical means of eradication. He recalls writing with regard to the 1914–18 war that one cannot seek the permission of politicians and generals to abolish wars and armies. But today he no longer feels that humankind can be saved from the prospect of war. Hermann believes that Europe and the wider world will not be peaceful and able to breathe happily until Germany — the most backward, least free and most dangerous country, populated by semi-barbarians who live under the thumb of full-blooded barbarians lacking even a shred of human emotion or intelligence — has ceased, in its present form, to exist. As long as this *Amokläufer* among the European countries is not rendered impotent, a constant threat of war in the world will persist and Europe cannot count on lasting peace.[6]

Twenty or so years ago, Hermann continues, the German state was not his enemy. He could lead his life quietly and in safety. Because, whatever objections one might have against the German state before 1914, it was not at that time a hindrance in the lives of its citizens. The change came with the war. Everyone was expected to be fervid in their support for it, and yet:

> Trotzdem aber, vergiß nie: Dieser Krieg ist ein deutscher Krieg und kein jüdischer Krieg. Du darfst dich und deine Kinder zwar in ihm totschießen lassen, du darfst dein Vermögen in Kriegsanleihen vernichten [lassen], du darfst hungern — aber du mußt dich dafür als Jude ständig von deinen Vorgesetzten im Feld und in den Kasernen beschimpfen lassen. Du bist Jude, also feige, als Arier und Deutscher bist du *eo ipso* tapfer. Siehst du als Jude die Gefahr, so nur, damit die andern nicht sehen, wie feige du eigentlich bist. Wirst du aber gar Offizier, so hast du dich vorgedrängt. Wurdest du als Arbeitssoldat des Nachts im vordersten Graben zum Krüppel geschossen, so bist du doch nicht des großen deutschen Fronterlebnisses teilhaftig geworden [...] Wenn du die

Wirtschaft — die ohne die Juden nach einem Vierteljahr zusammengebrochen
wäre — organisiertest, warst du Drückeberger, wenn du aber als Deutscher [...]
Granaten auf einer Drehbank fabrizieren ließest und dir die Taschen fülltest oder
ein Dutzend Schweine als kleiner Agrarier züchtetest, warst du ein deutscher
Held, auch wenn du leider unabkömmlich warst und dein Heldentum eben nur
in dieser Form manifestieren konntest.

[Nevertheless, never forget, this war is a German war and not a Jewish war.
Your children may fight in this war, your fortune may be destroyed in war
bonds, you may go hungry but you must always, as a Jew, accept the abuse
of your superiors in the field and in the barracks. If you are a Jew you are a
coward. If you are an Aryan and a German you are *ipso facto*, courageous. If
you as a Jew see dangers, it is only so that others do not notice how cowardly
you really are. If you are an officer then you have pushed yourself forward. If
you are a Jewish soldier on the front line, shot in the night in the trenches, you
still have not participated in the great German front experience. Never mind
that the German economy would have collapsed after three months without the
efforts of Jewish businessmen, they were merely slackers and opportunists. [...]
But if you were a small landowner with a dozen pigs, then your efforts were
indispensable and you were a German hero.][7]

These things and also what occurred next in Germany if one happened to be a
left-wing Jewish writer, are too well-known to need spelling out again, Hermann
writes. The avalanche which started rolling in August 1914 proved to be unstop-
pable. Those who tried to lead a counter-movement: Haase,[8] Luxemburg, Eisner,
Rathenau, Erzberger[9] and Landauer, were all murdered. That some Jews became
active in politics was, with hindsight, a regrettable mistake, and stemmed from the
erroneous assumption that the 'abgrundtiefe[n] Borniertheit' [bottomless bigotry]
of the German mindset could somehow be transformed and steered towards
universal human goals, that the Germans could lose their *Unteroffiziersgeist* and
inherent submissiveness.[10]

Had he happened to have been born in a different country, Hermann believes
that he might not now feel such a deep disgust with the world, the construct of the
state and mankind's lowly condition. In France, where people share his receptiveness
to sensory perceptions, Hermann suggests that a talent like his would hardly have
been noticed. He believes that as an Englishman and an English speaking Jew, he
would have written works which were broader in scope since there is always a
relationship between the novelist and his wider society. Had he been born in these
other countries, Hermann feels he would have been able to develop his talent for
portraying people and connecting their stories with the character of the period
further than he has been able to do in Germany. The circumstances in which he has
lived and the consequential mental depression, he believes, have retarded his craft
and made it too inwardly focused.

Hermann's thoughts then turn to his Judaism. By nature one of life's observers,
he recognized the changing nature of the Jewish question much earlier than others,
so early in fact that he was disbelieved and accused of exaggeration. Before the
war, like most of his fellow-Jews, Hermann, thank God, cared very little about it.
Anti-Semitism existed but it was annoying like mosquitos on a summer's evening

— they could be chased away — as one kept enjoying the soft and warm air outside. He expressed his Judaism latently. It had certainly dominated his literary work in that ninety per cent of his characters were Jewish city dwellers but his Judaism was like a warm and comfortable waistcoat worn underneath his jacket. It would never have occurred to Hermann, as is now the international Jewish fashion, to wear the waistcoat over the jacket.[11]

While he has no desire to observe what he regards as its anachronistic religious demands, from a sense of tradition, Hermann does feel an attachment to Judaism. He would never want to swap it for another faith — and he states that he has felt his Judaism in his blood from early on in his life. What attracts Hermann to today's Jews are their intellectual and moral faculties, their capacity for self-development and desire to realize their full potential. '... daß auch Neunzehntel der Juden ein widerliches Gesindel sind mit sehr üblen menschlichen und ethischen Qualitäten vielleicht nicht ganz so übel wie ihre Umgebung, aber wahrlich übel genug... [That is not to pretend that nine tenths of the Jews are not a terrible rabble — lacking in ethical qualities, not perhaps quite as bad as those that surround them but, all the same, bad enough].[12]

But Hermann is reconciled to the rabble for the other tenth and the contribution it makes to the world's cultural and social development. This last tenth makes him proud to be a Jew and he includes himself as belonging to it, or at least as eligible to being placed near to it.[13] He looks to the future of European Jewry and his wish is that his children and his children's children will be able to develop and express their views unhindered. He hopes that in the future, Europeans will become a supra-national people who have outgrown all that prevents them today from fulfilling their own and their communities' potential. Support will be given in this future world to the most vulnerable so that they do not end up in the gutter. Access to all of the cultural and life-enhancing aspects of life will be guaranteed. Hermann dreams that this world will be so illuminated with the bright lights of culture that it will penetrate even the dullest brains. The state will no longer be able to act with impunity:

> Ich träume von dem Zentralstaat, der in viele Departements geteilt, in denen man überall gleiches Recht und gleiche Sicherheiten und gleiche Lebens-möglichkeiten im Kleinen findet und deren große Aufgaben von eben jener Zentrale aus gemeinschaftlich geregelt werden. Ein normierter Staat, dem es nicht mehr gestattet ist, das zu tun, was das Individuum nicht tun darf: Mord, Erpressung des anderen Individuums und lügen und betrügen.

> [I dream of a centralized state that is subdivided into many autonomous regions where everyone enjoys equal rights, equal security and equal opportunities in their microcosm and where the big tasks are jointly regulated by the aforementioned central government. It will be a standardized state that is no longer permitted to do what the individual may not do: to murder, to extort another individual, to lie and to cheat.][14]

His disgust with the military, Hermann feels, he needs not reiterate. He shivers inwardly with rage when armed bulldog-faced soldiers intimidate ordinary people going about their normal business. 'Die Welt wird sie nicht vermissen, wenn sie nicht mehr vorhanden sein werden.' [The world will not miss them when they are no more].[15] The only problem that will have to be resolved on the dissolution of the army is that a flood of criminals will be poured out into the world. These trained killers will need to be educated and turned into socially useful members of the human race.

They say, Hermann writes, that a blind man should not speak of colour. In that case, he should not talk about religion. At that spot where the organ for religion sits in other people, Hermann says, there is just a vacuum in him. He finds all the tenets on which religion is based, all the claims that are made by it and what flows from them, incomprehensible. He understands neither the diversity of religions, nor their inability to change. He believes that religions were formulated by and for people with no scientific knowledge or skills and of a quite different mindset, and quotes Goethe's dictum, 'Wer Wissenschaft und Kunst besitzt, hat auch Religion; wer jene beiden nicht besitzt, der habe Religion.' [He who has science and art has religion as well; he who possesses neither of them, had better have religion].[16] For certain, the incomprehensible nature of life is the root of all religion; together with the fear of nothingness, having once tasted 'being'. But how ironic it is, Hermann reflects, that man who is so destructive of other forms of nature cannot comprehend his own death.

The fact that there are still state religions Hermann takes to be evidence of the outrageously primitive nature of the present day world where churches and temples continue to be built but the shortage of housing for ordinary people remains unaddressed. In Hermann's view, religions spread far more misery and unhappiness than they do joy. Above all, through their institutions, religions have appropriated a place in the life of the populace that knows no bounds, from the chief priests in Egypt, Babylon and Jerusalem to St Peter's Church in Rome. In this way, religion has played a hugely life-inhibiting, even life-destroying part in man's story. Hermann believes that religion, in particular Christianity, has established a reign of terror as dark as any that could be imagined:

> Die Welt kennt keine Rohheit, keine Lüge und Verruchtheit — angefangen von Menschenopfern bis zu Hexen- und Ketzerverbrennungen, Inquisition und Religionskriegen, Vertreibungen Andersgläubiger und Bartholomäus Nächten — die nicht von den Verkündern und Anhängern [...] der Religionen begangen worden wären und jede Stunde wieder begangen werden könnten. [...] Keine Religion ist seit zweitausend Jahren so mit Blut gesalbt wie die des Mannes, der da sagte oder übernahm: Du sollst nicht töten, liebe deine Feinde, liebe deinen Nächsten wie dich selbst.

> [The world knows no brutality, no lies and infamy — from human sacrifices to the burning of witches and heretics, Inquisitions and religious wars, expulsions of people of different faith and St. Bartholomew's Day Massacre — which have not been committed in the name of religion and could be committed again any time. And no religion has for two thousand years been as anointed with blood as that which purports to follow the man who said or reiterated, 'Thou shalt not kill, love thy enemies and love thy neighbour as thyself.'][17]

Hermann contends that he would have had to go through life deaf and blind not to have felt and shared Nietzsche's antipathy towards Christianity. Rather than carrying through its ethical programme and its egalitarianism, Hermann argues that Christianity has allied itself to the powerful and consistently helped elites to rob and plunder with impunity, and to enslave. It was Christianity which caused the collapse of the Ancient World, the finest culture, in Hermann's view, that the world has ever known — the culture which created everything: music, sculpture, architecture, drama, philosophy, the arts, poetry, the novel, painting, mathematics, the sciences, the republic and municipal government, sports and games — everything on which our present-day life is still based.

> ... so würde nichts in der Welt die Kulturschuld sühnen können, die es auf sich lud mit der Zerstörung und Ablösung der antiken Welt. Wenn ich an die Bronze eines attischen Epheben denke und an die Externsteine mit ihren schlechten [Kreuzabnahme] Reliefs und mir sage: Das also ist tausend oder zwölfhundert Jahre später geschaffen worden, bis zu dieser Verwilderung sanken Kunst und Kultur, so kommen mir [...] die Tränen in die Augen.

> [... nothing in the world can expiate Christianity's guilt in destroying and replacing the Ancient World. When I think of the bronze sculpture of Ephebe of Marathon and compare it with the Externsteine with their lamentable reliefs of the descent of the cross, I say to myself, "that bronze was created a 1000 or 1200 years before yet now art and culture have fallen to such barbarism!" then my eyes fill with tears.][18]

From religion, Hermann's focus turns to nationalism and his misfortune to be living in a period of soft-brained patriotism. It was much to the German people's advantage in the eighteenth century and the first half of the nineteenth century, Hermann argues, that they did not know this patriotism for everything that is great and good belongs to the world as a whole. There is no such thing as national art or national science. Reflecting on the spirit of the Enlightenment and the German people's subsequent regression to philistinism, Hermann continues,

> Nichts hat die Mentalität des Deutschen so heruntergewirtschaftet wie sein falscher Patriotismus und sein eingebildetes Ariertum, das Leuten, die gar nichts waren, den Dünkel gab, sie wären etwas, und zwar etwas Hehres und Herrliches, nämlich Arier, jener Rasse Mitglieder, die alles Große in der Welt geschaffen und die in Wahrheit unendlich spät und nur zerstörend ...

> [Nothing so much has brought the Germans to the brink of ruin than this false patriotism and imaginary Aryanism, that gave people who were nothing the delusion that they were something noble and glorious, members of a race which created everything great in the world.][19]

In fact, rather than being its architects, Hermann argues that Germans came late to culture. The Mediterranean basin was the cradle of civilisation, the culture of Europe and the wider world. The part Germans have played has been destructive. They have acted like a 'cultural torpedo' in world history.[20]

This plague of patriotism and nationalism, Hermann writes, is characterized by stupidity, egotism, self-praise, lies, emotional confusion, empty rhetoric, a rampant mindlessness, war-mongering hatred, an inability to understand different, more sophisticated mentalities, and a whipping-up of mob instincts at the expense of humanity. He himself is a victim of this German patriotism, the '*kalte Pogrom*' which has forced him into exile.[21]

Already in 1914, Hermann continues, the wave of German nationalism at the outbreak of the war aroused in him feelings of revulsion. He recalls his attempts at challenging the nationalistic fervour of the times, citing the article he published in 1915 on world literature[22] and *Randbemerkungen*. Hermann thought that what he was saying was self-evident but he found to his astonishment that he stood alone. And while there were some who in private might have shared his views, they lacked the courage to speak out on the side of the simplest common sense.

These negative experiences, Herman writes, had the effect of silencing him prematurely. Not because his opinions changed but because he questioned the point of speaking out to people so unreceptive to his views. He came to realize that in Germany, at least, between his friends and his foes, there were differences only in degree. They shared the same mentality, only the topcoat of paint was different, and from both sprang the same mob-spirited war-mongering. 'Schade um jeden braven jüdischen Jungen, der ab 1914 bis 1935 für diese Bande seinen Kopf hinhielt.' [Pity any good Jewish boy who from 1914 till 1935 put his head on the block for that gang].[23]

Hermann states that he has never believed in the notion of social democracy as socialism accommodated within strongly authoritarian capitalism and claims it was the treachery of Ebert, Noske, and Scheidemann which thwarted the November 1918 Revolution.[24] Even at that time and in Munich in 1919 he saw that Germany and its people were beyond help. But neither is Hermann a strong proponent of Bolshevism. The Russian form of government may be a good thing, he writes, but only for the Russians, not for other Europeans and not for somebody who has drawn all his life from a western culture and is essentially bourgeois, not proletarian, an outspoken individualist. An idolisation of the factory, the worker and production is not for Hermann. Improving people's living conditions, ensuring that they are properly fed, it is an impressive experiment, but ultimately what matters most, he argues, is the development of mankind, not the class consciousness of the proletariat.

One disappointment, Hermann reflects, that shocked him more than anything was the opportunity squandered in 1918:

> ... die Ideen, die damals in der Luft lagen: das Paneuropa, die allgemeine Entwaffnung, Freihandel, Aufhebung der Zollgrenzen, Weltgeld, Weltrecht, kurz alle die Umstellungen, die ein neues Friedensleben [...] erforderte, [zu verwirklichen]. Da war ich also wirklich der Ansicht, das wäre die allgemeine Meinung der Erde, und Wilsons vierzehn Punkte wären kein Bluff, sondern ein europäischer Anfang gewesen. Und zu meinem kaum zu bändigenden Staunen hörte ich allseits, daß diese Leute, die wie ich an eine Umgestaltung der Welt glaubten oder sich ihr widmen wollten, nicht nur als Narren verfolgt, verlacht, bespien und gemeuchelt, sondern als Verbrecher gebrandmarkt wurden, daß Krieg als etwas Heiliges und Gottgewolltes aufgezogen und Revolution als etwas Teuflisches erklärt wurde, daß "Pazifist", das erst einen Depp bezeichnet

nur hatte, ein Schimpfwort wurde, nachdem zehn Millionen Menschen — die Hoffnung der Welt — geschlachtet worden waren, und nachdem ein leidlich konsolidiertes Europa und Amerika zugrunde gerichtet waren. Das ging über meinen Horizont.

[The ideas that were in the air at that time: a European union, general disarmament, free trade, the abolition of custom barriers, a worldwide currency and a worldwide legal system, in short, all the changes that were required for a new peaceful life to be realized. I really thought that was the public opinion all over the globe and Wilson's Fourteen Points were not bluff; they were Europe's opportunity for a fresh start. But to my utter amazement, I found everywhere that people who thought like me and wanted to transform the world were not only ridiculed as fools, spat upon and murdered, but branded as criminals. War was celebrated as something sacred and willed by God; revolution declared diabolical and "pacifist", originally designating a fool, became a term of abuse after ten million people — the hope of the world — had been slaughtered and Europe, at the verge of consolidation, and America, had been ruined. That went over my head.][25]

At this point, the essay becomes more personal as Hermann switches his focus to literature and in particular to his own work. Today, he says, he has grown weary and he struggles on with many unpaid bills. Where formerly he was carried along by a sense that people were listening to what he had to say, now he feels that nobody is really interested in hearing his voice.[26] Hermann cannot but be depressed by this because he believes that one of the primary tasks of the writer is to tell other people about things, sometimes things they don't want to hear.[27]

Nevertheless, Hermann continues to find the act of writing therapeutic. It enables him to express painful feelings, even deflecting suicidal thoughts. Moreover, he has always had a profound fear that nothing will be left of his existence and that when he dies he shall be gone and forgotten. That fear has made him repeatedly try to capture what has already passed into non-existence. Even if what he writes is completely transformed into a pseudo-reality and largely symbolic, he still likes to peddle his take on what he has experienced.

But the ultimate spring of his writing, the impulse for his work, Hermann continues, is a deep fear, not so much of non-being but of the transience of life and the passage of time:

Ich, der ich 1871 geboren bin und von jung an ziemlich bewußt mein Leben verbrachte — meine Erinnerungen gehen fast bis in mein erstes Jahr zurück [...] — , habe eigentlich jedes Jahrzehnt eine neue Schicht des Seins in mir und um mich versinken sehn, und je älter ich wurde, desto bewußter ist es mir geworden und um so mehr quälte es mich, daß das Dasein Geschichte wird. Und so habe ich, wie die Kinder, dann Sandburgen gebaut, die den Wellen trotzen sollten, wenn die nächste Flut kam, und ich habe auch nachher, nachdem die Flut schon gekommen war, immer von neuem wieder sie aufzurichten versucht. Daß sie bleiben, oder, wenn sie das nicht für andere Leute tun, daß sie wenigstens für euch bleiben.

[I, who was born in 1871, have led my life in a very conscious way; my memories go back almost to my first year — and I noticed how every decade

a layer of existence within me and around me would submerge and the older I
got the more I agonized over the awareness that life was becoming history. And
so I, like the children who build sandcastles on the beach, have sought to defy
the waves when the next tide comes flooding in. And even when the tide had
come, I have tried, again and again, to restore my castles. That they remain,
even if not for other people, they remain at least for you.][28]

Hermann acknowledges that he is a natural collector who accumulates old things
and does not like to be separated from them.[29] He is a curator not just of the
artefacts in his collection but also of his own life. It's not impossible, Hermann
suggests, that some things which he has written will be read long after he has
gone. That when his heart no longer even twitches, it may still set other people's
hearts a-quiver. While that knowledge may not compensate for his present severely
straitened circumstances,

> Gewiß, es ist ganz nett, sich sagen zu können, daß man, längst unvorhanden
> und stumm, doch zu Menschen noch reden kann und nicht gerade Trivialitäten,
> sondern sogar irgendeinen Kontakt damit findet von seinem Innersten zu dem
> Innersten jener.[30]

> [It is certainly quite nice to be able to say that in the future, despite being mute
> and no longer extant, one can still talk to people and not about trivialities but
> about matters touching on our innermost selves.]

Although, unlike many of his peers, he is not well-educated in the arts and sciences,
Hermann acknowledges that he does have a retentive mind, the ability to locate
just the right piece of knowledge at the right moment. So it always seems as if he
knows more than he actually does. An eye for detail coupled with this sharpness
of memory makes it easy for Hermann to reconstruct things, people, moods and
visual impressions. This goes hand in hand with an appreciation of well-chosen
words, expressions and anecdotes.[31] These natural traits have been supplemented by
his haphazard reading of thinkers such as Plato, Emerson, Montaigne, Nietzsche,
Schopenhauer, Goethe, Novalis, Simmel, Bergson and Ortega y Gasset. While he
would never choose to read novels as long as those he has written himself, Hermann
has from time to time willingly leafed through his books and he believes that they
have undeniable literary merit; they are not 'Makulatur' [trash].[32]

Hermann then turns his gaze on the state of German literature more generally.
The question he raised during the war about whether German literature was for the
world or only for domestic consumption, he says, has now been answered entirely
in favour of the latter. What is more, it has become increasingly clear to Hermann
over the last forty years how inferior German literature has become. German
writers whose works endure are rare, Hermann argues, and even the better ones
like Dehmel, Stehr or Holz — today seem dated.[33]

Now that all of the Jewish writers have been eliminated from German literature,
one sees what one never really suspected before, that nothing remains but indifferent
kitsch. If you wanted to compose a list of the German literature of international
ranking, Hermann writes, you would need to look no further than the list of burned
books. In his view, Germany has no really significant representatives which it could

send to an international literary parliament — not even Schnitzler or the Nobel Prize winners, Thomas Mann and Gerhart Hauptmann. According to Hermann, the country has produced no Realist writers who can match the style of a Flaubert; no writers able to portray society like England's John Galsworthy, no pioneers of new dramatic forms like Shaw and Ibsen, no Tolstoy, and no social critics like the great American writers of recent decades.

The explanation for this, Hermann believes, is that 'alle Literatur der Welt setzt einen gewissen Grad von seelischer Verfeinerung voraus' [all world literature presupposes a certain degree of mental refinement].[34] It is characterized by an acute receptivity to external stimuli, a tender and compassionate sensitivity about life and death; using language that is not everyday language yet is simple and clear and vivid and drills deeper. Writers of world literature, Hermann argues, are like a secret society of the educated strata on earth, a spiritual free-masonry, subject to certain laws. And it is only German literature which excludes itself because of its singular false mentality. It is that mentality, Hermann believes, which stops it from finding international literary esteem.

Taking a more personal turn, Hermann considers what it is that he looks for from literature. First and foremost, he says, he wants to get to know a person, to understand the most subtle parts of their being. So he reads writers like Hamsun, Fontane, Verlaine, Tolstoy, Flaubert and Stendhal. He also likes to read letters and diaries like Rousseau's *Confessions* and autobiographies. Hermann believes that he shares the same spiritual and cultural outlook as these writers and though they may be very far away, he feels a certain connection to them. With others like Jack London and Dostoevsky, he gets frustrated. If he knew them in life he would probably not get much further than giving them a pat on the shoulder and saying, 'fine fellow'. He would sooner go back to those with whom he feels more of a personal affinity, those who reveal to him new subtleties about human nature.

Although he has written in the German language, Hermann is clear that his work has never had the slightest relationship to the kind of writing now making up the Nazi state-sanctioned patriotic literature:

> ... als Juden doch, ohne daß ich es ahnte, eine derartige Mentalität seelisch unzugänglich war. Ich habe nichts damit zu tun — auch wenn meine Romane so etwas wie berlinisch märkische Heimatkunst waren und eine Geschichte der Berliner Juden in hundert Jahren umfassen.

> [Because, as a Jew, without my even suspecting it, such a mentality was emotionally inaccessible to me. I have nothing to do with it — even if my novels are something like Berlin folk art and portray the history of Berlin Jews over a hundred years.][35]

He cannot close his essay, Hermann writes, without some words about the man who now leads Germany to an abyss of meaninglessness, who has destroyed hundreds of thousands of those of his race and religion, driven them out of the country and tortured people for their thoughts, not their deeds, in concentration camps. Believe me, Hermann writes, there is not a gallows too high, no bullet too fast, no poison gas too agonizing for Hitler and his cronies. He would feel this even if Hitler had not fallen into the atavistic bigotry of anti-Semitism because Hitler's deeds represent an attack upon all humanity. Had he the means, Hermann would put a premium on Hitler's head — not for himself but to try to safeguard the future of thousands of young Jews.[36]

He has always been a poor man, Hermann writes, but his name has become known in the world to millions. His novels have been published in many languages and he has worked with film makers, operetta producers, theatre companies and newspaper owners. There have been many people who have enjoyed what he has written and to whom he has brought pleasure. He takes comfort from the fact that while many memories, little experiences and impressions will be lost from the world when he departs it, he has written enough that his children and anyone else who should have a desire to be with him, can share his thoughts, although he will be unavailable:

> Wenn ich mal nicht mehr sein werde, wird es nur so sein, als ob ich mit unbekanntem Ziel verreist bin, auch wenn ich keine Ansichtspostkarten schicke. Aber endlich habe ich soviel Briefe geschrieben in tausenderlei Form, in denen braucht man nur zu blättern, dann bin ich wieder — und wenn man es nicht will, so schadet es auch nichts, Kinder. Außer euch habe ich niemand, von dem ich mich hier verabschieden mußte; macht es gut.

> [It will be as if I am travelling to an unknown destination, even if I don't send any picture postcards. But I have written so many letters in a thousand different forms, you need only dip into my work and then I am back with you — and if one doesn't want to do that, then there is no harm done, either, children. Except for you there is no one here from whom I need to take leave. Be well!][37]

Notes to Chapter 12

1. The essay remained as a manuscript until Laureen Nussbaum published it together with Hermann's letters to Hilde in *Unvorhanden und stumm* (1991), pp. 221–61.
2. Ibid., p. 224.
3. Ibid., p. 226.
4. Ibid., p. 228.
5. Ibid.
6. Ibid., p. 231.
7. Ibid., p. 233.
8. Hugo Haase, chairman of the Independent Social Democratic Party of Germany (USPD) was assassinated in October 1919.
9. As head of the German delegation, Matthias Erzberger signed the armistice ending the war and was subsequently Minister of Finance from 1919 to 1920. He was murdered by Organisation Consul in 1921.
10. Hermann, 'Weltabschied', *Unvorhanden und stumm*, p. 234.
11. Ibid., p. 236.
12. Ibid., p. 238.
13. Hermann's view of his own status would not have been regarded as unjustified by contemporaries. Cecil Roth, for example, in *The Jewish Contribution to Civilisation* (first published in 1938) makes reference to Georg Hermann and describes him as 'an imaginative writer of the first rank.' (New York: Harper and Brothers, 1940), p. 131.
14. Hermann, 'Weltabschied', *Unvorhanden und stumm*, p. 239.

15. Ibid., p. 241.

16. From *Die Xenien* (1797), a collection of epigrams written with Friedrich Schiller. See Johann Wolfgang von Goethe, 'Zahme Xenien IX', *Werke*, vol. 1 (Hamburg: Wegner, 1952), p. 367.

17. Hermann, 'Weltabschied', *Unvorhanden und stumm*, pp. 243–44.

18. Ibid., p. 245. The sculpture of the Marathon Boy was discovered in the Aegean Sea in the bay of Marathon in 1925. It is now dated to around 340–330 BC.

19. Hermann, 'Weltabschied', *Unvorhanden und stumm*, p. 247.

20. Ibid.

21. Ibid.

22. Hermann, 'Weltliteratur oder Literatur für den Hausgebrauch?', pp. 67–106.

23. Hermann, 'Weltabschied', *Unvorhanden und stumm*, p. 248.

24. SPD politicians: Friedrich Ebert was the first president of the Weimar Republic; Gustav Noske its first Defence Minister and Philipp Scheidemann its second head of government.

25. Hermann, 'Weltabschied', *Unvorhanden und stumm*, p. 251.

26. Ibid., p. 252.

27. Virginia Woolf makes a similar point in *A Room of One's Own* (1928). She argues that the writer has the chance to live more than other people in the presence of reality and that whatever reality touches it fixes and makes permanent. 'It is [the writer's] business to find it and collect it and communicate it to the rest of us.' (London: Penguin, 2000), p. 108.

28. Hermann, 'Weltabschied', *Unvorhanden und stumm*, pp. 252–53.

29. In his introduction to the 1941 Hebrew edition of *Jettchen Gebert*, Sammy Gronemann makes reference to this trait. He writes that just as Hermann collected butterflies and stamps in his youth, and later sculptures and porcelains, his writing shows that he has collected all of the idiosyncrasies of *Homo sapiens*. Gronemann, preface to Georg Hermann, *Jettchen Gebert*, p. xii.

30. Hermann, 'Weltabschied', *Unvorhanden und stumm*, p. 253.

31. Ibid., p. 254.

32. Ibid.

33. The novelist Hermann Stehr (1864–1940) was nominated four times in the 1930s for the Nobel Prize in Literature. Arno Holz (1863–1929) was a dramatist and poet, best known for *Phantasus* (1898).

34. Hermann, 'Weltabschied', *Unvorhanden und stumm*, p. 256.

35. Ibid., p. 258.

36. Ibid., p. 259.

37. Ibid., p. 261.

CHAPTER 13

❖

The Exile Novels

In 1935 Hermann published two new novels. Although now well into his sixties, there was nothing to suggest that he was slowing down in terms of his creative output.

The first, *Rosenemil*, was published by Allert de Lange, which felt obliged to honour its contract with Hermann, despite the difficulties over *Eine Zeit stirbt*.[1] The novel's protagonist, Emil Lehmann, actually makes his first appearance early on in *Der kleine Gast*, the second novel in *Die Kette*, when he tries to sell Fritz Eisner one of his long-stemmed roses, outside the Wertheim department store.[2] In *November achtzehn* Emil is a beggar. He pretends to be a *Kriegszitterer* and mimics the uncontrollable shaking which was one of the symptoms of the ex-soldiers who suffered from the disorder. But subsequently, while always remaining a minor character, Emil is one of the beneficiaries of the hyper-inflation years and for the first time in his life he escapes the lumpen-proletariat and becomes prosperous.

Hermann obviously felt an affection for Emil and decided to give him a book of his own. He wrote the novel between July and October 1933, so it is evident that he spent most of his first months in the Netherlands working on the book — escaping perhaps from the reality of his exile by turning his mind back to the Berlin demimonde of the turn of the century.

When we first meet Emil in the novel, he is hawking cheap paperbacks on street corners for a living. Handsome, articulate and athletic, Emil Lehmann is certainly not without charm. He is also described as 'nett' [kind] and 'anständig' [decent], if weak. The novel tells of his meeting and falling in love at first sight with Polenliese (Lissi), a prostitute. Hermann likens Lissi to Hippolyta. She is the uncrowned queen of this netherworld and Emil, whom she nicknames 'Rosenemil', because he brings her a rose at their first meeting, becomes her Prince Consort.

The story, which unfolds between spring and autumn 1903, takes place in the eastern part of the city — Lothringer Straße (today's Torstraße), home to peddlers, prostitutes and petty criminals. Hermann's impressionistic depiction of underworld life in Berlin reveals the city in all its tones — vital and corrupt, colourful and wretched. Reinhard Zachau describes the book as a 'superb dedication to the old Berlin that [Hermann] had made so famous in his earlier novels.'[3] The novel found favour with Sigmund Freud who wrote to Hermann in February 1936,

> Unterdes habe ich Ihren Rosenemil gelesen und bin noch voll von ihm, so voll, dass ich ihn kaum genug loben kann. Und er ist Ihre eigenste Besonderheit. Ein großes Stück von seltsamem Zauber des garstigen Berlin ist darin.

FIG. 13.1. Heinrich Zille, *Berlinerinnen*, 1905 (Staatliche Kunstsammlungen Dresden).

[Meanwhile, I have read your *Rosenemil* and am still full of it, so full that I can scarcely praise the novel enough. And it displays your characteristic trademark. A large slice of the strange magic of the dark side of Berlin is in it.][4]

Freud goes on to describe his memories of the time he spent in the German capital between 1928 and 1930 and tells Hermann, 'Ihr Buch hat Berlin bei mir aufgeweckt.' [Your book has awakened Berlin for me].

Hermann attributed the authenticity of his portrait of turn of the century Berlin to Heinrich Zille's illustrations — 'Einfach abgeschriebene Zilles, aber durch die Brille von Georg Hermann angesehn.' [Simply copied from Zille but viewed through the eyeglasses of Georg Hermann].[5] As the story unfolds, we get to know Lissi's friends, the other prostitutes of Lottumstraße, and a gang of thieves led by Palisadenkarl. Emil unwisely allows himself to be drawn into the gang and it is through Palisadenkarl that he meets the elegant, sophisticated Brillantenberta, a high-class 'companion'. Despite the happiness he has found with Lissi, Emil easily succumbs to Berta's charms. The novel's narrator tells us that he is in part a victim of his own nature, his own weakness, but also that he is subject to the law that says a woman's love starts to bloom just as that of her man's begins to wane. Brillantenberta takes Emil on as her latest toy boy, buying him a new suit to smarten him up. Emil escorts her to the races and enjoys the pleasures of her bed. Betrayed, Lissi, whose health is already fragile due to tuberculosis, goes into a decline and she attempts suicide. Emil returns to her but it is too late, and the novel ends with Lissi's death.

Rosenemil is notably terser than Hermann's previous novels and provides more action and suspense.[6] Love, love betrayed, denunciation and repentance, sickness, death and suicide constitute its fixed points. The narrator's voice stays in close proximity to the characters in the novel and at times he even takes over their speech and offers his own insights.[7] Anecdotal and humorous, he comes across as a somewhat laconic, worldly-wise figure but with his heart in the right place. His experience and perception is applied to almost all areas of life — from relationships to philosophy and the natural world. There are parallels between the narrator's voice and the character of Dr Levy, the humane physician who seeks to do his best for Lissi and his other patients. Cultured and caring, Dr Levy makes repeated references to the beauty and value of life as well as conversing on favourite Hermann subjects such as the art and architecture of northern Italy and German literary history.[8]

Hermann portrays the diverse nature of the developing city and how it is composed of many contrasting districts. Each is like a little empire in itself, with its own hierarchies and conventions. He is keen to show that despite the criminality of the underworld he is depicting, there is a moral code in operation, that honour really does exist among thieves. When Emil and Palisadenkarl are about to fight a duel, the narrator says that while the two men made no attempt to express themselves, principles were at stake because every district and every type of human activity has its unwritten code of honour; pimps no less than officers, bank managers, civil servants or student societies. Similarly, when Brillantenberta seeks to get her revenge on Emil, the narrator puts her response into the wider context of power relationships. She is accustomed to dominating men and younger men in particular and cannot tolerate that one should leave her. It was an idea with her, a principle, we are told, that this should not be. And there is no dynamite, the narrator says, which explodes so early or is as dangerous as such an idea.

While Hermann does not gloss over the wretched living conditions of Emil, Lissi and their associates, his depiction is infused with humour and empathy. Through the compassionate Dr Levy and his affectionate portrayal of the inherent decency of his protagonists, Hermann presents a picture of the ethical norms he believed characterized society before 1914 and which he detailed in his *Die Bilanz des Vorkriegsmenschen* essay. Hence, Weiss-Sussex argues, *Rosenemil* is perhaps less a literary response to the experience of exile than a picture of a long-lost world in which concern for one's fellow human beings was axiomatic.[9]

Hermann's second novel of 1935, *B. M. Der unbekannte Fußgänger* [B. M. The Unknown Pedestrian] was published by Menno Hertzberger.[10] Hermann first mentions the book in a card he sent to Hilde in February 1934, explaining that he has written 'einen hübschen kleinen Roman' (a charming little novel) of about 120 pages, two-thirds of which takes place in Paris and the other third in the sky above the city over an eighteen hour period.[11] The novel's anti-hero, Benno Meyer, is a Jewish-German writer past his prime who has fled Germany for Paris. There, the traffic policemen regard Meyer as a German and he reflects on the paradox that it is only within Germany that he is not considered to be a German.[12] Disorientated and uprooted, Meyer comes to realize that from now on, he is first and foremost a Jew. He experiences one last passionate infatuation before the novel ends with his death in a strange car accident by the Arc de Triomphe.[13] Van Liere was unable to ascertain the print run but indicates that probably only about 750 copies were produced.[14] It has never been reprinted and is now something of a rarity. Bassenge, the Berlin auction house, sold a copy of the novel in April 2016 for €295.

Although keeping busy with work, it is clear from his letters to Hilde during this period that family concerns were occupying Hermann. In particular, he remained anxious that Eva, Siegfried and little Beate, remained in Germany. In spring 1935 they finally moved to Berlin where Siegfried had managed to get a temporary job working on luminescence with the industrial firm, Auergesellschaft.[15] My grandmother always recalled the outraged reaction of friends in Heidelberg when she explained that they were leaving for Berlin — 'You are going to the Prussians!' In a poem written shortly after they had left Heidelberg, Eva writes about gazing up at the moon hanging rigid in the empty sky above Berlin. It looks to her like a monocle and to be exuding an air of arrogance. You can almost hear it praising itself, admiring its great height. The crowded houses above which it presides are lined up like regiments. She had hoped that the beautiful moon she used to admire in the south would at least be unchanged but now she realizes she was mistaken. It is a different moon she is seeing. This moon is a menacing Prussian presence.[16]

In April 1935 Hans Hinkel, the Nazi Commissar for 'non-Aryan' culture, agreed that the Berlin Jewish Kulturbund could stage *Jettchen Gebert*, so long as it avoided showing assimilation in a positive light. In a letter to Hilde written at the end of May, Hermann regrets that he is unable to see the play. He imagines that other

FIG. 13.2. *B. M. Der unbekannte Fußgänger.*

FIG. 13.3. Eva and Siegfried Rothschild, April 1935.

cultural societies may also stage the production but doubts if he will make any money from the performances.[17] The Kulturbund production was adapted from the novel by its director, Fritz Jessner, and performed throughout July 1935.[18] Jason Gebert's speech about the family's pride in being looked upon and respected as Jews in Berlin and in the fact that his father had not chosen to be baptized was retained in the production. But the second part of Jason's speech in which he speculates that had his father converted, the family might now be von Geberts and government officials, could not be spoken by a Jew in Germany in 1935. Jessner advised his actor to 'break-off' mid-sentence.

The play appears to have been positively received. Hermann wrote to Hilde in August that he had heard the performances were quite good.[19] But Hilde Cohen, in her review for the *Frauenbund*, warned that while the audience might identify with the German-Jewish milieu on stage, it would be a mistake to draw simple inferences about 'our contemporary problems'. Hermann Sinsheimer in a review for *Gemeindeblatt* complained that Walter Hertner's portrayal of Dr. Kössling strayed into melodrama.[20]

While the Kulturbund was staging its production of *Jettchen Gebert*, Goebbels' Institut zum Studium der Judenfrage (Institute for the Study of the Jewish Question) was putting the finishing touches to its magnum opus, *Die Juden in*

Deutschland.[21] The book includes nine pages of polemic against Georg Hermann. It draws exclusively on things he wrote in his wartime notes (*Randbemerkungen*) which are denounced as an exhaustive defamation of the government, the army and of the German people and their character. Hermann's comments that he could live quite contentedly outside of Germany and his lack of religious commitment is taken to be indicative of the rootlessness of all Jews. Instead of being committed to serving the fatherland he wants to lead a parasitic life.

Unsurprisingly, the institute seizes upon Hermann's own connection of his Jewishness with his opposition to the war and his argument that Jews are generally less susceptible than younger races to mass suggestion. This is seen as further evidence of Hermann's arrogance and lack of patriotism. Hermann's assertion that the human race would be much more advanced culturally and socially had it not been blessed with such a large number of so called great leaders and generals is also quoted.[22] What would Athens have been without Pericles? Rome without Caesar? England without Cromwell and Elizabeth I? France without Napoleon? Germany without Frederick the Great and Bismarck? asks the institute's anonymous author. What, indeed, would western culture be without the formation of states? The absence of the state would mean anarchy and a relapse into barbarianism. Hermann, of course, believed the opposite, that it was the state (as evidenced by the war) which was the agent of the return to barbarity.

The institute characterizes Hermann as a revolutionary anarchist. Those entries where Hermann voices his hostility towards the social elites he held responsible for the war are likened to the language of Marxist masterminds who during the war, it is alleged, undermined the country by stirring up class hatred and preaching the guilt of the ruling classes for the war. Hermann shows no appreciation of military service and in fact glorifies insubordination. The blind hatred of the Jews as exemplified by Hermann is contrasted with the ideal of heroic sacrifice in the service of the fatherland.

At the bottom of the final page of *Randbemerkungen*, Hermann had quoted a statement from Max Hilzheimer's *Geschichte unserer Haustiere* [History of our Domesticated Animals] explaining that the European pig does not originate from India but is in fact indigenous. Hermann probably intended it as a satirical note on which to end his wartime notes but for the author of *Die Juden in Deutschland* it is merely further evidence of Hermann's lack of patriotism. All Hermann has to offer is foreign Jewish pacifist materialism. He has no conception of German idealism, which is as closed to him as the book with seven seals.

Hermann, however, had more immediate problems than his lack of appreciation for the military ideals of the fatherland: money matters were assuming ever-increasing importance. With his novels proscribed in Germany, he was denied any income from previous books. New novels could only be published outside of Germany and he was unable to work as a journalist. After his 'Bilanz' essay in 1933 Hermann did not publish any further articles in Dutch periodicals and his last piece in a German paper was his 'Erinnerungen an Jakob Wassermann', published in *Central-Verein-Zeitung* on 25 January 1934. His letters to Hilde during the spring and summer of 1935 reveal his growing financial concerns and the steady erosion of his confidence that he would be able to make a new start in the Netherlands.

In June he and Usche spent a few days with friends in Belgium. Back in Hilversum and writing to Hilde, Hermann reflects that Holland, for all its good points, is *a la longue* a terribly dull place to live. Belgium is a thousand times more pleasant — the people are lively and engaging, the cafés full of life and the scenery is more akin to that of southern Germany. He would prefer to live somewhere warmer now that he is getting older but then Usche, more than the rest of us, he writes, has settled in Holland. Her schooling is going quite well, should he disrupt her life again by another move? But Hermann recognizes that,

> An sich wäre natürlich England oder Frankreich besser gewesen, weil die Zukunftsmöglichkeiten besser — am besten sogar Amerika, was mich auch sehr gereizt hätte, denn da ist man wirklich frei und ziemlich weit vom Schuß des zukünftigen europäischen Krieges, den ich euch und Uschchen gern erspart hätte.

> [Of course, England or France would have been better [than Holland] because they'd have offered greater future possibilities — even America, which would have been very invigorating for me, because there you are really free and quite far removed from the shots of the future European war, from which I would have liked to spare you and Uschchen.][23]

At the end of August, Eva, Siegfried and my mother stayed with Hermann and Usche in Hilversum. He writes to Hilde about playing games with Ate and reading her stories. Eva and Siegfried seem more comfortable, he tells her. He wishes it was possible that they could stay and it could continue *ad aeternitatem*.[24]

In the same letter Hermann expresses again his scepticism regarding Palestine as a possible home for Jewish refugees from Western Europe and makes reference to an essay on which he is working, 'Was sollen wir Juden tun?' [What Should We, the Jews, Do?]. Hermann hoped that the essay would be published by the Paris-based Carrefour publishing house which specialized in publishing anti-Nazi books and leaflets.[25] In the essay, Hermann considers, now that anti-Semitism is enshrined as state doctrine in Germany, whether the Jew should still seek to be a culturally orientated European or instead turn to his Jewish identity. Should Jews strive to form a united people? Or should they, lacking any inner identity other than their religious practice, continue to live largely assimilated amongst others but always in peril of being the object of those others' aggression, of being beaten or expelled?[26]

Hermann acknowledges that Germany has probably always been the cradle of anti-Semitism. But now it is being used as a means to an end by fanatics who rage about world domination and seek to liberate the whole planet from Judaism. To preserve their human dignity, the Jews have had to leave Germany. Hermann says that he personally has no desire to live in a land where a large proportion of the population enjoin the battle cry 'Juda verrecke' and SA men parade through the streets chanting combat songs like 'Wetzt die langen Messer auf dem Bürgersteig, laßt die Messer flutschen in den Judenleib' [Sharpen the long knives on the pavement, let the knives slip into the Jew's body].

He is convinced that it is the international duty of other countries to facilitate a mass emigration. Their failure to do so serves to promote the idea of Jewish self-reliance and unity. But for Hermann such self-reliance carries risks of the insularity which he associates with the traditions of Eastern Judaism and religious orthodoxy. He acknowledges that Jews have something in common wherever they might be living and that they recognize this about one another. But just as he had done in his 1919 essay 'Zur Frage der Westjuden' Hermann asserts that the advantage of the Jews lies in their freedom from the trappings of statehood (nationalism, administration and the military) which he believes hinder the development of the soul. His preference is still for a multi-cultural pan-European society founded upon the principle that all men are equal, a society in which the Jew could take his natural place.

A few weeks after Hermann stopped work on the incomplete essay, on 15 September 1935, the Reichstag unanimously approved the Nuremberg Laws. The new 'Law for the Protection of German Blood and German Honour' made marriage and sexual intercourse between Jews and non-Jews criminal offences. Only German citizens who had so-called German or similar blood could enjoy full civil rights and be classed as citizens of the Reich.

★   ★   ★   ★   ★

Hermann increasingly saw films as a way of generating some income. He believed that *Tränen um Modesta Zamboni*, *Träume der Ellen Stein* and *Grenadier Wordelmann* would all make good movies.[27] But his immediate focus was on *Jettchen Gebert* as around this time he was engaged with a project to develop an American film version of the Jettchen operetta. Hermann hoped that if the film was successful it would rekindle interest in the English translation of the novel which had not been reprinted since 1928.

A synopsis of the proposed film survives in the Georg Hermann Collection in the Leo Baeck Institute.[28] The scene remains Biedermeier Berlin but the action is put back (for no apparent reason) seven years, to 1832. The synopsis introduces a new character, one Madame Boulanger, who runs a fashionable clothing boutique. Julius Jacoby cuts a much more dashing figure than in the novels and is quite the man of the world. It transpires that he and Madame Boulanger are old friends from Posen and that her French persona is an act. The main storyline remains the love affair between Jettchen and Kössling but there is also a subplot focusing on Julius and Madame Boulanger's on/off relationship. Uncle Eli provides intermittent comic relief. Kössling, rather than being the frustrated serious writer of the novel, is a fashion journalist but he remains a man of limited means and a Christian. Uncle Salomon is staunch in his opposition to the projected match. Jettchen will marry the man he has chosen for her, he tells Jason, and that is all there is to it. That man, of course, is Julius.

As the wedding celebrations are coming to a close, and the moment drawing nearer when the bride and groom should be departing together, Jettchen retreats to her room. Sobbing, she tells her maid that she can't go through with the marriage and rushes off. She seeks sanctuary in Jason's house and has not been there long before Kössling also turns up. He and Jettchen, on being reunited, embrace passionately. Julius and members of the family arrive soon afterwards looking for Jettchen but Jason tells them that she will be staying at his house tonight. 'Don't worry, my girl,' he smiles at Jettchen fondly, 'we'll let fate take its course without silly human interfering. You must be happy now. The family you can leave to Uncle Jason!'

The hope was that Hollywood would want to sprinkle some of its magic on Jettchen's story. Hermann's letters to Hilde make repeated reference to the project, in particular to the terms of the contract with Arthur Hirsch of Westend Verlag. He had been offered a ten per cent cut of any profits but he wanted Hilde, who was acting on his behalf in the matter, to try to secure him a twenty per cent stake.[29] But it was not to be. The film was never produced and proved to be only another disappointment.

Writing to Hilde on Christmas Eve, 1935, Hermann tells her that it is a perfect winter's day and he wishes that she was with him to share it, or that he was with her in Copenhagen. *Rosenemil* has been well-received, he writes, but he makes no money from it. He is becoming increasingly conscious of the constraints placed on his life by his financial circumstances. He feels frustrated. He is still working a little and remains hopeful that his prospects will improve. But he needs a film or a gold nugget from Klondike.[30]

Soon after Hermann went into exile in the Netherlands, his brother Heinrich had also left Germany. An architect by profession but also a dabbler in the antiques trade (Eva remembered him doing business with Harrods), he realized that he had no future in Germany, and although sixty-six years old when Hitler came to power, decided to emigrate. Heinrich had remained a bachelor his whole life. According to Eva, this was because of a failed relationship in his youth, after which his former girlfriend had taken her own life.[31]

Heinrich promised his mother shortly before her death in 1910 that he would take care of his unmarried sister, Else, and they lived together in an apartment in Berlin until 1933. In her recollections, Usche recalls her childhood memories of the pair:

> I knew Uncle Heinrich and liked him; and also knew Aunt Else. [...] She and Heinrich shared one of those old-fashioned flats in Berlin. Neither of them ever married. Heinrich, an architect, was always the perfect gentleman. However, the two of them regularly quarrelled and yelled at one another! I remember the flat as having a rather gloomy atmosphere with very long corridors, and Uncle Heinrich had his room somewhere near the entrance. There was a live-in maid in the household, and Else kept a very large Alsatian dog. [...] I remember that she was a rather stern person. She and Uncle Heinrich adopted a boy who later ended up being a criminal. This was a very unfortunate chapter in their lives which they tried to cover up. However, they were regularly called to attend the juvenile court because of the problems of their adopted son.[32]

Family correspondence in the Swiss Institute for Egyptian Architectural and Archaeological Research in Cairo sheds more light on the difficulties linked to this adopted son, Walter.[33] It appears that, amongst other things, he had been secretly

FIG. 13.4. Heinrich Borchardt.

meeting with Else for some time to extort money from her. When Heinrich relocated to Rome, she also left Germany and went to live in Rapallo. However, in January 1935 Ludwig and Mimi decided that Else should return to Berlin to live in an old people's home. They thought she would be more comfortable in the familiar surroundings of the city and that the home would offer protection against Walter. Heinrich, however, was opposed to Else returning to Germany. He had written to Mimi in December 1934 to say that contrary to what she and Ludwig thought, most Jews now lived there as if in the ghetto and felt a sense of helpless anger at their deep humiliation. In another letter to his sister-in-law from February 1935 he reiterated that there could be no future for the Jews in Germany: 'Die ganze, ganze Jugend steht gegen uns. Die Jugend ist die Zukunft — unsere Zukunft in Deutschland. Unser Kampf ist verloren.' [All of the young people stand against us. The young people represent the future, our future in Germany. Our struggle is lost].[34]

Heinrich was just one of an estimated three thousand German Jews who sought refuge in Mussolini's Italy in the first years after Hitler's rise to power.[35] But not long after he had settled in Rome, his health deteriorated. We know from one of Hermann's letters to Hilde, for instance, that he was in the city's *Ospedale Israelitico*, in March 1935.[36] Heinrich was back in the hospital six months later and died there in his sleep on 16 September.

Hermann was closer to Heinrich than he appears to have been to Ludwig and Else and the news of his brother's death hit him hard. Only ten days before he died Heinrich had written to thank Hermann for sending him a copy of *Rosenemil*. He praised the book as a *glückliches Produkt* [delightful work] and said that there was a more rapid flow of action than was normally the case with a Georg Hermann novel. He looked forward to the success the book's merits must surely guarantee and which in turn he hoped would enable his younger brother to visit him in Rome.[37]

Although, according to Hermann, Heinrich was somewhat irascible (*ein Bullerkopp*) he was in the final analysis the most sensitive, artistic and humane of the siblings.[38] Characteristically, Hermann felt that the loss of his brother signified the passing of a former time. Within a decade, if not five years, he wrote to Hilde, the whole of the 'Borchardt generation' would be no more.[39] Knowledge of their life and times should be passed on, Hermann tells Hilde, but he fears that it will fade away and become little more than a fable.

It emerged when Heinrich's will was read that Else was his sole heir although provision was made for Eva, Hilde and Usche in the event of her death.[40] Under the terms of the will, however, Else was unable to dispose of anything without Ludwig and Mimi's consent. Presumably Heinrich had added this condition to stop Walter, their adopted son, from getting his hands on the estate. Heinrich requested that his ashes be buried in the Weißensee Jewish Cemetery, either in his sister Rose's grave or next to it. He asked that the words 'Es sei, wie es sei — es war so doch schön' [Let it be as it may — yet it was beautiful in its own way] should be inscribed on the grave.[41]

Hermann dedicated his next novel *Der etruskische Spiegel* [The Etruscan Mirror] to his brother's memory.[42] Its protagonist, the sixty-one year old Harry Frank, not

FIG. 13.5. Else Borchardt.

only shares Heinrich's forename but, like him, is a bachelor and a Jewish-German architect who leaves Hitler's Germany for Italy. We learn that Harry's family has long been resident in Berlin and that his Jewish origins have never been of great significance to him. His point of reference is North Germany. He identifies himself as a German, consistently thinking in his mind of 'we Germans'. It is only towards the end of the novel that Harry starts to think in terms of 'we Jews' and comes to regret that he knows so little about his Jewish heritage.

Although Harry shares Hermann's antipathy for all things military and abhors the autocratic nature of the regime of *Il Duce*, he is not someone driven by political ideology. He would happily bequeath a golden laurel wreath, we are told, on whoever can ensure that as many people as possible have a materially secure existence, whether they do so via capitalism, socialism, fascism or communism. That said, he does his best to ignore the fascism of the Italian state, turning a blind eye, for instance, to the effects of Mussolini's changes to Rome and the way in which the ugly four lanes of the Via dell'Impero have cut through the heart of the city's most prominent ancient excavations.

Harry's inner monologues dominate large sections of the novel and, as Nussbaum notes, to a degree the author's own experiences can be felt shimmering behind those of his fictional creation.[43] Like Harry, Hermann, now well into his second year in exile, was experiencing a sense of disorientation and loneliness. The trials of getting older were compounded by the challenges of living in a different country, and as Hermann had written in 'Weltabschied' the truth is 'alte Bäume gehen nicht an, wenn man sie verpflanzt.' [old trees don't grow as well when they are transplanted].[44]

Harry still longs for human warmth, for beauty and to be loved, and as well as dealing with issues of displacement and emigration, *Der etruskische Spiegel* is a love story. When travelling on the train to Rome, Harry meets Bellissima, the beautiful young widow of a Florentine archaeologist. She is in the carriage with her fifteen-year-old son, Achille, who is a jockey. They get talking and Bellissima offers lodgings to Harry in a *pensione* in their palatial home which is close to the Spanish Steps. Spending time with Bellissima, Harry experiences the city in an entirely new way and becomes increasingly immersed in its history and increasingly infatuated with her. The attraction is mutual — Bellissima finds Harry charming and cultivated and she appreciates his knowledge and affection for Italy. They become lovers.

On a whim, Harry buys a replica of an Etruscan hand mirror which he exchanges surreptitiously for an authentic one in an archaeological museum. The mirror proves to have magical properties and reveals scenes from the ancient time of the Etruscans. One of the visions which Harry sees in the mirror is of an Etruscan chariot race. A young charioteer who resembles Achille, on the verge of winning the race, is brought down and falls to his death. Harry believes that the vision is a premonition that Achille, who is due to ride in a horse race later that day, will be killed. He rushes to the racetrack to warn him not to take part but when he arrives, he hears that one of the boy jockeys has fallen. Without waiting to learn more, Harry leaves

FIG. 13.6. Charles Eyck's cover illustration for *Der etruskische Spiegel*

and goes to Ostia to the beach, with the intention of sinking the magic mirror in the sea. He believes that Achille's death will mean the end of his relationship with Bellissima. But Harry is mistaken. He has misinterpreted the images he saw in the mirror. Achille has survived the accident. It is his own death that the mirror has foretold. As he tries to sink the mirror into the sea, Harry drowns.

Hermann uses the mirror metaphor throughout both his fiction and non-fiction and *Der etruskische Spiegel* provides further evidence that he found something sinister and other-worldly about them: 'Die Spiegel haben für mich immer etwas Unheimliches gehabt, etwas von Totenbeschwörung.' [For me, mirrors have always had an unsettling, eerie quality, something of necromancy].[45] As Simone Langer has highlighted, there is a reference in the novel to Lafcadio Hearn's story *Of a Mirror and a Bell* (1904) which Hermann may have drawn upon in writing *Der etruskische Spiegel*. In the tale a young woman, after giving away a bronze mirror which has been in her family for many generations, ends up drowning herself.[46]

Der etruskische Spiegel and *B. M. Der unbekannte Fußgänger* were reviewed by Alfred Döblin in *Pariser Tageblatt*.[47] In his review, Döblin describes the novels as strange but interesting works, combining reportage and fantasy and emphasizes the poetic sense of melancholy which permeates both books. *Der etruskische Spiegel* was also reviewed positively a few days later in *Algemeen Handelsblad*. After drawing parallels with Hermann's *Tränen um Modesta Zamboni*, which Querido had published in 1928, the reviewer outlines the plot and key themes in the novel before concluding,

> Men geniet bij dit boek vooral van den rustigen, harmonischen stijl en van den fijnen, wijsgeerigen weemoed, waarmede het geschreven is, twee eigenschappen, die zich zeer gunstig onderscheiden van het gebrek aan distinctie, dat het gros der hedendaagsche Duitsche literatuur kenmerkt, onverschillig of zij in of buiten de grenzen van het Derde Rijk is ontstaan.

> [In this book, one particularly enjoys the calm, harmonious style and the fine, philosophical melancholy with which it is written, two qualities which differentiate it very favourably from the majority of contemporary German literature, whether originating from inside or outside the Third Reich.][48]

Hermann hoped that Döblin's review, in particular, would boost sales of the new books. He also had high hopes of an English translation of *Der etruskische Spiegel*, believing that the enticing descriptions of the Roman ambience would appeal to English readers. Nussbaum suggests that for this reason he may have played down the refugee aspect in the novel.[49]

But *Der etruskische Spiegel* failed to bring about any upturn in Hermann's circumstances. He continued to make no money. During the first six months of 1936 his total earnings amounted to just six guilders.[50] Earlier in the year he had written to Hilde, saying that although he was pleased that three of his books were in the shop window of a Hilversum bookseller (side-by-side, like three coquettish girls walking arm-in-arm, showing off their new outfits) he still felt that professionally he was making absolutely no headway in the Netherlands.[51]

With the German market closed to him, Hermann tried unsuccessfully to get Hachette which had published *La dette de Jettchen Gebert* back in 1911 to produce

French translations of *Rosenemil* and *B. M. Der unbekannte Fußgänger*. He also continued to seek a film adaptation of *Ellen Stein* and his letters to Hilde suggest that he had not entirely given up hope of a new movie of *Jettchen Gebert*. But it appears that Hermann had limited savings and increasingly he realized that things could not continue the way they were. Periodically, he considered selling pieces from his collection. By autumn 1936 he had to resort to taking money from the Amsterdam Jewish Refugee Committee and when there was a hiatus in the stipend being provided for Usche by Lotte's family, he was also tided over with some money from his brother Ludwig. It was a precarious existence.

In his letters Hermann suggests that if his circumstances were less insecure and he enjoyed greater piece of mind, he would probably be writing more but he is beset by the difficulty of getting any of his new work published. Accustomed to seeing his words in print on an almost daily basis for thirty years, now he was finding that his new works were little more than soliloquies. While Hilde, now Danish by marriage, was able to visit Berlin, it was not safe for Hermann to do so and his letters to his daughter evidence his growing sense of isolation. He did, however, remain aware of the deteriorating situation of the Jews within Germany. A visit from a former Ullstein editor early in 1936 reinforced his sense of their helplessness. When Eva told him in March that year that she was expecting a child, he was not altogether pleased at the news, given the family's current circumstances and the future being so uncertain. 'Über Evas Baby?! Sehr glücklich bin ich auch nicht drüber. Es ist nicht die Zeit, um Menschen in die Welt...' [About Eva's baby?! I am not very happy. Now is not the time to be bringing people into the world...].[52] However, he was confident that Ludwig and Mimi would not let the family go to rack and ruin.

Hermann's confidence in his brother and sister-in-law was not misplaced. That summer Eva met with Ludwig and Mimi when they were visiting Berlin. Mimi's biographer, Cilli Kasper-Holtkotte, believes that this meeting was pivotal and that thereafter she and Ludwig were committed to trying to help the family to leave Germany and get to the safety of England.[53] Ludwig was able to draw upon his network of contacts, most notably Sir Robert Mond with whom he had been friends for over forty years. Mond had worked with some of the principal Egyptologists of the time and helped set up a British School of Archaeology in Jerusalem. He was also an important figure in the British chemical industry, with a particular interest in luminescence, Siegfried's specialist area of expertise.

Eva's baby was born at Paul Strassman's clinic in Berlin, just before midday on 11 July 1936, and named Georg Heinrich Ludwig (Rothschild). Hermann told Hilde that it would have been better had the boy been called 'Georg Hermann' as Georg was a ubiquitous name whereas 'Georg Hermann' was more special and in the future would have reminded people of 'G. H.'[54] In any case and in keeping with family tradition, the baby was soon known by a completely different name (Bibi). Martha went to visit the new arrival in September but it does not appear that Hermann met his grandson in person during 1936. Nonetheless, he told Hilde that a picture which Eva sent him in September made him feel a very proud grandfather.[55]

Family matters take on increased significance in Hermann's letters from this time. Responding to Hilde's news that she has quit her job in the antiques trade, Hermann says that having worked in business for four years and been an office slave for half a year he understands the dreary sense of desolation that slowly eats away at you. But he shows a fatherly concern about what Hilde is going to do next. How does she spend her days now? Does she have any goals or is she just living day by day? Whereas his generation, he writes, felt a sense of purpose, he believes that Hilde and her peers — ravaged by war, revolution, inflation and political extremism — are like trees that have been stunted. When he comes across young people, especially young German Jews, he always finds the same thing — a sense of futility, a crippling lack of hope. Never, he says, has a generation been marked by such deep melancholy.[56]

Hermann's growing concern at the deteriorating political situation in Europe is also apparent in his letters of this period. He despairs at the lack of international response to Italy's invasion of Abyssinia and again wonders how much longer everybody can continue living with the powder keg that is Germany in their midst. How long, he asks, will it be before the continent goes up in flames?[57] He is very conscious of the Netherlands' proximity to Germany and the increasingly precarious nature of his own position: 'Der Boden, auf dem man stehen will, wird immer enger, und eine Scholle nach der andern bröckelt von der kleinen Insel in das Meer des Faschismus.' [The ground upon which one tries to stand becomes ever narrower and one clod of earth after another crumbles from the small island into the sea of fascism].[58]

In another letter, Hermann quotes from *Zarathustra* 'Das Leben ist ein Born der Lust; aber wo das Gesindel mit trinkt, da sind alle Brunnen vergiftet.' [Life is a well of delight; but where the rabble also drink, there, all fountains are poisoned].[59] But what Nietzsche probably never anticipated, Hermann tells Hilde, is that now the rabble drink everywhere.[60] Still, he was encouraged by the success of the Social Democrats in Scandinavia and believed that the Dutch, unlike their German neighbours, were not given to blind obedience and were generally too individualistic to ever succumb to the leader principle. Already, he writes, 120 years ago, Stendhal observed 'D[eutschland] ist der Tempel der Servilität, das Volk ist auf den Knien geboren.' [Germany is the high temple of servility, the people are born on their knees].[61]

In September 1936 Hermann was among a number of exiled German-Jewish writers who responded to a request from the Jewish literary journal *Der Morgen* to give their views on the present state and prospects of Jewish literature.[62] Hermann distinguishes in his response two broad groups of Jewish literature. One is insular in nature, concerned with, and targeted at Jews only. The other seeks to represent Jewish thought and what Hermann calls the 'specific Jewish mentality' in the world at large. Hermann says that he can only speak of this second type as that is what he is familiar with — German Jews writing as part of German literature in the same way that French, English and Russian Jews do in their countries. He points out that seeking to find a common denominator amongst these German, French, English and Jewish writers is only a recent pursuit and what's more, something that was first done by non-Jews. Yet, although the works of the likes of Altenberg and Schnitzler are evidently rooted in their experiences and impressions of the country of their birth, there is something common to these Jewish writers, Hermann believes, albeit very hard to put into words. This sensibility may be recognized more by what is absent rather than present.

The time has come, Hermann argues, when the preservation of this form of Jewish literature cannot be left to individual private initiative. Without institutional backing its position is hopeless and although it is a vital component of European culture, it will be expunged from it. Émigré writers require support, and he proposes that a publishing house should be established to enable them to publish their new works and issue new translations of existing novels to help foster the idea of unity among Jews of different languages and countries. Hermann's fear is that without this kind of support, the voices of these writers will cease to be heard and Judaism will be thrown back from the west to the east. Out of the European of 1936 will emerge the twelfth century 'östliche gothische Mensch' (Eastern Gothic man).

Notes to Chapter 13

1. Georg Hermann, *Rosenemil* (Amsterdam: Allert de Lange), 1935.
2. Hermann, *Der kleine Gast*, p. 24.
3. Reinhard Zachau, 'Writing under National Socialism', in *The Cambridge Companion to the Literature of Berlin*, ed. by Andrew J. Webber (Cambridge: Cambridge University Press, 2017), p. 120.
4. Letter from Sigmund Freud dated 28 February 1936, GHC; AR 7074; Box 1; Folder 1, LBI, 159/991.
5. Letter to Hilde, Autumn 1935, *Unvorhanden und stumm*, p. 67.
6. Nussbaum, 'Georg Hermann Attacks the Special Issue of *Der Jude*', p. 452.
7. Irmela von der Lühe, 'Versuch, im Schreiben zu überleben: Georg Hermanns *Rosenemil*', in Schoor (ed.), *Der Schriftsteller Georg Hermann*, pp. 203–09.
8. Godela Weiss-Sussex, 'Der Blick auf Berlin in Romanen exilierter Schriftsteller 1933–1936', in *Berlin Wien Prag: Modernity, Minorities and Migration in the Inter-War Period*, ed. by Susanne Marten-Finnis and Matthias Uecker (Bern: Peter Lang, 2001), p. 202.
9. Weiss-Sussex, 'Der Blick auf Berlin', p. 203.
10. Georg Hermann, *B. M. Der Unbekannte Fußgänger* (Amsterdam: Hertzberger, 1935).
11. Postcard to Hilde, 28 February 1934, *Unvorhanden und stumm* p. 36.
12. Hans Scholz, 'Georg Hermann und die Berliner Dichtung. Nachwort zur Neuauflage von *Rosenemil*' (Munich: Süddeutscher Verlag, 1962), p. 361.
13. Nussbaum, 'Georg Hermann Attacks the Special Issue of *Der Jude*', p. 453.
14. van Liere, *Georg Hermann: Materialien*, p. 217.
15. The family's address was Gundelfinger Straße 25, Berlin-Karlshorst.
16. Eva Rothschild, 'Berlin Reinickendorf 1935', in Rothschild, *Talking To Myself*, p. 84.
17. Letter to Hilde, 28 May 1935, *Unvorhanden und stumm*, p. 56.
18. Set design was by Heinz Cordell. Ruth Reimer played Jettchen, Walter Hertner, Kössling and Herbert Grünbaum, Julius Jacoby. See Rebecca Rovit, *The Jewish Kulturbund Theatre Company in Nazi Berlin* (Iowa City, IA: University of Iowa Press, 2012), pp. 69–71.
19. Letter to Hilde, 12 August 1935, *Unvorhanden und stumm*, p. 62.
20. Rovit, *The Jewish Kulturbund Theatre Company in Nazi Berlin*, p. 71.
21. (Munich: Franz Eher, 1935). The book was reprinted nineteen times in the six years to 1941.

22. Hermann, *Randbemerkungen*, p. 90.

23. Letter to Hilde, 20 June 1935, *Unvorhanden und stumm*, p. 60.

24. Letter to Hilde, end of August 1935, *Unvorhanden und stumm*, p. 63.

25. Letter to Hilde, 25 April 1936, *Unvorhanden und stumm*, p. 93.

26. Georg Hermann, 'Was sollen wir Juden tun', *c.* 1936, GHC; AR 7074; Box 5. Folder 66; LBI, p. 23. See also Kerstin Schoor, 'Was sollen wir Juden tun, Der Schriftsteller Georg Hermann zur Situation und den Perspektiven deutsch-jüdischer Existenz nach 1933', in Weiss-Sussex (ed.), *Georg Hermann: Deutsch-jüdischer Schriftsteller und Journalist*, p. 116.

27. Letter to Hilde, 30 March 1935, *Unvorhanden und stumm*, p. 52.

28. Ralf Roland, 'Jettchen Gebert — film synopsis', 1935, GHC; AR 7074; Box 4; Folder 17, LBI.

29. Hermann writes about the proposed contract in letters to Hilde throughout the last four months of 1935.

30. Letter to Hilde, 29 December 1935, *Unvorhanden und stumm*, p. 79.

31. Private family recording, 1991.

32. Ben-Dror, 'Recollections 1919–44'.

33. Details of this correspondence are provided in Cilli Kasper-Holtkotte, *Deutschland in Ägypten: Orientalistische Netzwerke, Judenverfolgung und das Leben der Frankfurter Jüdin Mimi Borchardt* (Oldenbourg: De Gruyter, 2017), pp. 305–10.

34. Ibid., p. 310.

35. See Klaus Voigt, 'Refuge and Persecution in Italy, 1933–1945', in *Simon Wiesenthal Center Annual*, vol. 4, ed. by H. Friedlander and S. Milton (Millwood, NY: Krauss International, 1987), pp. 3–64.

36. Letter to Hilde, 30 March 1935, *Unvorhanden und stumm*, p. 52.

37. Letter to Hilde, Autumn 1935, *Unvorhanden und stumm*, pp. 65–68.

38. Letter to Hilde, 6 October, *Unvorhanden und stumm*, p. 64.

39. Letter to Hilde, Autumn 1935, *Unvorhanden und stumm*, p. 66.

40. Eva had already written to say that if she, Hilde and Usche inherited anything in the future they should split it with Liese. *Unvorhanden und stumm*, p. 68.

41. Johann Wolfgang von Goethe, *Faust Part 2*, Act V, Scene IV, in *Works*, vol. 3 (Basel: Birkhauser, 1944), p. 344.

42. Georg Hermann, *Der etruskische Spiegel* (Amsterdam: Hertzberger, 1936). The novel included pictures by the Dutch Expressionist, Charles Eyck. The dedication reads 'Dem Andenken meines Bruders, des Architekten Heinrich Borchardt, gestorben in Rom 1935.'

43. Laureen Nussbaum, 'Assimilationsproblematik in Georg Hermanns letztem Exilroman, *Der etruskische Spiegel*', in *Deutsch-jüdisches Exil — und Emigrationsliteratur im 20. Jahrhundert*, ed. by Itta Shedletzky and Hans Otto Horch (Tübingen: Niemeyer, 1993), pp. 195–203.

44. *Unvorhanden und stumm*, p. 258.

45. Georg Hermann, *Der etruskische Spiegel* (Berlin: Das Neue Berlin, 1998), p. 149.

46. Ibid., p. 130. The story can be found in Lafcadio Hearn, *Kwaidan: Stories and Studies of Strange Things* (New York: Dover, 1968), pp. 24–28.

47. Alfred Döblin, 'Review of *B.M.* and *Der etruskische Spiegel*', in *Pariser Tageblatt*, 1 March 1936.

48. Chris de Graaff, 'Duitsche Literatuur', *Algemeen Handelsblad*, 7 March 1936, p. 3. Hermann wrote the following day to tell Hilde about the review. See his 8 March 1936 letter, *Unvorhanden und stumm*, p. 87. Later critiques of the novel have been less positive. Horch, for instance, notes its operetta-like features (Horch, 'Über Georg Hermann', p. 82).

49. Nussbaum, 'Georg Hermann Attacks the Special Issue of *Der Jude*', p. 453.

50. Letter to Hilde, end of June 1936, *Unvorhanden und stumm*, p. 100.

51. Letter to Hilde, 18 January 1936, *Unvorhanden und stumm*, p. 82.

52. Letter to Hilde, 8 March 1936, *Unvorhanden und stumm*, pp. 87–88.

53. Kasper-Holtkotte, *Deutschland in Ägypten*, p. 314.

54. Letter to Hilde, 13 July 1936, *Unvorhanden und stumm*, p. 103.

55. Letter to Hilde, Autumn 1936, *Unvorhanden und stumm*, p. 109.

56. Letter to Hilde, 3 September 1936, *Unvorhanden und stumm*, p. 108.

57. Letter to Hilde, 2 March 1936, *Unvorhanden und stumm*, p. 86.

58. Letter to Hilde, 9 July 1936, *Unvorhanden und stumm*, p. 101.
59. Friedrich Nietzsche, *Also sprach Zarathustra: Ein Buch fuer Alle und Keinen 1883–85*, ed. by Giorgo Colli and Mazzino Montinari (Berlin: De Gruyter, 1968), p. 254.
60. Letter to Hilde, 20 October 1936, *Unvorhanden und stumm*, p. 110.
61. Letter to Hilde, 3 November 1936, *Unvorhanden und stumm*, p. 112.
62. 'Gegenwart und Zukunft der jüdischen Literatur', *Der Morgen*, Berlin, September 1936, 245–65. Following an introductory essay by Hans Bach, the journal's editor, there are contributions from Hermann (pp. 251–54), Max Brod, Else Lasker-Schüler, Ernst Lissauer, Alfred Mombert, Soma Morgenstern, Jacob Picard, Kurt Pinthus, Alfred Wolfenstein, Otto Zarek and Stefan Zweig. For more about *Der Morgen*, see Sarah Fraiman, 'The Transformation of Jewish Consciousness in Nazi Germany as Reflected in the German Jewish Journal, *Der Morgen*, 1925–1938', *Modern Judaism*, vol. 20, no. 1 (2000), 41–59.

CHAPTER 14

❖

An Impecunious
Old Age

'God protect me from my friends; from my enemies I will protect myself.' So
opens Hermann's 1937 essay 'Eine Lanze für die Westjuden' [A Lance for the
Western Jews].[1] Like *Der doppelte Spiegel* the essay was triggered by something that
Hermann had read. In this case it was the 'unerhörte[r] und unbewiesene[r] Unsinn'
[outrageous and unproven nonsense] of Professor Förster. A leading German
academic and philosopher, Friedrich Wilhelm Förster was a 'friend' in the sense
that he was a committed pacifist and publicly opposed to Nazism. Like Hermann,
his books had been burned by the Nazis and as early as August 1933 his German
citizenship was revoked.

But although natural bedfellows in many respects, Hermann took great exception
to what he saw as Förster's unfounded criticisms of secular Western Jews in works
such as 1937's *Europa und die deutsche Frage* [Europe and the German Question]. In
particular, Hermann took issue with the way in which Förster and others were
vilifying assimilated Western Jews for having lost connection with their roots and
faith. Hermann asks how best we should judge the value of a human being's life. Is
it his piety, his relationship with God, the extent of his adherence to the religion
into which he was born? Do we judge a Jew by how often he goes to the synagogue,
how quickly he dons tefillin, how well his wife maintains religious rituals in the
home? Rather, Hermann argues, we should judge a person by the contribution he
makes to society at large, by his legacy and how it enriches the lives of others. Great
musicians, composers, painters, architects, poets and writers, doctors and inventors
— these are the people we should be celebrating. Does the fact that neither
Einstein nor Liebermann are religiously observant diminish their contribution to
society at large?

According to Förster, the Jews should confront their errors, the most prominent of
which on the part of the secular rootless Jews is their self-worship. The intellectual
power, imagination and willpower which before was invested in worshipping God,
has now been misdirected to the self. Hubris has supplanted faith. Hermann refutes
this notion of the pushy, self-aggrandizing Jew and draws a contrast between the
Jewish intellectuals he has known personally, some of them the leaders in their
fields, with the pomposity and megalomania of leading Nazis. Now in 1937 we
realize, as we did not in 1933, Hermann writes, that the slavish German mentality is

FIG. 14.1. Hermann with his grandson, Georg, Hilversum, 1938.

particularly receptive to the 'Führerprinzip'. Only those who are stupid, Hermann continues, can display such unshakeable self-confidence. If they understood a little more, they would realize the extent of their stupidity. The man of knowledge recognizes how small a span of understanding his single mind can attain.

Förster's mistake, Hermann contends, is that he sees the question of the Jews in purely religious terms, rather than as a people with a shared mentality predicated on a common belief in the sanctity of mankind. While assimilated Western Jews, like himself, do not want to lead lives that are circumscribed by age-old rituals, it is mistaken to equate assimilation and the lack of religious practice with a loss of Jewishness. Their Jewishness remains firmly a part of their lives, a sacred tradition. In his works, Hermann continues, he has represented Western Jews of all types — from the secure successful citizens to those on the margins of society. It is precisely because he knows this culture of the Jews before 1933 so well, both its perfections and imperfections, that Hermann feels entitled to defend Western Jewry from the unjustified accusations it now faces.

Although continuing to write, Hermann was increasingly hampered by health and financial problems. His diabetes worsened to the point where his heart became enlarged. His blood pressure reached 175/100 and from early October 1937 he started injecting insulin on a daily basis.[2] There were also problems with the stipend the Samters sent for Usche. Sometimes it would not arrive and then Hermann would have to ask Ludwig and Mimi if they could make up the shortfall. Meanwhile he was still procrastinating about selling pieces from his collection. In March 1937 the director of the Asian Museum in Amsterdam visited to look at his Japanese artworks but Hermann appears to have held off selling.[3] As he wrote to Hilde, his circumstances could change tomorrow if he found a publisher who would reissue his old works and agree to publish his new stories. Such optimism was not wholly unfounded. Shortly afterwards, the Amsterdam publishing house De Arbeiderspers paid Hermann money upfront for a new paperback edition combining the Dutch translation of the two Jettchen novels in a single volume.[4] 25,000 copies were printed the following year and presumably the sales generated some welcome royalties for Hermann.

Around the time of the museum director's visit, Hermann learned that Fritz Hirsch was going to revive the musical version of *Jettchen Gebert*. Hirsch, a former Berlin stage actor, had founded his company, the Fritz Hirsch Operetta in The Hague in 1929. The company first staged the musical the following year under the title *Wenn der weiße Flieder wieder blüht* [When the White Lilac is Again in Bloom].[5] It was a great success and ran for 175 performances. Hirsch had been invited back to Berlin to be the manager of Berlin's Schiller Theatre in 1932 but the appointment turned out to be short-lived. In February 1933 Hirsch was sacked (presumably because he was Jewish) and he returned to the Netherlands and re-formed his company. As before, Hirsch's popular romantic operettas proved to be very successful.

The revival of the musical occasioned an interview with Hermann published in the 16 March 1937 edition of *Het Vaderland*. The paper's literary affairs editor, Menno ter Braak, was the interviewer and he met Hermann in The Hague on

FIG. 14.2. Poster for *Wenn der weiße Flieder wieder blüht*.

the day the show opened at the Princesse Schouwburg, while final rehearsals were taking place. Much of what we know about Hermann during the late thirties comes from his letters to Hilde. They show us his private self but in ter Braak's article we catch a rare glimpse of Hermann's public persona — the distinguished writer, holding court. In the preamble to the interview, ter Braak emphasizes to his Dutch readers the extent to which Hermann is one of their own. He points out that in addition to *Jettchen Gebert* other Hermann novels like *Schnee, Die Nacht des Doktor Herzfeld* and *Kubinke* have been translated into Dutch. For a time, ter Braak suggests, Hermann was 'een der populairste auteurs van.... Nederland' [one of the most popular authors of the Netherlands].[6] Moreover, he has been living in the country for four years because '...want zijn bloed heeft enige fouten die ongeneeslijk zijn in bepaalde gewesten.' [his blood contains some flaws that are incurable in certain regions].[7]

Hermann's whole appearance and manner is that of the connoisseur, ter Braak observes. An indefatigable conversationalist, he flits from one subject to another but speaks with authority on them all. His conversation is sprinkled with a seemingly inexhaustible supply of anecdotes and *bons mots*, all garnished with Berlin humour. He takes pleasure and care in the telling of his stories, and, as is characteristic of the true connoisseur, he has an eye for detail — not necessarily because it has wider significance but simply for its own sake. Chatting with Georg Hermann, ter Braak writes, one experiences the joy of good conversation and old fashioned bonhomie.

It is clear from ter Braak's article that their conversation was wide-ranging. It encompassed Hermann's views on contemporary novels (overly concerned with action to the detriment of capturing ambience and that quiet and pensiveness which recommends a book to the more discerning reader), and dramatizations of his novels and other writers' such as Wassermann, Heinrich and Thomas Mann, Dostoevsky and Feuchtwanger. He tells ter Braak that Dutch literature remains too insular. What Dutch writers do, they do well but with the odd exception like Multatuli[8] they are rarely outstanding, in Hermann's opinion. He regrets that nowadays the only Dutch writer whose works are being translated into German is Jo van Ammers-Küller.[9]

The conversation also took in the actor Alexander Moissi about whom Hermann had written in *Die Zeitlupe*.[10] Hermann quips that he discovered Moissi almost unwillingly because he has never been a great theatregoer for the simple fact that the curtain goes up at the same time that he would otherwise be settling down to dinner. He talks about his appreciation for and friendships with German painters such as Liebermann and Slevogt, as well as sharing his thoughts with ter Braak on Dutch painters and on the idiosyncrasies of the Berlin dialect. Rather like a butterfly darting from one flower to the next, Hermann then lands on the subject of his readers who, he tells ter Braak fall into three groups, 'the Hermannophilien, the Hermannologen and the Hermannomanen'. In fact, Hermann tells ter Braak, 'Meine Hauptverehrer waren alle verrückt!' [my most enthusiastic admirers are all crazy]. His number one fan is to be found in 'een krankzinnigengesticht.' [a lunatic asylum].[11]

One has the feeling, ter Braak writes, that Hermann could go on chatting indefinitely, offering up a Berlin cornucopia of anecdotes and aperçus but eventually thoughts turn to that night's performance of the musical, and Hermann remarks, 'Eigenlijk heeft men niets nodig dan een goede schaar om van een roman een operette te maken!' [Actually it takes nothing more than a good pair of scissors to make an operetta of a novel!].[12] Hirsch who overhears this heresy only grins and Hermann also smiles because he does not really mean it. He just wants to conjure forth another *bon mot* from his collection.

Hermann seems to have enjoyed *Wenn der weiße Flieder wieder blüht*. Writing afterwards to Hilde, he said that taken as a whole the show was less idiotic than the average operetta or musical comedy. Moreover, it might sound arrogant, but he believed that there was something 'Unsterbliches' [eternal] about *Jettchen* which enabled it to withstand any treatment, some inherent quality that could not be completely extinguished.[13] Following that opening night in The Hague, Hirsch's company staged many successful performances of the musical all over the Netherlands.[14] Subsequent letters to Hilde show that Hermann took efforts to make sure that he was receiving royalties from the theatre agent and publisher, Kurt Reiss, for the current production and previous performances by Hirsch. However, it appears that he made only a small amount of money from the venture.[15]

In May 1937 a general election took place in the Netherlands and Hermann was naturally concerned to see how the Dutch Nazi Party would fare. The National Socialist Movement in the Netherlands (NSB) had been founded in 1931 but did not become openly anti-Semitic until 1936. Despite a well-organized campaign, it only gained four per cent of the votes. Hermann, writing to Hilde on the morning that the results were declared, described the election as a funeral for the Dutch Nazis and applauded the fact that the Dutch had not fallen for the same lies as the Germans. Moreover, he tells Hilde, 'das Beste ist, daß ja auch dadurch wir Fremden vorerst mal nichts zu fürchten haben, und daß man, statt die Zelte abzubrechen, noch ein paar Zeltstangen in den Boden rammen kann.' [The best thing is that we emigrants — for the time being at least — have nothing to fear and instead of having to unpitch our tents, can bang a few more pegs into the ground].[16]

But noting that only those aged over twenty-five could vote, Hermann remained concerned about the influence the NSB was exerting on young people and felt that more should be done to counter its impact. Hermann also believed that the other small democracies of Europe should band together much more closely. He feared that, if the Nazi-backed Fascists succeeded in Spain then 'Holland, Belgien, Tschechei — nachdem Österreich geschluckt wurde — das nächste, was drankommt oder doch auf dem Programm steht.' [Holland, Belgium, Czechoslovakia — after Austria has been swallowed up — would come next or at least be placed in the Fascists' sights].[17]

Nussbaum suggests that the May election results may have rekindled Hermann's affection for the Netherlands, as reflected in two unpublished essays which date from spring 1937. In 'Neue Heimat', Hermann writes about the pleasures of travelling on the Gooische Tram between Hilversum and Amsterdam, in particular the views of the beautiful Naarden countryside. He thanks that 'Billardspieler' Fate that he has arrived at this spot on the earth where despite all the woes in the world, he can still enjoy the sight and sweet smell of the blossoming apple trees and watch the tender new green leaves on the birches being ruffled in the breeze.[18] In the other essay, 'Vier Jahre Holland', Hermann gives an upbeat assessment of the Netherlands.[19] He praises its commitment to education and culture, the artistic talents of its people and the way that it maintains its traditions without becoming moribund. Hermann extols the quality of its libraries, the exhibitions he has been able to enjoy and the concerts. Even the children are cheerful despite seeming to be always having to sit school exams.

Since *Der etruskische Spiegel* Hermann had produced only short pieces — unpublished essays, short stories and personal reflections. We know that he was keeping some kind of diary. In his letter to Hilde of 7 January 1937 he makes reference to a fairly thick book he is compiling which comprises short pieces setting out his thoughts on the times. He likens it to *Randbemerkungen*. Sadly, it has not survived.[20] In March 1937, he was telling Hilde that he could not bring himself to write anything more substantial. His last three novels were good, had garnered reviews as if Goethe and Schiller had written them together, but had achieved zero sales. And the reason why, Hermann complained, was that there was no organisation to promote and support the works of refugees. They simply disappeared without a trace.[21]

But by early July, things had changed and Hermann was telling Hilde that he was 120 pages into a new novella.[22] 'Bist du es oder bist du's nicht?' [Is it you or is it not you?] takes its title from a nursery rhyme and, as with the Herzfeld novels, deals with questions of identity.[23] Indeed, Hermann described his new work as a *Nacht des Doktor Herzfeld* turned into fantasy. Like that earlier novel, there is very little in the way of action and the timeframe is compressed. Set in summer 1932 the story unfolds over just one evening and the following night. The protagonist, a maverick Bohemian who shares many of Hermann's traits, sits in his Berlin studio apartment, walks through the city's streets, all the time looking back on his life. The novella is dominated by memories, thoughts, conversations and essay-style expositions which appear like random individual strands but which are brought together by Hermann in the story's conclusion. Familiar Hermann themes feature — the atmosphere of Berlin on a summer's night, his ambivalence towards big city life and the chance encounter which has fatal consequences.

But what is different, as Weiss-Sussex highlights, is the background to the story: the description of the situation of Jewish intellectuals in the year before Hitler came to power. He presents a spectrum of ideological types from those who want to see German literature understood 'as a matter of the German people' to the increasingly embittered Jewish cosmopolitans. Among the latter circle, the institutionalized anti-Semitism is still a taboo subject although in reality it has already come to dominate their lives and goes far beyond literary considerations. It is experienced as a lethal threat and Weiss-Sussex notes that Hermann's depiction of the marginalisation and vulnerability of the German-Jewish intelligentsia in the novella is sharper than in any of his previous literary works.

Hermann had concerns about the possible consequences for Eva if 'Bist du es oder bist du's nicht?' was published, even though he purposefully set it in 1932. But he questioned how much longer she and the children could remain in Germany in any case. He told Hilde in July 1937, 'Auf die Dauer kann man ja doch da [in Deutschland] nicht bleiben [...], auch selbst wenn keine Pogrome mal kommen! [...] Denn daß das Pulverfaß Europa mal explodiert, ist ja doch nur eine Frage der Zeit.' [In the long run they cannot stay in Germany, even if no further pogroms come! That the powder keg will at some point cause Europe to explode is just a question of time].[24]

Usche celebrated her eighteenth birthday that summer. Due to the amount of schooling she had missed earlier in the year when she had been ill with pneumonia, she failed her final exams and, much to Hermann's frustration, refused to go back to school to retake them. In her recollections she recalls saying to her father, 'I'm not going to do these grades again, whatever you say or do, and I'm going to leave school!' He answered, 'so what will you do, be a salesgirl selling chewing gum or flowers?'[25]

Eventually, Hermann accepted that Usche was not willing to continue her studies for the time being. The truth remained however, he wrote to Hilde, that she would have a better chance of a decent life and of being able to fully enjoy the cultural riches of this world as an educated woman. But she shows no interest. Hermann complains that although he has over 1500 books in the house covering all kinds of subjects, Usche doesn't read them and barely looks over the titles on their spines. He sees her apparent lack of interest as being at odds with family tradition:

> Ich hasse aber nichts so wie *Niedergang*. [...] wir kommen wenigstens von einer Seite, seit 180 Jahren (denn Moses Mendelssohn und Felix Mendelssohn Bartholdy stehen uns nahe, sind aus der *gleichen* Mischpoche!) aus Ställen, bei denen es als selbstverständlich galt, daß das Geistige wertvoller und wichtiger war als das Materielle — wo sie schon vor *vier* Generationen und *früher* studiert haben, etc. etc. *Geld* haben wir *nicht mehr* — aber 'runterkommen und uns auf die andere Seite der Unkultur schlagen und zu den Bowkes flüchten und herabsinken, das wollen und dürfen wir nicht.

> [I hate nothing so much as *decline*. [...] we come from a family where — at least on one side — for 180 years (since Moses Mendelssohn and Felix Mendelssohn-Bartholdy are related to us and from the same *mischpoche*!) it has been taken for granted that the spiritual cultural side of life was of more importance than the material — where going back *four* generations and earlier, all of the members of the family studied etc. etc. We do not have money anymore but to cross over to the other side and sink into the ranks of the uncultured and good-for-nothings, that we do not want and cannot be allowed.][26]

It was decided that Usche should go abroad. She had a gift for languages and Hermann believed that a spell in London would enable her to further improve her English. She would also benefit from being in a different atmosphere and encouraged to become more independent in her intellectual interests, he told Hilde. Then, he anticipated, she would return to Holland and finish her education.

Usche sailed from Ostend to Dover on 7 December 1937:

> Because we did not have much money, Peps talked the Jewish Committee in Amsterdam [...] into sending me to their equivalent centre in Woburn House in London. They agreed that I could go for an intensive one month course in English, and covered my fees and fares. [...] I was booked into the Masterman-Smith English Language Institute near Victoria Station to which I commuted by the Number 2 bus from Swiss Cottage. [...] Coming across to London on my own as a late teenager suited me because I was both naïve and independent! I was ignorant of the risks for a girl on her own because my father had left me to fend for myself so much. I recall that I had the time of my life over there — meeting people in buses and so on![27]

Usche did very well at the English Language Institute, getting almost full marks in her final exams, much to Hermann's pleasure. The purpose of the exercise, he said, had been achieved. She now had learned to speak decent English but what she should do next, he told Hilde, he really did not know.[28]

In late October 1937 Eva had come for a visit to the Netherlands with the children. They stayed with Martha in Amsterdam. Hermann wrote to Hilde that Eva was much better for being away from Germany and how he had noticed that after a few days she seemed more her old self. Living in Germany has a corrosive effect on the soul, he tells Hilde. You don't have to be a Jew to experience that, just 'ein Mensch'.[29]

As Hermann recognized, the situation for Jews in Germany was becoming increasingly untenable. The early months of 1938 saw a fresh wave of radical anti-Semitism sweeping the country. It was particularly virulent in Berlin. The year before, the rabidly anti-Semitic Julius Lippert, one of the men who had assassinated Walther Rathenau in 1922, had become the city's mayor. Goebbels announced that the capital would soon be 'uncontaminated by Jews' and told a meeting of 300 of the city's policemen that 'law is not the order of the day but harassment'.[30]

It seems that Siegfried was again out of work, presumably a victim of the increased clampdown on the employment of Jews in the city. It was probably his lack of work, coupled with the ever more intimidating atmosphere in the capital that finally made him and Eva decide they must leave Germany. What that period in their lives was like, the five years they remained in the Third Reich, one dreads to imagine. That both Eva and Siegfried had been actively seeking opportunities outside Germany is evidenced by their inclusion in a 1936 London publication entitled, *Displaced German Scholars: A Guide to Academics in Peril in Nazi Germany* which was intended to help those listed find suitable positions abroad.[31]

By February 1938 Eva had told her father of their decision to leave Germany.[32] They could not take up residence in Amsterdam, due to new restrictions placed on refugees which had come into effect on 1 January. But, having exhausted all possibilities within Germany and reached breaking point, Hermann informed Hilde, one way or another, they will be coming to Holland. With Eva's departure, the only member of Hermann's immediate family still left in Germany, more than two hundred years after his ancestor Samuel of Jever first entered Berlin, was now his sister, Else.

The position of the Dutch government towards refugees had hardened significantly since Hermann's flight five years earlier. In the wake of the Great Depression, the 1930s were proving to be a period of prolonged recession in the Netherlands, marked by levels of unemployment as high as nineteen per cent.[33] From the introduction of the first restrictions in 1935, the government sought to justify its refugee policy by a perceived need to protect job opportunities for Dutch citizens. The Dutch government also consistently refused financial assistance to refugees. The Jewish Relief Association in Amsterdam which funded Usche's trip to England and helped Hermann when he was without means, relied entirely on private support. New restrictions on the ability of refugees to work were introduced just before Eva's arrival in the Netherlands. Hermann wrote to Hilde of his concern about what they might mean for Liese's job. Naturalisation was a complicated and expensive process and he realized that the family's German passports were likely to be withdrawn or not renewed.[34]

Hermann was also becoming increasingly conscious of the likelihood of another military conflict. He told Hilde,

> ... der Krieg ist eine Gewitterwolke über der ganzen Welt mit schwefelig gelber Beleuchtung, die schon jetzt jeden vor den Blitzen zittern macht. [...] weil eben schon morgen die Gewitterwolken da oben nicht nur über Europa, sondern über die ganze Welt sich entladen können.

> [War is a storm cloud hanging over the entire world, the flashes of its sulphurous yellow lightning already make us tremble. [...] Just tomorrow the storm clouds above can shed their load not only over Europe but over the whole world.][35]

Germany's invasion and annexation of Austria on 12 March 1938 only increased Hermann's sense of foreboding. In a postcard to Hilde, nine days later, he tells of his deep sense of despair at what has happened and what will happen. He can find no solace even in his revered trinity of Goethe, Stendhal and Fontane.[36] As with Dr Herzfeld in *Schnee*, Hermann's cultural icons could no longer offer any relief. He continued to write — he was busy with a new short story, 'Erste Liebe' (First Love) during this period — but it was becoming ever harder for him to earn his livelihood:

> Ich bin jener Georg Hermann, der die beiden *Jettchen-Gebert-Bände* — zusammen deutsch in über dreimal hunderttausend Exemplaren erschienen, und in ein Dutzend Sprachen übersetzt — *Kubinke, Nacht des Dr. Herzfeld* etc., und noch über ein Dutzend mehr oder minder bekannte Romane geschrieben hat und eigentlich Georg Hermann-Borchardt heißt, am 7. X. 1871 in Berlin geboren ist, und augenblicklich in Hilversum N H Siriusstraat 59 wohnt. Wenn Sie, da ich eigentlich von Tag zu Tag mehr in Bedrängnis komme, für mich etwas tun könnten, wäre ich Ihnen aufrichtig dankbar.

> [I'm that Georg Hermann of the two *Jettchen Gebert* volumes which have sold over 300,000 copies since they first appeared in Germany and were translated into a dozen languages. I also wrote *Kubinke, Die Nacht des Dr Herzfeld* etc. plus a dozen other more or less well-known novels. [...] I am currently living in Hilversum, [...]. Every day my situation becomes more distressed and if you could do something to help me I would be sincerely grateful.][37]

Fig. 14.3. Ludwig Borchardt

So wrote Hermann in a letter dated 13 March 1938 to the American Guild for German Cultural Freedom. The guild had been founded in New York three years earlier by Prince Hubertus zu Löwenstein, a prominent opponent of the Nazis who like Hermann had left Germany soon after they came to power following a tip-off that he was about to be arrested and sent to a concentration camp.[38] Hermann was one of those invited to become a member of the academy but he appears to have been perceived as a writer whose best days were behind him. Thomas Mann in a note to his daughter Erika (they were both actively involved with the guild) wrote, presumably in connection with Hermann's March letter, 'Georg Hermann-Borchardt: old jewish [sic] writer. Has been *very* famous, because of some novels on the Jewish bourgeoisie. If he is to be helped, so more because of his past than of his future.'[39]

Hermann was not helped. Despite subsequent letters like that of March 1938, the guild which provided Germany Academy in Exile scholarships to over 160 individuals including Bertolt Brecht, Elisabeth Castonier, Alfred Döblin, Egon Erwin Kisch, Robert Musil, Alfred Neumann, Joseph Roth and Arnold Zweig between 1938 and 1940 did not see fit to award one to Hermann. Neither was the guild receptive to Hermann's suggestions that it should step up its activities to support exiled writers. He proposed that it should bring out a series of cheap books of their best known novels and also promote young writers who otherwise would have no opportunities. In addition, Hermann advocated the development of a 'Jewish Cultural Library' which would document the role of Jews in European culture. What the guild did do in 1938 was to organize a literary contest with a prize of $5,365. Hermann was among the 177 writers who entered. The guild's archives show that he submitted *Bist du es oder bist du's nicht?* but it did not make the shortlist.[40]

On 8 May 1938, my mother's seventh birthday, she, together with my grandparents and little Georg, finally left Germany, travelling second class on the train to Amsterdam where they arrived that evening and were met by Hermann, Martha and Liese. They stayed for a few days in the city before going on to Hilversum where they moved in with Hermann and Usche. Initially on arrival, Siegfried and Eva were granted a residency permit for just eight days and classified as 'lästige Ausländer mit Kindern' [Undesirable Aliens with Children]. 'Reizend!' [Charming!] commented Eva in a letter to Ludwig and Mimi.[41]

In her recollections Usche describes the months after Eva arrived with the children as being a very happy time for her:

> I had a great time with George, who was so receptive to everything and amongst other things, I taught him to speak. I was able to spend time with Ipi, Eva and the children, right up until the time that they all left for England.[42]

My mother had started school in autumn 1937 at Volksschule 29 in Karlshorst. After two terms there she now enrolled at the Openbare Lagere School No. 17 in Hilversum and suddenly had to adjust to everything being in Dutch. But she managed to pick up the language quickly and soon made new friends. Hermann wrote to Hilde in October that Ate was loving school in Holland, unlike in Berlin,

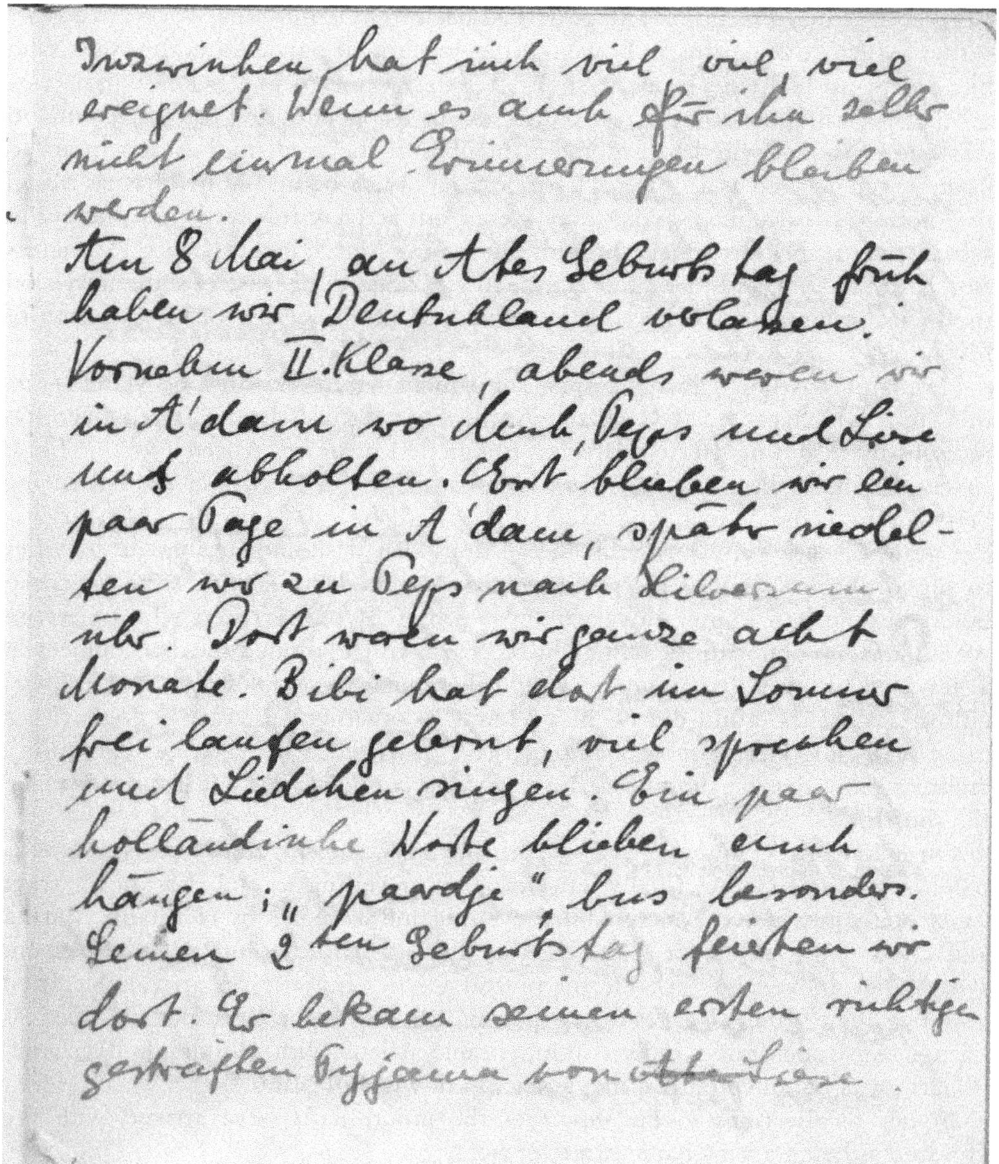

Inzwischen hat sich viel viel, viel
ereignet. Wenn es auch für ihn selbst
nicht einmal Erinnerungen bleiben
werden.

Am 8 Mai, an Abes Geburts tag früh
haben wir Deutschland verlassen.
Vornehm II.Klase, abends waren wir
in A'dam wo denk, Peps und Lise
uns abholten. Dort blieben wir ein
paar Tage in A'dam, später siedel-
ten wir zu Peps nach Hilversum
über. Dort waren wir ganze acht
Monate. Bibi hat dort im Sommer
frei laufen gelernt, viel sprechen
und Liedchen singen. Ein paar
holländische Worte blieben auch
hängen; "paardje" bus besonders.
Seinen 2 ten Geburtstag feierten wir
dort. Er bekam seinen ersten richtigen
gestreiften Pyjama von ~~Abe~~ Lise.

FIG. 14.4. Extract from Georg's baby-book.

and that she already had as much Dutch as she needed.[43] Bibi, he told Hilde, talked a great deal and ran around like a hedgehog, roaring and shrieking like a whole zoo, yet was also utterly adorable.[44] Eva recorded in Georg's baby-book that he was picking up some Dutch words and that there had been an enjoyable family celebration of his second birthday in July. Tante Liese gave Bibi his first pair of pyjamas. Hermann liked having the children around although he found it very hard to work. He and Usche had to share a bedroom, with the other rooms in the house given over to the Rothschilds.[45]

From the outset my grandparents only saw the Netherlands as a temporary option. Siegfried had excellent written and spoken English and his plan was to try to settle in England. But given the British government's restrictions on refugees, getting the family to the safety of England was conditional on securing permanent employment. In January 1938 — five months before they finally left Germany — the British physicist Henry Guinness de Laszlo had sought to make contact with Siegfried via his former colleague, Dr Ludwig Vanino.[46] De Laszlo was the eldest son of the Hungarian portraitist, Philip de László and his wife Lucy Guinness, who were good friends with Sir Robert Mond. After studies at Cambridge and Zurich and a spell as an associate professor at the Massachusetts Institute of Technology, de Laszlo had founded in 1931 a company which specialized in producing and providing rare organic chemicals to research laboratories across the world. De Laszlo wanted to meet with Siegfried, in connection with a book published the previous year — *Die Leuchtfarben, ihre Herstellung, Eigenschaften und Verwendung* [Luminous Colours: their Production, Characteristics and Use]. The book had been published under Vanino's name but the main work had been done by Siegfried. Vanino passed on de Laszlo's letter to Siegfried and they met in March 1938 in Berlin. At the meeting de Laszlo invited Siegfried to be part of a new company he was establishing in England.[47] He promised to send a formal invitation to the UK and to accompany Siegfried to the Home Office to assist with obtaining the necessary work and residency permits. Siegfried was to be paid £300 a year and share in fifteen per cent of the company's profits.

De Laszlo was not however simply offering Siegfried a job. He was also seeking investment in the proposed new company and to this end he wrote to Ludwig Borchardt on 31 March 1938, reporting on his meeting with Dr Rothschild. He explained that,

> Owing to a demand which has recently arisen from Government circles for certain products for use in Air Raid shelters and the prevention of fire in houses, I have been investigating the possibilities of manufacturing these substances in Great Britain.[48]

De Laszlo was confident that with Siegfried's knowledge it would be possible to produce the required luminescent materials but to get the business off the ground he needed investors. Two weeks later, de Laszlo informed Ludwig that Sir Robert Mond had now confirmed he was willing to take up 500 shares (each share was a pound sterling) in the new company being formed to utilize Dr. Rothschild's knowledge.

But Ludwig, who was being asked to buy 1000 shares, had reservations about investing large sums of money in the new company. He wrote to Sir Robert seeking more information about de Laszlo. Sir Robert sought to reassure his old friend about his credentials. Eva and Siegfried also made their own enquiries about de Laszlo and found that he was unanimously described to be reliable. Yet they also continued to have misgivings about the enterprise. In her letters to Ludwig and Mimi, Eva questions why de Laszlo had given up previous well-paid positions. It is also the case that his father had died in November 1937 and Kasper-Holtkotte suggests that he would have inherited a significant sum (possibly £160,000). For some reason, Eva does not appear to have entirely trusted de Laszlo. In a private family recording from 1979 she describes him as 'a bit of a crook'.

On 14 May 1938 Ludwig wrote to Eva to say that while he did not want to hinder the family's chances of settling in England, he had decided not to invest in the new company. Instead he wanted to make a gift to Eva of £1000. This was a sum of money he had already earmarked as a legacy. His intention now was to transfer the money directly to Eva and Siegfried. In return he asked her to keep him informed about their *Vertreibung* [expulsion]. *Auswanderung* [emigration] was not an adequate term, he wrote.[49]

On 2 June, Eva replied, asking her uncle to send a notarial certificate stating that he would pay £1000 on her resettlement in England. In his reply, Ludwig explained that he wanted to be very careful about how the money was transferred to make sure it could not be seized by the German government. She should let him know as soon as Siegfried was out of Germany. At the end of the month, Ludwig and Mimi left Alexandria on board the *Marco Polo* for Venice. From there they went to Basel where most likely Ludwig settled the safe transfer of the money.

On 26 June Siegfried left for London, probably in connection with these arrangements, but on arrival at Dover, was refused entry. The British government had introduced a new visa requirement for immigrants from Germany and Austria earlier in the year, ostensibly so that they could be selected 'at leisure and in advance'.[50] But despite having a visa which had cost him 10 Mark from the British Consulate General in Berlin and numerous letters of recommendation in his pockets from British residents, Siegfried was not permitted to disembark. He was made to return in a squalid little cabin, in what proved to be a very stormy crossing. It seems probable that Siegfried was sent back in error by a local immigration officer. Government policy was interpreted by staff working at the ports of entry and there were often discrepancies between policy decisions and how those decisions were implemented. As Louise London observes 'the more generous aspects of the government's practice went largely unacknowledged.'[51]

Hermann was appalled at his son-in-law's treatment. He was in the middle of a letter to Hilde when Siegfried's telegram arrived to say that he had not been allowed ashore and that he would be re-appearing around eleven o'clock that night. How outrageous it is, Hermann wrote to Hilde, that a decent, respectable man, a doctor with a visa, should be denied entry in this way. He saw Siegfried's deportation as symptomatic of '... der elenden Chamberlain-Politik...' [the wretched policies of the British Prime Minister, Neville Chamberlain].[52]

Increasingly aware that the Netherlands was no longer the safe haven it had been in 1933, Hermann recognized the importance of the family getting to England. Anti-Semitic pamphlets were now flooding the country and the protests and petitions of Dutch Christian intellectuals against the disgrace of the government's recent measures against foreigners (i.e. Jews) were proving to be entirely ineffective. In their clubs, the Germans could dress in their SA uniforms and do as they pleased. The Dutch Nazis, despite their poor showing in the elections, enjoyed a voice in government. There was no bourgeois newspaper anymore which in Hermann's opinion was not latently pro-Nazi. He believed that all of the left-leaning Liberal Democratic journalists had been dismissed. 'In short,' he wrote to Hilde,

> Holland bereitet sich langsam darauf vor, ein drittes oder viertes Österreich zu werden [...]. Also, wenn ich hätte, was ich nicht habe, nämlich: Geld — so würde ich mir morgen die Schiffsplätze nach USA besorgen lassen. Man ist Deutschland hier viel zu nahe — ja, man sitzt grade auf dem Puffer zwischen Deutschland und England eigentlich. Und die englische Politik ist nicht dazu angetan, um diesen Sitz als besonders gemütlich zu empfinden. Das weiß natürlich die Regierung — die im Gegensatz zum Volk steht! — ganz genau und macht jetzt schon nicht einen Ruck, sondern eine ganze Schwenkung nach ...[Deutschland] herüber.

> [Holland is preparing to become a third or fourth Austria. [...] If I had what I have not, namely money, I would get myself tickets for a ship to America tomorrow. Germany is much too close to us here. Holland is perched precariously like a buffer between Germany and England and the policies of the British make it a far from comfortable place to be. Of course, the Dutch government realizes this and contrary to the wishes of the people it already doesn't just tilt but actually shifts strongly towards Germany.][53]

Ludwig and Mimi were continuing their journey that summer, travelling by rail from Basel to Paris, when Ludwig suffered a heart-attack on the train. He died in a Paris hotel on 12 August 1938. Ludwig's sudden death meant that Mimi returned immediately to Zurich and no meeting with Siegfried took place. However, Eva always said that it was the £1000 which Ludwig and Mimi gave her which made it possible to get to England, so her uncle's sudden death did not prevent the payment from being made.[54]

Soon after being turned back at Dover, Siegfried did manage to enter the UK on a temporary basis and by November Hermann was able to inform Hilde that he had secured a good job.[55] He would be working for a chemical company where he could utilize his knowledge of fluorescence and phosphors. An increasingly important application of cathode ray tubes was radar screens and my mother believed that the contribution her father could make to developing radar detection systems also helped the family come to England. Eva always maintained that Siegfried met a physicist friend by chance soon after his arrival in London and that this fortunate encounter led to the job. Whatever the exact truth, by the end of the year, plans were proceeding for her and the children to join Siegfried in Woodford Green, a suburb to the east of London.[56]

Hilde's father-in-law Holger Hansen died on 8 November, shortly after she and

Villum had moved from Copenhagen to Aarhus. Hermann's letter of condolence to Hilde and Villum was written two days after the horror of Kristallnacht, a pogrom in Germany, Hermann writes, worse than what used to take place in Czarist Russia.[57] He was appalled by the lack of international response and the way in which Socialist leaders such as Belgium's Camille Huysmans placated the Nazis while their former friends were beaten to death or left languishing in concentration camps.

In Germany, Kristallnacht was swiftly followed by a host of new measures. On 12 November a decree was issued which excluded Jews from German economic life and summarily closed all Jewish-owned businesses. Three days later, all Jewish children were expelled from public schools. On 28 November the Reich Ministry of the Interior restricted Jews' freedom of movement. The following month all state contracts held with Jewish-owned firms were cancelled. A week later Jews were banned from being midwives. But despite all of this, as Hermann noted, other countries were not prepared to act against public opinion and to provide refuge for Germany's Jews. He told Hilde,

> Leibniz hat zwar, wie schon Voltaire in seinem *Candide* nachwies, *nicht* recht, wenn er behauptet, wir leben in der *besten* aller Welten, aber GH hat unwiderlegbar recht, wenn er behauptet, wir leben in der wahnsinnigsten aller Welten.
>
> [Leibniz, as Voltaire shows in *Candide*, was *not* right in asserting that we live in the *best* of all possible worlds but G. H. is irrefutably right when he asserts that we live in the most insane of all worlds].[58]

Hermann appears to have written very little during 1938. He simply found it too disruptive with the children in the house. He did complete a long treatise entitled 'Einige simple Tatsachen, naiv dargestellt' [Some Simple Facts Plainly Presented], shortly before the family's arrival.[59] In it, Hermann sets out his vision of a 'United States of Europe'. It would be a union of states whose common interest would be directed and led from one place but where individual states would still retain their national peculiarities. Such a union, he argues, would serve as a guarantee against future wars.[60] Hermann's favourite philosopher during this period in his life was José Ortega y Gasset and essays such as 'Einige simple Tatsachen' reflect his influence on Hermann's thinking. A call for European integration is at the heart of Ortega's best known work, *La rebelión de las masas* [The Revolt of the Masses]. Ortega shared Hermann's antipathy towards nationalism which he regarded as Europe's 'mania'. Nationalism for Ortega was merely an expression of provincialism; perhaps that same kind of petty provincialism which all those years before Heinrich Levin had complained of when he revisited his boyhood home of Massow.

Notes to Chapter 14

1. The essay, which is in the Georg Hermann Collection in the Leo Baeck Institute (GHC; AR 7074; Box 5; Folder 65), was not published until 1999 when it appeared in Schoor (ed.), *Der Schriftsteller Georg Hermann*, pp. 283–306.
2. Letter to Hilde, 31 October 1937, *Unvorhanden und stumm*, p. 142.

3. Letter to Hilde, 8 March 1937, *Unvorhanden und stumm*, p. 128.
4. Georg Hermann, *Jetje Gebert/Henriette Jacoby*, trans. by Jeannette Keizer (Amsterdam: De Arbeiderspers, 1938).
5. Franz Doelle's song 'Wenn der weiße Flieder wieder blüht' was a popular hit in 1928. The song spawned a silent movie in 1929 and in the 1950s a popular West German film starring Willy Fritsch, Magda Schneider and Romy Schneider. They are not connected with *Jettchen Gebert*.
6. Menno ter Braak, 'Georg Hermann Plaudert', *Het Vaderland*, 16 March 1937. There is an extract from the article together with a German translation in van Liere, *Georg Hermann: Materialien*, pp. 57–59.
7. Ibid.
8. Pen name of Eduard Douwes Dekker (1820–1887), best known for his satirical novel *Max Havelaar* (1860), set in the Dutch East-Indies.
9. Van Ammers-Küller's most successful novel, 1925's *De opstandigen* [The Rebel Generation] was widely translated. Her pro-Nazi stance during World War II contributed to the subsequent waning of her popularity in the Netherlands.
10. *Die Zeitlupe*, pp. 73–77.
11. Hermann had actually come up with this typology seven years earlier when he was among a number of writers including Döblin, Heinrich Mann and Wassermann who were asked by *Central-Verein-Zeitung* to write about how their readers perceived them. See Lars-André Richter, *Die Intellektuellen haben das Wort: Eine Auswertung von Presserundfragen unter Intellektuellen der Weimarer Republik* (Saarbrücken: VDM, 2013), p. 77.
12. Menno ter Braak, 'Georg Hermann Plaudert', *Het Vaderland*, 16 March 1937.
13. Letter to Hilde, 26 May 1937, *Unvorhanden und stumm*, p. 133.
14. van Liere, *Georg Hermann: Materialien*, p. 77.
15. Nussbaum, 'Georg Hermann Attacks the Special Issue of *Der Jude*', pp. 453–54.
16. Letter to Hilde, 27 May 1937, *Unvorhanden und stumm*, pp. 133–34.
17. Ibid., p. 135.
18. Nussbaum, 'Verliebt in Holland', p. 190. GHC; AR 7074; Box 4; Folder 32, LBI.
19. GHC; AR 7074; Box 6; Folder 22, LBI. Nussbaum gives a more detailed summary of the essay in *Verliebt in Holland*, pp. 190–91.
20. *Unvorhanden und stumm*, pp. 121–22. Hilde believed that it may have been buried in a tin in the garden of Hermann's friend, Hugo de Groot. In 1985 an unsuccessful attempt was made to find the tin. See Nussbaum, 'Georg Hermanns *Randbemerkungen*', p. 174.
21. Letter to Hilde, 14 April 1937, *Unvorhanden und stumm*, p. 130.
22. Letter to Hilde, 2 July 1937, *Unvorhanden und stumm*, p. 136.
23. Georg Hermann, 'Bist du es oder bist du's nicht?', in *Georg Hermann: Deutsch-jüdischer Schriftsteller und Journalist*, ed. by Weiss-Sussex, pp. 137–255. The novella was not published until 2004 when my uncle, George Rothschild, found a top copy of the manuscript which was believed to have been lost, amongst Eva's papers. Godela Weiss-Sussex edited the text and published it.
24. Letter to Hilde dated 2 July 1937, *Unvorhanden und stumm*, p. 136.
25. Ben-Dror, 'Recollections 1919–44'. Usche dates this conversation in July 1936 but from Hermann's letters to Hilde it is clear that it would have taken place in July 1937.
26. Letter to Hilde dated 2 July 1937, *Unvorhanden und stumm*, p. 137.
27. Ben-Dror, 'Recollections 1919–44'.
28. Letter to Hilde dated 12 February 1938, *Unvorhanden und stumm*, p. 149.
29. Letter to Hilde dated 31 October 1937, *Unvorhanden und stumm*, pp. 142–43.
30. Martin Kitchen, *A History of Modern Germany 1800 to the Present* (Oxford: Wiley-Blackwell, 2012), p. 254.
31. (San Bernardino, CA: Borgo Press, 1993), p. 15 and p. 24.
32. Letter to Hilde, 12 February 1938, *Unvorhanden und stumm*, p. 149.
33. Jan L. van Zanden, *The Economic History of The Netherlands 1914–1995* (London: Routledge, 1997), p. 91.
34. Letter to Hilde, 12 February 1938, *Unvorhanden und stumm*, p. 150.
35. Ibid., pp. 152–53.

36. Postcard to Hilde, 21 March 1938, *Unvorhanden und stumm*, p. 154.
37. Quoted in Irmela von der Lühe, 'Versuch, im Schreiben zu überleben. Georg Hermanns *Rosenemil*', in Schoor (ed.), *Der Schriftsteller Georg Hermann*, p. 197.
38. Volkmar Zühlsdorff, *Hitler's Exiles: The German Cultural Resistance in America and Europe*, trans. by Martin H. Bott (New York: Continuum, 2004), p. 16.
39. 10th May, 1938. Quoted in van der Lühe, 'Versuch, im Schreiben zu überleben', p. 199. The original is in English.
40. For more information about the contest see Zühlsdorff, *Hitler's Exiles*, pp. 146–53.
41. Kasper-Holtkotte, *Deutschland in Ägypten*, p. 323.
42. Ben-Dror, 'Recollections 1919–44'.
43. Letter to Hilde, 14 October 1938, *Unvorhanden und stumm*, p. 159.
44. Ibid.
45. Letter to Hilde, 11 November 1938, *Unvorhanden und stumm*, p. 162.
46. Ludwig Vanino (1861–1944) is mainly remembered for his two volume *Handbuch der präparativen Chemie* [Handbook of Synthetic Chemistry] which was first published in 1913.
47. Kasper-Holtkotte, *Deutschland in Ägypten*, p. 319.
48. Ibid.
49. Ibid., p. 323.
50. Anonymous Whitehall official quoted in Louise London, *Whitehall and the Jews, 1933–1948: British Immigration Policy, Jewish Refugees and the Holocaust* (Cambridge: Cambridge University Press, 2001), p. 59.
51. London, *Whitehall and the Jews*, p. 46.
52. Letter to Hilde, 27 June 1938, *Unvorhanden und stumm*, p. 156.
53. Ibid.
54. In today's money (2019) the sum given by Ludwig and Mimi would be the equivalent of about £60,000.
55. Letter to Hilde, 11 November 1938, *Unvorhanden und stumm*, pp. 160–62.
56. Letter to Hilde, 27 December 1938, *Unvorhanden und stumm*, p. 163.
57. Letter to Hilde, 11 November 1938, *Unvorhanden und stumm*, pp. 160–62.
58. Letter to Hilde, 27 December 1938, *Unvorhanden und stumm*, p. 165.
59. Georg Hermann, 'Einige simple Tatsachen', 1938, GHC; AR 7074; Box 5; Folder 24, LBI.
60. Ibid., p. 53.

CHAPTER 15

❖

War and Occupation

Early in 1939, Hermann found himself, once again, denounced as a traitor in a long article in *Völkischer Beobachter*. The piece included extracts from *Randbemerkungen 1914–17* such as Hermann's observation that his only interest in the war was the revolution which would surely follow in its aftermath. Hermann joked to Hilde that he would like to send them a postcard saying 'Am nächsten auch!!!' [The next one, too!].[1]

Hermann was also vilified in another tract produced by the Institut zum Studium der Judenfrage. Credited to Dr. Friedrich Karl Wiebe and first published in Germany in 1938, *Germany and the Jewish Problem* purports to make an intellectual case for persecution by showing how the 'unceasing encroachment of the Jews on the entire public life of Germany within the last few decades resulted in a terrible national catastrophe.'[2] In a section on literature, Hermann is singled out for special mention, and as always the focus is on his wartime notes:

> Georg Hermann represented a somewhat different, but by no means superior, type of Jew [to Alfred Kerr] occupying a conspicuous position in the German literary world. In his political diary entitled *Randbemerkungen* — Marginal Notes — (Berlin 1919) he reveals the credo of a weak, utterly decadent man of literary ambitions, devoid of moral backbone and support: "As a Jew, I belong to a race much too old to be duped by mass suggestion. Such words as Nation, War and State are endowed with neither sound nor colour for me."
>
> The cosmopolitan, international mentality of Ahasuerus's sons is clearly reflected in the following confession: "I feel at home in any country of the world whose language I speak, where there are beautiful women, flowers and art, a good library, a chess board, pleasant and cultivated society and where the climate is healthy and agreeable and the landscape attractive." Nevertheless, Hermann is honest enough to admit that the Jewish race is responsible for the dissemination of the negative attitude towards State and patriotism. He declares: "The Jew's rejection of all nationalistic ideology is the principal source of his evolutionary quality and intrinsic value." Hermann's standpoint which, as a matter of fact, is a purely anarchistic one, even goes so far as to frankly betray personal cowardice: "Five minutes of cowardice are preferable to being dead for the rest of one's days."[3]

On 1 February 1939 Eva, Siegfried, and the children finally left for England. They spent four weeks in London and then on 1 March moved to Buckhurst Hill, a suburban town in Essex. Two weeks later my mother started at Knighton

Preparatory School in Woodford Green. Beate became Beatrice and she was faced with adapting to another new country and learning another new language.

After they had left, Hermann bought some white and blue hyacinths. Their scent filled the house which must have felt empty now it was just him and Usche again after the bustle of the previous eight months. The children had thrived during their stay, he told Hilde.[4] Ate had grown by eight centimetres and Bibi had developed into a perfect little gentleman. If he retains his dimples and his winning smile in two decades' time, Hermann writes, he is going to be strikingly handsome. Siegfried, on his return to Hilversum said that he would not have recognized the boy. It goes to show, Hermann continues, what a better diet, clean air and above all, a less anxious atmosphere can do for children, even if they are too young to fully understand what is happening around them.[5]

The following month, and a week before the German occupation of Prague, Hermann took the first steps required for him and Usche to be naturalized in the Netherlands. But he was aware that the process could take years. He managed to get his passport extended to 10 April 1940 and wrote to Hilde asking her to secure him an official invitation to Denmark.[6] One never knows, these days, he says, when one might suddenly need to 'up sticks'. With peace and quiet restored to Siriusstraat 59, Hermann was writing again — 'Meine Liebesgeschichten' (for my grandson) — two love stories covering about a hundred pages.[7] One of the stories was humorous and Hermann likened it to Anatole France's short story, 'The Seven Wives of Bluebeard'. The other, he said, was out of his top drawer.[8]

At this time Hermann was also harbouring hopes that he might be able to go to the United States on a lecture tour. This was probably related to a letter he had received from the American academic, Solomon Liptzin. Liptzin was researching a book about the attitude of German authors of Jewish origin towards the 'duality within their soul' and had contacted a number of writers, including Hermann, to seek their thoughts on the subject. In his response, Hermann tells Liptzin that the subject of his project has been the chief concern of writers like himself since the first days of August 1914 when the schism between Jewish-German and Aryan German writers began.

> Mehr und mehr hat sich zwischen uns und jenen ja nun das vollzogen, was schon beim Turmin zu Babel sich vollzogen hat: Wir, die wir dachten, daß wir den Riesenturm einer Weltkultur einmal in den Himmel hinaufbauen wollten, ehedem, wir verstanden uns plötzlich nicht mehr. Aber, was schlimmer ist: wir erkannten, daß wir von je aneinander vorbeigeredet hatten.

> [More and more what has taken place between us and them, can be likened to what happened at the Tower of Babel: we thought that we were building a giant tower of world culture which would reach up into the sky but suddenly we found that we did not understand each other anymore. Worst of all, we realized that we had always been talking past each other.][9]

Hermann advises Liptzin never to forget, if he wants to see things in their proper light, that in Germany, even the most significant writers were never embraced in the same way as in England and France or pre-revolutionary Russia. In fact, he argues that the great champions of German high culture for over 150 years have been the Jews.[10] Hermann muses that this may be because the Jew has retained more of the disposition of the men of the old Mediterranean. He has preserved a stronger sense of justice and a taste for criticism. He is not a man who is easily captivated. This is one pole of the Jewish soul epitomized in Börne's political and literary activities which, Hermann argues, can be traced from him to the theatre critic Otto Brahm and the novelist Ludwig Lewisohn. Such people have always been at the forefront of Jewish-German culture, he writes, but they are not there now. The second pole of German-Jewish talent, at least until 1890–1900, Hermann suggests, flows from Heine to writers like Schnitzler and Werfel.

Hermann argues that Aryan-German writers rarely produce an oeuvre, failing to sustain the writing of their youth. Along with Dehmel and Holz, Hermann also cites as an example of this Hauptmann, whose play *Vor Sonnenaufgang* had made such an impact on him exactly fifty years ago.[11] Now we recognize, Hermann writes, that,

> Assimilation konnte immer nur bis zu einem gewissen Punkt gehen. Nämlich nur gerade so weit, wie die Mentalität davon noch nicht berührt wurde. Sowie die mitgehen sollte, zeigten sich zwischen der spezifisch "arischen" Mentalität und der um dreitausend Jahre älteren "jüdischen" Mentalität derartige ... [*sic*] fundamentale Unterschiede, daß sich so oder so: gewünscht, unabsichtlich, gewollt, erzwungen! ... einfach ihre Wege trennen mußten und sich getrennt hätten. Vielleicht auch ohne Hitler!

> [Assimilation could only ever reach a certain point. Namely only just as far as the difference in mentalities was not touched. There were such fundamental differences in the "Aryan" mentality and the "Jewish" mentality, which is three thousand years older, that one way or another: intentionally or not, voluntarily or by compulsion, their paths must inevitably diverge. Possibly even without Hitler!][12]

Given that a writer cannot but give voice to the mentality of the group of people from which he comes, according to Hermann, it was only natural that Jewish writers who hardly suspected that they were Jewish should be first and foremost in the clash of conscience.

It seems from Hermann's response to Liptzin that he had come to believe that the incompatibility in the 'Aryan' and 'Jewish' world views was so profound that it could not be reconciled. However, he does point out that this is a German phenomenon. In other countries like America, Holland, France and England, he tells Liptzin, the acculturated Jew has not been made to feel so far removed from his surroundings as in Germany since 1914.

Despite his acceptance that assimilation had failed in Germany, Hermann continued to be opposed to the creation of a Jewish homeland. By now, Hilde had come to support the Zionists but in a long letter to his daughter written two weeks after his response to Liptzin, Hermann sets out his 'diametrically opposed' views regarding the Jewish state.[13] For practical reasons he still believes its creation is unworkable. In addition, having lived for almost fifty years without anti-Semitism, he tells Hilde that he has known a time when it was associated with the lowest, most barbaric, echelons of society and he believes that those days will return. But above all, Hermann continues to believe that the creation of a Jewish state would be a misfortune as 'die Juden werden, staatlich gebunden, genauso beschränkt werden wie die andern Esel auch.' [once the Jews are bound by the state, they will be as confined as the other donkeys].[14] For Hermann, individual nation states, drenched in the idiocy of patriotism, are a construct which must be overcome.

At this time, Hermann was becoming increasingly disillusioned with the Dutch government. He found Holland's 'pseudo-democracy' more and more intolerable from month to month. In the same letter he writes of his shock at the government's creation in Drenthe of a refugee camp for Jews, the Centraal Vluchtelingenkamp Westerbork, describing it as a *Konzentrationslager*.[15] He also says that the local police are starting to act like the Gestapo, citing an incident that had taken place the day before at the Koco ice cream parlour in Rijnstraat, Amsterdam, which was run by two German-Jewish refugees, Alfred Kohn and Ernst Cahn. A group of Dutch Nazis had launched an attack on the premises, using knuckledusters and batons. Several people were wounded, glasses smashed and chairs and tables turned over. A number of members of the NSB were subsequently arrested and convicted.[16]

It is evident from Hermann's letters to Hilde that there were some difficulties between her and Eva. Hermann maintained that whatever the nature of their differences, they were nonsensical. One only had to look, he said, at the disagreements between him and his siblings, the bad relationship with Else, to see the pernicious effects of such arguments.[17] The family should knit together more closely, Hermann tells Hilde, not least because he might not live that much longer. He explains that he has recently been diagnosed with *angina pectoris*. This news about his health has made Hermann think that he would like to spend time with everyone in London — Hilde, Eva, Siegfried, and the children. They could go to see the Parthenon Sculptures in the British Museum and perhaps for one last time she can enjoy seeing some of the best paintings in the world under the expert tutelage of her father.[18]

On 1 September 1939 a million German soldiers swept into Poland and two days later Chamberlain declared war on Germany. The conflict which Hermann had regarded as inevitable for so long was now underway. The following month he celebrated his sixty-eighth birthday with Martha and Liese, who gave him purple asters and copper-coloured chrysanthemums.[19] There was no prospect now, of course, of any trip to London but Hermann was busy writing again. He was working on a set of four inter-linked but self-contained novels which together would form the two volumes of 'Die daheim blieben' [Those That Stayed Home]. It was to be a chronicle of recent times. Focusing on a well-to-do elderly Berlin Jewish couple who lived in Matthäikirchstraße[20] in the west of the city, Hermann's plan was to tell the story of the fate of the Jews in Germany through the experiences of one family by focusing on four key historical moments. Already by the end of November he had typescripts of the two stories which would form the first volume: 'Max und Dolly' and 'Ilse und Liese'.

'Max und Dolly' is set in Berlin on a Sunday morning in March 1933 and 'Ilse und Liese' takes place on the afternoon and evening of 15 September 1935, the day the Nuremberg Laws were enacted. The second volume was going to comprise 'Georg der Doktor', set in Florence in September 1938 when the exodus of the Jewish community in the wake of Mussolini's *Manifesto della razza* took place, and 'Heinrich und Agnes' set in Berlin on Kristallnacht when the elderly couple perish: the old man from the shock of the pogrom and his wife by her own hand.[21]

As well as being engaged with his new work, Hermann felt that there might be renewed interest in *Schnee* and *Träume der Ellen Stein* since both novels deal with the psychological effects of war. As ever, he harboured hopes that Hilde might be able to interest publishers in re-prints as well as in the manuscripts of 'Max und Dolly' and 'Ilse und Liese' which he asked her to share with the publisher Bermann Fischer who had recently relocated from Vienna to Stockholm.[22]

There is no doubt that Hermann's years of exile in the Netherlands were often difficult. He was dogged by ill-health as the years went by and often very short of money. But he found solace in the fact that he was still able to work. He told Hilde in November 1939 that exile had provided him with more time to himself than he had ever known. He had never previously had such space for self-reflection, never such scope to talk to himself, never so much time with his good old books. And although life had dragged him through the mud, Hermann told his daughter, the *homme de lettres* learns more from hardship than happiness.[23]

But Hermann's burst of creativity regarding 'Die daheim blieben' proved short-lived. By January 1940 he found he had lost the desire to write and could not bring himself to continue with the novels. It was less about technique, he told Hilde, than finding the determination and patience to construct a mosaic from his mountains of notes and fragments. Nussbaum discovered forty-three of these notes among Hermann's papers in the Leo Baeck Institute. They are bundled together on seventeen pages, on the top of which Hermann has written 'Ich will einmal sehen ob diese alten Blätter noch zu brauchen sind.' [I want to see if these old sheets are still needed].[24] Myriad ideas and thoughts are captured in the bundle which Hermann clearly intended to draw upon in writing the novels. They include, among other things, reflections on the experience of exile, Hermann's views on the way that Marxism, rather than building a more humane society, had merely replaced one set of power relations with another, his indignation at the Moscow show trials, thoughts on the *Anschluss* ('Finis Austriae') and observations about the League of Nations. Here and there the names of the fictional characters in 'Die daheim blieben' have been added in pencil. More often, Hermann has written 'wichtig' or 'gut' in the margin against points that he wanted to pick up in the novel.[25]

The bundle provides an interesting insight into Hermann's working methods, containing as it does examples of those notes which Hilde had told the Friends of German Literature in Copenhagen in 1933 she had come to respect:

> ... mein Vater arbeitet immer. Und jeder Spaziergang, den er macht, ist ein neues Sehen, Fühlen und Empfinden. Wenn wir zusammen gehen und er mitten im Gespräch, meist mitten auf dem Fahrweg, stehenbleibt, ein kleines Notizbüchelchen herauszieht, um rasch einen Gedanken festzuhalten, ist mir das so vertraut, daß ich nur Obacht gebe, daß wir nicht überfahren

werden. Nicht nur Beobachtungen und eigene Einfälle, sondern auch nette Bemerkungen, die er von anderen hört, und sei es nur von seinen Kindern, finden Platz in diesem Büchelchen.

Wenn mein Vater sich an den Schreibtisch setzt, hat er meist schon die schwierigste Arbeit hinter sich. Der Schreibtisch ist dann überfüllt mit Notizzettelchen, bei denen der Rot- und Blaustift eine große Rolle spielt, die mächtig eng beschrieben sind und furchtbar unordentlich durcheinanderliegen. Wir haben Respekt vor all den Zettelchen, vielleicht auch nur, weil wir das Prinzip, nach dem mein Vater mit ihnen umgeht, nicht ergründen können.

[... my father is always working. Every walk he makes is a means to new ways of seeing, feeling and sensing. When we go out together and he stops, in the midst of a conversation, and most often in the middle of the road [...] and takes out a small notebook to quickly capture a thought, I am so used to it that my only concern is that we don't get run over. Not only does he jot down his own observations and ideas, but also the interesting remarks he hears from others, including his children, all find a place in his little book.

When my father sits down at his desk, he has usually already done the most difficult work. The desk will be crowded with numerous little notes, annotated densely in blue and red pencil and scattered about in what appears to be a terrible mess. [...] We have respect for all these scraps of paper perhaps only because we cannot fathom the principle upon which my father deals with them.][26]

Assembling these disparate observations to produce a cogently structured novel can never have been straight-forward and in January 1940 Hermann was struggling to find the energy for the task he had set himself. He tells Hilde in a subsequent letter that he has always found the most difficult aspect of writing a novel to be the challenge of maintaining its coherence while working on it over a prolonged period.[27]

Mimi was continuing to send money but the German occupation of Poland meant that Lotte's family could no longer make the payments to Usche, and Hermann was again finding himself very short of funds. He hoped that Hilde and Eva would be able to stand surety for 700 guilders between them, as this would enable him to receive further money from the Dutch Jewish Relief Committee, which was now under huge pressure, given the wave of refugees who had crossed the border after Kristallnacht.[28]

The German invasion of the Netherlands began in the early hours of 10 May 1940. Five days later, in the wake of the destruction of the centre of Rotterdam by the Luftwaffe, the Dutch army surrendered. Martha and Liese were extremely lucky, amid the pandemonium, and managed to get passage from Ijmuiden on one of the last of the small boats that made it out. Martha was able to bring nothing with her other than her handbag which still contained the knitted booties of Ilse, the baby daughter she had lost to diphtheria in 1903. 'Mu and Liese fled straight to the quay with just the clothes on their back', Eva later recalled.[29] Upon their arrival in England they were detained in Holloway Prison.

Hundreds, if not thousands, of people went to Ijmuiden by bike, taxi or any other way that they could, only to find that there was absolutely no passage to be had. The Dutch authorities had closed off the area around the harbour from concern for public safety on 14 May with the result that the gigantic passenger ship *Bodegraven* sailed to England almost empty. Another passenger ship, the *Coen*, was scuttled.[30] In her recollections Usche recalls the sense of shock everyone felt on seeing the first German warplanes flying over the country and how hard it was to think rationally. Hermann's former girlfriend, Mies Blomsma, together with her husband, the journalist Gerth Schreiner, committed suicide in Amsterdam in the first days of the German occupation. Hermann was terribly upset by her death, according to Usche.[31] Menno ter Braak, who had interviewed Hermann in March 1937 at the opening of *Wenn der weiße Flieder wieder blüht*, committed suicide on 14 May after a failed attempt to flee to England. He was thirty-eight.

Soon after the Dutch surrender, Arthur Seyss-Inquart, the Austrian Nazi whom Hitler had made Reichsstatthalter of 'Ostmark' two years before, was appointed Reichskommissar of the Netherlands. Seyss-Inquart quickly took measures to remove Jews from the government, the press and leading positions in industry.

From May 1940 all of Hermann's cards and letters to Hilde were subject to the censor. They are stamped with the eagle and swastika and the words 'Geprüft Oberkommando der Wehrmacht.' [Checked by the Wehrmacht High Command]. Hermann sought to express his true feelings to Hilde in his first communication after the occupation by sending her a picture postcard of a Hashihime mask used in Japanese Noh theatre to represent the madness of despair. Other than a few bland observations on the lovely summer weather, the only piece of information which he seeks to impart to Hilde is that Martha and Liese are now with Eva. In other words, that they had escaped to England.[32]

By the time that Hermann was writing his postcard to Hilde, Eva, Siegfried, George, and my mother had already been interned as 'enemy aliens' on the Isle of Man for a month. In George's baby book, Eva records the date of the family's internment as 25 May 1940.[33] They were to remain there for a total of 266 days. At the outbreak of the war all German and Austrians over the age of sixteen had been grouped into one of three categories. 'Category A' individuals were identified as high security risks and immediately interned. Around 6,500 doubtful cases were placed in 'Category B' and subject to restrictions. 'Category C' were classified as no security risk and left at liberty. Of the 64,000 people in this group, more than 55,000, the great majority of whom were Jewish, were recognized as refugees from Nazi oppression. Presumably Siegfried and Eva would have been placed in 'Category C'. However, once the decision was made — three days into the fighting in the Netherlands and Belgium — to round up and intern people in Categories B and C, they appear to have been in the first wave, and were among the 10,000 Germans and Austrians already interned by 11 June.[34]

Kempton Park was used as the collecting station for the London region so most likely Siegfried, Eva and the children were taken there, prior to making the journey by rail to Liverpool and then by boat to Douglas. Years later Eva would recall one of the dockside workers saying, 'Have we sunk so low that we can treat women and children this way?' She also used to remember (with exasperation) being asked by one of the legal officials arranging the internment, 'So, why did you leave

FIG. 15.1. Hermann's postcard from June 1940.

FIG. 15.2. Usche and Herbert.

Germany?' Women and children were billeted in boarding houses in Port Erin and Port St. Mary. 'We were like their summer guests,' Eva would later say. Siegfried was interned in House 15, Central Camp. The camps were blocks of commandeered houses, mostly boarding houses which were cut off from the main quarters of the seaside towns by barbed-wire fences. A minimum of furniture was left in the houses and the internees were left to run things themselves.[35]

No attempt was made to separate pro-Nazi Germans from Jewish refugees. Eva would tell a story about how one day jellyfish were spotted in the sea but one 'Nazi woman' had ignored the warnings and insisted on going for a swim, only to be so badly stung that she had to be taken to hospital. Later in life, Eva talked quite a lot about her internment. She emphasized the positive aspects — she gave lectures while on the island and took part in the range of interesting activities organized by the internees. In addition, she would point out, they were well away from the German bombing of the mainland. When the children finally got to see their father again, George apparently said, 'We had one the same as him at home.'

In July 1940 Usche turned twenty-one. She'd had a steady boyfriend, Herbert Kalmann, for some time. Herbert's family, also refugees from Germany, had established a cloth factory producing fittings for coats, and Usche would sometimes work there, operating machines or packing the finished products. Herbert also worked in the factory.[36] In August, Hermann wrote to Hilde to let her know that Usche and Herbert would soon be getting married.[37] Usche was in the early months of pregnancy.

Hermann was not optimistic about their prospects. He tells Hilde that he hopes Usche will treat this marriage like an exam you sit the first time just for practice so that you can make a better fist of it the second time around. Moreover, he disapproves of the Kalmanns and says she is not marrying into a family suitable for the daughter of 'G. H.'. Hermann's objections seem to be based on his view that the family was too materialistic and lacked any appreciation for the finer things in life. He feared that Usche would find herself mired in a completely foreign *Mischpoche*.[38] As Usche later recalled 'he was prejudiced against the family because in his eyes they were Eastern Jews and therefore less intellectual and more orthodox.'[39]

Usche and Herbert were married by a rabbi in September at the Kalmanns' home, 132 Goudenregenlaan, which was a few miles away from Siriusstraat. Hermann's prejudice against the Kalmanns comes through in his note to Hilde about the wedding. He tells her that Usche's new family was less embarrassing than he had feared. They were warm and welcoming towards him and came across as fine independent business types. But even still, he does not believe the marriage will last.[40]

A more positive picture of Hermann's relations with the Kalmanns emerges from Herbert's own recollections of this time.[41] He recalls that he was first introduced to Hermann and Usche one Sunday afternoon by the journalist and broadcaster Frank Warschauer.[42] Soon, he was spending a great deal of time at the house in Siriusstraat which he found very much to his liking:

> Zij nam mij ook mee naar huis en daar had ik het wel naar mijn zin. Ik kon het erg goed met haar vader vinden, hoewel ik veronderstel dat hij mij voornamelijk als vaak beschikbare praatpaal gebruikte. De man praatte onophoudelijk maar wat hij zei was wel bijzonder geestig, onderhoudend en ook wel leerzaam. Te zeggen dat hij belezen was is een understatement. Ik heb het idee dat er niets gedrukt was dat hij niet uit zijn hoofd kende. Ik kreeg nooit genoeg van zijn verhalen. Hij woonde met Usche in een museum. Ik geloof dat zijn huis inderdaad op de lijst van de nederlandse musea stond. Het rijtjes-huis was van onder tot boven gevuld met kunstvoorwerpen. Gothische madonna's, biedermeier engelen, egyptische graf-attributen, chinees aardewerk, japans houtsnijwerk. Stoelen, kasten en banken gingen schuil onder de antiquiteiten; op de tafels moest men voor de maaltijden van alles verplaatsen om een eetplek te vinden. Men struikelde over de objekten die zo maar over de grond verspreid lagen. De muren waren bepleisterd met schilderijen en tekeningen van alle tijden en streken. Maar vooral van min of meer contemporaine duitsers zoals Zille, Liebermann, Kollwitz, Menzel en Grosz. En dan waren er nog de duizenden boeken, in kasten, op de grond, op de tafels en in de bedden. Dit alles was zeer matig schoon gehouden door Usche die na het beeindigen van haar schoolcarriere de huishoudelijke plichten op zich had genomen. Er lagen dikke vlokken stof op de gothische engelen. Ik vond het prachtig.

> [I got along very well with Usche's father, although I guess that he saw me primarily as someone who was readily available who he could chat with [...]. The man talked incessantly but what he said was very witty, entertaining and also instructive. [...] To say that he was well-read would be an understatement. I had the feeling that there was nothing in print that he didn't know off the top of his head. I never tired of his stories. He lived with Usche in a museum. [...] Their terraced house was [...] chock-a-block with artefacts — Gothic Madonnas, Biedermeier figurines, Egyptian relics, Chinese pottery and

Japanese woodcarvings. Chairs, cabinets and sofas were hidden under the antiquities. At meal times one had to move everything aside to make room at the tables to eat. It was impossible not to stumble over the objects which were simply scattered on the floor. The walls were covered with paintings and drawings from different periods and places but especially more or less contemporary German artists such as Zille, Liebermann, Kollwitz, Menzel and Grosz. And then there were also thousands of books, in cabinets, on the floor, on the tables and in the beds. All of this was kept minimally clean by Usche, who had assumed the household duties after leaving school. There were thick flakes of dust on the Gothic angels. I loved it.][43]

Herbert would stay overnight at the house:

Ik bleef vaak slapen in het huis van G.H.B, woonde er eigenlijk half. 's Zondags kwam G.H.B altijd bij mijn ouders voor het eten, daarvoor en daarna las hij uit zijn werken voor. Ik vond dat wel feestelijk. Hij nam altijd afscheid van mijn moeder met de woorden: "Es war sehr gut, gnä Frau, nicht ganz so fett wie sonst bei jüdische Leuten."

[I would often sleep at G.H.B.'s house and was really living there half the time. Every Sunday G.H.B. would come to my parents for dinner, before and after which he would read aloud from his works. [...] He always said farewell to my mother with the words, "The dinner was very good, madam, not quite as rich as is usual with Jewish folk."][44]

Initially, following Usche's departure to live with her new in-laws, Hermann was not on his own. He had three lodgers: a couple and the wife's eighty-five-year old mother. But he missed Usche. He had become accustomed to having his children close, he told Hilde. He hears from Mimi now and again, he says, but otherwise he does not hear anything. 'Arbeiten habe ich mir fast abgewöhnt' [Work, I have almost stopped doing].[45] Instead, Hermann was escaping into the world of Stendhal's *Roman Journal*.

Despite the restrictions placed by the censor, some of Hermann's letters to Hilde from this period are particularly illuminating. In an extended letter written in late November 1940, when Seyss-Inquart was dismissing all Jews employed in the Dutch Civil Service, Hermann sets out in some detail his approach as a novelist.[46] He confesses that he has never been an ardent reader of novels. In his youth he enjoyed Dickens, Turgenev and Fritz Reuter and then later Scandinavian writers such as Jonas Lie, Alexander Kielland and Jens Peter Jacobsen. But he was never an avid reader of the novelists of the time, writers like Paul Lindau, Berthold Auerbach and Gustav Freytag.[47] Indeed, he was so ignorant that when he started at university in 1896, he had never even heard the name Gottfried Keller[48] and was barely familiar with *Faust*. But this ignorance, Hermann tells Hilde, was very much to his advantage. It meant that he wrote directly from life. His approach was not influenced by an excess of literary awareness. So when *Spielkinder* was compared by reviewers with the Norwegian Realist Arne Garborg's contemporary novel, *Trætte Mænd* (Weary Men), it came as a surprise. Hermann had simply set out to portray himself and the far from satisfactory nature of his life.

As his style has developed, Hermann tells Hilde, it has become more akin to that of the Late Impressionists but his works have remained very personal since, '... nämlich letzten Endes das, was mich auf der Welt am meisten interessiert, ich selbst bin.' [ultimately, what interests me most in the world is myself].[49] Narcissistic though this sounds, a preoccupation with the self is by no means unusual in writers. What A. N. Wilson has written of Tolstoy seems equally applicable to Hermann:

> Tolstoy was profoundly self-obsessed, and it is this self-obsession which made him a writer. But the truth could be told the other way around. It could be said that it was only through the artifice of literature that he was able to comprehend or impose a shape on the inchoate business of existence.[50]

Hermann's desire to make sense of his own existence and thereby the wider world not only provided the impetus for much of his writing but also underpinned what he wrote. Hermann states in his letter to Hilde that all of the best novelists seek to capture 'die ganze umhergewirbelte Hoffnungslosigkeit dieses Daseins' [the whole swirling hopelessness of this existence].[51] For him, a novel like *Joie de Vivre* has only limited appeal because there is so little of Zola himself in it. Hermann prefers those who, like the Danish Impressionist author Herman Bang, write directly about their lives as they see them.[52] Hermann places his faith in this directness and cautions against over-analysis. He recalls one time when his old friend Max Liebermann had shown him a detailed questionnaire he had been sent by a scholar: ninety-five questions, asking him things like how he feels when he dips his brush into his paints. If he knew the answers to such questions, Liebermann told Hermann, he would not be an artist.[53]

Hermann returned to the theme of writing in one of his last letters to Hilde.[54] Hilde must have intimated that she was thinking of taking up writing herself and this prompted Hermann into a discourse on 'The Art of Being a Famous Danish Writer in 24 Hours'.[55] He probably had in mind Börne's satirical essay 'The Art of Becoming an Original Writer in Three Days'. According to Börne, there is nothing one needs to learn to become an original writer, only much one needs to *unlearn*. The trick, he maintains is to take a few sheets of paper and write.

> Write everything that goes through your mind for three consecutive days with neither hesitation nor hypocrisy. Write down what you think of yourself, what you think of your wife, what you think of the war with the Turks, what you think of Goethe, of Fonk's trial, of the Last Judgement, of your superiors. At the end of three days you will scarce believe what new and unheard-of thoughts have come to you. And that, my friends, is how to become an original writer in just three days![56]

Hermann advises Hilde that you must write as you speak and read aloud everything you write. One should write for the ear and not for the page. He continues,

> Das Wichtigste ist nicht, was du schreibst, sondern daß du schreibst. Das heißt: dein persönlichstes Ich, das einmalig auf der Welt ist und, wenn du redest und erzählst, ja so nett seinen Ausdruck findet. Das heißt: das Beste an guten Büchern ist ja doch das persönliche Ich — die Gesamtfärbung des Wesens des Schreibenden — , das durch die Geschichten hindurch leuchtet. Sei unverziert und aufrichtig und kümmere dich einen Dreck um den sogenannten Leser. — Man schreibt für sich, zur Selbstentlastung und um über Teile seines

Daseins hinwegzukommen, an denen man sonst leidet wie an eingeklemmten Affekten.

[The most important thing is not what you write but that you write. That you find the way to express your unique inner self. For the best thing about good books is how the personality — the essence of the writer's character — radiates through the stories. Be plain and sincere and don't give a damn about your so-called reader. — One writes for one's self, for one's self-relief and to get over aspects of one's life which otherwise would cause suffering, as happens with emotions that are suppressed.][57]

It is no surprise that Hermann advises that the aspiring writer should make notes. Rather than letting their thoughts escape them they must write them down immediately. In fact, Hermann argues that you cannot have too many notes. The smallest observations and thoughts captured in one's notes can develop into something much bigger. Writers should avoid extravagance — they should be simple but not simplistic and write for educated people. Feeling is everything, he tells Hilde, but as a writer you should remember to stay unsentimental and composed.

Hermann advises Hilde not to get caught up with 'isms'. She should develop her own literary personality, avoid being influenced too much by other writers, and write instinctively:

Du mußt nicht beim Anfang des Schreibens, aber bald danach das Gefühl haben, als ob dir die Worte diktiert würden, das heißt, du hörst sie und schreibst sie nach — oftmals so schnell, daß man kaum mitkommt. [...] Denn die Hauptarbeit dabei ist ja nicht bewußt, sondern unterbewußt.

[You don't have to feel as if the words are being dictated to you when you first begin to write but soon afterwards, it should be as if you are hearing them and then writing them down, so fast that you can hardly capture it all. [...] For the main work is not conscious, but subconscious.][58]

It appears that things started going wrong for Usche only weeks into her marriage. Already, it had become a sham, Hermann was telling Hilde in October 1940.[59] The differences between her and Herbert had proved too great. Usche, like all the younger generation, has always been dismissive of culture, he writes, but now she realizes she cannot stand a life without it. Rather like her father, Hermann says, she is a slow developer. If years ago she had possessed the understanding that she is gaining now, she would not find herself in her current predicament. But since it's happened, the main thing, he writes, is working out how best she can extricate herself.

Around this time Hermann's lodgers moved out and he found himself living alone. Alone, that is, except for a Siamese cat. His long-running feud with his unreliable coal stove came to a head in the snows of January 1941. He tells Hilde that many times he would have liked to smash it to bits with a mallet and would have done so had it not been made of wrought iron. But now he has finally given up, and he is making do with a small stove upstairs.[60]

The winter of 1940/41 witnessed a marked stepping up of the persecution of the

Jewish population. The same month Hermann finally admitted defeat with his iron stove, a new German decree ordered the registration of all Jewish persons: full Jews, half-Jews, quarter-Jews, orthodox or not. Upon registration, Jews were issued with a yellow card. Dr H. Böhmcker, the Special German Representative in Amsterdam, subsequently wrote to Seyss-Inquart that as a result of registration, 'all Dutch Jews are now in the bag' (erfasst).[61] Around the same time, the NSB and its defence section, the Weerbaarheidsafdeling (WA), began targeting Jewish neighbourhoods in Amsterdam. This in turn led to street fights between the WA and Jewish self-defence groups which culminated in a pitched battle on the Waterlooplein on 11 February 1941. The next day German soldiers encircled the old Jewish neighbourhood, creating the Amsterdam ghetto. It was cordoned off from the rest of the city, police checkpoints were established, and non-Jews were barred from entering. A week later the Van Woustraat Koco ice-cream salon was raided by the German 'Grüne Polizei'. A violent fight ensued in which several police officers were wounded.

There was a ruthless reprisal on the weekend of 22/23 February when the Germans unleashed a pogrom in which 425 Jewish men were taken hostage and imprisoned. The co-owner of Koco, Ernest Cahn, was one of those arrested. The men were deported from Amsterdam first to Buchenwald and then to Mauthausen where they were all murdered. The banned Dutch Communist Party called a general strike in protest against the pogrom. About 300,000 people joined the Februaristaking which brought much of Amsterdam to a halt and spread to other areas including Hilversum. But the Germans brutally suppressed the strike after three days, effectively crippling Dutch resistance organisations.

The day before the pogrom, Hermann had responded to Hilde's news that she and Villum were going to Teheran. Villum had managed to get a job working as an engineer on a Danish project there. It was of course a means of escaping occupied Denmark and Hermann thought it could be a springboard for getting to America. For Hermann it was bittersweet news. He felt pleased for them but sad that Hilde should be going so far away. Where would he now spend his summers, he asks, if not with her and Villum in Aarhus?[62]

In April a new decree forbade Jews from moving from Amsterdam to other parts of the country. It was followed in August by decrees enabling the disposal of Jewish estates and requiring that Jewish children should be educated separately. In September Jews were prohibited from parks, cafés, hotels, buffet-cars, theatres, cinemas, sportsgrounds, bathing beaches, swimming pools, art exhibitions and concerts, public libraries, reading rooms, museums and markets.

This was the world into which Usche and Herbert's son, Micky, had been born on 13 March 1941. As the historian Jacob Presser writes with regard to the German and Austrian Jewish refugees in the Netherlands, 'Anxious for their families, often scattered over the face of the earth, subject to all sorts of humiliating regulations, hounded from pillar to post — one can only admire the way so many managed to carry on at all.'[63]

By the summer of 1941, Hilde and Villum, after travelling through the USSR, were in Iran and it proved impossible to maintain the correspondence that she and her father had kept since March 1933. Hermann's second but last card to Hilde came back to him undelivered, although he said he would try sending it again via Baghdad.[64] He wanted to let her know that he had been in hospital for a week the previous month because of heart spasms and that subsequently he had fallen down a flight of stairs and suffered a slight concussion, cuts and bruises.

From the time of Georg Hermann's last communications with Hilde, there exists a short reflection, a charming, witty balance sheet entitled *Bekenntnis* [Confession], which shows that at least his sense of humour remained intact.

> Niemals hat jemand Rücksicht auf mich genommen. Zum mindesten auf den Schriftsteller in mir. Erst habe ich doch etwas Vernünftiges werden sollen, einen anständigen bürgerlichen Beruf ergreifen sollen, da habe ich schon deshalb nicht schreiben dürfen — nur so insgeheim. Dann habe ich mich verheiratet. Hat mich meine Frau daran gehindert zu schreiben. Wäre ich Anwalt gewesen oder Arzt, hätte sie mich doch nie gehindert, meine Praxis wahrzunehmen. Dann die Kinder. Dann habe ich ein zweites Mal geheiratet. Ist alsbald das gleiche Lied losgegangen. Dann habe ich als Witwer mit einer Tochter gelebt, allein. War's auch nicht viel besser. Nun hat auch die geheiratet, und ich lebe nunmehr als Solokrebs — nachdem mich auch meine Untermieter verlassen haben — mit einer siamesischen Katze im Haus, die mich beim Schreiben stört. Duldet das Biestchen doch nicht, daß ich selbst dieses Bekenntnis hier tippe. Haut mit ihren Tatzen auf die Tasten. Und wenn alles nicht hilft, setzt sie sich auf das Manuskript und streichelt mich leise mit ihrer Sammetpfote ins Gesicht: ich soll lieber doch mit ihr spielen, statt diese wertlosen Dummheiten zu treiben!! Nie habe ich, solange ich denke und mich zurückerinnern kann, schreiben dürfen.
>
> Nun denke man nur mal. Einige vierzig Bände habe ich herausgegeben. Mindestens ebenso viel ist in Zeitschriften und Zeitungen noch verstreut. An fünfzehn Bände, sagen wir, mag noch ungedruckt herumfahren. Ins siebzigste Jahr bin ich nun allgemach gekommen — und nie, nie, nie habe ich schreiben dürfen.
>
> Was aber hätte ich nun wirklich geschrieben erst, wenn ich wirklich ungestört hätte schreiben können und dürfen, und Frauen, Kinder, Katzen — auch Hunde nicht zu vergessen! — jemals auf mich und meine Arbeit und meine Ruhe dazu irgendwelche Rücksicht genommen hätten?!
>
> Ich will es euch ganz im Geheimen anvertrauen: gar nichts!!

[Nobody has ever shown consideration for me; at least, for the writer in me. In the first place I was meant to take up some sensible bourgeois profession and had to do my writing in secret. Then when I got married, my wife prevented me from writing. Had I been a lawyer or a doctor, she would never have sought to stop me from practising my profession. Then the children. Then I married a second time and it was the same old story. Then I lived alone as a widower with a daughter. It wasn't much better. Now she's married and I live alone, as solitary as an old crab, after my sub-tenants left me, too. Except that there is a Siamese cat in the house [...] which bothers me when I am writing. The little temptress won't even suffer me to write this confession. Her paws are at the keys of the typewriter. If all else fails, she sits down on the manuscript and strokes my face softly with her velvet paw. I should be playing with her rather than writing this worthless nonsense! Never, as long as I can remember, have I been allowed to write!

Now just think, some forty books I've published and at least as much again is scattered about in magazines and newspapers. There are texts for about fifteen more books as yet unprinted. And now I am in my seventieth year and never, never, never have I been permitted to write.

But what would I have written had I really been allowed to write and women, children and cats — not to mention dogs — had ever shown the least consideration for me and my work and the concentration it requires?

I'll tell you but it's a secret: nothing at all!]⁶⁵

Notes to Chapter 15

1. Letter to Hilde, February 1939, *Unvorhanden und stumm*, p. 168.
2. F. K. Wiebe, *Germany and the Jewish Problem*, published on behalf of the Institute for the Study of the Jewish Problem (Berlin: Muller, 1939), pp. 20–21.
3. Ibid., p. 67.
4. Letter to Hilde, February 1939, *Unvorhanden und stumm*, p. 167.
5. Ibid.
6. Postcard to Hilde, 13 April 1939, *Unvorhanden und stumm*, p. 172.
7. Georg Hermann, 'Meine Liebesgeschichten', 1939, GHC; AR 7074; Box 4; Folder 29, LBI.
8. Postcard to Hilde, 3 April 1939, *Unvorhanden und stumm*, pp. 171–72.
9. Gelber, 'Georg Hermann's Late Assessment of German-Jewish and Aryan-German Writers', pp. 10–11.
10. One example of this is the Jewish-German contribution to Goethe scholarship. See Klaus L. Berghahn and Jost Hermand (eds.), *Goethe in German-Jewish Culture* (Rochester, NY: Camden House, 2001).
11. Since 1933 Hauptmann had remained in Germany and been public in his support for the Nazi regime, describing Hitler as the greatest German since Luther. See Anthony Grenville, 'The Case of Gerhart Hauptmann', *Journal of the Association of Jewish Refugees* (2012), 1–2.
12. Gelber, 'Georg Hermann's Late Assessment of German-Jewish and Aryan-German writers', p. 11.
13. Letter to Hilde, 25 May 1939, *Unvorhanden und stumm*, pp. 175–80.
14. Ibid., p. 176.
15. Ibid. Here, p. 178.
16. R. W. Jansen, *Anne Frank. Silent Witnesses — Reminders of a Jewish Girl's Life*, (Hoogeveen: RWJ Publishing, 2014), p. 108.
17. Letter to Hilde, 21 August 1939, *Unvorhanden und stumm*, p. 180. Mimi continued to be in touch with Else who remained in Berlin. By the end of the year, Else was seriously ill with brain convulsions and required twenty-four hour nursing (see Hermann's letter of 27 December 1939, *Unvorhanden und stumm*, p. 189). She died in 1940.
18. Ibid.
19. Postcard to Hilde, 10 October 1939, *Unvorhanden und stumm*, p.184.
20. The street was renamed Herbert-von-Karajan-Straße in 1998.
21. This outline of the novels comes from Hermann's letter to Hilde dated 27 November 1939, *Unvorhanden und stumm*, pp. 185–86. A copy of the unpublished partial text of 'Max und Dolly' and 'Georg der Doktor' is in the GHC; AR 7074; Box 3; Folder 29; LBI. Laureen Nussbaum has explored the notes that Hermann made for the stories, in particular a notebook which bears the title 'Holland Liese'. See Nussbaum, *Verliebt in Holland*, p. 187.
22. Ibid.
23. Letter to Hilde, 27 November 1939, *Unvorhanden und stumm*, p.187.
24. Nussbaum, 'Georg Hermanns *Randbemerkungen*', pp. 165–66.
25. Ibid.
26. *Unvorhanden und stumm*, p. 12.
27. Letter to Hilde, 19 January 1941, *Unvorhanden und stumm*, p. 211.

28. Letter to Hilde, 23 January 1940, *Unvorhanden und stumm*, pp. 192–93.
29. Private recording, 1979.
30. Geert Mak, *Amsterdam: A Brief Life of the City*, trans. by Philipp Blom (London: Vintage, 2001), p. 251.
31. Ben-Dror, 'Recollections 1919–44'.
32. Postcard to Hilde, 24 June 1940, *Unvorhanden und stumm*, pp. 194–95.
33. It would have been some time before Hermann would have learned of their internment. Once the Netherlands were occupied there was no mail service between it and the UK. News could only be exchanged via neutral countries: Switzerland, Sweden and until December 1941, the USA.
34. François Lafitte, *The Internment of Aliens*, 1940. Reprinted 1988 (London: Libris, 1988), p. 76.
35. Ibid., p. 134. On 8 January 1941 Albert Einstein wrote to Frederick Lindemann, the government's chief scientific advisor, seeking his help in securing Siegfried's release, in part because of his potential contribution to the war effort. Lindemann shared the letter with Anthony Bevir, Churchill's private secretary. See the Papers of F. A. Lindemann, Viscount Cherwell, Nuffield College Library, Oxford. (Reference D. 65).
36. Ben-Dror, 'Recollections 1919–44'.
37. Postcard to Hilde, 13 August 1940, *Unvorhanden und stumm*, pp. 196–97.
38. Letter to Hilde, 9 September 1940, *Unvorhanden und stumm*, p. 200.
39. Ben-Dror, 'Recollections 1919–44'.
40. Postcard to Hilde, 18 September 1940, *Unvorhanden und stumm*, p. 200.
41. Herbert Kalmann, *Overpeinzingen voor mijn nakomelingen — een overlevingsbericht* (Bunschoten: ABEM, 1993).
42. Ibid., pp. 144–45.
43. Ibid., pp. 146–47.
44. Ibid., p. 149.
45. Postcard to Hilde, 24 September 1940, *Unvorhanden und stumm*, pp. 200–01.
46. Letter to Hilde, 24/25 November 1940, *Unvorhanden und stumm*, pp. 202–07.
47. Paul Lindau (1839–1919), novelist and dramatist. Berthold Auerbach (1812–82) is best known for his *Schwarzwälder Dorfgeschichten* (Black Forest Village Stories). Gustav Freytag (1816–1895), novelist and dramatist. His 1855 novel *Soll und Haben* (Debit and Credit) made him famous across Europe.
48. Gottfried Keller (1819–1890). Swiss poet and novelist who was at the forefront of literary realism in the nineteenth century.
49. Letter to Hilde, 24/25 November 1940, *Unvorhanden und stumm*, p. 203.
50. A.N. Wilson, *Tolstoy* (London: Penguin, 1988), p. 88.
51. Letter to Hilde, 24/25 November 1940, *Unvorhanden und stumm*, p. 203.
52. Hermann's *Die Zeitlupe* (pp. 19–27) includes an essay about Bang.
53. Letter to Hilde, 24/25 November 1940, *Unvorhanden und stumm*, p. 204.
54. Letter to Hilde, 19 January 1941, *Unvorhanden und stumm*, pp. 207–12.
55. Postcard to Hilde, 7 February 1941, *Unvorhanden und stumm*, p. 213.
56. Börne's article first appeared in 1823. This translation is by Leland De La Durantaye, *Harvard Review*, 31 (2006), 64. Peter Anthony Fonk was a Cologne merchant who was sentenced to death for murder in 1822 after a legal process that lasted six years.
57. Letter to Hilde, 19 January 1941, *Unvorhanden und stumm*, p. 208.
58. Ibid., p. 211.
59. Letter to Hilde, 25 October 1940, *Unvorhanden und stumm*, p. 206.
60. Letter to Hilde, 19 January 1941, *Unvorhanden und stumm*, p. 207.
61. Jacob Presser, *Ashes in the Wind — the Destruction of Dutch Jewry*, trans. by Arnold Pomerans (London: Souvenir, 2010), p. 35.
62. Letter to Hilde, 21 February 1941, *Unvorhanden und stumm*, pp. 213–14.
63. Presser, *Ashes in the Wind*, p. 223.
64. Postcard to Hilde, 9 July 1941, *Unvorhanden und stumm*, pp. 216–17.
65. *Unvorhanden und stumm*, pp. 219–20. The original is in the GHC; AR 7074; Box 8; Folder 10, LBI, 549/827.

CHAPTER 16

❖

The End

The intensification of the persecution of the Jewish population in the Netherlands continued during the exceptionally cold winter of 1941/42. On 5 December 1941 a decree ordered all non-Dutch Jews to report for 'voluntary emigration' to the 'Zentralstelle für jüdische Auswanderung' [Central Office for Jewish Emigration]. The measure resulted in another wave of suicides.[1] On 29 January 1942, 137 of Hermann's Jewish neighbours in Hilversum were selected, probably at random, ordered to leave and taken to Westerbork, the camp established by the Dutch in 1939 to accommodate undocumented Jewish refugees. They were allowed to take only what they could carry.[2]

But this was just the start. In March the Germans required the Jewish Council to find 3,000 Amsterdam Jews aged between eighteen and fifty-five to work in the Drenthe labour camps.[3] From May, all Jews over six years old appearing in public were required to wear the yellow star sewn on the left breast of their outer garment. The Germans issued 569,355 of these yellow stars to the Jewish Council for distribution. As Presser writes, 'there is little doubt that [the yellow star] helped to seal the fate of Dutch Jewry, that it marked them out for slaughter.'[4]

The impact on daily life of all these measures is described by Anne Frank, shortly before the Franks went into hiding, in her 20 June 1942 diary entry:

> After May 1940 the good times were few and far between: first there was the war, then the capitulation and then the arrival of the Germans, which is when the trouble started for the Jews. Our freedom was severely restricted by a series of anti-Jewish decrees: Jews were required to wear a yellow star; Jews were required to turn in their bicycles; Jews were forbidden to use trams; Jews were forbidden to ride in cars, even their own; Jews were required to do their shopping between 3.00 and 5.00 p.m.; Jews were required to frequent only Jewish-owned barbershops and beauty salons; Jews were forbidden to be out on the streets between 8.00 p.m. and 6.00 a.m.; Jews were forbidden to go to theatres, cinemas or any other forms of entertainment; Jews were forbidden to use swimming pools, tennis courts, hockey fields or any other athletic fields; Jews were forbidden to go rowing; Jews were forbidden to take part in any athletic activity in public; Jews were forbidden to sit in their gardens or those of their friends after 8.00 p.m.; Jews were forbidden to visit non-Jews in their homes; Jews were required to attend Jewish schools, etc. You couldn't do this and you couldn't do that, but life went on.[5]

The wholesale rounding-up and deportation of Dutch Jewry began in July 1942 and continued through to September 1943. On the 14 July German forces seized 700 Jews in the streets in Amsterdam. These people were held as hostages until the Jewish Council was able to ensure that the 4000 people who had been designated by the Nazis for removal to the transit camps presented themselves.[6] On 6 August, the same tactic was deployed again in the 'Raid of the Two Thousand' when the Germans picked up Jews in the street or dragged them out of their homes, often with a great deal of brutality.[7] Three days later hundreds more Jews were hauled from their homes in parts of Amsterdam South. Those arrested were herded into the Hollandse Schouwburg and kept there until their transfer to Westerbork. At one point over 1400 people were confined in the theatre.[8]

Presser quotes the contemporary description in the underground newspaper *Vrij Nederland* of the nightmare Jews faced every evening, once the curfew fell:

> At the stroke of eight, as darkness falls, the dread ordeal of waiting begins once again for our Jewish fellow-citizens. Each footstep is a threat, each car approaching doom, each bell a sentence. The squad cars are out, the boys in green and the Dutch Jew-baiters ready for their deadly night's work. Every evening the doors are flung open and women, children, old people, the sickly and the rest are dragged out [...] defenceless, without appeal, hope or help. Night after night. By the hundred, dragged away, always to one and the same destination: death. When the morning comes, those left behind do the rounds of their friends and relatives to see who is left. Next come the removal vans, taking away what furniture is left, and in the evening it all starts over again.[9]

In autumn 1942 Usche and Herbert's marriage came to an abrupt end:

> One day, I still remember the date, 7 October 1941, clearly, I had a terrible row with my mother-in-law. I took Micky in his stroller and walked all through Hilversum in the morning, ending up at the door of Peps' place. I said to him, "Here I am and I'm never going back, and no one will force me to do so." Well, Peps was not unhappy about this. He was on his own, and was already prejudiced against the family because, in his eyes, they were Eastern Jews and therefore less intellectual, and more orthodox. So there I was with a young baby and an old father and not much experience in looking after either![10]

In January 1943, a German officer visited Hermann and Usche and ordered them to move to one of the neighbourhoods now designated for Jews in Amsterdam. The Commander of the German Security Police, Ferdinand aus der Fünten, had first threatened to evacuate all provincial Jews on 23 November 1942. He repeated his threat on 10 December and then again at an unspecified date before 25 January 1943. On 10 February 1943 a decree was issued ordering all Jews to Amsterdam. In her recollections Usche recalls:

> Quite a few of our friends in Hilversum had already disappeared by this time, or gone underground, or moved into the ghettos in Amsterdam. One day, a German officer came to our place. He was not at all interested in Peps, the author, but had heard that we possessed a large art collection. The officer was friendly and had a good look around at what was in the flat. He was obviously visualizing what would look good in his villa. Peps being naïve was so attached to his things, that, even when we had no money and he might at least have sold some things, he never did so. This would have helped us a lot, because with

just a few things sold, there was still a huge amount left. The whole flat was just crammed full with art objects.

Before leaving, the German officer said, "You will move out within forty-eight hours." Peps said, "What will happen to the things in the apartment?" and the officer said "Don't worry, they are valuable so they will be taken good care of." Again, Peps' naivety revealed itself. I recall that during that forty-eight-hour period, I used the baby stroller in the evening and made trips to take some things to Elsje (de Goot) and to other people, in order to hide them. I already understood that I had to do this otherwise all would have been lost. This was in January 1943.

The Germans had arranged for the Jewish community in Amsterdam to compulsorily take-in other Jewish people from the provinces. So, we three went with our hand luggage by train to Amsterdam and were given the address of a Dutch Jewish couple in the ghetto area in the south of the city. We got two very small rooms up on the second floor. I was not allowed to cook there, so I obtained food through the equivalent of "meals on wheels". The food was awful, and with Peps being diabetic, things became very difficult.

By this time we were already becoming aware of the extent of the anti-Semitism. We had to wear [...] the yellow Star of David at all times. Elsje came over sometimes to take Micky, now two years old, for a walk in the stroller, as I could not do so. There was a curfew at 8.00 p.m. and a total blackout at night. By this time we could already hear the Germans knocking on doors along the street and people shouting and screaming, so it was apparent that things were getting worse.

Then the Germans began another evacuation program of the whole street that we were in, and said that they had another flat allocated for us. We went on foot, with my stroller and hand luggage, to another part of Amsterdam south, where most Jews were living. The house that we were told to go to had very steep stairs leading up to it, with a "peep hole" in the door for the occupant to see who was coming (Peps wrote about such a house as the "Steile Treppe")[11]. We rang the doorbell, and stood there while a woman answered the door. On seeing us, she became hysterical and shouted 'No, no, not with a child, off with you!' So there we were — in the street with nowhere to go. We did not know what to do. We could not go back to where we had come from, so we just stood there.

After quite some time, the woman's husband appeared, and after some discussion we were eventually allowed to stay. Apparently the woman was so upset at seeing us because they had a son of around sixteen years old, and the Germans had come the evening before and said to the boy, "Just come down for a moment with us and sign a paper in the car." The parents were not allowed to come down and the boy had just vanished. After this, the mother had become quite crazed, and seeing a child like Micky had led to her outburst.

I can't realistically begin to describe what these times were really like. You had this feeling that you were not actually alive, and that what was happening could not be real. After a few days, somebody approached me and said, "you should get your child underground." We had no money, but were told that there were people who were willing to hide children for the rest of the war. I was told, "please think it over". In making this suggestion, no one said directly to me, "if you are taken by the Germans you won't ever come back", but that was, of course, implied.

I thought long and hard about it all. I knew that Micky was the last remaining joy for Peps and to take him away would deprive him of that. For him to see a small innocent child first thing in the morning was his last real ray of sunshine, but I also realized that hiding Micky might save his life. Finally I said, "take him". I was then not allowed to go near him again, and they dressed him towards evening. He was crying all the time. When he had gone, I felt as though I was under an anaesthetic. I could not recall anything about those days, except that Micky was not there. Then, after three days, someone came back with him. He had been crying non-stop from the moment they took him away, and would have betrayed the presence of other children being hidden — even in a village. Also, he would not eat, go to the toilet or do anything else. So there he was, back with his mother and grandfather for better or for worse. That whole incident remains unforgettable for me.[12]

It was during this period in Amsterdam that Hermann handwrote a poem which he dedicated to Eva.

Seelenwanderung

Nun hab ich genug vom Seelenwandern
Immer von neuem stets in den andern.
Weder in Cohn will ich, noch in Schmidt
Kurz gesagt: ich mach nicht mehr mit!!
Doch in Fünfzigtausend Jahren dann
Da sehe ich noch mal den Schwindel mir an,
Falls dann die Erde noch nicht vereist ist
Und der Trottel von Mensch noch nicht völlig vergreist ist
Und, wenn die Bestie noch *immer* nicht gezähmt ist,
Und seine Dummheit und Mordgier *noch* stets ungelähmt ist,
Und, wenn dann diese Weltordnung immer noch in Kraft ist
Und die Weltgeschichte noch nicht abgeschafft ist
Man den Menschen noch immer vorn und hinten belügt
Und wie ein Sandkorn ihn unterpflügt,
dann schlaf ich weiter in Ruh und gut zugedeckt,
Und zeige die Kehrseite jedem, der mich weckt.

[Reincarnation

I've had my fill of reincarnation
This eternal soul migration.
I don't want to be back as Cohn nor Schmidt[13]
In short: I no longer want to go along with it!!
But perhaps in fifty thousand years, then
I might re-enter the dizzy caper again,
If the earth is not under an icy sheet
And that half-wit man become obsolete
And, if the beast that *always* lies within him has not been tamed,
And his stupidity and murderous lust continues *still* the same,
And if this current world order persists
And world history has not ceased to exist
If people are still being deceived as they are now
And treated like grains of sand under the plough,
Then I shall sleep in peace, well covered up,
And turn my back on anyone who wakes me up.][14]

In May 1943 the Germans told the Jewish Council that 7000 of its staff must be transported. When the council failed to bring forward that number, 3000 Jews were summarily rounded up on 26 May.[15] On 8 June Hermann wrote to his friend, the well-known conductor and composer Peter van Anrooy, to see if he could help arrange for Usche, Micky and himself to be placed on the list of Jews to be moved to Kamp Barneveld, about forty kilometres east of Hilversum. From 1942 onwards, around 700 so called 'privileged' Dutch Jews, intellectuals and artists, had been detained near Barneveld at Castle De Schaffelaar and at a private estate, De Biezen.[16] Hermann makes it clear in the letter that he is only interested if his daughter and grandson can accompany him.[17] Whether Peter van Anrooy acted upon the request, and if so whether it was ever considered, is unknown.

Twelve days later, there was a massive offensive. Otto Bene, the German Foreign Office Delegate to the Netherlands, said that the round-the-clock operation had 'bagged' 5500 Jews, bringing the total up to 100,000.[18] Hermann, Usche and Micky were among the victims:

> [...] on the 20th June 1943, a Sunday, we were included in a large roundup of Jews and put on special trams that went to the central railway station. I remember the three of us sitting in one of these trams and riding through Amsterdam. It was sunny weather and there were families going for walks, while we and our fellow travellers were possibly being transported to our deaths. It was so incongruous, but no one shouted out or screamed. We were all in deep shock. Then we arrived at central station where the train, composed of cattle wagons, was waiting for us. We were loaded in and then transported to Westerbork, a very large transit camp halfway between Amsterdam and Groningen. The camp had originally housed German Jews who had fled to Holland from Germany later than us, but had not been granted permits to settle. About 1,000 people were transported from this camp every week, so you can imagine how large it was. Most of this transportation was to death camps.
>
> On arrival, I recall being met off the train by a tall woman in overalls, who took Micky, saying, "Give me Peter" (Micky's other name) and immediately talked to him. He did not cry at all and soon went around with her. It turned out that she had three children in hiding, and of course every child that she saw was, in effect, her own. [...] When we got off the train, Peps was then taken to a separate wooden barrack for old people — not for the sick ones.
>
> Well, there we were and one had to make the best of it. There was a bathhouse where one could have a shower, and there was always someone there to provide a jug of hot water for Micky. It was basically okay, but every now and again people committed suicide by hanging themselves, especially just before transportations were due.
>
> There were large shacks, each with dormitories of bunk beds that were three-high. I was put in one room where I met Dini [Bernadina Polac], who was four years younger than me (and later went to our kibbutz). She had already been in the camp for some time, having been rounded up while training for an agricultural project for youths in Palestine. Another camp inmate was Rutje [Ruth Cohen], eight years my junior, who also ended up on our kibbutz.
>
> My ex-husband (we had divorced in absentia) had not been transported, but had wanted me to come to Belgium where his whole family had gone — before they all ended up in an internee camp in Switzerland. He had not

wanted my father to join us, as all he and his family really wanted was Micky. He eventually married the non-Jewish daughter of the doctor who treated his family in the internee camp.

One day, Micky fell ill and he was taken to hospital in what resembled a primitive wheelbarrow. I was not allowed to go with him. I had been in the hospital myself so I knew that it was ramshackle and improvised [...] Also, I recall that when I had to go there I was very sick but was not told what was wrong. Anyway, Micky was in this "hospital" and being kept in isolation. Although there were many young girls in the camp who worked in the hospital as nurses, none of them was granted access to him. So, I had no idea what was wrong with him. It was awful.[19]

The lawyer and writer Abel Herzberg who was deported to Westerbork in November 1943 describes it thus:

> Westerbork was another word for purgatory. There was nothing to sustain one materially or spiritually. Each was thrown on his own resources, utterly alone. Desperation, total and absolute, seized everyone. People sought help but seldom found it and, if they did, knew that it could not possibly prevail. Deportation to Poland might at best be postponed — for a week, perhaps, or for a few weeks at most. Husbands were powerless to protect their wives, parents had to watch helplessly while their children were torn away from them for ever. The sick, the blind, the halt, the mentally-disturbed, pregnant women, the dying, orphans, new-born babies — none was spared on the Tuesdays when the cattle-trucks were being loaded with human freight for Poland. Tuesdays, week in, week out, for two interminable years.[20]

The seasoned Dutch journalist Philip Mechanicus, who like Hermann had once worked on *Algemeen Handelsblad*, kept a diary during his nine months of incarceration in Westerbork. In his entry from 9 September 1943, we catch a glimpse of Hermann. Mechanicus writes,

> De oude letterkundige Georg Hermann, de schrijver van *Jettchen Gebert*, loopt als een deur zo stijf, maar in stranddracht met een pet en een wandelstok rond en vraagt iedereen: Na, mein Freund, gibt's Neues? Sie wissen doch so viel. En vertelt gemoedelijke grapjes, zoals in *Jettchen*.

> [The old literary man, Georg Hermann, author of *Jettchen Gebert* walks around as stiff as a door, but in beach wear with a cap and a walking stick and asks everyone, "well, my friend, what's new? You know so much." And tells jovial jokes, as in *Jettchen*.][21]

Hermann was still in touch with Mimi. He wrote to her on 1 October, saying that he was receiving assistance from his fellow inmates in Barrack 54, among whom there were a number of physicians, but that medicines were not available.[22] Mimi was continuing to try to rescue Hermann, Usche and Micky, but, every Tuesday, camp inmates were taken away on the deportation train, and in November Hermann was selected:

> One day in mid-November, Peps was given a slip bearing his name by the head of the barrack, who then told him to be ready to go for transportation the following morning. [...] We were given the same instructions. The trains always

left before dawn, while all other inmates had to remain inside. I remember that I went over to Peps' barrack, and said "look you're going tomorrow morning, let's try to be together in the same wagon." [...] Then, I went back to my barrack (still without Micky who remained in hospital) where a lot of people were already getting their belongings together for the morning's transportation. The mood of everyone was "sub-zero" but you always did what you were told to do. There was no choice, but people tried as long as possible to stay together.

Then, at about 10.00 p. m., an errand boy came from headquarters in the barracks with a slip saying, "the child named (Micky's details) is untrans-portfàhig", meaning untransportable. The Germans were meticulous with detail as always, and the rules stated that mothers remain with children up to the age of three — after which everyone could be disposed of / killed separately. Micky was not yet three. I know that Peps had already had his birthday, so this transportation must have been at the end of October or the beginning of November 1943.[23] So my transportation was delayed for another week, to go with the next batch of 1,000 people. I was sorry not to be going with my father — one did not think of consequences beyond that.

Dini and all other able-bodied people were taken to the railway station to push the transported people into the trains. Dini has traumas to this day about all this. She was thus the last person to see Peps — because she knew him. No one will ever know how Peps died — whether this was during the transportation or later. I did get a notice from the Red Cross saying that he died "on arrival". As he was a diabetic, I know that it would have been a traumatic trip for him. I had done a similar trip in the cattle wagons from Amsterdam to Westerbork. The wagons were sealed from the outside, and there was no food or water, toilet facilities or any other amenities.

During that same week, and with the next transport pending, there was an outbreak of scarlet fever in the camp, but Micky did not have this illness. I believe that he may have had polio, as another small boy with him in the sickbay did definitely have this disease (Micky also had lice at this time, and so his head had to be shaved). The German troops, mostly young, who were recruited to accompany these weekly trains, refused to go into the camp because of the scarlet fever outbreak. So there were no transports for three weeks. During this period, prominent Jewish writers in Palestine (one name I recall was Sammy Gronemann) had got together and sent an "SOS" saying that something must be done urgently to save Georg Hermann in Westerbork as he was on the verge of being transported. Two documents, like affidavits, arrived at Westerbork via the Red Cross, one for Peps and one for me and Micky. They provided authorization for us to enter Palestine.

The appalling conditions in the camp and everything that had gone on with Peps' transportation meant that, strangely, I did not really react to this good news as one might have imagined. Still, at least I now had a paper that would prevent me from going on the next transportation. So, I went to the Jewish people in the barracks HQ carrying Peps' paper and said "Can't you send this to him with the next transportation?" The people there, knowing what was going on, just shrugged their shoulders, and could not say more.

On 17 November Usche wrote to her friend Elsje de Groot in Hilversum to give her news of what had happened. Choosing her words carefully to get past the censors she wrote,

Peter's Opa läßt dich grüssen; er war einige Tage in der Krankenbaracke, aber ist jetzt nicht mehr da. Er war sehr tapfer. Fratello hat sich Mühe gegeben, aber für einen von uns ist es schon zu spät.

[Peter's Grandpa (i.e. Hermann) sends you greetings. He was some days in the patients' barrack. He was very brave. Fratello (i.e. Herbert Kalmann) gave himself trouble, but for one of us it is already too late.][24]

The notice from the Dutch Red Cross information bureau to which Usche refers in her recollections is quoted by van Liere:

Daß laut der ihm zur Verfügung stehenden Angaben GEORG BORCHARDT [...] am 16. November 1943 aus rassischen Gründen und zwar wegen jüdischer Abstammung, vom K. L. Westerbork nach Auschwitz deportiert wurde. Obengenannte Person gilt als gestorben am 19. November in Auschwitz.

[According to the information we have, Georg Borchardt was deported from K. L. Westerbork on 16 November 1943 to Auschwitz for racial reasons and because of his Jewish descent. The above mentioned person is considered to have died on 19 November in Auschwitz.][25]

The Kalendarium der Ereignisse im K. Z. Auschwitz-Birkenau [Calendar of Events] states:

17.11.1943 RSHA-Transport, 995 Juden aus dem Lager Westerbork: 166 Kinder, 281 Männer und 291 Frauen unter 50 Jahren und 257 Personen im Alter von über 50 Jahren. Nach der Selektion lieferte man 275 Männer als Häftlinge ins Lager ein. Sie bekamen die Nr. 163798–164072; 189 Frauen bekamen die Nr. 68724–68912. Die restlichen Personen wurden vergast.

[17.11.1943 RSHA-Transport, 995 Jews from Camp Westerbork: 166 children, 281 men and 291 women under the age of fifty and 257 people aged fifty or more. After the selection, 275 men were taken as prisoners to the camp. They were given the numbers 163798 to 164072. 189 women were given the numbers 68724 to 68912. The remaining [531] people were gassed.][26]

Notes to Chapter 16

1. Presser, *Ashes in the Wind*, p. 93.
2. Ibid., p. 112. Westerbork was declared a transit camp by the Germans on 1 July 1942.
3. Ibid., p. 102.
4. Ibid., p. 127.
5. Anne Frank, *The Diary of a Young Girl*, trans. by Susan Massotty (London: Penguin, 2001), p. 8.
6. Presser, *Ashes in the Wind*, p. 143.
7. Ibid., p. 152.
8. Ibid., p. 163.
9. *Vrij Nederland*, 10 October 1942, quoted in Presser, *Ashes in the Wind*, p. 162.
10. Ben-Dror, 'Recollections 1919–44'. 7 October 1941 was also Hermann's seventieth birthday.
11. *Der kleine Gast* was published together with *Einen Sommer lang* as a novel in two volumes in 1925 by DVA under the title *Die steile Treppe*.
12. Ben-Dror, 'Recollections 1919–44'.
13. 'Cohn' and 'Schmidt' are stereotypical Jewish and German names (respectively).
14. The poem is dated 26 April 1943. On the reverse of the final page, Hermann wrote 'For Dr Eva Rothschild / Bukkershill (Essex) / Russel Road 19'. This was Eva's old address; the family were

no longer living in Buckhurst Hill at this time, having moved to Cambridge in summer 1941. The poem is in the archives of the publisher Das Neue Berlin and is reproduced in Schoor (ed.), *Der Schriftsteller Georg Hermann*, p. 56.

15. Presser, *Ashes in the Wind*, p. 205.

16. In September 1943, all those in Kamp Barneveld were sent to Westerbork and from there were deported to Theresienstadt, where several dozen of the group perished, but the majority survived.

17. Private letter dated 8 June 1943 in the Peter van Anrooy-Archiv des Gemeentemuseums Den Haag, quoted in van Liere, *Georg Hermann: Materialien*, p. 53.

18. Presser, *Ashes in the Wind*, p. 206. On 29 September 1943 a further 3,000 to 5,000 Jews were rounded-up and taken to Westerbork and the Jewish Council was dissolved.

19. Ben-Dror, 'Recollections 1919–44'.

20. Abel Herzberg, 'Introduction' to Jacob Presser, *De nacht der Girondijnen* (Amsterdam: Vereeniging ter Bevordering van de Belangen des Boekhandels, 1957), p. viii. Quoted in Presser, *Ashes in the Wind*, p. 406.

21. Philip Mechanicus, *In Dépôt: Dagboek uit* Westerbork (Amsterdam: Van Gennep, 1964), p. 156.

22. van Liere, *Georg Hermann: Materialien*, p. 54.

23. 16 November 1943. There were eight transports from 24 August to 16 November 1943 (seven from Westerbork and one from Vught). A total of 8,127 people were transported on them. See Presser, *Ashes in the Wind*, p. 483.

24. van Liere, *Georg Hermann: Materialien*, pp. 54–55.

25. Ibid., p. 56.

26. Ibid.

EPILOGUE

❖

> History is not something that's behind us [...] it's something we are moving through. It's the element we move through, like a fish through water, but like the fish, we are unconscious of that element and the ripples spread out around us.
>
> HILARY MANTEL, interview with James Naughtie,
> BBC Radio 4 *Bookclub*, 6 October 2013.

November 2007: My uncle George Rothschild and I are staying at the Hotel Friedenau, known as Das Literaturhotel Berlin, in Fregestraße. It is seventy years since George left Germany for the Netherlands and this is the first time that he has been in Berlin since then. It is also my first time in the German capital. Why would anyone in the family want to go back to Berlin? But we are here now.

The hotel is elegant. The dining room is laid out like a Biedermeier salon, replete with period furniture. In the main hallway there is a gallery of black and white photographs of German writers. Georg Hermann is among them. It is the same photograph that Eva kept in a frame on a bookshelf in her flat in Wallington. The same photograph that in her old age she would kiss at night.

Bundesallee (formerly Kaiserallee) is just around the corner from the hotel. The house where Hermann, Martha and Eva lived when she was first born has gone but there remains a building on the site. Number 108 is now a launderette, with flats above and a Chinese restaurant next door. This is where Hermann wrote *Jettchen Gebert*. There's a massive Toys R Us opposite. We walk back up Bundesallee to find where it meets Stubenrauchstraße, and eventually spot the Georg Hermann memorial. It is surrounded by a green fence and within the grounds of a Pestalozzi school. There's no public access, so we stand in the adjoining children's playground and look at it through the barricade. A white plastic chair lies on the ground next to the memorial, adding to the general air of neglect. The untended past.

It was in 1962, a year after the Berlin Wall went up, that the memorial was erected. On 28 August, Goethe's birthday. A little park which had previously been called Ulmenhof, site of today's playground, was renamed Georg-Hermann-Garten and that late summer's day the mayor of Schöneberg, other local dignitaries, two or three press photographers and a small group of mainly older people gathered for the unveiling ceremony. The mayor spoke a few words. Children from the Pestalozzi school looked on, surprised. The writer and director Hans Scholz, best known for his 1955 novel *Am grünen Strand der Spree* [On the Green Beach of the Spree River], was amongst those present and wrote about the occasion.[1] We know from Scholz's account that there was an elderly woman at the ceremony who was a second cousin of Hermann. Her grandmother and Hermann's mother were sisters.[2] Lovis Corinth, with whom Hermann once corresponded, set up a school for women painters in October 1901 and the elderly woman's mother was one of his students, she told Scholz. There was, then, a family representative that day in 1962.

What can one say about the neglected memorial, today? The butterfly at the top is a nice touch but the year of Hermann's death is wrong and there is no mention of what happened to him, how he died. And what is the memorial doing inside the school grounds?

George and I have been invited to Berlin by Evelyn Weissberg of Friedenauer Brücke to be present at the launch of her and her husband's new book *Friedenau erzählt: Geschichten aus einem Berliner Vorort 1871 bis 1914* [Friedenau Recounted: Stories from a Berlin Suburb 1871–1914].[3] It is a collection of articles and stories about Wilhelmine Friedenau, together with photographs and maps showing its growth during the period. There are a number of short prose pieces and extracts from works by Georg Hermann in the collection and Evelyn has used a quotation from *Jettchen Gebert* for the introduction. That evening, we gather in a comfortable modern hall close to the station in Friedenau. There are perhaps fifty or so people. Two actors read extracts from the book, including some humorous pieces by Hermann which make the audience laugh.

The next day we find the block of 'scheußlich' flats in Laubenheimer Straße where Hermann and Usche lived from August 1931 to March 1933. There is a white plaque on the outside of the building which records that Hermann lived there before his emigration, mentions three of his novels and his death at Auschwitz-Birkenau.

We go on to Grunewald to find Trabener Straße 19. Opposite the house where Hermann lived we see Engelbert Humperdinck's former home. It is marked with a similar white plaque explaining that the composer and Isadora Duncan had once lived there. I picture in my mind, little Eva, Hilde and Liese, popping across the road to go and play in the Humperdinck garden. Grunewald has a leafy upmarket feel about it, spacious and comfortable.

On our way back to Grunewald Station, we see a memorial, surrounded by flowers. It is a monument to the 50,000 Jews who lived in the Grunewald area and were transported from the station to concentration camps. There are 186 cast steel objects, representing the number of transports that left Berlin, embedded in the gravel along track seventeen, which was the track the trains used. About 160 meters of the loading bay have been reconstructed and as I look out at it and the tracks receding into the distance, I see a solitary young woman walking alongside the rails. She seems to be looking for something. Like us, I think.

It begins to rain. We take the train to Hermann's beloved Potsdam and head to the north of the city to find Georg-Hermann-Allee. The boulevard was built between 1999 and 2001 on land which had previously been used as an exercise ground for Soviet troops. Streets in the Bornstedter Feld, a newly developed part of Potsdam, were mostly named for resistance fighters and army officers of the resistance, who lived in the town. But others were also honoured and documents in the archives at the Stadtverwaltung show that it was in recognition of Hermann's writing about Potsdam and because of his murder at Auschwitz that his name was given to one of the major streets in the Bornstedter Feld.[4] At Georg-Hermann-Allee 99 there is now the Potsdam Biosphere, home to 20,000 tropical plants and, amongst other things, a butterfly house. Where thirty years ago Soviet troops exercised, today you can step into the colourful world of the tropics. It is a change of which, one can safely assume, Hermann would have approved.

★   ★   ★   ★   ★

Although Usche had learned of her father's death from the Dutch Red Cross in 1945, it was some time until it became more generally known. It was not before July 1947, for instance, that the British Association of Jewish Refugees published news of his death:

> Only now, two years after the defeat of the Nazis do we hear some facts about the bitter fate that befell our exiled poets and writers. [...]. We remember Georg Hermann, Berlin's poet, the author of the wonderful Biedermeier novel, *Jettchen Gebert*. [...] At first the writer had found safety in Holland, where friends hid him from the Gestapo. Yet eventually he shared the fate of so many other Jews who had found refuge in Holland. For a considerable time he was held in the transit camp of Westerbrock [*sic*]. Dutch scholars and writers pleaded for his release. The result of this petition to the occupation authorities was that Georg Hermann was immediately singled out for deportation to the East, where he found his death in an extermination camp.[5]

Usche and Micky were moved from Westerbork to Bergen-Belsen on 1 February 1944 where they remained until 30 June. Their inclusion (facilitated by Aunt Mimi) in an exchange with a group of German civilian internees from Palestine was finally confirmed and took place on 6 July in Istanbul. Four days later, Usche and Micky were in Palestine. Saved.[6]

When the war was over, Hilde and Villum returned to Copenhagen, together with Heinz, an orphaned boy they had adopted while they were in Teheran. Released from internment on the Isle of Wight in February 1941, Eva, Siegfried, and the children were living in Cambridge by the summer of that year. My mother always retained happy memories of the five years that the family spent in Cambridge and stayed in contact with the school friends she made at that time for the rest of her life. Liese remained in London throughout the war and shortly afterwards met and married a journalist, Walter Kuhnberg, originally from Silesia.

Hermann's first wife, Martha, settled initially in Newmarket and then, after the war, moved to Brighton. She was seventy-eight when she died in March 1954. Her story is largely untold. We know a great deal about what Hermann was thinking and feeling but almost nothing about Martha's inner life. We learn a little about her, however, from Usche's recollections. She recalls the kindness Martha (Mu) showed her in the years after her mother's death in 1926:

> After my mother died, while there was no contact with Uncle Ludwig, Mu was really fantastic and a very sweet-natured person. She was still in Neckargemünd

FIG. E.I. (from left to right) Liese, Siegfried, Eva, Beate, George, Villum, Martha and Hilde, England (May, 1947)

when I was there and later lived in Heidelberg just across the river Neckar. At that time she was renting out a number of rooms in her flat to students. This must have been before I was twelve years old, because I had not yet gone to Berlin. I went to school on the other side of the Neckar River in central Heidelberg, and used to call on Mu regularly. She was always happy to see me, and being an excellent cook used to make me special treats such as lemon mousse. She also knew that I liked music and played the piano for me. Her own children had, of course, already left home. [...] As a child one never questions deeper issues and it did not occur to me that Mu might have had any problems in spending time with me (being the child of her husband's second marriage). I don't think that she ever had such thoughts. She invited me to come at any time and to stay overnight as well. She certainly never ever used me as a means of getting extra support from Peps.[7]

Martha's sister, Tante Paula, did not survive the war. She died in a concentration camp in 1941 when she was sixty-three.[8] Their mother, Elise, died the year before, after receiving her deportation order.[9]

FIG. E.2. Mimi Borchardt (after the war)

Mimi Borchardt remained in Switzerland where she died in 1948. She did a huge amount before and during the war to help not only members of the extended family but also other friends and their relatives.[10] She saved Usche and Micky from Auschwitz and, together with Ludwig, was also instrumental in enabling Eva and Siegfried to settle in England. My mother used to say that her whole life had been a bonus, and now dotted around the globe in Australia, America, Israel and England are an ever-increasing number of family members who, knowingly or not, owe a debt of gratitude to Mimi.

Although much of Hermann's personal collection was lost, a remarkable amount seems to have been saved, presumably as a result of Usche's efforts back in January 1943. After the war Eva and Siegfried returned to the Netherlands to collect what had been stowed away and make arrangements for it to come to England. Together with pieces from Hermann's collection — paintings, furniture, clocks, ornaments

— were boxes of his papers. It is no surprise given Hermann's acute sense of the fleeting nature of human existence, that he kept so much, but what is surprising is that it should have remained intact.

In the mid-1970s, Eva and Hilde approached Arnold Paucker, the director of the London branch of the Leo Baeck Institute, with the suggestion that their father's papers should find a permanent home with the institute. The LBI collects and preserves for posterity the history and culture of German-speaking Jewry. In Dr Paucker's words, 'Alles ist Zeugnis einer unwiderruflich verlorenen Vergangenheit, die nicht in Vergessenheit geraten darf.' [Everything bears testimony to a past that is irrevocably lost but must not be forgotten].[11] Paucker travelled to Copenhagen to collect the papers that Hilde had, among them her father's letters from 1933 to 1941 which offer such an insight into his years of exile. But by far the largest part of the estate was in London and many years later Paucker recalled the numerous boxes which were delivered to his office in Devonshire Street, and the time he spent arranging the handover with Eva, whom he found charming and generous.[12] The transfer proved to be straight-forward but there was one strict condition. Eva and Hilde insisted that Paucker put in writing that their father's estate would never in any circumstances be transferred to Germany.

But what of Hermann the writer, whose once cherished books had been first burned and then banned during the Nazi years? He was not wholly forgotten in Germany. In East Germany, Das Neue Berlin — a publishing house set up in 1946 — appears to have been the first to reissue Hermann's works after the war. Its initial focus was on Berlin literature, in particular his works and those of Fontane, although it later branched out into crime and science fiction, and became one of the largest and highest-circulation publishers in the Deutsche Demokratische Republik (DDR).

In 1949 Das Neue Berlin published a short collection of extracts mainly from Hermann's novels entitled *Nur für Herrschaften* [Only for Ladies and Gentlemen]. A new edition of *Kubinke* appeared in 1951. I now have my mother's copy in which Eva wrote 'For Ate — in memory of your grandfather, October 1951'. In the next five years new editions of *Jettchen Gebert*, *Henriette Jacoby* and *Grenadier Wordelmann* followed. All of the books included editorial comments by Christfried Coler. The choice of Hermann's earlier works and the more plot-driven *Wordelmann* may have reflected Coler's view that Hermann's later works are less accessible for those looking to be entertained in the ordinary sense of the word. However, for the more discerning reader, Coler argued, they offer a wealth of erudite reflections on human nature and the problems of our imperfect existence.[13] In addition to the books, there were television adaptations of *Kubinke* in 1962 and 1967 and one for radio in 1973.

From the mid-1960s, Das Neue Berlin began publishing Hermann's selected works in large single editions under the editorship of Dr Bernhard Kaufhold. Between 1963 and 1977 eight volumes appeared.[14] Hilde and Villum worked with Kaufhold on the books. They had remained active leftists and, unusually for the times, they were able to travel back and forth between East Germany and the West.[15] We were given copies of the books, sometimes together with incredibly robust Dresden-made Ihagee cameras Hilde and Villum had acquired on their visits. Kaufhold must have been a Hermann enthusiast but sadly his analyses are often so pre-occupied with reinforcing Hermann's regime-friendly credentials that they tend to shed more light on the nature of East German society than on the novels. There is indeed heavy irony in the fact that Hermann should have been embraced by the DDR. It embodied all those aspects of the modern state which he most despised.

Sales figures for the Hermann novels which Das Neue Berlin published between 1949 and 1973 suggest that the books did quite well. By the time of the 1973 collection of short prose, *Die Reise nach Massow. Erzählungen und Skizzen*, 130,000 copies had been sold of the various re-issues.[16] Van Liere wrote to Kaufhold to ask him why he felt Hermann was popular in the DDR and whether he appealed more to particular age groups. Kaufhold responded that he believed the people buying and reading Hermann's books were probably not young. One needs a certain amount of experience of life, Kaufhold argued, to be attracted to the novels. Their success in the DDR, he attributed to the fact that the books were cheaper than in West Berlin because the profit motive was not the primary consideration, resulting in the possibility of moulding taste and popularity.[17]

New editions of Hermann's books were also appearing during this time in West Germany. In Cologne, Kiepenheuer & Witsch published a new edition of *Jettchen Gebert*, with illustrations by Beate Obsieger in 1955. In 1962 came the Süddeutscher Verlag edition of *Rosenemil* which includes the essay by Hans Scholz. Ullstein, Hermann's old publisher (the publishing house was restored to the family after the war), produced a paperback version of *Jettchen Gebert* in 1963 which sold 50,000 copies. Another edition was published by Herbig in 1971. S. Fischer Verlag, the publishing house which had decamped to Sweden during the war and which Hermann hoped would publish his never completed 'Die daheim blieben' novels, produced a new version of *Kubinke* in 1974, which included an afterword by its then managing director, the well-known writer and poet Peter Härtling. In March 1978 came a new stage adaptation of the Jettchen novels by Reinhart Baumgart,[18] which prompted the London Association of Jewish Refugees to talk of a 'Georg Hermann Renaissance'. The play, which was directed by Horst Zankl, premiered at the Freie Volksbühne in West Berlin. Jettchen was played by Susanne Tremper, Jason by Michael Degen and Kössling by Ulrich Hass. It was not only Hermann's novels which were reissued in West Germany. There were also new editions of *Das Biedermeier im Spiegel seiner Zeit* and *Spaziergang in Potsdam*.

During this period, interest in Georg Hermann also began to develop in academic circles. Van Liere started to publish articles in the early 1970s, ahead of his 1974 doctoral dissertation, *Georg Hermann: Materialien zur Kenntnis seines Lebens und seines Werkes* (Georg Hermann: Materials for the Knowledge of his Life and Work). Van Liere's book laid the foundations for Hermann scholarship and forty years after its publication his meticulous study remains an invaluable resource.[19]

Van Liere's critical analysis, in particular his argument that there is something specifically Jewish about the structure and style of Hermann's novels has, however, proved problematic as the elements he labels Jewish are also found in non-Jewish

Der 'jüdische Fontane'

GEORG HERMANN

German-Jewish Writer
and Journalist 1871-1943

ONE-DAY CONFERENCE

AT THE

INSTITUTE OF GERMANIC
STUDIES
UNIVERSITY OF LONDON

ON

FRIDAY, 28 SEPTEMBER 2001

DE MONTFORT UNIVERSITY
INSTITUTE OF GERMANIC STUDIES
UNIVERSITY COLLEGE LONDON

IN ASSOCIATION WITH THE

LEO BAECK INSTITUTE, LONDON
AND THE
EMBASSY OF THE FEDERAL REPUBLIC
OF GERMANY

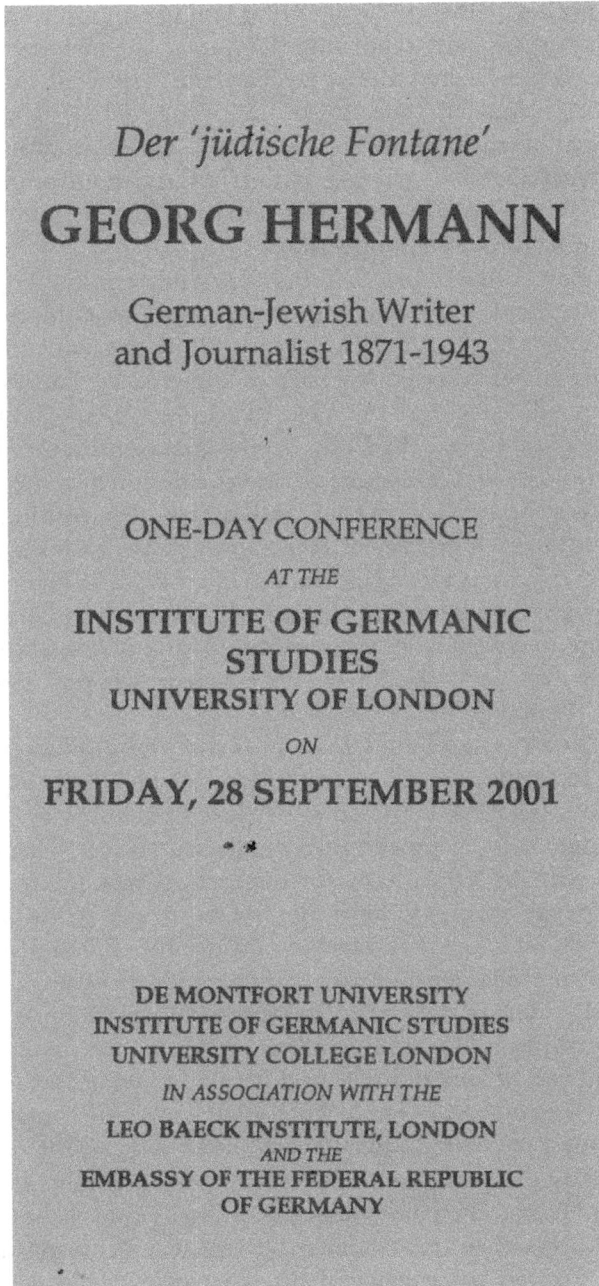

FIG. E.3. Georg Hermann London Conference, 2001.

literature of the period.[20] It seems to me that trying to define writers in this way can do them a dis-service by shoehorning them into categories with a neatness that belies the untidy, multi-faceted and ever-changing nature of human identity. As Arthur Miller once observed, 'The evil in the urge to *identify* is the urge to freeze and fix forever what in truth is fluid and flowing.'[21] One thinks of the young Georg Hermann, insect net in hand, chasing butterflies and then pinning his captured specimens in the display boxes where they remain today, frozen in time and faded like the photographs in the old family album.

The emphasis that van Liere places in his dissertation on the importance of 'fate' as an over-arching theme in Hermann's novels has also come to be questioned. Hermann was, of course, a keen chess player and the analysis of his novels by van Liere suggests that his characters' lives are as directed by fate as the pieces on a chessboard are powerless to resist the hand that moves them. Taking his cue from the leitmotif in *Jettchen Gebert*, 'Es kam, wie es kommen mußte' [And everything came, as come it must], van Liere argues that it is a design principle with Hermann, that his protagonists should be powerless in the face of onrushing fate.[22] It is true that in the foreword to *Henriette Jacoby*, Hermann writes '... ich könnte ja die Karten anders mischen; aber — was würde es nützen?' [I could shuffle the cards otherwise, but what difference would it make?].[23] Similarly, as noted in Chapter 7, Hermann sets a fatalistic tone in *Schnee* from the very beginning of the novel with the quote from Goethe, 'Da ist's denn wieder, wie die Sterne wollten' [So back it comes, what's written in the stars].

But other scholars, among them Christian Rehse, have subsequently challenged van Liere's interpretation, arguing convincingly that on closer inspection it is clear that Hermann does not seek to portray the development of events as being pre-determined by some unseen power and wholly outside his characters' control.[24] That Rosenemil wins his court case, for instance, is not due to fate but because Brillantenberta can pay for him to have a good lawyer, in a world where the judicial system can only guarantee the same level of injustice for all. Jettchen is not as passive a figure as she is sometimes depicted and grapples with the constraints placed on her by her family and wider social norms. The hapless Emil Kubinke falls prey to the inequities and social ills of big city life; social problems that the novel hints there is no appetite to address. Schmitzdorff is undone in *Grenadier Wordelmann* not by his own lack of willpower but as a result of a dehumanising bureaucracy, social injustice and the powerlessness of the individual against the might of the state.

Rather than being predicated on a belief in the immutability of social relations, Rehse argues that Hermann portrays how the outside world shapes, often negatively but avoidably, the lives of his protagonists. In this way his novels reflect his wider social criticism, so often the subject of his journalism. One of the reasons why Rehse's argument convinces is because it aligns with what we know of Hermann's writing technique and the way he sought to interpolate his political and social concerns into the fabric of his novels, and sometimes into his characters' mouths, using his bundles of notes. And that so many of Hermann's protagonists take their own lives at the conclusion of his novels is not, then, as van Liere contends, because they are too weak to escape a tragic fate but rather because, as Hilde suggested in her 1933 lecture, they are sensitive and insecure people who simply can no longer endure the world as it is.

In January 1985 a leading literary scholar, Hans Otto Horch, chose Hermann as the subject for the inaugural lecture to the Koblenzer Gesellschaft für Christlich-jüdische Zusammenarbeit [Koblenz Society for Christian-Jewish Cooperation] in Aachen. He delivered the lecture two years later at the Leo Baeck Institute in Jerusalem and that year, it was published in the LBI's annual bulletin.[25] In the lecture, Horch argues strongly for a re-evaluation of Hermann's works. The most important task of philology, he states, is to understand the world of the past and what it means for the present and the future. Horch argues that for the modern-day reader, Hermann's novels offer the opportunity to better understand a German-Jewish bourgeois culture which is irretrievably lost. He describes Hermann as a successor to such writers as Jens Peter Jacobsen, Peter Altenberg, Peter Hille and to the painter Max Liebermann, emphasizing his naturalistic descriptions and his Impressionist ability to capture mood and ambience.

1985 also saw an exhibition in Berlin organized by the LBI and the Berlinische Galerie entitled *Jettchen Geberts Kinder*. The exhibition presented art works and documents from the LBI's collection, through them seeking to convey the contribution of German Jewry to German culture from the eighteenth to the twentieth century. The exhibition catalogue included a short biography of Hermann, the etching of him by Hermann Struck and reproductions of some of the letters he received from Jakob Wassermann, Heinrich Zille, Walther Rathenau, Kurt Tucholsky, Thomas Mann, Julius Bab, Alfred Döblin and Max Liebermann.

To an extent, Horch's plea for a re-discovery of Hermann was heard, as more articles about his works appeared and an increasing number of his novels were studied and re-evaluated. In 1993 a feature film of *Rosenemil* was made by the Romanian director, Radu Gabrea,[26] and three years later, on the 125th anniversary of his birth, a colloquium on Georg Hermann was hosted by the Berliner Literaturhaus. The colloquium reflected the gradual increase in scholarly interest in Hermann's works during the preceding decades as other academics, most notably, Laureen Nussbaum, began to explore his life. Nussbaum's collection of Hermann's letters to Hilde which she edited and published in 1991 together with her analysis of some of his exile novels and journalism have shed a great deal of light on a period of Hermann's life which had hitherto been neglected.

Since 1997, when Laureen Nussbaum wrote that sadly there existed next to nothing on Georg Hermann in the English language, there have appeared a growing number of articles about his novels in English and indeed other languages.[27] Godela Weiss-Sussex's *Metropolitan Chronicles: Georg Hermann's Berlin Novels (1897–1912)* was the first book about Hermann in English to be published (in 2001) and it was she who organized a Georg Hermann Conference in London in September that year.

Opening the conference, Martin Swales, Professor of German at University College London from 1976 to 2003, raised the question of Hermann's literary credentials:

Where are we to situate Hermann within the canon of German literature? One answer is as simple as it is brutal: nowhere. Clearly Hermann neither is, nor can we by any stretch of the imagination claim that he ought to be, installed in the Pantheon of twentieth century German literature alongside Kafka, Thomas Mann, Broch, Hesse, Musil, Döblin, Grass.[28]

Swales does suggest, however, that Hermann 'has a great deal to offer us, more than his current marginal status would suggest'.[29] He goes on to say that while Hermann may never figure in the company of the 'all time greats' his creativity does rub shoulders with authors like Max Brod, Jakob Wassermann, Sammy Gronemann and Lion Feuchtwanger. Such writers, Swales argues, make a weighty contribution to German letters. 'Hermann', he posits, 'as a characteristically assimilated Western Jew, had great need of German culture. What we may now be beginning to realize is just how much it had need of him.'[30]

In the early 1920s when Hermann's collected works were being published and *Jettchen Gebert* was widely regarded as a classic, the idea that one day Hermann would occupy only a marginal a place in German literature would have seemed implausible. But, as the novelist David Lodge remarks in his portrait of H. G. Wells, a writer much admired by Hermann, 'there are eccentric orbits in literary history'.[31]

Gundel Mattenklott and her late husband Gert, who were both at the London Conference, did much to try to re-establish Hermann's literary credentials. Beginning in 1996 they embarked on what was to be a twenty-one volume series of Hermann's complete works; beautifully presented new hardback editions of his novels, essays and letters, published by Das Neue Berlin. The first volumes to appear were *Der etruskische Spiegel* and *Spaziergang in Potsdam*. They were soon followed by *Kubinke,* the Herzfeld novels, *Rosenemil,* the two Jettchen novels,[32] the five novels comprising *Die Kette* and *Spielkinder*. But after the publication of these thirteen volumes, the other planned books in the series were never produced due to poor sales. In his review of one of the new volumes for *Die Zeit*, noting their lack of commercial success, Rolf Vollmann, wrote that perhaps once again, Hermann's time had not come.[33] As a consequence of the poor sales, still today, *Der unbekannte Fußgänger* (which the Mattenklotts had intended to issue with the unfinished 'Die daheim blieben') has never been re-issued. Sadly, it also means that the volume of short stories, three volumes of essays and two of Hermann's letters, also never saw the light of day. Most of this material continues to be not readily accessible.

While awareness of Hermann has steadily increased, it remains the case that he is sometimes more conspicuous by his absence. For instance, in Amos Elon's lengthy consideration of the response of Jewish writers to the outbreak of the First World War, he makes no reference to Hermann's dissenting voice, although at that time Hermann was at the peak of his success. Similarly, the international art exhibition 'Biedermeier: The Invention of Simplicity' (2006) and its accompanying 400 page catalogue found no space to mention Hermann, despite his role in rekindling interest in the period which for a long time had been deemed unworthy of serious attention. The Knoblauchhaus, a museum devoted to the Biedermeier era in Berlin, also has nothing to say about Hermann or *Jettchen Gebert*.

The absence of Hermann, the erosion of his reputation, may simply reflect the vagaries of literary fashion. After all, the work of only a select few writers endures. Possibly the extent of the commercial success of *Jettchen Gebert* and its subsequent adaptations may have undermined Hermann's credentials as a serious writer. The novel certainly came to overshadow his other works and it has recently been suggested that Hermann's negative depiction of the *Ostjuden* Jacobys in the book has contributed to his marginalisation.[34] But it is impossible not to wonder how far his silencing by the Nazis, the fact that his books were first burned and then banned, that he was forced into exile and died at Auschwitz, has contributed to Georg Hermann's marginalisation and subsequent neglect. Van Liere considers the same question and points to Hermann's continuing popularity in the Netherlands during the 1930s — the success of the new paperback editions of the Jettchen novels and of *Wenn der weiße Flieder wieder blüht*. Nussbaum notes Hans Elema's assessment that Georg Hermann was the most read German author in the Netherlands during the first three decades of the twentieth century, more popular than the Mann brothers, Hesse, Döblin and Rilke.[35] But once under German occupation, Hermann's books were banned and since 1945 no Dutch editions of his novels have ever appeared again. Even when the news of Hermann's death in Auschwitz became known, no Dutch newspaper saw fit to mention it.[36] Similarly in Denmark where the translation of *Jettchen Gebert* sold 35,000 copies before the war, Hermann's fame did not survive beyond 1945. Reinhard K. Zachau, who describes Hermann as *the* Berlin novelist, argues Hermann's post-war popularity in East Germany had an adverse effect on his reception in the West, in the same way that others such as Heinrich Mann and Hans Fallada suffered from the literary division of Germany.[37]

Hermann was never a writer motivated by commercial considerations. Even with his first novel *Spielkinder*, Hermann was willing to sacrifice the much needed money he was being offered for a magazine serialisation rather than accept the cuts the editor wanted to make. He had a strong sense of his own artistic integrity and preferred to experiment rather than to rest on his laurels. His publishers and the public might have wanted him to write more *Alt-Berlin* romances similar to *Jettchen Gebert* but he left that to other writers such as Adele Gerhard and Felix Philippi. Philippi even borrowed from Hermann the leitmotif, 'Und so kam es...' for his bestselling novel of 1916, *Lotte Hagedorn*.

The act of writing enabled Hermann to capture and preserve personal experiences, as well as providing an outlet where he could re-evaluate his life and give expression to his innermost feelings. It was clear as early as *Spielkinder* that he had few qualms in making his private world public in his work. But then, as the critic James Wood argues, for any serious writer, the private self is the writing self; the writing is the living. 'You feel in the greatest novels', Wood suggests, 'the ghost of the author's soul rustle into life.'[38]

Hermann certainly regarded himself as a serious writer. He wanted to write about the things that mattered most to him, and increasingly after 1914 that meant writing about the anti-Semitism which came to dominate every aspect of his life. Just as Hermann was one of the few writers not to get caught-up in the nationalistic fervour of 1914, so he was one of the first to write unpalatable truths about how the war had transfigured the way that German Jews were perceived by their co-nationals. During the 1920s he found himself increasingly isolated. He kept writing novels, publishing articles and essays but he found that his values and his whole outlook were out of step with the tenor of the times. Even before he went into exile he had become more and more displaced. Once in the Netherlands, Hermann continued to write and his letters to Hilde show his determination and commitment to his craft, in the most difficult of circumstances. Even as the prospect of getting his work published diminished, he carried on writing.

★   ★   ★   ★   ★

After that significant first visit to Heidelberg in 1897, Hermann wrote a short story, 'Der Wert des Lebens'.[39] It was inspired by a student meeting Hermann had attended. He had been frustrated by the philosophical nature of the discussion that took place about the *Wert des Lebens* and the smug self-satisfaction with which the other young people appeared to believe that they had answers to everything. Hermann said nothing at the time but later that evening he wrote the speech he would have liked to have made, and afterwards in writing the story, he put the words into the mouth of a young bookseller whose heartfelt passionate outburst expressing all of the confusion and anxiety he feels about life, leaves the cerebral arguments of the self-assured students in tatters.[40] The bookseller's speech finishes with these lines:

> Hoch oben soll man mich begraben, wo mein Hügel weit über das Land sehen kann, auf die roten Dächer der Dörfer hinab, über Wald und Äcker und Felder bis zu dem fernen Münster; das Flußband soll wie eine silberne Schlange sich mir zu Füßen ringeln ... und jeden Frühling werden neue Blumen sprießen, Krokus und Veilchen, weiße und gelbe Anemonen.

> [I want to be buried high above the valley, from where my mound will overlook the land, the red roofs of the villages below, across the forest and the fields, all the way to the distant cathedral, with the river like a silver serpent winding its way at my feet ... and every spring the new flowers will appear, crocuses and violets, white and yellow anemones.][41]

Hermann cites the speech in his 1928 essay about his first visit to Heidelberg. He writes that he could never have anticipated how his words of thirty years before would be borne out:

> Damals, als ich vor dreißig Jahren diese Worte schrieb, ahnte ich nicht, daß meine Sehnsucht einmal Wahrheit werden würde. Denn gerade dort, wo man vom Hügel herab das Münster von Speier sieht und Rhein und Neckar manchmal weit draußen im Licht aufschimmern, wird über kurz oder lang meine Asche ruhen, neben meiner wundervollen jungen Frau, die mir vorangegangen ist — "Die herrlichsten Gottesgeschenke werden zuerst zurückgefordert" — und so werde ich dem Heidelberger Frühling ewig verbunden bleiben...

> [Back when I wrote these words, thirty years ago, I had no idea that what I yearned for would ever come true. For it is just at that point on the hill with its

view of the cathedral of Speyer and the Rhine and Neckar glimmering at times in the sunlight that my ashes before long will be buried, next to my wonderful young wife who has gone before me — "the most magnificent of God's gifts are the first be to to be reclaimed" — and I will remain forever linked to the Heidelberg spring...][42]

The hills are still there. The forest and the fields are still there, the cathedral steeples. The River Neckar is still winding its way through the valley. The Bergfriedhof cemetery is still there, the cemetery on the hill with Lotte's grave. Each spring the crocuses, the violets and the anemones still reappear, that Heidelberg spring which Hermann believed he would be a part of forever. It is all the same and yet, in conscience, it can never be the same again. But as Hermann always understood, however ephemeral our lives may be, the written word bears testimony. The written word remains. *Litera scripta manet.*

Notes to the Epilogue

1. Scholz's essay, 'Georg Hermann und die Berliner Dichtung', is included as an afterword to a reissue of *Rosenemil* (Munich: Süddeutscher Verlag, 1962), pp. 343–68. Scholz describes the unveiling on pages 364–68.
2. Berta had two sisters, Jenny and Johanna, so the woman at the ceremony must have been the granddaughter of one or the other.
3. Hermann Ebling, *Friedenau erzählt — Geschichten aus einem Berliner Vorort 1871 bis 1914* (Berlin: Friedenauer Brücke), 2007.
4. I am very grateful to Andreas Goetzmann, the head of the city planning department at the Stadtverwaltung Potsdam, for providing me with this information about Georg-Hermann-Allee.
5. Karl Escher, 'Allzu früh und fern der Heimat', *Association of Jewish Refugees Information*, July 1947, 51. Usche's account does not suggest that friends hid Hermann from the Gestapo nor that petitioning for his release expedited the decision to transport him.
6. Usche's memories of her time in Bergen-Belsen and her subsequent journey to Haifa are set out in her 'Recollections'. A detailed account of the exchange can be found in A. N. Oppenheim's, *The Chosen People: The story of the '222 Transport' from Bergen-Belsen to Palestine* (London: Vallentine Mitchell, 1996).
7. Shulamith Ben-Dror, 'Recollections'.
8. van Liere, *Georg Hermann: Materialien*, p. 27.
9. Private family recording, 1979.
10. For more information, see Kasper-Holtkotte, *Deutschland in Ägypten*.
11. Arnold Paucker, 'Zur Geschichte von Georg Hermanns Nachlass: Ein Geleitwort' in Weiss-Sussex (ed.), *Georg Hermann: Deutsch-jüdischer Schriftsteller und Journalist 1871–1943*, p. 134.
12. Ibid.. p. 135.
13. Christfried Coler, 'Es kam alles, wie es kommen mußte: Erinnerungen an Georg Hermann', *Aufbau*, 3:2 (1947), 182–83. The reference to Hermann's later novels is in his article, 'Georg Hermann, Dichter und Mahner' in *Das Goldene Tor*, 3 (1948), 31–33.
14. See bibliography for details.
15. For more information on Villum's political work, see Rasmus Mariager, 'Surveillance of peace movements in Denmark during the Cold War', *Journal of Intelligence History*, vol. 12 (2013), 60–75.
16. van Liere, *Georg Hermann: Materialien*, p. 228.
17. Private letter from Dr. Bernhard Kaufhold to van Liere, December 1973. Ibid., p. 225.
18. Association of Jewish Refugees in Great Britain, *Information*, vol. XXXIII, no. 2, February 1978, 9.

19. Sadly, van Liere died only two years after completing his dissertation. In the 1977 Das Neue Berlin edition of *Tränen um Modesta Zamboni*, Bernhard Kaufhold dedicates his afterword to van Liere whom he describes as a dedicated and tireless Georg Hermann researcher.

20. Weiss-Sussex, *Metropolitan Chronicles*, p. 20. See also Horch, 'Über Georg Hermann', pp. 79–80.

21. Arthur Miller, 'On True Identity', in *Collected Essays: Echoes Down the Corridor*, ed. by Steven R. Centola, (London: Methuen, 2000), pp. 159–60.

22. van Liere, *Georg Hermann: Materialien*, p. 162. Van Liere even appears to suggest (p. 60) that Hermann himself was so fatalistic that he failed to make serious efforts after May 1940 to escape his 'drohenden Schicksal' [impending fate].

23. Georg Hermann, *Henriette Jacoby* (Berlin: Das Neue Berlin, 1998), p. 5.

24. Christian Rehse, 'Nehmen wir die Dinge nicht so ernst. Zum "fatalistischen Grundzug" in Georg Hermanns Werken', in Schoor (ed.), *Der Schriftsteller Georg Hermann*, pp. 175–88.

25. Horch, 'Über Georg Hermann', pp. 73–94.

26. See Dominique Nasta, *Contemporary Romanian Cinema: The History of an Unexpected Miracle* (New York: Columbia University Press, 2013), pp. 227–28.

27. For instance, see Luis S. Krausz, *Ruínas Recompostas: Judaísmo centro-europeu em Aharon Appelfeld, Joseph Roth e Georg Hermann* (São Paulo: Humanitas, 2013).

28. Martin Swales, 'Introductory Remarks', in Weiss-Sussex (ed.), *Georg Hermann: Deutsch-jüdischer Schriftsteller und Journalist 1871–1943*, pp. 3–4.

29. Ibid, p. 1.

30. Ibid., p. 4.

31. David Lodge, *A Man of Parts* (London: Vintage, 2012), pp. 558–59.

32. Das Neue Berlin collaborated with Albin Michel to produce a new French translation of the two novels which was published in a single volume in 2002. It includes a thoughtful introduction by the translator, Serge Niémetz and detailed notes. Georg Hermann, *Henriette Jacoby*, trans. by Serge Niémetz (Paris: Albin Michel, 2002).

33. Rolf Vollmann, 'Die Kunst des Kunstlosen: Ein letzter Versuch, Leser für den großen Romancier Georg Hermann zu gewinnen', *Die Zeit*, 10 February 2000.

34. Franka Marquardt, 'Durchaus ein jüdischer Roman?' Judentum, Antisemitismus und die wechselhafte Rezeptionsgeschichte von Georg Hermanns *Jettchen* Gebert', *Zeitschrift für Religions- und Geistesgeschichte*, vol. 67, issue 1 (2015), 64–84. Evelyn Weissberg has suggested to me that the prominent literary critic Marcel Reich-Ranicki was not a Hermann admirer, in part because of his negative depiction of the Jacobys in *Jettchen Gebert*.

35. *Verliebt in Holland*, p. 182.

36. van Liere, *Georg Hermann: Materialien*, p. 224.

37. See Reinhard K. Zachau, 'The City as Political Space: Modernism in Georg Hermann's Novels of Jewish Life in Berlin', in *Berlin's Culturescape in the Twentieth Century*, ed. by Thomas Bredohl (Regina, Saskatchewan: University of Regina Press, 2008), pp. 33–52.

38. James Wood, 'Sins of the Father', *New Yorker*, 22 July 2013, 70–74. Hermann, I think, would have been in agreement. In 'Weltabschied' (p. 257) he says that in reading the works of writers such as Fontane, Tolstoy, Flaubert and Stendhal, first and foremost he wants to become acquainted with them, to understand the most subtle parts of their being.

39. The story is included in vol. 5 of Hermann's *Gesammelte Werke* (Stuttgart: DVA, 1922), pp. 260–69.

40. Hermann, 'Wie ich auf Heidelberg kam', p. 189.

41. 'Wert des Lebens' in *Gesammelte Werke*, vol. 5, p. 268.

42. Hermann, 'Wie ich auf Heidelberg kam', p. 190.

BIBLIOGRAPHY

❖

1. Texts by Georg Hermann

1.1. Collected Works

Gesammelte Werke, 5 vols (Stuttgart: DVA, 1922) vol. 1: *Jettchen Geberts Geschichte*; vol. 2: *Spielkinder, Kubinke*; vol. 3: *Nachbar Ameise, Heinrich Schön jun., Einen Sommer lang*; vol. 4: *Doktor Herzfeld, Die Nacht* und *Schnee*; vol. 5: *Novellen und Essays*. Specific reference is made to the following stories and essays from vol. 5: 'Wert des Lebens', 260–69; 'Rückblick zum Fünfzigsten', 423–54; and 'Die Unstetheit des Schriftstellers', 600–11

Ausgewählte Werke in Einzelausgaben, ed. by Bernhard Kaufhold (Berlin: Das Neue Berlin, 1963–85) *Kubinke*, 1963; *Jettchen Gebert*, 1964; *Henriette Jacoby*, 1965; *Heinrich Schön jun.*, 1967; *Rosenemil*, 1969; *Grenadier Wordelmann*, 1970; *Die Reise nach Massow. Erzählungen und Skizzen*, 1973; *Tränen um Modesta Zamboni*, 1977; *Spaziergang in Potsdam*, 1985

Specific reference is made to the following stories and essays from *Die Reise nach Massow. Erzählungen und Skizzen*:

'Also — ein Jubiläum', pp. 292–300

'Das Biedermeier', pp. 359–401

'Meine Eltern', pp. 287–91

'Pro Berlin', pp. 355–58

'Die Reise nach Massow', pp. 7–18

'Das Schönste auf der Welt', pp. 201–05

'Im Spiegel (Pfeilerspiegel, ganze Figur)', pp. 301–09

'Die Zukunftsfrohen', pp. 86–118

Werke und Briefe ed. by Gert and Gundel Mattenklott and others (Berlin: Das Neue Berlin, 1996–2001) *Der etruskische Spiegel*, 1996; *Spaziergang in Potsdam*, 1996; *Doktor Herzfeld (Die Nacht* und *Schnee)*, 1997; *Kubinke*, 1997; *Heinrich Schön jun.*, 1998; *Henriette Jacoby*, 1998; *Jettchen Gebert*, 1998; *Spielkinder*, 1998; *Der kleine Gast*, 1999; *Einen Sommer lang*, 1999; *November achtzehn*, 2000; *Eine Zeit stirbt*, 2001; *Ruths schwere Stund*, 2001

1.2. Other publications (in chronological order)

Modelle: Ein Skizzenbuch (Berlin: Fontane, 1897)

Die Zukunftsfrohen: Neue Skizzen (Berlin: Fontane, 1898)

'Der Simplicissimus und seine Zeichner' (Berlin: Die Welt am Montag, 1900)

Die deutsche Karikatur im 19. Jahrhundert (Bielefeld: Velhagen und Klasing, 1901)

'Max Liebermann', in *Jüdische Künstler*, ed. by Martin Buber (Berlin: Jüdischer Verlag, 1903), pp. 105–35

Rudyard Kipling: Eine Studie (Berlin: Vita Deutsches Verlagshaus, 1909)

Sehnsucht. Ernste Plaudereien (Berlin: Fleischel, 1909)

Um Berlin (Berlin: Cassirer, 1912)

Das Biedermeier im Spiegel seiner Zeit (Berlin: Bong, 1913)

Vom gesicherten und ungesicherten Leben — Ernste Plaudereien (Berlin: Fleischel, 1915). Specific reference is made to the following essays from this collection:

'Vom gesicherten und Gesicherten Leben', pp. 1–51

'Der tote Naturalismus', pp. 52–66

'Weltliteratur oder Literatur für den Hausgebrauch?', pp. 67–106

Der Guckkasten — Altes und Neues (Berlin: Fleischel, 1916)

'Zur Frage der Westjuden', *Neue jüdische Monatshefte*, 10 July 1919, 400–05

Randbemerkungen 1914–17 (Berlin: Fleischel, 1919)

Hetty Geybert, trans. by Anna Barwell, (London: George Allen & Unwin, 1924)

Foreword to Felix Eberty, *Jugenderinnerungen eines alten Berliners* (Berlin: Verlag für Kulturpolitik, 1925), pp. 5–16

'Das Jüdische in meinem Wesen und Schaffen', *Jüdisch–liberale Zeitung*, no. 42, vol. 5, Berlin, 16 October 1925, 1

'In Memoriam Lotte Hermann-Borchardt' (Berlin: Verlag der Jüdische-Liberalen Zeitung, 1926)

Der doppelte Spiegel (Berlin: Alweiss, 1926)

'Am Neckar und Am Maine: Eine Autoreise', *Die Dame*, May 1928, 2–7

Die Zeitlupe und andere Betrachtungen über Menschen und Dinge (Stuttgart: DVA, 1928)
Specific reference is made to the following essays from this collection:

'Bang. Reger', pp. 19–27

'Dostoevsky', pp. 78–83

'Der junge Hauptmann und seine Modelle', pp. 54–62

'Liebknecht', pp. 31–36

'Moissi', pp. 73–77

'Der Politisierung der Schriftsteller', pp. 165–75

'Rathenau', pp. 41–48

'Wie ich auf Heidelberg kam', pp. 186–94

Vorschläge eines Schriftstellers (Baden Baden: Merlin-Verlag, 1929). Specific reference is made to the following essays from this collection:

'Die Generation von heute und morgen: Das Disinteressement vom Buch', pp. 225–36

'Meine Generation', pp. 209–21

'Die Kinder des Geschiedenen', pp. 95–111

'Was Wäre, Wenn (§218)', *Die Weltbühne*, 25, II (1929), 444–48

Various letters and postcards from exile to his daughter Hilde (1933–1941), in *Unvorhanden und stumm, doch zu Menschen noch reden, Briefe aus dem Exile 1933–41 an seine Tochter Hilde*, ed. by Laureen Nussbaum (Mannheim: persona verlag, 1991), pp. 19–218

'Die Bilanz des Vorkriegsmenschen', *De Stem*, XIII (1933), reprinted in *... Aber ihr Ruf verhallt ins Leere hinein. Der Schriftsteller Georg Hermann*, ed. by Kerstin Schoor (Berlin: Weidler, 1999), pp. 235–82

'Holland und Liebermann', *Central-Verein-Zeitung*, Berlin, no. 1, 4 January 1934

'Weltabschied' (1935), published in *Unvorhanden und stumm, doch zu Menschen noch reden, Briefe aus dem Exile 1933–41 an seine Tochter Hilde*, ed. by Laureen Nussbaum (Mannheim: persona verlag, 1991), pp. 221–61

'Eine Lanze für die Westjuden' (1937), published in *... Aber ihr Ruf verhallt ins Leere hinein. Der Schriftsteller Georg Hermann*, ed. by Kerstin Schoor (Berlin: Weidler, 1999), pp. 283–306

'Bist du es oder bist du's nicht?' (1937), published in *Georg Hermann: Deutsch-jüdischer Schriftsteller und Journalist 1871–1943*, ed. by Godela Weiss-Sussex, (Tübingen: Niemeyer, 2004), pp. 137–255

'Autobiographisches' (1938), trans. by Hub Nijssen and published in *... Aber ihr Ruf verhallt ins Leere hinein. Der Schriftsteller Georg Hermann* ed. by Kerstin Schoor (Berlin: Weidler, 1999), pp. 231–33

Henriette Jacoby, trans. by Serge Niémetz (Paris: Albin Michel, 2002)

1.3. Unpublished sources

'Der deutsche Jude und das Großstadtproblem', *c.* 1926–32, GHC; AR 7074; Box 5, Folder 6, LBI

'England... Stichworte von Georg Hermann', *c.* 1920s (the article is undated but it is clear from the text that the trip took place after 1918), GHC; AR 7074; Box 6; Folder 25, LBI

'Warum Goethe?', March 1932, GHC; AR 7074; Box 5; Folder 37; LBI

'J'accuse', 1933, GHC; AR 7074: Box 5, Folder 67, LBI

'Was sollen wir Juden tun', *c.* 1936, GHC; AR 7074; Box 5; Folder 66, LBI

'Neue Heimat', 1937, GHC; AR 7074; Box 4; Folder 32, LBI

'Vier Jahre Holland', 1937 GHC; AR 7074; Box 6; Folder 22, LBI

'Einige simple Tatsachen', 1938, GHC; AR 7074; Box 5; Folder 24, LBI

'Antisemitismus! Ach ja — Antisemitismus!!', *c.* 1938, GHC; AR 7074; Box 5; Folder 22, LBI

'Meine Liebesgeschichten', 1939, GHC; AR 7074; Box 4; Folder 29, LBI

'Max und Dolly' und 'Georg der Doktor' , 1939, GHC; AR 7074; Box 3; Folder 29; LBI

2. Other primary sources

BANG, HERMAN, *Tina*, trans. by Paul Christophersen (London: Athlone), 1984

BELLOW, SAUL, *To Jerusalem and Back: A Personal Account* (Harmondsworth: Penguin), 1976

BEN-DROR, SHULAMITH, 'Recollections 1919–44', Center for Jewish History Digital Collections, PID: 411295; Call Number: ME 1312. MM III 6

BORCHARDT, HILDE, 'Georg Hermann', in *Georg Hermann — Unvorhanden und stumm, doch zu Menschen noch reden, Briefe aus dem Exile 1933–41 an seine Tochter Hilde*, ed. by Laureen Nussbaum (Mannheim: persona verlag, 1991), pp. 7–16

BÖRNE, LUDWIG, 'How to Become an Original Writer in Three Days', trans. by Leland de la Durantaye, *Harvard Review*, 31 (2006), 63–70

ELLISON, RALPH, *Invisible Man* (London: Penguin, 2001)

FLAUBERT, GUSTAVE, *Sentimental Education*, trans. by Robert Baldick (Harmondsworth: Penguin, 1964)

FONTANE, THEODOR, *Effi Briest*, trans. by Hugh Rorrison and Helen Chambers (London: Penguin, 2000)

——*Jenny Treibel*, trans. by Ulf Zimmermann (New York: Ungar, 1976)

FRANK, ANNE, *The Diary of a Young Girl*, trans. by Susan Massotty, ed. by Otto H. Frank and Mirjam Pressler (London: Penguin, 1997)

GOETHE, JOHANN WOLFGANG VON, *Selected Poetry*, ed. by David Luke (London: Penguin, 2005)

GRONEMANN, SAMMY, *Utter Chaos*, trans. by Penny Milbouer (Bloomington, IN: Indiana University Press, 2016)

HAUPTMANN, GERHART, *Dramatic Works*, vol. 1, trans. by Ludwig Lewisohn (London: Secker, 1912)

HEARN, LAFCADIO, *Kwaidan: Stories and Studies of Strange Things* (New York: Dover, 1968)

HESSEL, FRANZ, *Walking in Berlin*, trans. by Amanda DeMarco (Melbourne: Scribe, 2016)

JACOBSEN, JENS PETER, *Niels Lyhne*, trans. by Tiina Nunnally (London: Penguin, 2007)

LODGE, DAVID, *A Man of Parts* (London: Vintage, 2012)

MANN, THOMAS, *Buddenbrooks — The Decline of a Family*, trans. by H. T. Lowe-Porter (London: Vintage Classics, 1996)

MECHANICUS, PHILIP, *In Dépôt: Dagboek uit Westerbork* (Amsterdam: Van Gennep, 1964)

MILLER, ARTHUR, *Echoes Down the Corridor: Collected Essays 1944–2000*, ed. by Stephen R. Centola (London: Methuen, 2000)

MORRISON, TONI, *Conversations*, ed. by Carolyn C. Denard (Jackson, MS: University Press of Mississippi, 2008)

OZ, AMOS, *A Tale of Love and Darkness*, trans. by Nicholas de Lange (London: Vintage, 2005)

ROTH, JOSEPH, *What I Saw: Reports from Berlin 1920–33*, trans. by Michael Hofmann (New York: Norton, 2004)

ROTHSCHILD, EVA, *Talking To Myself and Collected Poems 1919–78* (Charleston: Create Space, 2012)

ROTHSCHILD, GEORGE, 'Mein Großvater Georg Hermann', preface to Georg Hermann's *Spaziergang in Potsdam* (Berlin: Verlag für Berlin-Brandenburg, 2013), pp. 7–9

SCHNITZLER, ARTHUR, *My Youth in Vienna*, trans. by Catherine Hutter (London: Weidenfeld and Nicholson, 1971)

TROLLOPE, ANTHONY, *The Way We Live Now* (London: Vintage, 2012)

TURGENEV, IVAN, *Spring Torrents*, trans. by Leonard Schapiro (London: Methuen, 1972)

WILDE, OSCAR, *Plays, Prose Writings and Poems* (London: Campbell, 1991)

WOOF, VIRGINIA, *A Room of One's Own* (London: Penguin, 2000)

ZWEIG, STEFAN, *The World of Yesterday*, trans. by Anthea Bell (London: Pushkin Press, 2009)

——*Messages from a Lost World: Europe on the Brink*, trans. by Will Stone (London: Pushkin Press, 2016)

Secondary sources

ALLEN, ANN TAYLOR, *Satire and Society in Wilhelmine Germany: Kladderadatsch and Simplicissimus, 1890–1914* (Lexington, KY: University Press of Kentucky, 1984)

ANDERSON, MARK M., 'Ludwig Börne Begins His Career', in *The Yale Companion to Jewish Writing and Thought in German Culture, 1096–1996*, ed. by Sander L. Gilman and Jack Zipes (New Haven, CT: Yale University Press, 1997), pp. 129–35

ARAD, DAVID, 'Memories of Eduard Meyerstein', *International Association of Jewish Lawyers and Jurists*, 22 (1999), 20–22

ASCHHEIM, STEVEN E., *Brothers and Strangers: The East European Jew in German and German-Jewish Consciousness 1800–1923* (Madison WI: University of Wisconsin Press, 1982)

BARTELS-ISHIKAWA, ANNA, *Theodor Sternberg — einer der Begründer des Freirechts in Deutschland und Japan* (Berlin: Duncker & Humblot, 1998)

——*Post im Schatten des Hakenkreuzes. Das Schicksal der jüdischen Familie Sternberg in ihren Briefen von Berlin nach Tokyo in der Zeit von 1910 bis 1950* (Berlin: Duncker & Humblot, 2000)

BEN-DROR, SHULAMITH, 'Erinnerungen an eine unbehelligte Kindheit', in *Erinnertes Leben: Autobiographische Texte zur judischen Geschichte Heidelbergs*, ed. by Norbert Giovanni and Frank Moraw (Heidelberg: Wunderhorn, 1998), pp. 61–64

BENN, GOTTFRIED, *Absinth schlürft man mit Strohhalm, Lyrik mit Rotstift. Ausgewählte Briefe 1904–1956*, ed. by Holger Hoff (Göttingen: Wallstein, 2017)

BERGHAHN, KLAUS L., and JOST HERMAND (eds) *Goethe in German-Jewish Culture* (Rochester, NY: Camden House, 2001)

BERMAN, RUSSELL A., *The Rise of the Modern German Novel: Crisis and Charisma* (Cambridge, MA: Harvard University Press, 1986)

BIEBER, HUGO, *Heinrich Heine: A Biographical Anthology*, trans. by M. Hadas (Philadelphia, PA: Jewish Publication Society of America, 1956)

BILSKI, EMILY D., *Berlin Metropolis: Jews and the New Culture 1890 to 1914* (Jewish Museum, New York, 1999)

BITHELL, JETHRO, *Modern German Literature 1880–1950* (London: Methuen, 1959)

BORCHARDT, LUDWIG and HERBERT RICKE, *Egypt: Architecture, Landscape, Life of the People* (New York: Westermann, 1929)

BORCHARDT, LUDWIG, *Porträts der Königin Nofret-ete. Aus den Grabungen 1912/13 in Tell El-Amarna* (Leipzig: Hinrichs, 1923)

BRENNER, ARTHUR DAVID, *Emil J. Gumbel: Weimar German Pacifist and Professor* (Boston, MA: Brill, 2001)

BRENNER, MICHAEL, *The Renaissance of Jewish Culture in Weimar Germany* (New Haven, CT: Yale University Press, 1996)

BRY, GERHARD, *Wages in Germany, 1871–1945* (Princeton, NJ: Princeton University Press, 1960)

CASTONIER, ELISABETH, *Stürmisch bis heiter. Memoiren einer Außenseiterin* (Munich: dtv, 1964)

COLER, CHRISTFRIED, 'Es kam alles, wie es kommen mußte: Erinnerungen an Georg Hermann', *Aufbau*, 3:2 (1947), 182–83

—— 'Georg Hermann, Dichter und Mahner', *Das Goldene Tor*, 3 (1948), 31–33

COURT, SOPHIE, R. A., 'Review of *Träume der Ellen Stein* by Georg Hermann', *Books Abroad*, vol. 4, no. 2, April 1930 (University of Oklahoma), 140–41

CRAIG, GORDON A., 'Rahel's Jewish Sofa', *New York Review of Books*, 12 May 1988, 41–42

DEAKIN, MOLLY F., *Rebecca West* (New York, NY: Twayne, 1980)

DEGLER, FRANK, 'Die verschlafene Revolution in Georg Hermanns *November achtzehn* (1930) in Kontext des Romanzyklus Kette', in *Friede, Freiheit, Brot! Romane zur deutschen Novemberrevolution*, ed. by Ulrich Kittstein and Regine Zeller (Amsterdam: Rodopi, 2009), pp. 197–220

DÖBLIN, ALFRED, 'Review of *B.M. der unbekannte Fußgänger* and *Der etruskische Spiegel*', *Pariser Tageblatt*, 1 March 1936

DORTMANN, ANDREA, *Winter Facets: Traces and Tropes of the Cold* (Oxford: Peter Lang, 2007)

EBLING, HERMANN, *Friedenau erzählt — Geschichten aus einem Berliner Vorort 1871 bis 1914* (Berlin: Friedenauer Brücke, 2007)

—— *Friedenau erzählt 1914 bis 1933* (Berlin: Friedenauer Brücke, 2008)

ELON, AMOS, *The Pity of It All — A Portrait of the German-Jewish Epoch 1743–1933* (New York, NY: Picador, 2003)

ESCHER, KARL, 'Allzu früh und fern der Heimat', *London Association of Jewish Refugees Information*, July 1947, 51

FINK, CAROLE, 'The Murder of Walther Rathenau', *Judaism*, 44:3 (1995), 249–70

FLÜGGE, MATTHIAS and HANS JOACHIM NEYER (eds.), *Heinrich Zille — Zeichner der Großstadt* (Dresden: Verlag der Kunst, 1997)

FRAIMAN, SARAH, 'The Transformation of Jewish Consciousness in Nazi Germany as Reflected in the German Jewish Journal *Der Morgen 1925–1938*', *Modern Judaism*, 20: 1 (2000), 41–59

FRIEDLANDER, FRITZ, 'The author of Jettchen Gebert: Centenary of Georg Hermann's Birth', *London Association of Jewish Refugees Information*, October 1971, 7

GELBER, MARK H., 'Georg Hermann's Late Assessment of German-Jewish and Aryan-German Writers', *Monatshefte* 82:1 (1990), 6–16

GERARDS, MARIANNE, 'Naar aanleiding van Georg Hermann's *Träume der Ellen Stein*', *Groote Nederland*, 32, I (1934)

GILBERT, BARBARA, C., (ed.), *Max Liebermann. From Realism to Impressionism* (Seattle, WA: University of Washington Press, 2005)

GRADY, TIM, *The German-Jewish Soldiers of the First World War in History and Memory* (Liverpool: Liverpool University Press, 2012)

GRAAFF, CHRIS DE, 'Duitsche Literatuur', *Algemeen Handelsblad*, 7 March, 1936, 3

GRENVILLE, ANTHONY, 'The Case of Gerhart Hauptmann', *Journal of the Association of Jewish Refugees* (2012), 1–2

GRONEMANN, SAMMY, preface to *Jettchen Gebert*, trans. by Itzhak Schönberg (Tel Aviv: 'Ligvulam' with Bialik Institute, 1941), pp. i–xv

GRUBEL, FRED and EBERHARD ROTERS, *Jettchen Geberts Kinder. The Contribution of German Jewry to German Culture from the Eighteenth to the Twentieth Century* (New York, NY: Leo Baeck Institute of New York, 1985)

GUMBEL, E. J., *Vier Jahre politischer Mord* (Berlin: Verlag Gesellschaft und Erziehung, 1922)

HELT, BENJAMIN CARTER, *Burning the Reichstag — An Investigation into the Third Reich's Enduring Mystery* (Oxford: Oxford University Press, 2014)

HENKE, BURKHARD ET AL, *Unwrapping Goethe's Weimar: Essays in Cultural Studies and Local Knowledge* (Rochester, NY: Camden House, 2000)

HESSEL, FRANZ, 'Georg Hermann *November achtzehn*', *Die literarische Welt*, 7 July 1932, 5

HILL, LEONIDAS E., 'The Nazi Attack on "Un-German" Literature 1933–1945', in *The Holocaust and the Book: Destruction and Preservation*, ed. by Jonathan Rose (Amherst, MA: University of Massachusetts Press, 2001), pp. 9–46

HIRSCH, FRIEDA, 'Von Heidelberg nach Haifa. Lebenserinnerungen einer Zionistin 1918–1933', in *Erinnertes Leben: Autobiographische Texte zur jüdischen Geschichte Heidelbergs*, ed. by Norbert Giovannini and Frank Moraw (Heidelberg: Wunderhorn, 1998), pp. 21–49

HIRSCH, LEO, 'Die neue Georg Hermann: *Eine Zeit stirbt*', *Central-Verein-Zeitung*, no. 12, 22 March 1934

HOBSBAWM, ERIC, *Age of Extremes* (London: Abacus, 1995)

—— 'Homesickness', *LRB*, vol. 15, no. 7, April 1993, 20–21

HOLL, KARL, 'Review of *Dichtung und Dichter der Zeit. Ein Schilderung der deutschen Literatur der letzten Jahrzehnte* by Albert Soergel and other works', *MLR*, 7 (1912), 416–21

HORCH, HANS OTTO, 'Über Georg Hermann: Plädoyer zur Wiederentdeckung eines bedeutenden Deutsch-Jüdischen Schriftstellers', *Bulletin des Leo Baeck Instituts*, no. 77 (1987), 73–94

HUPPERT, GEORGE, *Comrade Huppert: A Poet in Stalin's World* (Bloomington, IN: Indiana University Press, 2016)

JACOBI, PAUL J., 'Geschichtliche Grundlagen zu Georg Hermanns *Jettchen Gebert*', *Bulletin des Leo Baeck Instituts*, no. 51 (1975), 114–21

JACOBSON, JACOB, ed., *Die Judenbürgerbücher der Stadt Berlin 1809–1851: Mit Ergänzungen für die Jahre 1791–1809* (Berlin: De Gruyter, 1962)

JANSEN, R. W., *Anne Frank. Silent Witnesses — Reminders of a Jewish Girl's Life,* (Hoogeveen: RWJ Publishing, 2014)

JELAVICH, PETER, *Berlin Cabaret* (Cambridge, MA: Harvard University Press, 1993)

JENSON, ERIK N., *Body by Weimar: Athletes, Gender and German Modernity* (Oxford: Oxford University Press, 2014)

KAES, ANTON and OTHERS, *The Weimar Republic Sourcebook* (Berkeley, CA: University of California Press, 1994)

KALMANN, HERBERT, *Overpeinzingen voor mijn nakomelingen — een overlevingsbericht,* (Bunschoten: ABEM, 1993)

KAPLAN, MARION, 'Redefining Judaism in Imperial Germany', *Jewish Social Studies*, 9:1 (2002), 1–33

KASPER-HOLTKOTTE, CILLI, 'Vom Main an den Nil. Zur Geschichte der Familie Cohen in Frankfurt und des Ehepaares Borchardt in Kairo', in *Sahure. Tod und Leben eines großen Pharao. Eine Ausstellung der Liebighaus Skulpturensammlung*, ed. by V. Brinkmann (Frankfurt a/M: Liebighaus, 2010), pp. 122–41

——*Deutschland in Ägypten: Orientalistische Netzwerke, Judenverfolgung und das Leben der Frankfurter Jüdin Mimi Borchardt* (Berlin: De Gruyter, 2017)

KITCHEN, MARTIN, *A History of Modern Germany 1800 to the Present* (Oxford: Wiley-Blackwell, 2012)

KRUMMEL, RICHARD FRANK, *Nietzsche und der deutsche Geist* (Berlin: De Gruyter, 2006)

LAFITTE, FRANÇOIS, *The Internment of Aliens* (London: Libris, 1990)

LAQUEUR, WALTER, *The History of Zionism* (London: Tauris, 2003)

LANDSHOFF, FRITZ H., *Amsterdam, Keizersgracht 333. Querido Verlag — Erinnerungen eines Verlegers. Mit Briefen und Dokumenten* (Berlin: Aufbau-Verlag, 1991)

LANGER, SIMONE, *Deutschtum — Judentum — Europa. Das Werk Georg Hermanns im Kontext seiner Epoche* (Wuppertal: Arco, 2018)

LAYTON, ROLAND V., JR., 'The *Völkischer Beobachter* 1920–1933: The Nazi Party Newspaper in the Weimar Era', *Central European History*, 3:4 (1970), 353–82

LEVI, ERIK, *Music in the Third Reich* (London: Palgrave Macmillan, 1994)

LIPTZIN, SOLOMON, *Germany's Stepchildren* (Philadelphia, PA: Jewish Publication Society of America, 1944)

LONDON, LOUISE, *Whitehall and the Jews, 1933–1948: British Immigration Policy, Jewish Refugees and the Holocaust* (Cambridge: Cambridge University Press, 2001)

LOWENSTEIN, STEVEN M., *The Berlin Jewish Community: Enlightenment, Family and Crisis, 1770–1830* (Oxford: Oxford University Press, 2000)

MAITLAND, CATHERINE, 'Dora and her Sisters: Control and Rebellion in Hermann and Schnitzler' (doctoral thesis, Chapel Hill, NC: University of North Carolina Press, 2006)

MALTERUD, KATHRINE, 'Review of *Die Zeitlupe und andere Betrachtungen über Menschen und Dinge* by George Hermann', *Books Abroad*, vol. 3, no. 3, July 1929, 305–06

MALTHANER, JOHANNES, '*November achtzehn* by Georg Hermann', *Books Abroad*, vol. 5, no. 2 (April 1931), University of Oklahoma, 155

MAK, GEERT, *Amsterdam: A Brief Life of the City*, trans. by Philipp Blom (London: Vintage, 2001)

MARIAGER, RASMUS, 'Surveillance of peace movements in Denmark during the Cold War', *Journal of Intelligence History*, 12 (2013), 60–75

MARQUARDT, FRANKA, 'Durchaus ein jüdischer Roma?' Judentum, Antisemitismus und die wechselhafte Rezeptionsgeschichte von Georg Hermanns *Jettchen Gebert*', *Zeitschrift für Religions — und Geistesgeschichte*, 67: 1 (2015), 64–84

MATTENKLOTT, GERT, '*Der doppelte Spiegel*. Georg Hermann über Juden in Deutschland (vor 1933)', in *Georg Hermann: Deutsch-jüdischer Schriftsteller und Journalist*, ed. by Godela Weiss-Sussex (Tübingen: Niemeyer, 2004), pp. 103–13

MAURER, WARREN, R., 'Gerhart Hauptmann's Character Names', *German Quarterly*, 52:4 (1979), 457–71

MINDEN, MICHAEL, 'The First World War and its aftermath in the German Novel', in *The Cambridge Companion to the Modern German Novel* ed. by Graham Bartram (Cambridge: Cambridge University Press, 2004), pp. 138–51

MOORE, BOB, 'Jewish Refugees in the Netherlands 1933–40: The Structure and Pattern of Immigration from Nazi Germany', *Leo Baeck Institute Year Book* XXIX (1984), 73–101

MOSSE, GEORGE L., *German Jews beyond Judaism* (Bloomington IN: Indiana University Press, 1985)

——*Masses and Man: Nationalist and Fascist Perceptions of Reality* (Detroit, MI: Wayne State University Press, 1987)

MÜLLER, LOTHAR, 'Franz Hessel und Georg Hermann: Zwei Spaziergänger im Berlin der

Neuen Sachlichkeit', in ... *Aber ihr Ruf verhallt ins Leere hinein. Der Schriftsteller Georg Hermann*, ed. by Kerstin Schoor (Berlin: Weidler, 1999), pp. 119–35

NASTA, DOMINIQUE, *Contemporary Romanian Cinema: The History of an Unexpected Miracle* (New York, NY: Columbia University Press, 2013)

NISBET, HUGH BARR, *Gotthold Ephraim Lessing: His Life, Works, and Thought* (Oxford: Oxford University Press, 2013)

NUSSBAUM, LAUREEN, 'A Sampling of Georg Hermann's Letters about German Literature', in *Georg Hermann: Deutsch-jüdischer Schriftsteller und Journalist 1871–1943*, ed. by Godela Weiss-Sussex (Tübingen: Niemeyer, 2004), pp. 73–86

——'Assimilationsproblematik in Georg Hermanns letztem Exilroman, *Der etruskische Spiegel*', in *Deutsch-jüdische Exil — und Emigrationsliteratur im 20. Jahrhundert*, ed. by Itta Shedletzky and Hans Otto Horch (Tübingen: Niemeyer, 1993), pp. 195–204

——'Georg Hermann Attacks the Special Issue of *Der Jude*', in *The Yale Companion to Jewish Writing and Thought in German Culture, 1096–1996*, ed. by Sander L. Gilman and Jack Zipes (New Haven, CT: Yale University Press, 1997), pp. 448–54

——'Nachwort' to *Unvorhanden und stumm, doch zu Menschen noch reden. Briefe aus dem Exil 1933–41 an seine Tochter Hilde* (Mannheim: persona verlag, 1991), pp. 263–69

——'Verliebt in Holland: ein wichtiges und wechselndes Verhältnis in Georg Hermanns reiferen Jahren', in *Interbellum und Exil*, ed. by Sjaak Onderdelinden (Amsterdam: Rodopi, 1991), pp. 181–98

——'Wenn Deutschland die ganze Welt gewänne, nichts könnte den Kummer dieses Krieges gutmachen: Georg Hermanns *Randbemerkungen (1914–1917)*', in ... *Aber ihr Ruf verhallt ins Leere hinein. Der Schriftsteller Georg Hermann*, ed. by Kerstin Schoor (Berlin: Weidler, 1999), pp. 153–74

OPPENHEIM, A. N., *The Chosen People: The Story of the '222 Transport' from Bergen-Belsen to Palestine* (London: Valentine Mitchell, 1996)

ORTEGA Y GASSET, JOSÉ, *The Revolt of the Masses* (New York, NY: Norton, 1994)

OTTOMEYER, HANS, ET AL., *Biedermeier: The Invention of Simplicity* (Milwaukee Art Museum: Hatje Cantz, 2006)

PARET, PETER, *The Berlin Secession: Modernism and Its Enemies in Imperial Germany* (Cambridge, MA: Belknap Press of Harvard University Press, 1980)

PAUCKER, ARNOLD, 'Zur Geschichte von Georg Hermanns Nachlass: Ein Geleitwort', in *Georg Hermann: Deutsch-jüdischer Schriftsteller und Journalist 1871–1943*, ed. by Godela Weiss-Sussex (Tübingen: Niemeyer, 2004), pp. 133–36

PETZINA, DIETER, 'Germany and the Great Depression', *Journal of Contemporary History*, 4:4 (1969), 59–74

PRESSER, JACOB, *Ashes in the Wind — The Destruction of Dutch Jewry*, trans. by Arnold Pomerans (London: Sovereign Press, 2010)

RANDALL, ALEC, W. G., 'Wandering Germans and the Bread of Banishment', *TLS*, 25 January 1936, 70

REHSE, CHRISTIAN, 'Nehmen wir die Dinge nicht so ernst. Zum "fatalistischen Grundzug" in Georg Hermanns Werken', in ... *Aber ihr Ruf verhallt ins Leere hinein. Der Schriftsteller Georg Hermann*, ed. by Kerstin Schoor (Berlin: Weidler, 1999), pp. 175–88

REICHART, WALTER A., 'Review of *Das Letzte Geheimnis: Eine psychologische Studie über die Brüder Gerhart und Carl Hauptmann* by Jean Jofen', *Journal of English and Germanic Philology*, 72:4 (1973), 599–603

RICHTER, LARS-ANDRÉ, 'Die Intellektuellen haben das Wort: Eine Auswertung von Presserundfragen unter Intellektuellen der Weimarer Republik' (doctoral thesis, Berlin: Humboldt University, 2008)

RIGG, BRYAN MARK, *Hitler's Jewish Soldiers* (Lawrence, KS: University Press of Kansas, 2002)

RIPPMANN, INGE, *Vormärz im Biedermeier — Zu Georg Hermanns Doppelroman* Jettchen Gebert *und* Henriette Jacobi (Bielefeld: Aisthesis, 2014)

RITCHIE, J. M., 'The Nazi Book-Burning', *MLR*, 83:3 (1988), 627–43

ROBERTSON, RITCHIE, 'Cultural Stereotypes and Social Anxiety in Georg Hermann's *Jettchen Gebert*', in *Georg Hermann Deutsch-jüdischer Schriftsteller und Journalist 1871–1943*, ed. by Godela Weiss-Sussex (Tübingen: Niemeyer, 2004), pp. 5–21

RÖNNEBECK, ARNOLD, 'Books in German', *Books Abroad*, vol. 3, no. 3, July 1929 (University of Oklahoma), 280

ROPER, KATHERINE, 'Fridericus Films in Weimar Society: Potsdamismus in a Democracy', *German Studies Review*, 26: 3 (2003), 493–514

ROTH, CECIL, *The Jewish Contribution to Civilisation* (New York, NY: Harper and Brothers), 1940

SCHEFFLER, HERBERT, 'Recent Historical Fiction in Germany', *Books Abroad*, vol. 7, no. 3, July 1933 (University of Oklahoma), 277–80

SCHIFF, GERT, 'Review of *The Berlin Secession: Modernism and Its Enemies in Imperial Germany* by Peter Paret', *Art Journal*, 42: 4 (1982), 357 and 359

SCHOLZ, HANS, 'Georg Hermann und die Berliner Dichtung. Nachwort zur Neuauflage von *Rosenemil*' (Munich: Süddeutscher Verlag, 1962), pp. 343–68

SCHOOR, KERSTIN, 'Aber ihr Ruf verhallt ins Leere hinein. Georg Hermann — Ein Autor und seine Leser', in *... Aber ihr Ruf verhallt ins Leere hinein — Der Schriftsteller Georg Hermann*, ed. by Kerstin Schoor (Berlin: Weidler, 1999), pp. 9–56

SIMMEL, GEORG, *Die Grosstädte und das Geistesleben*, reprinted in *The Blackwell City Reader*, ed. by Gary Bridge and Sophie Watson (Oxford: Wiley, 2010), pp. 103–10

SINGER, ISIDORE, ed., *The Jewish Encyclopedia* (New York, NY: Funk and Wagnalls, 1906)

SOISTER, JOHN T., *Conrad Veidt on Screen: A Comprehensive Illustrated Filmology* (Jefferson, NC: McFarland, 2002)

SPRENGEL, PETER, 'Der Dreschflegelgraf. Antisemitismus als Tendenz der Epoche in Georg Hermanns *Der kleine Gast*', in *... Aber ihr Ruf verhallt ins Leere hinein — Der Schriftsteller Georg Hermann*, ed. by Kerstin Schoor (Berlin: Weidler, 1999), pp. 189–96

——'Nachwort zu Georg Hermanns *Der kleine Gast*' (Berlin: Das Neue Berlin, 1999), pp. 579–90

STANOMIR, GHEORGE, 'Georg Hermann und das Haus Poststraße 2', *Neckargemünd Jahrbuch*, vol. 5, Stadt Neckargemünd (1993), 85–105

STEPHAN, INGE, 'Nachwort zu Georg Hermanns *Ruths schwere Stunde*' (Berlin: Das Neue Berlin, 2001), pp. 321–33

STROTE, NOAH B., 'The Birth of the "Psychological Jew" in the Age of Ethnic Pride', *New German Critique* 115, vol. 39, no.1 (2012), 199–224

SWALES, MARTIN, 'Introductory Remarks', in *Georg Hermann Deutsch-jüdischer Schriftsteller und Journalist 1871–1943*, ed. by Godela Weiss-Sussex (Tübingen: Niemeyer, 2004), pp. 1–4

TER BRAAK, MENNO, 'Georg Hermann Plaudert', *Het Vaderland*, 16 March 1937

TYLDESLEY, JOYCE A., *Nefertiti: Egypt's Sun Queen* (London: Penguin, 1998)

VANELLEPUTTE, MICHEL, 'Eine Stadt und dreierlei Garten in Georg Hermanns Roman *Jettchen Gebert* (1906), in *Literarische Mikrokosmen. Begrenzung und Entgrenzung. Festschrift für Ernst Leonardy*, ed. by Christian Drösch, Hubert Roland and Stéphanie Vanasten (Brussels: Peter Lang, 2006), pp. 107–21

VAN LIERE, C. G., *Georg Hermann: Materialien zur Kenntnis seines Lebens und seines Werkes* (Amsterdam: Rodopi, 1974)

VAN ZANDEN, JAN L., *The Economic History of The Netherlands 1914–1995* (London: Routledge, 1997)

VOIGT, KLAUS, 'Refuge and Persecution in Italy, 1933–1945', *Simon Wiesenthal Center Annual*, vol. 4, ed. by H. Friedlander and S. Milton (Millwood, NY: Krauss International, 1987), pp. 3–64

VOLKOV, SHULAMITH, *Germans, Jews, and Antisemites: Trials in Emancipation* (Cambridge: Cambridge University Press, 2006)

VOLLMANN, ROLF, 'Die Kunst des Kunstlosen: Ein letzter Versuch, Leser für den großen Romancier Georg Hermann zu gewinnen', *Die Zeit*, 10 February 2000

VOLTAIRE, *Œuvres complètes de Voltaire*, ed. by Louis Moland, 50 vols (Paris: Garnier, 1877–83)

VON DER LÜHE, IRMELA, 'Versuch, im Schreiben zu überleben: Georg Hermann's *Rosenemil*', in ... *Aber ihr Ruf verhalt ins Leere hinein — Der Schriftsteller Georg Hermann*, ed. by Kerstin Schoor (Berlin: Weidler, 1999), pp. 197–210

WARD, JOHN, *Jews in Business and Their Representation in German Literature, 1827–1934* (Oxford: Peter Lang, 2010)

WEISS-SUSSEX, GODELA, *Metropolitan Chronicles: Georg Hermann's Berlin Novels 1897–1912* (Stuttgart: Hans-Dieter-Heinz, 2001)

—— 'Naturalist Metaphor of Destruction or Impressionist Panorama? A Re-evaluation of Georg Hermann's Berlin Novel, *Kubinke*', *Comparative Literature Studies*, 35:4 (1998), 356–79

—— 'Confronting Stereotypes: Department Store Novels by German-Jewish Authors, 1916–1925', in *Konsum und Imagination. Tales of Commerce and Imagination*, ed. by Godela Weiss-Sussex and Ulrike Zitzlsperger (Oxford: Peter Lang, 2015), pp. 89–106

—— 'Der Blick auf Berlin in Romanen exilierter Schriftsteller 1933–1936', in *Berlin Wien Prag: Modernity, Minorities and Migration in the Inter-War Period*, ed. by Susanne Marten-Finnis and Matthias Uecker (Bern: Peter Lang, 2001), pp. 185–206

—— 'Impressionismus als Weltanschauung. Die Kunstkritik Georg Hermanns', in *Georg Hermann Deutsch-jüdischer Schriftsteller und Journalist 1871–1943*, ed. by Godela Weiss-Sussex (Tübingen: Niemeyer, 2004), pp. 87–101

WIEBE, F. K., *Germany and the Jewish Problem* (Berlin: Muller, 1939)

WILDT, MICHAEL, *Hitler's Volksgemeinschaft and the Dynamics of Racial Exclusion: Violence against Jews in Provincial Germany*, trans. by Bernard W. Heise (New York, NY: Berghahn, 2012)

WILSON, A. N., *Tolstoy* (London: Hamish Hamilton, 1988)

WOOD, JAMES, 'Sins of the Father', *New Yorker*, 22 July 2013, 70–74

ZACHAU, REINHARD K., 'The City as Political Space: Modernism in Georg Hermann's Novels of Jewish Life in Berlin', in *Berlin's Culturescape in the Twentieth Century*, ed. by Thomas Bredohl and Michael Zimmermann (Regina, SK: University of Regina Press, 2008), pp. 33–52

—— 'Writing under National Socialism', in *The Cambridge Companion to the Literature of Berlin*, ed. by Andrew J. Webber (Cambridge: Cambridge University Press, 2017), pp. 111–29

ZÜHLSDORFF, VOLKMAR, *Hitler's Exiles: The German Cultural Resistance in America and Europe*, trans. by Martin H. Bott (New York, NY: Continuum, 2004)

INDEX

❖

www.ingramcontent.com/pod-product-compliance
Lightning Source LLC
Chambersburg PA
CBHW080540090426
42734CB00016B/3162